PREPARING COMPANY ACCOUNTS

2013–14

PREPARING COMPANY ACCOUNTS 2013–14

for small companies accounting under the Companies Act 2006

Katie White and Mark Worsey

Buzzacott LLP

Twenty-first Edition

CCH
a Wolters Kluwer business

Disclaimer

This publication is sold with the understanding that neither the publisher nor the authors, with regard to this publication, are engaged in rendering legal or professional services. The material contained in this publication neither purports, nor is intended to be, advice on any particular matter.

Although this publication incorporates a considerable degree of standardisation, subjective judgment by the user, based on individual circumstances, is indispensable. This publication is an 'aid' and cannot be expected to replace such judgment.

Neither the publisher nor the authors nor Buzzacott LLP can accept any responsibility or liability to any person, whether a purchaser of this publication or not, in respect of anything done or omitted to be done by any such person in reliance, whether sole or partial, upon the whole or any part of the contents of this publication.

Wolters Kluwer (UK) Limited
145 London Road
Kingston upon Thames
KT2 6SR
Tel: 0844 561 8166
Fax: 0208 547 2638
E-mail: cch@wolterskluwer.co.uk
www.cch.co.uk

ISBN 978-1-84798-662-7

No responsibility for loss occasioned to any person acting or refraining from action as a result of any material in this publication can be accepted by the authors, Buzzacott LLP or publisher.

Views expressed in this publication are the authors' views and are not necessarily those of Buzzacott LLP or of the publisher.

British Library Cataloguing-in-Publication Data

A catalogue record for this book is available from the British Library.

Typeset by Integra Software Services Pvt. Ltd., Pondicherry.
Printed by Gutenberg Press Ltd, Malta.

Preface

Preparing Company Accounts 2013–14 represents the twenty-first edition of the book. For over thirty years, it has focussed on what has come to be known as the 'small companies regime' – the statutory accounting requirements for the 'small' company.

GAAP (generally accepted accounting practice) has developed considerably over this period. The FRSSE (Financial Reporting Standard for Smaller Entities), originally introduced in November 1997, is now widely adopted and underpins the statutory accounting framework of company legislation under the CA 2006. The availability of audit exemption has afforded a measure of relief for some companies from the burden of statutory compliance.

Nevertheless, for smaller companies, discerning the requirements can still be difficult and the detailed legislation often remains complex – exemptions and opportunities (or the rules to take advantage of them) can be easy to miss or misinterpret.

The main objective of this book remains the same; it has always been intended to be a companion rather than a comprehensive technical treatise in its own right – a quick and, we hope, relatively straightforward guide, simplifying where possible, concentrating on basic principles, suggesting appropriate tools and illustrating changes and opportunities.

In itself, implementation of the CA 2006 was a major landmark. However, the dawn of this new era of company legislation is now to be followed by the end of another – UK GAAP as we currently know (and love) it.

This edition of the book reached its publication date before the issue of the new UK financial reporting standard (FRS 102 *The Financial Reporting Standard applicable in the UK and Republic of Ireland*), but the final proposals in relation to the future of financial reporting in the UK are discussed at greater length in this edition. Companies will soon need to start planning for the implications of whichever is their applicable part of the new financial reporting framework which FRS 100 *Application of financial reporting requirements* has confirmed will be mandatory for accounting periods starting on or after 1 January 2015.

Initially, the least change may be for the largest (public companies which are already applying IFRS) and the smallest (those entities which can currently apply the FRSSE), as the current FRSSE (effective April 2008), although slightly amended by FRS 100, will remain in force as the FRSSE (effective January 2015). In time it is likely that the FRSSE will again require amendment and be impacted further by International Accounting Standards and European proposals for smaller companies.

For the future, European proposals approved by the European Council in February 2012, if adopted in the UK, may have a significant effect on the financial reporting requirements for very small companies ('micros').

This is the fourth year that Buzzacott LLP has provided the authors of the book. At the very start, the author was Ray Mayes who was a partner in Buzzacott and continued writing the book following his retirement from the partnership. For the last two editions the author was Kay Morrow, technical director of the firm. This is the first year of co-authorship and we hope that we have maintained the high standards set by our two predecessors.

We are indebted for their assistance to Jenny Carter at the FRC and to our colleagues at Buzzacott LLP and particularly Vesna Sowden, from our company secretarial team, who has directed us in the preparation of Chapter 14 and Sharon Kilbane who assisted in editing the book. We are grateful for all the comments received in the past; please keep them coming and we wish you good luck in braving the world of new UK GAAP.

Katie White and Mark Worsey
March 2013

Contents

Abbreviations

AAC	Audit and Assurance Council (part of the FRC)
APB	Auditing Practices Board (disbanded in July 2012, replaced by the FRC's Audit and Assurance Council)
ASB	Accounting Standards Board (disbanded in July 2012, replaced by the FRC's Accounting Council)
BIS	Department for Business, Innovation and Skills
C(AICE) 2004	Companies (Audit, Investigations and Community Enterprise) Act 2004
CA 2006	Companies Act 2006
CCAB	Consultative Committee of Accountancy Bodies
EC	European Commission
EEA	European Economic Area
ESOP	Employee share ownership plan
EU	European Union
EU Regulation	Regulation (EC) No. 1606/2002 of the European Parliament (dated 19 July 2002) on the application of international accounting standards
FA	Finance Act
FASB	US Financial Accounting Standards Board
FRC	Financial Reporting Council
FRED	Financial Reporting Exposure Draft
FRRP	Financial Reporting Review Panel (disbanded in July 2012, replaced by the FRC Monitoring Committee)
FRS	Financial Reporting Standard
FRSSE	Financial Reporting Standard for Smaller Entities (being the 'FRSSE (effective April 2008)' unless otherwise indicated or as the circumstances dictate)
FSMA 2000	Financial Services and Markets Act 2000
GAAP	Generally accepted accounting practice (or principles) (see also 'UK GAAP')
IAASB	International Auditing and Assurance Standards Board
IAS	International accounting standards issued or adopted by IASB
IAS Regulation	Regulation (EC) No. 1606/2002 of the European Parliament (dated 19 July 2002) on the application of international accounting standards
IASB	International Accounting Standards Board
ICTA	Income and Corporation Taxes Act 1988
IFRIC	International Financial Reporting Interpretations Committee (an IASB committee)
IFRS	International Financial Reporting Standards (including IAS and interpretations adopted by IASB)
IFRS for SMEs	International Financial Reporting Standard for Small and Medium-sized Entities
ISA	International Standard on Auditing ('ISA (UK and Ireland)': an ISA applicable within the UK and Ireland)
NIC	National Insurance contribution
MIFID	MiFID investment firm – an investment firm within the meaning of Article 4.1.1 of Directive 2004/39/EC of the European Parliament and of the Council of 21 April 2004 on markets in financial instruments (but see CA 2006 s. 474)
OFR	Operating and Financial Review
OPSI	Office of Public Sector Information
P & L account	Profit and loss account
PAYE	Pay as you earn
PN	APB Practice Note
POB	Professional Oversight Board (part of the FRC) (disbanded in July 2012, replaced by the FRC Conduct Committee)

Reg.	Regulation (for example, SI 2008/409 reg. 4(2) means regulation 4(2) of SI 2008/409)
s.	section (unless otherwise stated, section references refer to CA 2006, as amended or inserted from time to time)
Sch	Schedule (for example: 'CA 2006 Sch 7.7(2)' means CA 2006 Schedule 7, paragraph 7(2); or for SI 2008/409, 'SI 2008/409 Sch 4.5(2)' or simply 'Sch 4.5(2)' means Schedule 4 paragraph 5(2))
SI	Statutory instrument
SIC	Standing Interpretation Committee of IASB (or an interpretation of SIC e.g. 'SIC-1')
SME	Small or medium-sized entity (or enterprise)
SORP	Statement of Recommended Practice
SSAP	Statement of Standard Accounting Practice
SSRA	Statement of Standards for Reporting Accountants
STRGL	Statement of total recognised gains and losses
UCITS	Undertaking for Collective Investment in Transferable Securities (see CA 2006 s. 471(1))
UITF	Urgent Issues Task Force (part of FRC since July 2012, previously part of the ASB)
UK GAAP	Financial reporting requirements (as specified by the FRC) in the United Kingdom and the Republic of Ireland (see 'GAAP')
VAT	Value added tax

Statutory instruments

SI 2012/2301	The Companies and Limited Liability Partnerships (Accounts and Audit Exemptions and Change of Accounting Framework) Regulations 2012
SI 2012/952	The CA 2006 (Amendment of Part 23) (Investment Companies) Regulations 2012
SI 2011/2198	Companies (Disclosure of Auditor Remuneration and Liability Limitation Agreements) (Amendment) Regulations 2011
SI 2009/1802	The CA 2006 (Part 35) (Consequential Amendments, Transitional Provisions and Savings) Order 2009
SI 2009/1581	The CA 2006 (Accounts, Reports and Audit) Regulations 2009
SI 2008/2860	The CA 2006 (Commencement No. 8, Transitional Provisions and Savings) Order 2008
SI 2008/489	The Companies (Disclosure of Auditor Remuneration and Liability Limitation Agreements) Regulations 2008
SI 2008/410	The Large and Medium-sized Companies and Groups (Accounts and Reports) Regulations 2008
SI 2008/409	The Small Companies and Groups (Accounts and Directors' Report) Regulations 2008
SI 2008/393	The CA 2006 (Amendment) (Accounts and Reports) Regulations 2008
SI 2008/374	The Companies (Summary Financial Statement) Regulations 2008
SI 2007/3495	The CA 2006 (Commencement No. 5, Transitional Provisions and Savings) Order 2007

EC Regulations and Directives

EC 1004/2008	Adoption of certain IASs in accordance with regulation EC 1606/2002 (amending regulation EC 1725/2003) (15 October 2008)
EC 707/2004	Adoption of certain IASs in accordance with regulation EC 1606/2002 (amending regulation EC 1725/2003) (6 April 2004)
EC 1606/2002	Requirement for use of IASs by listed companies (by 2005) (19 September 2002)
2003/51/EC	The 'Modernisation Directive' amending earlier Directives on annual and consolidated accounts (18 June 2003)
2001/65/EC	The 'Fair Value Directive' on valuation rules for annual and consolidated accounts of certain companies (21 September 2001)

Summary of implementation dates

Company Law

Companies Act 2006

The CA 2006 received Royal Assent on 8 November 2006. Provisions under the Act were introduced by commencement orders and regulations. All parts of the Act were brought into force by 1 October 2009.

Accounts and reports – generally, the requirements on the form and content of accounts and reports in CA 2006 Part 15 (Accounts and reports) and new regulations made under it (including, for example, SI 2008/409 for small companies) were effective for accounts and reports for **periods beginning on or after 6 April 2008**.

Audit – the provisions of CA 2006 Part 16 (Audit) were effective on 6 April 2008, and, following the approach in Part 15 (Accounts and reports) above, most of the provisions became applicable to the audits of accounts for **financial years beginning on or after 6 April 2008**.

The CA 2006 is available via the Legislation.gov.uk website at:

www.legislation.gov.uk/ukpga/2006/46/contents

Regulations under CA 2006 are available via the Legislation.gov.uk website at:

The Small Companies and Groups (Accounts and Directors' Report) Regulations 2008 (SI 2008/409): www.legislation.gov.uk/uksi/2008/409/contents/made

The Large and Medium-sized Companies and Groups (Accounts and Reports) Regulations 2008 (SI 2008/410): www.legislation.gov.uk/uksi/2008/410/contents/made

Financial Reporting Standard for Smaller Entities (FRSSE)

Directors choosing to adopt the FRSSE must ensure that accounts are prepared in accordance with the appropriate version; the current version is:

- FRSSE (effective April 2008) – accounts prepared under CA 2006.

The FRSSE (effective April 2008) is available free of charge on the FRC website at:

www.frc.org.uk/FRC-Documents/ASB/FRSSE-(effective-April-2008).aspx

FRSSE (effective April 2008)

The Financial Reporting Standard for Smaller Entities (effective April 2008) was applicable for financial statements relating to accounting periods beginning on or after 6 April 2008.

International Accounting Standards and IFRS for SMEs

In accordance with SI 2004 No. 2947 *The Companies Act 1985 (International Accounting Standards and Other Accounting Amendments) Regulations 2004*, from 1 January 2005 all UK companies (other than charities and those automatically covered by the EU IAS Regulation) were permitted (but not required) to use international accounting standards (forming 'IAS accounts') as an alternative to the UK domestic reporting accounting framework ('Companies Act accounts').

As part of the preparations for adoption of the new financial reporting framework set out in FRS 100, the Companies Act was recently amended by the *Companies and Limited Liability Partnerships (Accounts and Audit Exemptions and Change of Accounting Framework) Regulations* (2012/2301) such that, for financial years ending on or after 1 October 2012, the directors of a company that has converted to IAS accounts in previous periods may choose to revert back to preparing Companies Act accounts. Prior to this revision, reverting to Companies Act accounts was only allowed following what the Companies Act defined as 'relevant changes of circumstance'. (See **4.7.4**)

In July 2009 the IASB issued the IFRS for SMEs – International Financial Reporting Standard for Small and Medium-sized Entities. The IFRS for SMEs will not be adopted in the UK in its current form, however the forthcoming FRS 102 will be based broadly on this standard. **Chapter 4** comments on the current status of the new accounting framework in the UK and Republic of Ireland and a fuller explanation of the status of small company reporting and the impact of IFRS and current EC proposals.

Company size thresholds

Size thresholds for small and medium-sized companies, as increased by Statutory Instrument *The Companies Act 2006 (Amendment) (Accounts and Reports) Regulations 2008* (SI 2008/393) are set out below.

The Regulations came into force on 6 April 2008 and apply in relation to financial years beginning on or after 6 April 2008.

Statutory Instrument SI 2008/393 is available via the Legislation.gov.uk website at:

www.legislation.gov.uk/uksi/2008/393/contents/made

Chapter 5 explains how these thresholds apply in the preparation of companies' accounts and **Chapter 11** covers the audit exemption limits.

	Thresholds (CA 2006)
Small companies – *see Chapter 5*	
Small company	
Turnover	£6.5 million
Balance sheet total	£3.26 million
Average number of employees (on a monthly basis)	50
Small group	
Aggregate turnover	£6.5 million net* (£7.8 million gross**)
Aggregate balance sheet total	£3.26 million net (£3.9 million gross)
Average number of employees (on a monthly basis)	50
Medium-sized companies – see *Chapter 5*	
Medium-sized company	
Turnover	£25.9 million
Balance sheet total	£12.9 million
Average number of employees (on a monthly basis)	250
Medium-sized group	
Aggregate turnover	£25.9 million net (£31.1 million gross)
Aggregate balance sheet total	£12.9 million net (£15.5 million gross)
Average number of employees (on a monthly basis)	250

**'Net' basis* – Aggregate figures for turnover and balance sheet totals after any set-offs and consolidation adjustments made for the elimination of group transactions.

***'Gross' basis* – Aggregate figures for turnover and balance sheet totals without such set-offs and consolidation adjustments.

Note on scope of book

Preparing Company Accounts 2013-14 is essentially concerned with the accounts of small companies (that is, 'small companies' as defined by the CA 2006) under the 'small companies regime' for financial years beginning on or after 6 April 2008.

The statutory accounting provisions for small companies under the CA 2006 are applicable for financial years beginning on or after 6 April 2008.

Statutory references are to CA 2006 itself (as amended from time to time) or to regulations made under the Act, unless otherwise indicated.

Changes to legislation and to accounting standards issued up to 31 December 2012 have been considered in the writing of *Preparing Company Accounts 2013-14*. As a result the book considers the impact of FRS 100 *Application of financial reporting requirements* and FRS 101 *Reduced disclosure framework*, but is not able to comment on the effect of the final version of FRS 102 *The Financial Reporting Standard applicable in the UK and Republic of Ireland* which had not been issued at this date.

The following topics are considered peripheral to this main objective and are not therefore covered in detail:

International accounting standards: Many small companies are adopting the FRSSE and also preparing abbreviated accounts. At present, international accounting standards (IAS) impinge on small companies only to the extent that some 'convergence' (that is, harmonisation) of domestic UK and international financial reporting standards is reflected within the UK FRSSE. The ASB *project: The future of UK GAAP* is developing the new framework for UK accounting. The framework as set out indicates that the current version of the FRSSE is likely to remain in force for the foreseeable future although EC proposals may require a revision if approved.

Medium-sized companies: Although medium-sized companies continue to benefit from certain exemptions, these are generally now more limited and less distinguishable from the requirements for larger companies. A medium-sized parent company is no longer exempt from the requirement to prepare group accounts. Statutory requirements for medium-sized companies may be found in *The Large and Medium-sized Companies and Groups (Accounts and Reports) Regulations 2008* (SI 2008/410) at:

www.legislation.gov.uk/uksi/2008/410/contents/made

Chapter 5 at **5.2** provides the qualifying conditions for 'small' and 'medium-sized' companies.

Fair value accounting: *Preparing Company Accounts 2013–14* does not cover the subject of fair value accounting as this is rarely adopted by small companies. Further, the FRSSE does not apply to companies preparing individual or group accounts in accordance with the fair value accounting rules for certain assets and liabilities set out in Section D of Schedule 1 of Statutory Instrument 2008/409 (see **Appendix B**). SI 2008/409 may be found at:

www.legislation.gov.uk/uksi/2008/409/contents/made

Consolidated accounts: Small parent companies (as defined) are not required to prepare group accounts. However, as well as preparing individual accounts, they *may* prepare group accounts if they wish to do so. **Chapter 9** provides details of the exemption opportunities and also the requirements where a small parent company prepares group accounts. *Preparing Company Accounts 2013–14* does not cover the detailed mechanics of consolidations and group accounting.

Summary financial statements: All companies subject to audit, including small companies, may be able to send summary financial statements to members and others instead of their full audited accounts (CA 2006 s. 426). Small companies rarely produce summary financial statements and such statements are not consequently covered.

The statutory requirements concerning summary financial statements may be found in *The Companies (Summary Financial Statement) Regulations 2008* (SI 2008/374) at:

www.legislation.gov.uk/uksi/2008/374/contents/made

Audit and assurance: *Preparing Company Accounts 2013–14* does not purport to provide professional guidance on auditing or the provision of assurance services by auditors. Many small companies are now increasingly able to take advantage of audit exemption. Consequently, the book does not comment in detail on audit exemption, audit reports and on the reporting requirements of auditors in circumstances where an audit may be appropriate. Reference should be made to **Chapter 11** (Determining small company audit exemption) and **Chapter 13** (Small company audit and assurance reports).

Charities: *Preparing Company Accounts 2013–14* does not cover the requirements of incorporated charities. Accounting for charities (incorporated or otherwise) has generally been brought under one roof by the introduction of the Charities Act 2011, which supersedes the Charities Act 1993 and the Charities Act 2006, and, to which reference should be made where appropriate. Further information is available at:

www.charity-commission.gov.uk/ (Charity Commission); or

www.legislation.gov.uk/ukpga/2006/50/contents

Limited Liability Partnerships (LLPs): *Preparing Company Accounts 2013–14* does not cover the requirements of LLPs. The CA 2006 is applicable to LLPs for accounting periods starting on or after 1 October 2008. The key regulations which set out how the CA 2006 applies to LLPs are *The Limited Liability Partnerships (Accounts and Audit) (Application of Companies Act 2006) Regulations* 2008 (SI 2008/1911), available at:

www.legislation.gov.uk/uksi/2008/1911/contents/made

The requirements for LLPs are set out in the CCH publication *Preparing Accounts for LLPs 2011-12*.

Part I General

Chapter 1 Introduction

1.1 Purpose of the book

1.1.1 Accounts of small companies

This book is essentially concerned with the accounts of small companies (that is, 'small companies' as defined by the CA 2006 under the 'small companies regime') preparing accounts under UK GAAP. No references are made to the requirements of previous legislation within this edition.

A company is treated as small (or medium-sized) if it does not exceed more than one of the following criteria:

	Small	*Medium-sized*
Turnover	£6.5 million	£25.9 million
Balance sheet total	£3.26 million	£12.9 million
Average number of employees (on a monthly basis)	50	250

Criteria amended (increased) by SI 2008/393

Chapter 5 sets out the qualifying criteria in detail.

Certain categories of company, regardless of size, will not be entitled to any exemptions. *s. 384*

The following companies are not eligible:

- public companies;
- members of 'ineligible' (basically, public) groups;
- companies carrying on an insurance market activity; and
- companies that are authorised insurance companies, banking companies, e-money issuers, MiFID investment firms or UCITS management companies.

Certain categories of small financial services companies that would otherwise be precluded from taking advantage of the exemptions are however now treated as 'small' companies (unless they are required to have an audit under European directives).

All companies are required to prepare full statutory accounts for members but those for small companies may contain less detailed information than medium-sized or large companies.

Small and medium-sized companies may also prepare 'abbreviated accounts' for filing.

Certain defined categories of small company are exempt from audit.

The book endeavours to simplify the still somewhat complex requirements for small company accounts. While not purporting to give comprehensive coverage of all accounting provisions, the aim of the book is to explain many of the company accounting requirements that affect small companies and the exemptions (both accounting and audit) that are available to them. The book concentrates on those matters of practical relevance as far as accounts are concerned. In essence, it aims to resolve the following issues:

What sort of statutory accounts are required? The Act, together with the regulations under *The Small Companies and Groups (Accounts and Directors' Report) Regulations 2008* (SI 2008/409), sets out the requirements for small company accounts.

Preparing abbreviated accounts. Many companies, that are able to do so, now prepare (additional) simplified 'abbreviated accounts' for filing with the Registrar of Companies.

Adoption of the FRSSE. The FRSSE (Financial Reporting Standard for Smaller Entities), avoiding the full rigours of UK accounting standards (and increasingly international standards), has become the basic standard for many small companies.

Is an audit required or necessary? Many companies, while qualifying as 'audit exempt', nevertheless consider whether a Companies Act audit or alternatively some form of assurance or accountants' report is appropriate.

International accounting standards. The smaller company currently has the choice of adopting international accounting standards, being full IAS accounts. **Chapter 15** sets out the new developments regarding the financial reporting framework in the UK.

What needs to be filed? With the advent of web-filing, the options for filing companies' accounts with the Registrar of Companies have added complexity.

The book is written from the perspective of the small company and focuses on matters currently relevant to small companies preparing accounts under current UK GAAP. It provides the following:

- a summary of statutory company accounts provisions in general – to put 'small companies' in context;
- an explanation of the company accounts provisions for small (and 'medium-sized') companies – for both full statutory and abbreviated accounts;
- an explanation of the audit exemptions available to certain small companies;
- guidelines and definitions – for accounting presentation, disclosure and terminology; and
- illustrative examples – including the full statutory accounts of a 'small company'.

Consolidated accounts and accounting for consolidations and group situations are generally not dealt with in detail, although the basic statutory provisions affecting small group accounts and group audit exemptions are inevitably covered.

1.1.2 Small companies in the 'small companies regime'

Legislation, of both domestic and European origin, has resulted in a measure of standardisation for company accounts, the codification of accounting rules and principles and, to some extent, the simplification of disclosure. Increasingly, the accounts provisions of company law have been supplemented by guidance in the form of Financial Reporting Standards issued by the UK Accounting Standards Board (ASB) and now, with the demise of the ASB in July 2012, adopted by the Financial Reporting Council (FRC).

UK company law, nevertheless, has remained comprehensive and complex. Preparers of accounts have to contend with a significant level of legislation and regulation.

With the aim of reducing the administrative burden on smaller companies, over the years, the whole process of accounts production for the small company has gradually been simplified, the result being that:

- small company accounts are less detailed than those of larger companies;
- 'abbreviated accounts' (as a filing option) afford a measure of further privacy and simplicity for small companies;
- there is statutory recognition of a dedicated regime of accounting for small companies (together with an accounting standard for such companies – the FRSSE); and
- audit exemption affords the opportunity for many smaller companies to avoid the cost and effort involved in what is sometimes regarded as a 'statutory burden'.

A significant number of companies fall into the category of 'small company' and are hence taking advantage of the accounting opportunities available – see **6.2**. Accounting and audit exemption thresholds for small and medium-sized companies were most recently updated by Statutory Instrument *The Companies Act 2006 (Amendment) (Accounts and Reports) Regulations 2008* (SI 2008/393).

Over 90% of all annual accounts filed with the Registrar of Companies in 2011/12 were classified as audit exempt accounts. A further 2.6% comprised audited small company abbreviated accounts.

Table 1.1 Annual accounts registered at Companies House by type 2011/2012

UK in total

	000s	*%*
Audited accounts		
Full individual accounts	119.6	5.8
Abbreviated accounts		
Small company	54.3	2.6
Medium-sized company	5.0	0.2
Group accounts	19.3	0.9
		9.5
Audit exempt		
Audit exempt accounts	1,470.0	71.4
Dormant company accounts	392.2	19.1
		90.5
Other		
Interim/Initial accounts	0.1	0.0
	2,060.5	100.0

Source: Companies House Statistical Tables on Companies Registration Activities 2011-2012 (Table F2) (as amended for roundings).
www.companieshouse.gov.uk/about/companiesRegActivities.shtml

1.2 Legislation – Accounting regime under the Companies Act 2006

The CA 2006 received Royal Assent on 8 November 2006. Running to 701 pages of primary legislation together with 59 pages of index and comprising 47 Parts, 1,300 sections and 16 Schedules, it is the longest Act ever. It consolidated virtually all existing companies legislation and introduced many reforms. Company law was re-written and re-presented in an attempt to make it easier to understand and more flexible – especially for smaller companies.

The accounts provisions of Part 15 of the CA 2006 are effective for all accounting periods commencing on or after 6 April 2008.

Reference should always be made to the actual legislation itself (CA 2006) in order to ensure full adherence to current and up-to-date legislation. *The Small Companies and Groups (Accounts and Directors' Report) Regulations 2008* (SI 2008/409) are reproduced in full in **Appendix B** and all UK legislation is available on the website www.legislation.gov.uk.

This book covers the legislation in force and guidance issued up to December 2012.

1.3 Financial Reporting Standard for Smaller Entities (FRSSE)

To reduce the burden for smaller entities of considering and complying with the whole range of accounting standards while producing clear financial reporting, the UK Accounting Standards Board (ASB) issued the FRSSE – Financial Reporting Standard for Smaller Entities. Originally issued in November 1997, the FRSSE has been subsequently updated on a number of occasions. The current version of the FRSSE is the amended version issued in June 2008, effective April 2008. The requirements of the FRSSE (effective April 2008) are set out in **Chapter 10**.

The FRSSE applies to all smaller entities (as defined) – not just companies – which prepare accounts showing a true and fair view and which choose to adopt the stand-alone document containing all the relevant standards. In essence, the FRSSE aims to be a 'one-stop shop FRSSE' in the sense of incorporating all relevant existing requirements of small companies legislation (covering small company accounts and directors' reports) and including, for example, statutory accounts formats.

FRS 100 *Application of Financial Reporting Requirements* (issued in November 2012) sets out the new financial reporting framework to be mandatorily applied for periods beginning on or after 1 January 2015. It also includes (in paragraph 16) a number of consequential amendments to the FRSSE and the FRSSE as amended by these will form the FRSSE (effective January 2015) and shall be regarded as standard in respect of financial statements beginning on or after 1 January 2015, although earlier application is permitted. It has not been decided yet whether a revised complete version of FRSSE (effective January 2015) reflecting these amendments will be published, but users should have regard to these consequential amendments contained in FRS 100. These have been considered in **Chapter 4**.

1.4 International accounting standards

In July 2003, the UK government announced its intention to permit (but not require) all companies subject to the Companies Act (other than those automatically covered by the EU Regulation) to use international accounting standards as an alternative to UK domestic accounting standards. This legislative change was subsequently implemented by statutory instrument *The Companies Act 1985 (International Accounting Standards and Other Accounting Amendments) Regulations 2004* (SI 2004/2947).

Despite the fact that the adoption of international accounting standards in the UK has affected primarily fully-listed and AIM-listed parent companies and subsidiaries preparing group accounts, there is an inevitability about the cascading effect of international harmonisation, so that all companies will sooner or later have to embrace international accounting practice and principles.

The impact of international accounting standards is explained more fully in **Chapter 4** and **Chapter 15** together with the developments which are coming to UK GAAP and which have their roots in international accounting standards.

1.5 The future of UK financial reporting

July 2009 saw the publication of the IFRS for SMEs (International Financial Reporting Standard for Small and Medium-sized Entities). This provided the opportunity for the ASB to issue a consultation paper, *Policy Proposal: the future of UK GAAP*, which set out its proposals for the future reporting requirements for UK and Irish entities. The ASB believed that the IFRS for SMEs would play a significant role in the future of financial reporting.

Based on the responses to the consultation on the policy proposal and the subsequent exposure drafts of the FRSME (Financial Reporting Standard for Medium-sized Entities) and the FRSPBE (Financial Reporting Standard for Public Benefit Entities), in January 2012 the ASB issued FRED 46 (The Future of Financial Reporting) and revised financial exposure drafts which set out the planned approach for the financial reporting framework in the UK and Republic of Ireland.

Two of these three exposure drafts have now been issued as new financial reporting standards. FRS 100 *Application of Financial Reporting Requirements* and FRS 101 *Reduced disclosure framework* were released in final form in November 2012. At the time of writing, the new UK financial reporting standard, FRS 102 *The Financial Reporting Standard applicable in the UK and Republic of Ireland*, is expected to be issued in the Spring of 2013.

The implementation date of the revised framework is accounting periods starting on or after 1 January 2015.

Further details of the developments in UK financial reporting are given in **Chapter 15**.

Chapter 2 Companies Act 2006

2.1 Annual accounts under CA 2006

2.1.1 Basic approach

The CA 2006 received Royal Assent on 8 November 2006. Running to 701 pages of primary legislation together with 59 pages of index and comprising 47 Parts, 1,300 sections and 16 Schedules, it was the longest Act ever. It consolidated virtually all existing companies legislation and introduced many reforms and company law was re-written and re-presented to make it easier to understand and more flexible – especially for smaller companies.

Working on the 'think small first' approach, company law is presented on a basis that clearly recognises each of the following categories of company or group (CA 2006 s. 380).

1. Small companies.
2. Larger private companies.
3. Public companies (other than quoted companies).
4. Quoted public companies.
5. All companies.

Different provisions apply to different kinds of company; the main distinctions are between:

- companies subject to the 'small companies regime' (CA 2006 s. 381) and companies that are not subject to that regime; and
- quoted companies (CA 2006 s. 385) and companies that are not quoted.

Provisions applying to companies subject to the small companies regime appear in the legislation before the provisions applying to other companies (CA 2006 s. 380(4)).

The small companies regime applies to a company for a financial year in relation to which the company:

- qualifies as small (CA 2006 s. 382–3); and
- is not excluded from the regime (CA 2006 s. 384).

The law, both within the Act itself and in supporting legislation issued in regulations under it, is clearly presented in its application. Small companies have their own separate comprehensive code of accounting and reporting requirements, defining the generally accepted accounting practice relevant to them.

2.1.2 Implementation

Provisions of the CA 2006 were introduced by statutory instrument by means of 'commencement orders' and other supporting regulations in the months leading up to October 2009, the date by which all parts of the Act came into force.

The accounts and report provisions of the Act relate to financial years ***commencing on or after 6 April 2008***.

2.1.3 Small companies accounts regime

The Act presents the 'small companies regime' (as it is termed) within:

- Part 15 (Sections 380 to 474) – 'Accounts and reports'; and
- Part 16 (Sections 475 to 539) – 'Audit' (where relevant for the smaller company).

Preparing small company accounts is governed by reference to:

- CA 2006 Part 15 (relevant sections) (the 'primary legislation'); and
- regulations made under statutory instruments for small companies ('secondary legislation'), covering the form and content of accounts and directors' report – *The Small Companies and Groups (Accounts and Directors' Report) Regulations 2008* (SI 2008/409).

2.1.4 Structure of SI 2008 No. 409

The Small Companies and Groups (Accounts and Directors' Report) Regulations 2008 (SI 2008/409). These Regulations specify the form and content of the accounts and directors' report of companies subject to the small companies regime under Part 15 of the CA 2006. CA 2006 s. 381 of the Act defines what is meant by 'small companies regime'.

Table 2.1 Contents and structure of SI 2008 No. 409

The contents and structure of *The Small Companies and Groups (Accounts and Directors' Report) Regulations 2008* (SI 2008/409) are as follows:

Schedule 1 – *Companies Act individual accounts*

- general rules and formats
- accounting principles and rules
- notes to the accounts

Schedule 2 – *Information about related undertakings where company not preparing group accounts (Companies Act or IAS individual accounts)*

- required disclosures
- interpretation of references to 'beneficial interest'

Schedule 3 – *Information about directors' benefits: remuneration (Companies Act or IAS accounts)*

- information required to be disclosed
- supplementary provisions

Schedule 4 – *Companies Act abbreviated accounts for delivery to Registrar of Companies*

- required balance sheet formats
- notes to the accounts

Schedule 5 – *Matters to be dealt with in directors' report*

Schedule 6 – *Group accounts*

- form and content of Companies Act group accounts
- information about related undertakings where company preparing group accounts (Companies Act or IAS group accounts)

Schedule 7 – *Interpretation of term 'provisions'*

Schedule 8 – *General interpretation*

The Small Companies and Groups (Accounts and Directors' Report) Regulations 2008 (SI 2008/409) is reproduced in full in **Appendix B**.

2.2 Contents of annual accounts and reports

Table 2.2 below compares the contents of the annual reports of small companies, large companies (public or private), and other companies (public or private) following company law reform:

Table 2.2 Contents of annual reports

Annual reports – CA 2006

	Small Companies	*Large Public or Private Companies**	*Other Public or Private Companies*
Primary Financial Statements			
Form and content determined by:			
• Statutory regulation	√	√	√
• Accounting Standards and international accounting standards		√	√
• FRSSE/Accounting Standards	√ (FRSSE optional)		
Abbreviated Accounts – statutory regulation	√ (optional)		√ (optional for 'Medium sized' private companies only)
Group Accounts	[√] (optional)	√	√
Business Review (OFR) – ASB 'best practice' Reporting Statement 'Operating and Financial Review (OFR)' (January 2006)		√ (Quoted companies only, others optional)	
Directors' Report – including enhanced Business review		√	√
Directors' Report	√		
Directors' Remuneration Report		√ (Quoted companies only)	
Summary Financial Statements (Optional) Summary Financial Statement (extended to include, where appropriate, 'OFR' matters)	√	√	√

2.3 Auditing and audit reports

Audit is covered in Part 16 of CA 2006, which contains provisions concerning, for example, the requirement for audited accounts, the appointment of auditors, the auditor's report, the duties and rights of auditors, and removal, resignation, etc.

The audit report must include an introduction identifying the annual accounts and the financial reporting framework under which they are prepared, together with a description of the scope of the audit identifying the auditing standards adopted.

In essence, under CA 2006 s. 495, the auditor is required to report his opinion on four elements.

1. ***True and fair view*** – whether the annual accounts show a 'true and fair view' (having regard to the directors' statutory duty under CA 2006 s. 393(1)).
2. ***Relevant reporting framework*** – whether the accounts have been prepared in accordance with the relevant financial reporting framework.

3. ***Appropriate legislation*** – whether the accounts have been prepared in accordance with CA 2006 (Part 15) or IAS (IAS Regulation Article 4), if applicable.
4. ***Form of report or emphasis*** – whether the report is 'unqualified or qualified' or contains reference to any emphasis of any matters without qualifying the report.

The auditor's report must state the name of the auditor and be signed and dated. Where the auditor is a firm, the report must be signed by the 'senior statutory auditor' in his own name, for and on behalf of the auditor (CA 2006 s. 504). This only applies to the set of the accounts provided to the members of the company. A signature is not required on the set of accounts delivered to Companies House. However, if the auditor wishes to physically sign the accounts for Companies House, they can be signed in the name of the firm rather than the individual.

The form of report by auditors to be adopted with respect to Companies Act accounts is determined by CA 2006 and also by international auditing standards applicable within the UK. Following the adoption of International Standards on Auditing (ISAs), auditors' reports on accounts are required to follow, inter alia, ISA (UK and Ireland) 700 (Revised) *The Auditor's Report on Financial Statements*, as commented on within **Chapter 13** – see **Example 13.1**.

Chapter 3 General accounting provisions

3.1 Introduction

This chapter summarises the accounting provisions of the CA 2006 which relate to the prescriptive formats of accounts, the content of accounts; and the principles and rules for determining amounts included in the accounts.

The chapter summarises accounts provisions of the CA 2006, insofar as they relate to accounts ('individual accounts') which the directors of the company have a duty to prepare in accordance with the CA 2006 s. 394. **Chapter 6** provides more detailed guidance on the company accounts provisions of the CA 2006 as they affect the accounts of companies under the 'small companies regime'. **Chapter 10** considers the additional impact on the accounts of small companies of the Financial Reporting Standard for Smaller Entities (FRSSE).

'Abbreviated accounts' (modified statutory accounts) are considered separately in **Chapter 8**. Matters relating to small groups of companies are covered in **Chapter 9**.

Annual accounts may be prepared:

- as 'Companies Act individual accounts' (CA 2006 s. 396) or 'Companies Act group accounts' (CA 2006 s. 404); or
- in accordance with international accounting standards ('IAS individual accounts' or 'IAS group accounts') (CA 2006 s. 395(1)).

Unless otherwise indicated, this chapter summarises and comments upon the accounts provisions of the CA 2006 insofar as they relate to Companies Act individual accounts, that is, prepared in accordance with the requirements of the CA 2006.

3.2 Accounts

Accounts must be prepared for members for all companies, irrespective of size (except some dormant companies – see **7.7**). *s. 394*

The full accounts of a 'small' company, however, are subject to reduced disclosure requirements compared to large or medium-sized companies (see **Chapter 6** 'Contents of small company accounts'). A small company may also take advantage of the FRSSE and the opportunities provided by the FRSSE are discussed further in **Chapter 10**.

A company qualifying as 'small' or 'medium-sized' (see **Chapter 5**) may, in addition, prepare 'abbreviated' accounts for filing with the Registrar of Companies.

Depending on certain size criteria, small companies may be exempt from the requirement for audit. Certain subsidiaries and dormant companies may also take advantage of audit exemption (see **Chapter 11**).

Company accounts are produced from the company's underlying financial records ('adequate accounting records') as explained at **3.10** (CA 2006 ss. 386–389 'Accounting Records').

Table 3.1 summarises the requirements which directors must follow in respect of a company's 'individual accounts' which are set out in CA 2006 s. 396.

Table 3.1 Individual accounts (CA 2006 s. 396)

For each financial year, the directors must prepare individual accounts comprising:

- a balance sheet; and
- a profit and loss account;

showing a true and fair view of:

- the state of affairs at the year end; and
- the profit or loss for the financial year;

complying with:

- the provisions of *The Small Companies and Groups (Accounts and Directors' Report) Regulations 2008* (SI 2008/409) (as to form, content and notes);

containing:

- any additional information (or departure from requirement) necessary to show a true and fair view.

3.3 'True and fair' view

As shown in **Table 3.1**, there is a fundamental requirement for full accounts (individual accounts
s. 393 or group accounts) to show a 'true and fair' view. The directors of a company must not approve accounts unless they are satisfied that they give a true and fair view of the company's assets, liabilities, financial position and profit or loss.

The requirement for full accounts to show a 'true and fair' view applies irrespective of whether or not the accounts are subject to audit. Any decision concerning the method of accounting or means of disclosing information must take this basic requirement into account.

The basic accounting principle is that annual accounts should show a 'true and fair' view, a term that has never been defined in statute or case law (but see **4.5.1**).

In essence, accounts are deemed to present a 'true and fair view' if they:

- comply with any relevant legislation or regulatory requirement;
- comply with accounting standards and generally accepted accounting practice (GAAP – see **Chapter 4**);
- provide an unbiased (fair and reasonable) presentation;
- are compiled with sufficient accuracy within the bounds of materiality; and
- faithfully represent the underlying commercial activity (the concept of 'substance over legal form').

The requirement for accounts to give a 'true and fair view' is also embodied within European Accounting Directives. In the case of IAS accounts, there is a requirement under international accounting standards that such accounts must achieve a 'fair presentation'.

A 'true and fair view' is required to be given of the state of affairs of the company (and/or consolidated undertakings) as at the end of the financial year and of the profit or loss of the company (and/or consolidated undertakings so far as concerns members of the parent company) for the financial year.

Where compliance with the provisions of CA 2006 as to the matters to be included in 'annual accounts' ('individual accounts' or 'group accounts') or the notes would not be sufficient to give a true and fair view, the necessary additional information must be given in the accounts or in a note to them.

If in *special circumstances* such compliance is inconsistent with the requirement to show a 'true and fair view', the directors must depart from the relevant provision of CA 2006 to the extent necessary to show a 'true and fair view' and must explain such departure in a note to the accounts (the true and fair 'override' principle). One common example of this circumstance concerns the non depreciation of fixed asset investment properties. *FRS 18*

The 'true and fair view' has the ultimate legal override; an entity may override accounting standards only to give a 'true and fair view' and this would be only in exceptional circumstances. A departure from an accounting standard must be justified and explained.

3.4 Format of accounts

The form and content of accounts is governed by regulations made under the CA 2006.

The form and content of Companies Act individual accounts is determined in accordance with:

- *the Small Companies and Groups (Accounts and Directors' Report) Regulations 2008* (SI 2008/409) for small companies; and
- *the Large and Medium-sized Companies and Groups (Accounts and Reports) Regulations 2008* (SI 2008/410) for medium-sized companies and large companies.

The Small Companies and Groups (Accounts and Directors' Report) Regulations 2008 (SI 2008/409) is set out in full in **Appendix B** and is discussed in greater detail in **Chapter 6**.

Schedules within SI 2008/409 and SI 2008/410 prescribe the required formats from which companies may choose for Companies Act individual and group accounts. Formats which are most commonly used by small companies are illustrated in **Chapter 6**.

Once a format has been adopted, the company must use the same format for subsequent years unless, in the directors' opinion, there are special reasons for changing; these must be disclosed in the year of change. *Sch 1.2, SI 2008/409*

Every balance sheet and profit and loss account must show the items listed in the adopted format if they apply either in the financial year or the preceding year. *Sch 1.1*

Adopting a particular format is not as restricting as it may seem, as there are a variety of options, for example: *Sch 1.3*

- departure from the format is allowed if it is made to ensure a true and fair view (see above); *Sch 1.10(2)*
- certain headings (which the Schedules identify by the use of Arabic numbers) may be combined (provided combination is disclosed); *Sch 1.4*
- immaterial items may be disregarded;
- information can be given in greater detail than prescribed and items not listed in a format may be included, if directors so wish; and
- certain information may be given in notes instead of on the face of the accounts.

Where there is no amount to be shown for a format item for the financial year, a heading or sub-heading corresponding to the item must not be included, unless an amount can be shown for the item in question for the immediately preceding financial year under the relevant format heading or sub-heading. *Sch 1.5*

For every balance sheet or profit and loss account item, the corresponding amount for the immediately preceding financial year must also be shown. Where that corresponding preceding year amount is not comparable, the prior year amount may be adjusted, but particulars of the non-comparability and of any adjustment must be disclosed in a note to the accounts. *Sch 1.7*

Every profit and loss account must show the amount of a company's profit or loss on ordinary
Sch 1.6 activities before taxation. (See **Chapter 6** at **6.5**.)

3.5 Accounting principles

Company accounts are required to be prepared in accordance with the principles set out in:

- Schedule 1 of SI 2008/409 – small companies;
- Schedule 6 of SI 2008/409 – small company groups;
- Schedule 1 of SI 2008/410 – medium-sized (and large) companies; and
- Schedule 6 of SI 2008/410 – medium-sized (and large company) groups.

These principles are the fundamental accounting concepts that underlie accounts and are also incorporated within accounting standards (FRSs and SSAPs) generally and (for small companies adopting it) the FRSSE.

The basic statutory accounting principles in SI 2008/409 are as follows.

1. *Going concern* – The company or reporting entity is presumed to be carrying on business as a going concern.
2. *Consistency* – Accounting policies must be applied consistently within the same accounts and from one financial year to the next.
3. *Prudence* – The amount of any item must be determined on a prudent basis and in particular:
   (a) only profits realised at the balance sheet date must be included in the profit and loss account; and
   (b) all liabilities having arisen in respect of the financial year (or preceding financial years) must be taken into account (including those liabilities becoming apparent up to the date of approval of the accounts (in accordance with CA 2006 s. 414)).
4. *Accruals* – All income and charges relating to the financial year to which the accounts relate must be taken into account, without regard to the date of receipt or payment.
5. *Individual determination* – In determining the aggregate amount of any item, the amount of each
Sch 1.15 individual asset or liability that is taken into account must be determined separately.
6. *Sch 1.8* *Netting* – Amounts in respect of items representing assets or income must not be set off against amounts in respect of items representing liabilities or expenditure (as the case may be), or vice versa.
7. *Substance of transactions* – In determining how amounts are presented within the accounts, regard should be had to the substance of the reported transaction or arrangement in accord-
Sch 1.9 ance with GAAP.

References to Sch 1 are to Schedule 1 of SI 2008/409.

If it appears to the company's directors that there are special reasons for departing from any of the accounting principles in preparing the company's accounts in respect of any financial year, they may do so. Particulars of the departure, the reasons for it and its effect must be given in a note to the accounts.

FRS 18, Accounting standards (FRSs generally) enhance the above principles by determining that
FRSSE accounting policies adopted should be relevant, reliable, comparable and understandable.

For fixed assets, stocks, investments and goodwill, rules regarding valuation, accounting and
Sch 1.16–29 disclosure are laid down in the Regulations.

Historical cost principles are stated as the normal method of accounting but alternative bases (e.g. revaluation and current cost) are allowed provided that details and related historical cost figures
Sch 1.30–35 are disclosed. The 'alternative accounting rules' are illustrated in **Appendix A (5)**.

Only 'realised' profits can be included in the profit and loss account. *Sch 1.13(a)*

In determining for accounting purposes 'realised profits' (and 'realised losses'), such profits or losses mean profits or losses of the company that fall to be treated as realised in accordance with principles generally accepted at the time when the accounts are prepared, unless the CA 2006 specifies some other treatment. *ss. 853(4)–(5)*

Financial instruments, including derivatives, may be included under the CA 2006 at fair value. *Sch 1.36–41*

It should be noted, however, that companies adopting 'fair value accounting' rules cannot apply the FRSSE, although this does not preclude accounting for fixed assets and investments at valuation.

3.6 Notes to accounts – disclosures

For small companies, Schedule 1 of *The Small Companies and Groups (Accounts and Directors' Report) Regulations 2008* (SI 2008/409) sets out the information required to be disclosed in the notes to a small company's accounts, covering the following heads: *Sch 1.42–63*

- reserves and dividends;
- disclosure of accounting policies;
- share capital;
- fixed assets;
- investments;
- assets and liabilities valued at fair value;
- investment property and living animals and plants at fair value;
- reserves and provisions;
- details of indebtedness (including payments by instalments and nature of security);
- guarantees and other financial commitments;
- particulars (analysis) of turnover;
- preceding year items included in profit and loss account – effect of inclusion;
- extraordinary and exceptional items;
- sums denominated in foreign currencies – basis of translation into sterling; and
- dormant companies acting as agent.

Schedule 1 of SI 2008/409 is included in **Appendix B**.

The enhanced disclosures for medium sized companies are contained in *The Large and Medium-sized Companies and Groups (Accounts and Reports) Regulations 2008* (SI 2008/410).

3.7 Directors' report – contents and requirements

The directors of a company must prepare a directors' report for each financial year of the company. *s. 415*

Where the company is a parent company, and the directors of the company prepare group accounts, the directors' report must be a consolidated report (a 'group directors' report') covering all the undertakings included in the consolidation. A group directors' report may, where appropriate, give greater emphasis to matters that are significant to the undertakings included in the consolidation, taken as a whole.

Small companies, however, are permitted to prepare a directors' report that is much reduced in content, omitting much of the information otherwise required to be included in the directors' report of a medium-sized or large company. (See **Table 6.6** at **6.7**.)

Companies which meet the definition of 'small' which are otherwise not able to take advantage of exemptions available to 'small companies' because they are part of an ineligible group (defined in **5.1**) are still entitled to small companies exemption in respect of their directors' report (s. 415A(1)(b)) in respect of the disclosures required by:

- s. 416(3) – the amount the directors recommend should be paid by way of dividend; and
- s. 417 – a business review.

Additionally, such a company need not file its directors' report with the Registrar of Companies (s. 446).

The directors of larger companies are required to prepare a directors' report complying with the following CA 2006 provisions:

- general matters (s. 416) including SI 2008/410 disclosures;
- business review (s. 417);
- matters covering company and subsidiaries (SI 2008/410) (parent company preparing group accounts); and
- statement as to disclosure of information to auditors (audited accounts) (s. 418).

The latter two are also required in small companies' directors' reports if the small companies are preparing group accounts and/or are subject to audit, respectively.

s. 420 Quoted companies are also required to prepare:

- a directors' remuneration report (s. 421), covering aspects of directors' remuneration such as remuneration details, company policy, service contracts, share options and pension disclosures; and
- operating and financial review (OFR).

In accordance with s. 385, a 'quoted company' means a company whose equity share capital has been included in the official list in accordance with the provisions of Part 6 of the Financial Services and Markets Act 2000 (c. 8), or is officially listed in an EEA State, or is admitted to dealing on either the New York Stock Exchange or the NASDAQ.

The directors' report of a small company is covered in **Chapter 6** at **6.7**.

3.8 Group accounts

A parent company (other than a small parent company (see **9.1**)) which has 'subsidiary undertakings' is required (with certain exceptions) to prepare group accounts in the form of consolidated accounts of the company and its subsidiary undertakings. Consolidation is not restricted to subsidiaries which are companies.

Group accounts (when prepared) are required to comply with the provisions of the CA 2006 as to the form and content of consolidated accounts and additional information to be given. Regulations under CA 2006 provided by SI 2008/409 Schedules 6 and 3 (Small companies) and SI 2008/410 Schedules 6 and 4 (large and medium-sized companies) require the following accounting for consolidations:

- elimination of group transactions;
- provisions for acquisition and merger accounting;
- treatment and disclosure of 'minority interests';

- non-consolidated subsidiary undertakings;
- joint ventures and associated undertakings; and
- preparation 'as if' the group were a single company.

A subsidiary may be excluded from consolidation on the grounds of immateriality and *must* be excluded in the following circumstances: *s. 405(2)*

- severe long-term restrictions; or *FRS 2*
- temporary control – holding with a view to subsequent resale. *FRS 2*

The exemptions available for small groups are explained in **Chapter 9**.

Exemptions from the requirement to prepare consolidated accounts otherwise available for groups generally are under:

- CA 2006 s. 400 (company included in EEA accounts of larger group);
- CA 2006 s. 401 (company included in non-EEA accounts of larger group); and
- CA 2006 s. 402 (company none of whose subsidiary undertakings need be included in the consolidation).

3.9 Audit reports

Full statutory accounts (together with an audit, if appropriate) are required for members for all companies (see **6.2**).

For companies other than those applying provisions for companies subject to the small companies regime, the availability or otherwise of audit exemption will determine whether the accounts should be accompanied by an auditor's report (see **Chapter 11**). *s. 475*

The auditor must consider whether the information given in the directors' report is consistent with the accounts and must state that fact in their report. There is no requirement to state in what respect it is inconsistent. *s. 496*

Where a company subject to audit prepares abbreviated accounts (under the 'small' and 'medium-sized' company filing provisions), a special auditor's report is required stating that in the auditor's opinion: *s. 449(2)*

- the company is entitled to deliver abbreviated accounts; and
- the abbreviated accounts have been properly prepared.

3.10 Adequate accounting records

Companies are required to keep 'adequate accounting records' in accordance with CA 2006 s. 386. Company accounts are produced from these underlying financial records.

CA 2006 s. 386 is summarised in **Table 3.2**.

Table 3.2 Adequate accounting records

A company is required to keep accounting records ('adequate accounting records') which are sufficient to show and explain the company's transactions. The accounting records must:

- disclose with reasonable accuracy, *at any time*, the financial position of the company *at that time*;
- enable the directors to ensure that any accounts required to be prepared comply with the requirements of CA 2006 (and, where applicable, of Article 4 of the IAS Regulation*);
- contain entries from day to day of all receipts and expenditure (with sufficient identifying detail); and
- contain a record of company assets and liabilities.

**Article 4 of the IAS Regulation relates to the consolidated accounts of publicly traded companies and explains the requirement for the preparation of the consolidated accounts in accordance with International Accounting Standards.*

If the company deals in goods, the accounting records must also contain statements of:

- stock held at the year end;
- stocktaking (records and procedures) underlying the year end stock; and
- all goods sold and purchased (except for retail sales), in sufficient detail to identify the goods and the buyers and sellers.

A parent company must ensure that any subsidiary undertaking keeps such accounting records as ensure compliance with CA 2006 or IAS.

(Directors should be constantly aware of the company's financial position and progress. The exact nature and extent of the accounting systems and management information needed to exercise adequate control will depend on the nature, complexity and extent of the company's business.)

Adequate control over records and transactions involves monitoring:

- cash;
- debtors and creditors;
- stock and work in progress;
- capital expenditure;
- contractual arrangements; and
- plans and budgets.

Accounting records are required by CA 2006 s. 388(4) to be preserved for:

- three years (private company); or
- six years (public company).

from the date on which they are made; although, having regard to other legislation, it is generally considered that documents should be kept for at least six years (and 12 years in the event of contracts under seal).

3.11 Approval and signature of accounts

The directors' report, statutory accounts and the auditor's report all require appropriate approval and signature.

A company's annual accounts must be approved by the board of directors and signed on behalf of the board by a director of the company. The signature must be on the company's individual balance sheet and the name of the signatory must be stated. *s. 414*

The directors' report must also be approved by the board of directors and signed on their behalf by a director *or* the secretary of the company; the name of the signatory must be similarly stated. On occasions when the secretary signs the directors' report this is generally 'by order of the board'. *s. 419(1)*

The above requirements also apply to the approval and directors' signature of abbreviated accounts. *s. 450(3)*

The auditor's report must state the name of the auditor and be signed and dated. Where the auditor is an individual, the report must be signed by him. Where the auditor is a firm, the report delivered to the members must be signed by the senior statutory auditor in his own name, for and on behalf of the firm of auditors. *s. 503*

The balance sheet and directors' report of a small company which have been prepared in accordance with the provisions applicable to companies subject to the small companies regime must each contain a statement by the directors to that effect in a prominent position above the signature (see **6.8**). *ss. 414(3) 419(2)*

3.12 Publication of statutory and non-statutory accounts

If a company publishes any of its statutory accounts (other than a summary financial statement under s. 426), they must be accompanied by the auditor's report on those accounts (unless the company is exempt from audit and the directors have taken advantage of that exemption). A company that prepares statutory group accounts for a financial year must not publish its statutory individual accounts for that year without also publishing with them its statutory group accounts. *s. 434*

If a company publishes non-statutory accounts, it must publish with them a statement indicating: *s. 435(1)*

- that they are not the company's statutory accounts;
- whether statutory accounts dealing with any financial year with which the non-statutory accounts purport to deal have been delivered to the Registrar of Companies; and
- whether an auditor's report has been made on the company's statutory accounts for any such financial year, and if so whether the report:
  (a) was qualified or unqualified, or included a reference to any matters to which the auditor drew attention by way of emphasis without qualifying the report; or
  (b) contained a statement under CA 2006 s. 498(2) (accounting records or returns inadequate or accounts or directors' remuneration report (where applicable) not agreeing with records and returns), or CA 2006 s. 498(3) (failure to obtain necessary information and explanations).

A company must not publish with any non-statutory accounts the auditor's report (i.e. the full audit report) on the company's statutory accounts. *s. 435(2)*

'Non-statutory accounts' are accounts or other published financial information that are not the company's statutory accounts (e.g. simplified accounting information such as an account in any form purporting to be a balance sheet or profit and loss account relating to the financial year of a company or group). *s. 435(3)*

Chapter 4 Accounts and accounting standards

4.1 Basic contents of financial statements

'Financial statements are a structured financial representation of the financial position of and transactions undertaken by an enterprise.'

In its *Statement of Principles for Financial Reporting*, issued in December 1999 (and to be withdrawn for accounting periods beginning on or after 1 January 2015), the Accounting Standards Board* (ASB) set out the concepts that underlie the preparation and presentation of financial statements. The ASB stated that the objective of financial statements is:

> 'to provide information about the reporting entity's financial performance and financial position that is useful to a wide range of users for assessing the stewardship of management and for making economic decisions.'

To meet this objective, accounting information is normally presented in the form of a structured set of financial statements comprising:

- primary statements; and
- the notes to the financial statements, including the accounting policies.

Together these will form the 'true and fair view accounts' (as the term is used in this book).

* On 2 July 2012, the Financial Reporting Council (FRC) replaced the ASB as the prescribed body for issuing standards and, in this chapter, documents which were issued originally by the ASB and which remained 'current' at the time of the replacement of the ASB, will be described as being issued by the FRC.

4.2 Primary statements

Primary statements under UK GAAP comprise the profit and loss account (the income statement); the statement of total recognised gains and losses (if necessary in addition to the profit and loss account); the balance sheet (assets, liabilities, and equity) and the cash flow statement. Notes to the financial statements amplify or explain items in the primary statements (for example, principal accounting policies).

The formats of the primary statements, as they apply to small companies, are determined as in **Table 4.1**.

Table 4.1 Formats of the primary statements

Primary statement	*Format determined by:*
Financial performance	
Profit and loss account	CA 2006 under SI 2008/409 Sch 1 (Small companies) amplified by FRSSE (if adopted)/relevant FRSs.
Statement of total recognised gains and losses (STRGL)	FRSSE (if adopted)/FRS 3 *Reporting financial performance* (see **4.3** below).
Financial position	
Balance sheet	CA 2006 under SI 2008/409 Sch 1 (Small companies) amplified by FRSSE (if adopted)/relevant FRSs.
Cash flow	
Cash flow statement	FRSSE (voluntary disclosure)/FRS 1 *Cash flow statements* (see **4.4** below).

4.3 Statement of total recognised gains and losses

A statement of total recognised gains and losses includes those items, being gains or losses, that are recognised in the period, but which do not pass through the profit and loss account. Gains, such as revaluation surpluses which are recognised but not necessarily realised in the period, are dealt with in this statement.

4.4 Cash flow statements

FRS 1 *Cash flow statements* requires, with exceptions, all entities producing true and fair view accounts to include a cash flow statement within the accounts drawn up in accordance with the FRS.

Companies which are eligible to adopt the small companies regime as set out in the CA 2006 are exempt from the requirement to produce a cash flow statement (but are, nevertheless 'encouraged' by the FRSSE to provide such a statement on a voluntary disclosure basis).

Medium-sized and larger companies and small ineligible companies (including, for example, a public, banking or insurance company or certain authorised entities under FSMA 2000), are required to prepare cash flow statements in accordance with FRS 1.

Subsidiary undertakings where 90 percent or more of the voting rights are controlled within the group, provided that consolidated financial statements in which those subsidiary undertakings are included are publicly available, are exempt from the requirement to prepare a cash flow statement.

For smaller entities, a form of cash flow statement indicated as voluntary disclosure is set out in the FRSSE, although where a small entity does choose to prepare a cash flow statement the format set out in FRS 1 is more commonly adopted.

If the parent company of a small group is entitled to the exemption from preparing group accounts, it is exempt from preparing a cash flow statement (whether its own individual statement or a consolidated one), whether or not group accounts are actually prepared.

4.5 Accounting standards

4.5.1 True and fair view

The concept of a true and fair view lies at the heart of financial reporting in the UK. As confirmed by the FRC in its July 2011 document 'True and Fair', the true and fair requirement remains of fundamental importance in both UK GAAP and IFRS.

CA 2006 s.393 requires that directors of a company must not approve accounts unless they are satisfied they give a true and fair view of the assets, liabilities, financial position and profit or loss:

- of the company (in the case of the company's individual accounts); and
- of the undertakings included in the consolidation as a whole, so far as concerns members of the company (in the case of the company's group accounts). *s. 393(1)*

For a company that is subject to audit, the auditor of the company, in carrying out his functions in relation to the company's annual accounts under CA 2006, must have regard to the directors' statutory duty in this respect. *s. 393(2)*

The term 'true and fair view' has never been defined precisely in statute or case law, although eminent authority has been given over the years in the form of legal opinion.

In essence, accounts are deemed to present a 'true and fair view' if they:

- comply with any relevant legislation or regulatory requirements;
- comply with accounting standards and generally recognised practice (GAAP – see below);
- provide an unbiased (fair and reasonable) presentation;
- are compiled with sufficient accuracy within the bounds of materiality; and
- faithfully represent the underlying commercial activity (the concept of 'substance over legal form').

The *Statement of Principles for Financial Reporting* states that 'it is inherent in the nature of the true and fair view concept that financial statements will not give a true and fair view unless the information they contain is sufficient in quantity and quality to satisfy the reasonable expectations of the readers to whom they are addressed.'

Companies that prepare Companies Act accounts in accordance with UK accounting standards are subject to the overriding requirement of CA 2006 (and regulations made under it) that accounts give a 'true and fair view', which, in all but highly exceptional cases, requires compliance with UK accounting standards.

UK tax legislation requires that the profits of a trade, profession or vocation be computed in accordance with generally accepted accounting practice on an accounting basis which gives a true and fair view, subject to any adjustment required by tax law in computing those profits.

Companies adopting international accounting and financial reporting standards (IFRS) are required to present accounts that are 'fairly presented'. Although in essence this may constitute a 'true and fair' view, unlike UK Accounting Standards, IFRS are explicitly part of the law rather than deriving from it.

In 2008, in the absence of statutory definition, the FRC commissioned legal opinion to confirm the continued relevance of the 'true and fair' concept to the preparation and audit of financial statements following the enactment of the CA 2006 and the introduction of IFRS. The opinion received is available at:

www.frc.org.uk/FRC-Documents/FRC/True-and-Fair-Opinion,-Moore,-21-April-2008.aspx

This legal opinion endorsed the analysis of previous opinions and confirmed the centrality of the 'true and fair view' concept in UK financial reporting. It also confirmed that 'fair presentation' under IFRS is equivalent to a true and fair view.

4.5.2 True and fair override

The 'true and fair view' has the ultimate legal override; an entity may override accounting standards only to give a 'true and fair view' and this would be only in exceptional circumstances. A departure from an accounting standard must be justified and explained.

The 'true and fair override' does not apply to companies which prepare their accounts in accordance with IFRS. Nevertheless, although the application of IFRS is presumed to result in a 'fair presentation', in extremely rare circumstances it may be necessary for a company to depart from strict compliance with IFRS in the interests of fair presentation.

4.5.3 Accounting standards

s. 464 Accounting standards are defined as 'such standards as are, in accordance with their terms, relevant to the company's circumstances and to the accounts'.

For the purposes of Part 15 of CA 2006 (Accounts and Reports) the term 'Accounting standards' means statements of standard accounting practice issued by such body or bodies as may be prescribed by regulations or the Secretary of State. Accounting standards applicable to a company's annual accounts are such standards as are relevant to the company's circumstances and to the accounts.

On 2 July 2012, the FRC replaced the ASB as the prescribed standard setting body for the purposes of CA 2006 s. 464.

'Accounting standards', in the context of this chapter, are UK accounting standards considered on the basis discussed in **4.5.1**, particularly the requirement to show a 'true and fair' view.

In its *Foreword to Accounting Standards (November 2012)* the FRC has stated that:

> 'Accounting standards are authoritative statements of how particular types of transaction and other events should be reflected in financial statements and accordingly compliance with accounting standards will be necessary for financial statements to give a true and fair view.'

Accounting standards are applicable to the accounts of a reporting entity which are intended to give a true and fair view of its state of affairs at the balance sheet date and of its profit or loss (or income and expenditure) for the financial period ending on that date.

Accounting standards do not need to be applied to items judged to be immaterial.

In preparing accounts giving a true and fair view, a company should therefore follow any applicable accounting standard (FRS or SSAP) unless there are good reasons for not doing so.

Accounting standards may comprise:

- Financial Reporting Standards (FRSs including the FRSSE) and UITF Abstracts;
- Statements of Standard Accounting Practice (SSAPs) (that is, accounting standards adopted by the ASB and now by the FRC but issued prior to the ASB's formation); and
- International Financial Reporting Standards (IFRSs including IASs and SIC interpretations) (for those companies adopting them – primarily, in the UK, quoted or publicly traded groups of companies only).

Recent years have seen a programme of increasing convergence (that is, harmonisation) of domestic UK and international (including US) financial reporting on the basis of globally accepted accounting standards (see **4.7**).

FRSs and SSAPs adopted by the FRC are 'accounting standards' for the purposes of the Companies Act legislation. The CA 2006 requires individual accounts, other than those prepared by small or medium-sized companies (as defined by the Act), to include a specific disclosure stating whether they have been prepared in accordance with applicable accounting standards and to give particulars of any material departure from those standards and the reasons for it. All companies, including small and medium-sized companies, must disclose and explain any departure from accounting standards necessary to provide a true and fair view.

References to accounting standards in the Act are contained in paragraph 45 of Sch. 1 *The Large and Medium-sized Companies and Groups (Accounts and Reports) Regulations 2008* (SI 2008/410), with the exemptions for medium-sized companies to be found in regulation 4(2) of SI 2008/410.

UITF Abstracts are published consensus pronouncements of the Urgent Issues Task Force (UITF)*, which deals with accounting issues and treatments requiring early authoritative interpretation. The pronouncements are made within the framework of the law and the principles established in accounting standards, and have a standing similar in authority to accounting standards. Once they had been accepted by the ASB (and now accepted by the FRC), a UITF Abstract is to be regarded as accepted practice in the area in question and therefore effectively has the force of an accounting standard. Amplification of accounting principles and treatment introduced by UITF Abstracts are invariably reflected within existing or subsequently revised FRSs.

The FRSSE was specifically written as a standalone standard for smaller entities and therefore many small companies choose to adopt the FRSSE instead of the whole range of FRSs and SSAPs which are more appropriate to larger entities (see **Chapter 10**).

* The role and responsibilities of the UITF were transferred from the ASB to the Accounting Council on 2 July 2012 as a result of the FRC reform.

4.5.4 Generally accepted accounting practice (GAAP)

There is no precise technical or legal definition of 'GAAP' in the UK. 'Generally accepted' means a practice that is accepted by accountants generally as being permissible in the particular circumstances of a business – the practice may not necessarily be the 'best' or 'only' accounting method available. GAAP may therefore be regarded as encompassing:

- accounting principles contained in 'Accounting Standards';
- Companies Acts and listing rules of quoted companies;
- industry-specific accounting treatments, including SORPs; and
- any other acceptable accounting treatment, including treatments for which there is currently no adopted Accounting Standard (for example, methods of 'revenue recognition').

4.6 Application of accounting standards to smaller companies

Although the *principles* of accounting (in terms of accounting methods and treatment, measurement criteria and estimation techniques) should apply equally to *all* companies, it is frequently recognised that the burden of complying with accounting standards falls more heavily upon the smaller company. Therefore within accounting standards there are a number of exemptions for smaller entities. A small company can alternatively choose to adopt the standalone FRSSE and **Chapter 10** provides guidance on the more significant impact of adoption of the FRSSE for smaller entities.

Table 4.2 gives an indication of the concessions that may be available to small or medium-sized companies in the application of the various Accounting Standards (SSAPs, FRSs and UITF Abstracts).

Unlike medium and large companies, a small company is not required by the Companies Act to make a statement in its individual accounts as to whether they have been prepared in accordance with applicable accounting standards and to give particulars of and reasons for any material departure from those standards (although if a true and fair override is applied, details of this must be disclosed – see **3.3**). However, this exemption relates only to disclosure – it does not diminish in any way the obligation of a small company to adopt and comply with appropriate accounting standards and prepare accounts which give a true and fair view.

Table 4.2 UK Accounting standards

This table shows the whole range of FRSs and SSAPs (excluding the new FRS 100 *Application of Financial Reporting Requirements* and FRS 101 *Reduced Disclosure Framework* and the soon to be released new UK accounting standard FRS 102 *The Financial Reporting Standard applicable in the UK and Republic of Ireland*) and comments on their application to and relevance for small companies. Exceptions and comments are made in the 'Application' column.

Statement	*Application*
Financial Reporting Standards (FRSs)	
FRS 1 *Cash flow statements*	Not applicable to those entities which can adopt the small companies regime (however can be voluntarily adopted)
FRS 2 *Accounting for subsidiary undertakings*	Applicable to parent undertakings preparing consolidated financial statements. However, a small parent undertaking exempt from preparing consolidated financial statements is required to provide disclosures in its individual accounts in accordance with SI 2008/409 Sch. 2.
FRS 3 *Reporting financial performance*	Applicable
FRS 4 *Capital instruments*	Substantially replaced by FRS 25 and FRS 26
FRS 5 *Reporting the substance of transactions*	Applicable for specific (generally more complex) transactions
FRS 6 *Acquisitions and mergers*	Applicable where appropriate for consolidated accounts
FRS 7 *Fair values in acquisition accounting*	Applicable where appropriate for acquisitions
FRS 8 *Related party disclosures*	Applicable
FRS 9 *Associates and joint ventures*	Where applicable
FRS 10 *Goodwill and intangible assets*	Where applicable
FRS 11 *Impairment of fixed assets and goodwill*	Applicable
FRS 12 *Provisions, contingent liabilities and contingent assets*	Applicable
FRS 13 *Derivatives and other Financial Instruments: Disclosures*	Substantially replaced by FRS 25 (IAS 32)
FRS 14 *Earnings per share*	Substantially replaced by FRS 22 (IAS 33)
FRS 15 *Tangible fixed assets*	Applicable
FRS 16 *Current tax*	Applicable
FRS 17 *Retirement benefits*	Applicable
FRS 18 *Accounting policies*	Applicable
FRS 19 *Deferred tax*	Applicable
FRS 20 *(IFRS 2) Share-based payment*	Applicable
FRS 21 *(IAS 10) Events after the balance sheet date*	Applicable
FRS 22 *(IAS 33) Earnings per share*	Not applicable
FRS 23 *(IAS 21) The effect of changes in foreign exchange rates*	Not applicable–but adoption permitted. Application as FRS 26
FRS 24 *(IAS 29) Financial reporting in hyperinflationary economies*	Rarely applicable–but adoption permitted. Application as FRS 26
FRS 25 *(IAS 32) Financial instruments: disclosure and presentation*	Presentation–application as FRS 26 Disclosure–replaced by FRS 29
FRS 26 *(IAS 39) Financial instruments: recognition and measurement*	Not applicable–other than listed companies or companies applying 'fair value accounting'

Table 4.2 UK Accounting standards (cont'd)

FRS 27 *Life assurance*	Not applicable (the small companies regime does not apply to authorised insurance companies and therefore this standard is not considered to be applicable)
FRS 28 *Corresponding amounts*	Applicable
FRS 29 *(IFRS 7)* Financial instruments: disclosures	Not applicable–other than entities applying FRS 26
Improvements to Financial Reporting Standards 2010	
FRS 30 *Heritage Assets*	Rarely seen in financial statements of small companies as heritage assets are generally held by not-for-profit entities
Statements of Standard Accounting Practice (SSAPs) adopted by FRC	
SSAP 4 *Accounting for Government grants*	Rarely seen in financial statements of small companies
SSAP 5 *Accounting for value added tax*	Applicable
SSAP 9 *Stocks and work-in-progress*	Applicable
SSAP 13 *Accounting for research and development*	Applicable but with disclosure exemptions
SSAP 19 *Accounting for investment properties*	Applicable
SSAP 20 *Foreign currency translation*	Applicable
SSAP 21 *Accounting for leases and hire-purchase contracts*	Applicable
SSAP 25 *Segmental reporting*	Not generally applicable
Urgent Issues Task Force (UITF) Abstracts	
Reporting entities applying the FRSSE are exempt from UITF Abstracts. (With the exception of UITFs 21, 24 and 28, no UITF Abstract is addressed or reflected within the FRSSE (see **Chapter 10**).)	
UITF 4 *Presentation of long-term debtors in current assets*	
UITF 5 *Transfers from current assets to fixed assets*	
UITF 9 *Accounting for operations in hyper-inflationary economies*	
UITF 11 *Capital instruments: issuer call options*	Adopted within FRS 26. Rarely applicable
UITF 15 *Disclosure of substantial acquisitions*	Rarely seen in financial statements of small companies
UITF 19 *Tax on gains and losses on foreign currency borrowings that hedge an investment in a foreign enterprise*	Rarely seen in financial statements of small companies
UITF 21 *Accounting issues arising from the proposed introduction of the euro*	Principles apply but disclosure exemption
UITF 22 *The acquisition of a Lloyds business*	Rarely seen in financial statements of small companies
UITF 23 *Application of the transitional rules in FRS 15*	
UITF 24 *Accounting for start-up costs*	Principles apply but disclosure exemption
UITF 25 *National Insurance contributions on share option gains*	Rarely seen in financial statements of small companies
UITF 26 *Barter transactions for advertising*	
UITF 27 *Revision to estimates of the useful economic life of goodwill and intangible assets*	
UITF 28 *Operating lease incentives*	Applicable

Table 4.2 UK Accounting standards (cont'd)

UITF 29 *Website development costs*	
UITF 31 *Exchanges of business or other non-monetary assets for an interest in a subsidiary, joint venture or associate*	
UITF 32 *Employee benefit trusts and other intermediate payment arrangements*	
UITF 34 *Pre-contract costs*	
UITF 35 *Death-in-service and incapacity benefits*	
UITF 36 *Contracts for sales of capacity*	Rarely seen in financial statements of small companies
UITF 38 *Accounting for ESOP trusts*	Rarely seen in financial statements of small companies. Amended within FRS 20
UITF 39 *Members' shares in cooperative entities and similar instruments*	
UITF 40 *Revenue recognition and service contracts*	
UITF 41 *Scope of FRS 20 (IFRS2)*	
UITF 42 *Reassessment of embedded derivatives*	Rarely seen in financial statements of small companies
UITF 43 *The interpretation of equivalence for the purposes of S 228A of the Companies Act 1985*	
UITF 44 *FRS 20 (IFRS2) – Group and Treasury share transactions*	
UITF *45 Liabilities arising from Participating in a Specific Market – Waste Electrical and Electronic Equipment*	Rarely seen in financial statements of small companies
UITF 46 *Hedges of a Net Investment in a Foreign Operation*	Rarely seen in financial statements of small companies
UITF 47 *Extinguishing Financial Liabilities with Equity Instruments*	
UITF 48 *Accounting implications of the replacement of the retail prices index with the consumer prices index for retirement benefits*	

4.7 International Accounting Standards

4.7.1 Introduction of IAS

The EU requirement to adopt international accounting standards (IAS) has been in place since 2005. Recent years have seen a continuing programme aiming at convergence (that is, harmonisation) of domestic UK, international and US financial reporting on the basis of globally accepted accounting standards.

Despite the fact that changes from 2005 onwards (in the UK) have impacted primarily on the consolidated accounts of quoted (that is, publicly traded) groups of companies, there has been an inevitability about the cascading effect of international harmonisation so that all companies, including small companies, will sooner or later have to embrace new procedures or principles. The recent arrival of FRS 100 *Application of Financial Reporting Requirements* and FRS 101 *Reduced Disclosure Framework* and the new UK accounting standard FRS 102 *The Financial Reporting Standard applicable in the UK and Republic of Ireland* (expected in March 2013) appears to confirm that UK GAAP will continue, albeit in a different form although one which has been derived from international GAAP, for the foreseeable future (see **Chapter 15**).

4.7.2 IASB standards

IFRSs are the financial reporting standards issued or adopted by the International Accounting Standards Board (IASB). The IASB is the independent body of the IFRS Foundation, formed in 2001 to succeed the International Accounting Standards Committee.

IASB and FRC (previously ASB) standards have over the years been very similar in many cases (although there were significant differences), having been developed on the basis of the application of general principles and the use of professional judgment. US accounting standards have traditionally incorporated a more rigid adherence to specific accounting rules and consequently convergence of IASB and US standards has posed a considerable challenge. Nevertheless, the IASB and the US Financial Accounting Standards Board (FASB) continue to work together on joint projects with the aim of achieving some harmonisation.

4.7.3 The EU Regulation on the Application of IAS

In July 2002, Member States of the EU adopted a Regulation (Regulation (EC) No. 1606/2002) on the application of accounting standards. Applying from financial years commencing 1 January 2005, the Regulation requires publicly traded companies (that is, companies whose securities are traded on a regulated market within the EU) to prepare their consolidated accounts on the basis of accounting standards issued by the International Accounting Standards Board that are adopted by the European Commission. The Regulation only applies to the detailed accounting provisions; domestic law implementing EU Accounting Directives where relevant will continue to apply in other areas such as the requirement to prepare individual accounts, auditing, enforcement and directors' reports.

Two main impacts of Regulation (EC) No. 1606/2002 for those UK companies affected are:

- such companies have to comply with adopted IASB accounting standards, rather than much of the CA 2006 and UK domestic standards issued by the ASB; and
- those IASB accounting standards have direct legal force within the UK, without the requirement for legislative action to turn them into UK statute law.

The EU Regulation applies directly to the preparation of consolidated accounts of publicly traded companies. In addition, the Regulation also permits each Member State to extend application to:

- the individual accounts of publicly traded companies; and
- the individual and/or consolidated accounts of some or all non-publicly traded companies.

Legislative change by statutory instrument was introduced by SI 2004/2947 to permit (but not require) all companies subject to the Companies Act (other than those automatically covered by the EU Regulation) to use international accounting standards (IASs – that is, EU-adopted IFRSs) as an alternative to UK domestic accounting standards.

Until such time as the EU Regulation is applied, by UK adoption, to private companies, the accounting requirements of such companies will continue to be governed by relevant UK GAAP determined by UK legislation (CA 2006) and FRC standards.

The adoption of IAS by smaller UK companies remains unusual and as such falls outside the scope of this book.

4.7.4 IAS accounts and the option to choose

The CA 2006 states that a company's individual accounts may be prepared either in accordance with UK GAAP (i.e. the accounting regulations specified by the Secretary of State as defined in

s. 396), which are referred to in the Act as 'Companies Act individual accounts', or in accordance with international accounting standards (s. 397) which the Act refers to as 'IAS individual accounts',
s. 395(1) subject to certain provisions.

The adoption of IAS in the UK can now be broadly illustrated as in **Table 4.3**.

Table 4.3 The adoption of IAS accounts by UK companies

	IAS accounts	*CA 2006 accounts*
Publicly traded companies (trading on an EU regulated market)	Required	Not permitted
Other publicly traded companies	Permitted (if not otherwise required by EU regulation)	Required (unless IAS accounts adopted)
Non-publicly traded companies	Permitted	Required (unless IAS accounts adopted)
Incorporated charities	Not permitted	Required

As part of the preparations for adoption of the new financial reporting framework set out in FRS 100, the Companies Act was recently amended by the *Companies and Limited Liability Partnerships (Accounts and Audit Exemptions and Change of Accounting Framework) Regulations* (SI 2012/2301) such that for financial years ending on or after 1 October 2012, the directors of a company that has voluntarily converted to IAS accounts in previous periods may choose to revert back to preparing Companies Act (UK GAAP) accounts (provided they have not changed to Companies Act accounts in the period of five years preceding the first day of that financial year). Prior to this revision, reverting to Companies Act accounts was only allowed under special circumstances as follows:

- the company becomes a subsidiary undertaking of another undertaking that does not prepare IAS individual accounts;
- the company ceases to be a subsidiary undertaking;
- the company ceases to be a company with securities admitted to trading on a regulated market in an EEA State; or
- a parent undertaking of the company ceases to be an undertaking with securities admitted to trading on a regulated market in an EEA State.

All companies within a group must consistently adopt the same accounting framework (that is, IAS or UK GAAP). Upon adopting IAS accounts, a company will still need to apply a variety of provisions of CA 2006 where the scope is beyond IAS (for example, disclosures of staff or directors' remuneration, or contents of the directors' report).

Small companies (as defined) should be alert to various factors if considering a move to full IAS accounts:

- no equivalent exemptions as afforded by CA 2006 or the FRSSE are available under IAS;
- the determinants to define a 'small company' are different within IAS formats;
- abbreviated accounts are not available for filing (although a small company is not required to file its IAS profit and loss account); and
- exemptions concerning audit exemption, the directors' report, and group accounts continue to be available.

4.8 The new financial reporting framework

The new framework to be applied by UK companies which will be mandatory for periods beginning on or after 1 January 2015 is discussed in **Chapter 15**.

Part II Smaller companies

Chapter 5 Qualifying as a small company

5.1 The 'small companies regime'

The CA 2006 provides for different provisions to apply in certain respects to different kinds of company. As far as the smaller (and unquoted) company is concerned, the main distinction is between:

- companies subject to the 'small companies regime'; and *s. 381*
- all other companies (companies that are not subject to that regime). *s. 380(3)*

The small companies regime applies to a company for a financial year in relation to which the company:

- qualifies as small; and *ss. 382–383*
- is not excluded from the regime. *s. 384*

The small companies regime does not apply to the following companies: *s. 384(1)*
(a) public companies;
(b) authorised insurance companies, banking companies, e-money issuers, MiFIDs, investment firms or UCITS management companies;
(c) companies carrying on insurance market activity*; or
(d) members of an ineligible group**.

Such companies are therefore excluded from the regime.

** As defined by the Financial Services and Markets Act 2000 section 316(3), 'insurance market activity' means a regulated activity relating to contracts of insurance written at Lloyd's.*

*** A group is ineligible if any of its members is a public company, a body corporate (other than a company) whose shares are admitted to trading on a regulated market in an EEA State, a person (other than a small company) who has permission under Part 4 of the Financial Services and Markets Act 2000 to carry on a regulated activity, a small company that is an authorised insurance company, a banking company, an e-money issuer, a MiFID investment firm or a UCITS management company, or a person who carries on insurance market activity.*

5.2 Qualifying conditions – 'small' and 'medium-sized' companies

Two classifications of companies – 'small' and 'medium-sized' – are entitled to certain special provisions with regard to the contents of the statutory accounts for filing with the Registrar of Companies.

CA 2006 s. 382(3) and 465(3) set out the conditions to be met by a company to qualify as 'small' or 'medium-sized' as appropriate.

Under the CA 2006, a company is treated as small or medium-sized if it does not exceed more than one of the following criteria: *s. 382(3) and s. 465(3)*

	Small	Medium-sized
Turnover	£6.5 million	£25.9 million
Balance sheet total	£3.26 million	£12.9 million
Average number of employees (on a monthly basis)	50	250
CA 2006 criteria amended (increased) by SI 2008/393		

s. 382(4) and s. 465(4) Turnover figures should be proportionately adjusted where the financial 'year' is not in fact 12 months.

s. 382(5) and s. 465(5) 'Balance sheet total' means the aggregate of the amounts shown as assets in the company's balance sheet (i.e. gross assets before deduction of liabilities, accruals and provisions; that is, the aggregate of headings A to D in Format 1 or the 'Assets' headings in Format 2).

The average number of employees is determined by using the number of persons employed under contracts of employment by the company each month and calculating an average. There is therefore no expectation that this is a measurement of 'full time' employees.

As a general rule, for a company to qualify as small or medium-sized, the criteria must be met for the current (Y1) and previous year (Y0). If the criteria are not met for the following year (Y2), a company may still continue to be treated as small or medium-sized, as appropriate, for that following year (Y2) if it met the criteria and qualified as small or medium-sized in the previous year (Y1). However, if the criteria are not met in the year after that (Y3), then the company must file accounts according to its size. Growing companies can therefore continue to be treated as small or medium-sized in the first year that they fail to meet the qualifying criteria.

If the company is in its first year and if the criteria are met for that first year, the company will qualify as small or medium-sized for that year.

Appendix C contains a decision chart to be used in determining whether small company accounts exemptions are available to a company for a particular year.

5.3 Parent companies and small groups

CA 2006 s. 383(4) and 466(4) set out the conditions to be met by a group for the parent company to qualify as 'small' or 'medium-sized' as appropriate.

s. 383 A parent company qualifies as a small company in relation to a financial year only if the group headed by it qualifies as a small group.

The size classification of a parent company is determined with regard to the aggregate qualifying criteria of the group taken as a whole (parent company and subsidiary undertakings), irrespective of the actual size qualification of the parent company itself (see **Chapter 9**).

Chapter 6 Contents of small company accounts

6.1 Introduction

This chapter summarises the company accounts provisions of the CA 2006 as they affect companies under the 'small companies regime'. The CA 2006 lays down provisions relating to:

- prescriptive formats of accounts;
- the content of accounts; and
- principles and rules for determining amounts included in the accounts.

This chapter summarises accounts provisions of the CA 2006, insofar as they relate to accounts ('Companies Act individual accounts') that are prepared in accordance with the CA 2006 s. 396. **Chapter 10** considers the additional impact on the accounts of small companies of the Financial Reporting Standard for Smaller Entities (FRSSE).

'Abbreviated accounts' (modified statutory accounts for filing purposes) are considered separately in **Chapter 8**. Small company 'group accounts' under CA 2006 s. 398 and s. 404 are considered in **Chapter 9**.

6.2 Accounts – provisions for small companies

For each financial year accounts must be prepared for all companies, irrespective of size. *s. 394 et seq*

The accounts of a 'small' company, however, are often less detailed with reduced statutory disclosure requirements compared to larger companies. A small company may also take advantage of the FRSSE.

In addition, a company qualifying as 'small' or 'medium sized' (see **Chapter 5**) may prepare 'abbreviated' accounts for filing with the Registrar of Companies. A company wishing to file abbreviated accounts with the Registrar of Companies has to produce two sets of accounts: the annual accounts for members and the abbreviated accounts.

By virtue of the provisions applicable for companies subject to the small companies regime set out in the CA 2006, a small company is therefore entitled to prepare:

- annual accounts for members – with a balance sheet and reduced disclosure requirements for the notes to the accounts and the directors' report (as determined by SI 2008/409); and
- abbreviated accounts for filing and delivery to the Registrar of Companies – under CA 2006 s. 444.

Company accounts prepared in accordance with the provisions of the CA 2006 s. 396 and requirements within the Regulations contained in Sch. 1 of SI 2008/409 are referred to as 'small company accounts' in this book. CA 2006 s. 396 and SI 2008/409 together determine the minimum disclosure required in a small company's annual accounts. However, a small company does not have to take advantage of all the exemptions and modifications permitted if it does not wish to do so.

For example, SI 2008/409 provides that Companies Act individual accounts 'are treated as having complied with any provision of Schedule 1 to these Regulations [i.e. the 'Small Companies Accounts Regs' SI 2008/409] if they comply instead with the corresponding provision of Schedule 1 to the Large and Medium-Sized Companies and Groups (Accounts and Reports) Regulations 2008 [SI 2008/410]'. *409 reg 3(3)*

Similarly, Companies Act group accounts 'are treated as having complied with any provision of Part 1 to Schedule 6 [of SI 2008/409 – "Form and content of Companies Act group accounts"] if they comply instead with the corresponding provision of Schedule 6 to the Large and Medium-Sized Companies Accounts Regs [SI 2008/410]'. *409 reg 8(2)*

The provisions applicable to small companies apply not only to the individual accounts of such companies but also to the group accounts where a small company produces them. If at the end of a financial year a company subject to the small companies regime is a parent company, the directors, as well as preparing individual accounts for the year, have the option to prepare group accounts for the year, if they so wish. *s. 399*

6.3 Format of small company accounts

6.3.1 SI 2008/409

Under the small companies regime of the CA 2006, the form and content of:

- Companies Act individual accounts for small companies;
- Companies Act group accounts for small companies; and
- Companies Act abbreviated accounts

are determined in accordance with *The Small Companies and Groups (Accounts and Directors' Report) Regulations 2008* (SI 2008/409).

The Regulations in SI 2008/409 prescribe the required formats for Companies Act individual accounts from which small companies may choose. Formats which are most commonly used are illustrated later in this chapter.

Once a format has been adopted, the company must use the same format for subsequent years unless, in the directors' opinion, there are special reasons for changing; these must be disclosed in the year of change. *Sch 1.2(1)*

6.3.2 Form and content of accounts prepared by small companies

The form and content of individual accounts prepared by small companies are determined in accordance with regulations provided by *The Small Companies and Groups (Accounts and Directors' Report) Regulations 2008* (SI 2008/409) and in particular Schedule 1.

Schedule 1 to SI 2008/409 (Companies Act individual accounts) is structured as in **Table 6.1**.

Table 6.1 Schedule 1 Companies Act individual accounts – The Small Companies and Groups (Accounts and Directors' Report) Regulations 2008 (SI 2008/409)

Part 1 General rules and formats

Section A	General rules
Section B	Required formats for accounts • Balance sheet formats (Formats 1 and 2) and notes thereon • Profit and loss account formats (Formats 1, 2, 3 and 4) and notes thereon

Part 2 Accounting principles and rules

Section A	Accounting principles • Accounting principles
Section B	Historical cost accounting rules • Fixed assets • Depreciation and diminution in value • Development costs • Goodwill • Current assets • Miscellaneous and supplementary provisions *(including determination of purchase price and production cost, and assets included at a fixed amount)*
Section C	Alternative accounting rules • Alternative accounting rules • Application of the depreciation rules • Additional information to be provided in case of departure from historical cost account rules • Revaluation reserve
Section D	Fair value accounting • Inclusion of financial instruments at fair value • Determination of fair value • Hedged items • Other assets that may be included at fair value • Accounting for changes in value • The fair value reserve

Part 3 Notes to the accounts

- Reserves and dividends
- Disclosure of accounting policies
- Information supplementing the balance sheet *(Share capital, fixed assets, investments, fair values, reserves and provisions, indebtedness, and guarantees and other financial commitments)*
- Information supplementing the profit and loss account *(including particulars of turnover)*
- Miscellaneous matters *(including foreign currencies and dormant companies acting as agents)*

Schedule 1 is reproduced in full in **Appendix B**.

6.3.3 The statutory formats

The accounts formats from which a small company may choose are given in SI 2008/409 Schedule 1 (Part 1 Section B – 'The required formats for accounts').

There is a choice of:

- *four* profit and loss account formats; and
- *two* balance sheet formats.

Two profit and loss account formats and one of the balance sheet formats are in the 'vertical' styling in which most accounts are prepared. The two 'horizontal' styles of profit and loss account (Formats 3 and 4) and balance sheet (Format 2) are not generally used.

Balance sheet

A small company must adopt in its annual (individual) accounts one of the formats of balance sheet set out in SI 2008/409 Schedule 1 (Part 1 Section B). If applicable, it must show the items listed in either of the formats, as set out in **Tables 6.2** and **6.3**. The individual balance sheet of a small company which adopts Format 1 would be as set out in **Table 6.4**.

Profit and loss account

The choice of profit and loss account formats for a small company is set out in SI 2008/409 Schedule 1 (Part 1 Section B) which is reproduced in **Appendix B**. The formats are also illustrated in **Table 6.5**. The principles governing the formats are as set out in **3.4**.

Accounting principles

Small company accounts are prepared in accordance with the principles set out in SI 2008/409 Schedule 1 (Part 2 Section A). These principles are the fundamental accounting concepts that underlie accounts and are also incorporated within FRSs and SSAPs generally, including the
Sch 1.9–15 FRSSE.

Accounting principles are explained further in **3.5** (**Chapter 3**).

6.4 Small company balance sheet

The formats of balance sheet set out in SI 2008/409 Schedule 1 (Part 1 Section B) from which a small company must choose for its annual (individual) accounts are set out in **Table 6.2**. **Table 6.2** illustrates the differences between the two balance sheet formats available.

Table 6.2 Small company balance sheets – the two formats compared

The items shown as boxed in Format 1 need not be disclosed in Format 2. For illustrative purposes, the Arabic number sub-headings (which are common to both formats) are not reproduced in this table but are set out in **Table 6.3**.

Format 1		Format 2	
	ASSETS		
A	Called up share capital not paid	A	Called up share capital not paid
B	Fixed assets	B	Fixed assets
	I Intangible assets		I Intangible assets
	II Tangible assets		II Tangible assets
	III Investments		III Investments
C	Current assets	C	Current assets
	I Stocks		I Stocks
	II Debtors		II Debtors
	III Investments		III Investments
	IV Cash at bank and in hand		IV Cash at bank and in hand
D	Prepayments and accrued income	D	Prepayments and accrued income
E	Creditors: amounts falling due within one year		– –
F	Net current assets (liabilities)		
G	Total assets less current liabilities		
	LIABILITIES		
H	Creditors: amounts falling due after more than one year	A	Capital and reserves
			I Called up share capital
			II Share premium account
			III Revaluation reserve
			IV Other reserves
			V Profit and loss account
		[ ]	Minority interests
I	Provisions for liabilities	B	Provisions for liabilities
J	Accruals and deferred income		
[ ]	Minority interests [*Alternative* (1)]		
	– – – – – – – – – – – – – – – –		
K	Capital and reserves	C	Creditors
	I Called up share capital		[*Amounts falling due within one year and after one year must be shown separately for each of the items in creditors and in aggregate unless the aggregate amounts within one year and after one year are disclosed in the notes.*]
	II Share premium account		
	III Revaluation reserve		
	IV Other reserves		
	V Profit and loss account		
[ ]	Minority interests [*Alternative (2)*]	D	Accruals and deferred Income

The dotted line above in Format 1 illustrates the usual 'break-point' in the balance sheet, although in practice the balance sheet total could be 'struck' after item G. Format 2 requires balance sheet totals of ASSETS and LIABILITIES to be given.

Table 6.3 Small company balance sheets – Arabic number sub-headings

B I INTANGIBLE ASSETS

1 Goodwill
2 Other intangible assets

B II TANGIBLE ASSETS

1 Land and buildings
2 Plant and machinery etc.

B III INVESTMENTS

1 Shares in group undertakings and participating interests
2 Loans to group undertakings and undertakings in which the company has a participating interest
3 Other investments other than loans
4 Other investments

C I STOCKS

1 Stocks
2 Payments on account

C II DEBTORS

1 Trade debtors
2 Amounts owed by group undertakings and undertakings in which the company has a participating interest
3 Other debtors

C III INVESTMENTS

1 Shares in group undertakings
2 Other investments*

CREDITORS: AMOUNTS FALLING DUE WITHIN ONE YEAR

1 Bank loans and overdrafts
2 Trade creditors
3 Amounts owed to group undertakings and undertakings in which the company has a participating interest
4 Other creditors

CREDITORS: AMOUNTS FALLING DUE AFTER MORE THAN ONE YEAR

1 Bank loans and overdrafts
2 Trade creditors
3 Amounts owed to group undertakings and undertakings in which the company has a participating interest
4 Other creditors

** For group balance sheets, the format headings are as set out in SI 2008/409 Schedule 6 (Part I paragraph 1(2) – see Note 1 to Table 6.4)*

The balance sheet format of a small company which adopts balance sheet Format 1 would be as set out in **Table 6.4**.

Table 6.4 Small company balance sheet (Format 1)

CALLED UP SHARE CAPITAL NOT PAID

FIXED ASSETS
Intangible assets
Goodwill
Other intangible assets

Tangible assets
Land and buildings
Plant and machinery, etc.

Table 6.4 Small company balance sheet (Format 1) (cont'd)

Investments *(Note 1)*
Shares in group undertakings and participating interests
Loans to group undertakings and undertakings in which the company has a participating interest
Other investments other than loans
Other investments

CURRENT ASSETS
Stocks
Stocks
Payments on account

Debtors *(Note 2)*
Trade debtors
Amounts owed by group undertakings and undertakings in which the company has a participating interest
Other debtors

Investments
Shares in group undertakings
Other investments

Cash at bank and in hand

PREPAYMENTS AND ACCRUED INCOME

CREDITORS: amounts falling due within one year
Bank loans and overdrafts
Trade creditors
Amounts owed to group undertakings and undertakings in which the company has a participating interest
Other creditors *(Note 3)*

NET CURRENT ASSETS (LIABILITIES)

TOTAL ASSETS LESS CURRENT LIABILITIES

CREDITORS: amounts falling due after more than one year
Bank loans and overdrafts
Trade creditors
Amounts owed to group undertakings and undertakings in which the company has a participating interest
Other creditors

PROVISIONS FOR LIABILITIES

ACCRUALS AND DEFERRED INCOME *(Note 4)*

CAPITAL AND RESERVES
Called up share capital
Share premium account
Revaluation reserve
Other reserves
Profit and loss account

Note 1 Where a small company prepares small group accounts, in a consolidated balance sheet the format for 'Investments' is:
1. *shares in group undertakings;*
2. *interests in associated undertakings;*
3. *other participating interests;*
4. *loans to group undertakings and undertakings in which a participating interest is held;*
5. *other investments other than loans; and*
6. *others.*

SI 2008/409 Sch. 6.1(2)

Table 6.4 Small company balance sheet (Format 1) (cont'd)

Note 2 A small company must disclose the aggregate total of 'debtors falling due after more than one year' but such disclosure (if the amount is not material) may be in the notes to the accounts rather than in the balance sheet.

Note 3 The amount of any creditors in respect of taxation and social security and convertible loans should be shown separately.

Payments received on account must be included in so far as they are not shown as deductions from stock.

Note 4 Accruals and deferred income may also be shown under 'other creditors'.

6.5 Small company profit and loss account

The choice of profit and loss account formats for a small company, as set out in SI 2008/409 Sch. 1 (Part 1 Section B), is illustrated in **Table 6.5**.

In practice, care needs to be taken in the choice of format and presentation of the profit and loss account. **Table 6.5** presents a comparison of the two formats (Formats 1 and 2) showing the differences in presentation and disclosure. It is particularly relevant to note:

- *gross profit or loss* is specifically disclosed only in Format 1 (it may also be readily ascertained from Format 3); and
- *depreciation* may require allocation over various cost headings in Format 1 (and 3) but needs only to be shown as one item in a Format 2 (or 4) profit and loss account.

The amount of a company's 'profit or loss on ordinary activities before taxation' must be included on every profit and loss account. (This item is not specified in the formats.)

All formats require similar information, except that Formats 3 and 4 require separate totals of 'charges' and 'income'.

All other items in the profit and loss account formats (being represented by Arabic numbers) could be combined and given in the notes to the accounts, provided the profit and loss account contains a summarised linking figure.

For small companies which are able and intend to file abbreviated accounts (which omit a profit and loss account) on the public record with the Registrar of Companies, the choice of profit and loss account formats in their full accounts may be of less consequence.

Table 6.5 Small company profit and loss account formats (SI 2008/409 Schedule 1 (Part I Section B))

Items boxed show the differences in disclosure required by the formats.

(Note: Formats 3 and 4 are not recognised under the FRSSE (see **Chapter 10**)).

Expenses classified by function	**Expenses classified by type**
Format 1	*Format 2*
Format 3 requires the same information in a different presentation	Format 4 requires the same information in a different presentation
1 Turnover	1 Turnover

Table 6.5 Small company profit and loss account formats (SI 2008/409 Schedule 1 (Part I Section B)) (cont'd)

2	Cost of sales	2	Change in stocks of finished goods and work in progress
3	Gross profit or loss	3	Own work capitalised
4	Distribution costs		
5	Administrative expenses		
6	Other operating income	4	Other operating income
		5	(a) Raw materials and consumables (b) Other external charges
	(In Format 1 staff costs must be allocated over items 2, 4 and 5. (Staff costs disclosure in the notes is not applicable for small companies (CA 2006 s .411))	6	Staff costs: (a) Wages and salaries (b) Social security costs (c) Other pension costs
	(In Format 1 depreciation must be allocated over items 2, 4 and 5 (Sch 1 Part I Section B note 11) and disclosed separately in Notes (Sch 1.19))	7	(a) Depreciation and other amounts written off tangible and intangible fixed assets
			b) Exceptional amounts written off current assets
		8	Other operating charges
7	Income from shares in group undertakings	9	Income from shares in group undertakings
8	Income from participating interests	10	Income from participating interests
9	Income from other fixed asset investments	11	Income from other fixed asset investments
10	Other interest receivable and similar income	12	Other interest receivable and similar income
11	Amounts written off investments	13	Amounts written off investments
12	Interest payable and similar charges	14	Interest payable and similar charges
12A	*Profit or loss on ordinary activities before taxation (Sch. 1.6 and FRSSE)*	*14A*	*Profit or loss on ordinary activities before taxation (Sch 1.6 and FRSSE)*
13	Tax on profit or loss on ordinary activities	15	Tax on profit or loss on ordinary activities
14	Profit or loss on ordinary activities after taxation	16	Profit or loss on ordinary activities after taxation
15	Extraordinary income	17	Extraordinary income
16	Extraordinary charges	18	Extraordinary charges
17	Extraordinary profit or loss	19	Extraordinary profit or loss
18	Tax on extraordinary profit or loss	20	Tax on extraordinary profit or loss
19	Other taxes not shown under the above items	21	Other taxes not shown under the above items
20	Profit or loss for the financial year	22	Profit or loss for the financial year

Extraordinary items, although included within the statutory formats, are now viewed by the FRSSE (and FRS 3 Reporting financial performance*) as being extremely rare.*

'Profit and loss on ordinary activity before taxation' must also be disclosed – see SI 2008/409 Sch. 1.6 and FRSSE.

Where a small company prepares group accounts, the items in **Table 6.5** headed 'Income from participating interests' in the above formats (item 8 (Format 1) and item 10 (Format 2)) become two items:

SI 2008/409 Sch 6.1(3)

- Income from interests in associated undertakings; and
- Income from other participating interests.

6.6 Notes to the accounts – small company

A small company must set out in the notes (if not given in the company's accounts) the following information specified in SI 2008/409 Sch. 1 paragraphs 42–63:

Information supplementing the balance sheet:

- Sch 1.46–47 *Share capital*
  Details of allotted share capital; information about redeemable shares; share allotments during the year for each class of shares.
- Sch 1.48–49 *Fixed assets*
  Additions, disposals, revaluations, depreciation and other movements for each category of fixed assets.
- Sch 1.50 *Investments*
  Listed investments; market valuation.
- Sch 1.51–53 *Fair value of assets and liabilities*
  Assumptions and techniques used; fair value and transfers to/from reserves for each category of financial instruments; terms and details of each class of derivatives.
  Details of investment property and living animals and plants at fair value.
- Sch 1.54 *Reserves and provisions*
  Movements and transfers to/from reserves and provisions.
  Details of each 'other provisions' which is material.
- Sch 1.55–56 *Details of indebtedness*
  Creditors payable or repayable in more than five years; security; arrears of fixed cumulative dividends.
- Sch 1.57 *Guarantees and other financial commitments*
  Particulars of charges on assets, contingent liabilities, capital commitments not provided for, pension commitments and other financial commitments.
- Sch 1.58 *Substituted price or cost of assets where price or cost unknown*
  Particulars must be given of any case where the purchase price or production cost of any asset is for the first time determined under paragraph 29.

Information supplementing the profit and loss account:

- Sch 1.60 *Turnover**
  Percentage attributable to geographical markets outside UK.

- Sch 1.61 *Miscellaneous**
  Effect of prior year adjustments and exceptional transactions, and particulars of extraordinary charges or income.

SI 2008/409 Reg 3(2) ** The profit and loss account of a company that falls within CA 2006 s. 408 (individual profit and loss account where group accounts prepared) need not contain the information specified in paragraphs 60-61.*

- Sch 1.62 *Sums in foreign currencies*
  Basis of translation of foreign currencies.

- *Dormant companies acting as agents* Sch 1.63
  Audit exempt dormant companies acting as agents.

Information about related undertakings (small groups):

Where the parent company of a small group does not prepare group accounts, it must set out in the notes to the company's accounts the information about related undertakings specified in SI 2008/409 Sch. 2 as specified by Regulation 4. The required disclosures are set out in **Chapter 9**.

Other information to be disclosed:

- *Reserves and Dividends* Sch 1.43
  Actual or proposed movements and transfers to and from reserves.
  Aggregate amount of dividends paid in the financial year (other than those for which a liability existed at the immediately preceding balance sheet date).
  Aggregate amount of dividends that the company is liable to pay at the year end.
  Aggregate dividend proposed before date of approval of accounts, not already disclosed above.

- *Disclosure of accounting policies* Sch 1.44
  Policies in respect of items on the balance sheet and used in determining the profit or loss of the company.

- *Directors' benefits – advances, credit and guarantees*
  CA 2006 s. 413 provides for the disclosure of advances and credits granted by a company to its directors, and guarantees of any kind entered into by a company on behalf of its directors (see **6.10**).

- *Liability limitation agreements*
  A company (subject to audit) which has entered into a liability limitation agreement limiting an auditor's liability must disclose in the notes:

  - the principal terms of the agreement; and
  - the date of the resolution approving the agreement (or its principal terms) or, in the case of a private company, the date of the resolution waiving the need for such approval.
    (CA 2006 s. 538 and SI 2008/489 reg 8.)

6.7 Directors' report of a small company

6.7.1 Small company directors' report – entitlement

A company is entitled to the small companies exemption in relation to the directors' report for a financial year if:

- it is entitled to prepare accounts for the year in accordance with the small companies regime; or
- it would be so entitled but for being or having been a member of an ineligible group (see **9.2**). s. 415A

The exemption enables a small company:

- not to provide a business review (otherwise required by s. 417);
- not to provide a statement of the amount recommended by way of dividend (under s. 416(3)); and
- to take advantage of matters set out in s. 444 to 446 (being the filing obligations of medium-sized or unquoted companies).

This latter exemption allows a company which is a member of an ineligible group, and which as a result cannot be treated as small for the purposes of preparing it financial statements, to dispense with the requirement to file a directors' report with its financial statements at Companies House.

6.7.2 Small company directors' report – contents

As a result of the available exemption, the directors' report of a small company is only required to provide the following information:

CA 2006 s. 416

- names of directors during the year; and
- principal activities.

SI 2008/409 Sch. 5 (see **Appendix B** for full disclosure requirements)

- political donations (to a party, organisation or election candidate) and expenditure (exceeding £2,000);
- charitable donations (exceeding £2,000);
- company acquiring own shares; and
- employment of disabled persons (where average weekly employees exceed 250).

CA 2006 s. 236

- qualifying third party indemnity provision.

For a company entitled to small companies exemptions in relation to the directors' report (CA 2006 s. 415A) to take advantage of the exemptions, the directors' report must contain a statement to that effect under s. 419(2). This statement is explained in **6.8**.

Table 6.6 compares the contents of a directors' report of a company entitled to the small companies exemption with the requirements for other unquoted companies, including medium-sized companies.

Table 6.6 Contents of directors' report

Entitled to small companies exemption	***Other companies***
Section 416	***Section 416***
Names of directors during the financial year.	Names of directors during the financial year.
Principal activities of the company and its subsidiary undertakings and any significant changes during the year.	Principal activities of the company and its subsidiary undertakings and any significant changes during the year.
	Amount of dividend payment, if any, recommended.
	Section 417
	Business review – a fair review of the business and description of the principal risks and uncertainties, development and performance of the company and its subsidiary undertakings during the financial year (including key performance indicators) and of their position at the end of it.
	(The extent of business review will depend on whether the company is medium-sized or quoted.)

Table 6.6 Contents of directors' report (cont'd)

SI 2008/409 Sch. 5	***SI 2008/410 Sch. 7***
	Asset values – including any significant and substantial difference in market value of interests in land at the year end from balance sheet amount.
Political and charitable gifts exceeding £2,000 (not applicable for wholly-owned subsidiaries).	Political and charitable gifts exceeding £2,000 (not applicable for wholly-owned subsidiaries).
	Disclosures relating to the use of financial instruments.
	Particulars of any important post balance sheet events affecting the company and its subsidiary undertakings.
	Indication of likely future developments in the business of the company and its subsidiary undertakings.
	Indication of research and development activities (if any), of the company and its subsidiary undertakings.
	Indication of the existence of branches outside the UK (unless company is unlimited company).
Particulars of any purchase by the company of its own shares.	Particulars of any purchase by the company of its own shares.
Statement of policy of the company concerning the employment of disabled persons. (*Only companies with average weekly employees of more than 250.*)	Statement of policy of the company concerning the employment of disabled persons. (*Only companies with average weekly employees of more than 250.*)
	Statement of arrangements adopted concerning employee involvement. (*Only companies with average weekly employees of more than 250.*)
	Statement of policy and practice on the payment of creditors. (*Public company and large (i.e. other than small or medium-sized) subsidiaries only.*)
	Additional disclosures required by certain publicly traded companies.

Disclosure of information to auditors (s. 418) *– Unless a company is exempt for the financial year in question from the requirements of CA 2006 Part 16 as to audit of accounts (and the directors take advantage of that exemption), the directors' report must also contain a statement as to disclosure of relevant audit information to auditors in accordance with CA 2006 s. 418.*

6.7.3 Drafting considerations

When drafting a small company's directors' report for full shareholders' (Companies Act individual) accounts, it is worth bearing in mind whether abbreviated accounts are going to be prepared.

In 'small company' abbreviated accounts, no directors' report is required.

The directors' report of a 'medium-sized company' is reproduced in full in abbreviated accounts and should be drafted with this in mind.

6.8 Directors' statements

A company which qualifies as a small company in relation to a financial year (other than a dormant company) and takes advantage of the provisions applicable to companies subject to the small companies regime with respect to the preparation of annual accounts and/or directors' report must include statements in its accounts, where appropriate, on the balance sheet, and in the directors' report confirming preparation in accordance with the small companies regime provisions.

For small (unquoted) companies, every copy of any balance sheet and directors' report that is published by or on behalf of the company must state the name of the person who signed it on behalf of the board. *s. 433*

6.8.1 Directors' statement – small company accounts preparation: Sections 414 and 419

A company's annual accounts must be approved by the board of directors and signed on behalf of the board by a director of the company. The signature must be on the company's balance sheet.

If the accounts are prepared in accordance with the provisions applicable to companies subject to the small companies regime, the balance sheet must contain a statement to that effect in a prominent position above the signature. *s. 414*

The balance sheet therefore must contain (in a 'prominent position' above the signature of a director required by s. 414(1-2)) a statement that the accounts have been prepared in accordance with the provisions applicable to companies subject to the small companies regime within Part 15 of CA 2006. Reference to the FRSSE (effective April 2008) should also be made in this statement, but only if applicable, as indicated by the tinted text in **Example 6.1** below.

> ***Example 6.1***
>
> **Section 414 Directors' statement – balance sheet**
> These accounts have been prepared in accordance with the provisions applicable to companies subject to the small companies regime as set out within Part 15 of the CA 2006 *[and with the Financial Reporting Standard for Smaller Entities (effective April 2008)].*

The directors' report must be approved by the board of directors and signed on behalf of the board by a director or the secretary of the company. *s. 419*

If the report is prepared in accordance with the small companies regime, the directors' report must contain (in a 'prominent position' above the signature of a director or secretary required by s. 419(1)) a statement that the report has been prepared in accordance with the provisions applicable to companies subject to the small companies regime as set out within Part 15 of CA 2006 relating to small companies.

> ***Example 6.2***
>
> **Section 419 Directors' statement – directors' report**
> The above report has been prepared in accordance with the provisions applicable to companies subject to the small companies regime as set out within Part 15 of the CA 2006.

6.8.2 Directors' statement – small company audit exemption entitlement: Section 475

A small company eligible for audit exemption is required to provide a statutory statement in accordance with CA 2006 s. 475(2) to appear in the balance sheet above the director's signature of approval.

> ***Example 6.3***
>
> **Section 475 Directors' statement – entitlement to exemption from audit (Balance sheet)**
> For the financial year ended [ ] the company was entitled to exemption from audit under s. 477* of CA 2006; and no notice has been deposited under s. 476.
> The directors acknowledge their responsibilities for complying with the requirements of the CA 2006 with respect to accounting records and the preparation of accounts.

** s. 477 relates to the exemption for small companies; if the company is dormant, replace s. 477 with s. 480.*

6.8.3 Directors' statement – directors' responsibilities

Where a small company is subject to audit, it is necessary (in order to accord with international standards on auditing) to prepare a more detailed statement appearing, generally, within the directors' report.

The ISA (UK and Ireland) 700 (revised in October 2012), *The auditor's report on financial statements*, requires the auditor's report to include a statement that those charged with governance are responsible for the preparation of the financial statements and a statement that the responsibility of the auditor is to audit and express an opinion on the financial statements in accordance with applicable legal requirements and International Standards on Auditing (UK and Ireland).

APB Bulletin 2010/2, *Compendium of illustrative auditor's reports on United Kingdom private sector financial statements for periods ended on or after 15 December 2010 (revised), (last updated March 2012)* envisages a 'Directors' Responsibilities Statement' within the financial statements or accompanying information (for example, in the directors' report) to include an adequate statement of directors' responsibilities. Specific reference is made to this statement in the auditor's report.

Example 6.4 provides an example directors' responsibilities statement based on APB Bulletin 2010/2 (Revised) (APB Bulletin Appendix 17 Example 47).

An independent accountants' report on unaudited (audit-exempt) accounts, should, on the same basis, include a statement that the directors are responsible for the preparation of the accounts.

> ***Example 6.4***
>
> **Example Directors' Responsibilities Statement**
> ***Auditor's reports on financial statements in the United Kingdom***
>
> **APB Bulletin 2010/2 (Revised)** ***Appendix 17 Example 47***
> **Directors' responsibilities statement**
>
> The directors are responsible for preparing the Directors' Report and the financial statements in accordance with applicable law and regulations.
>
> Company law requires the directors to prepare financial statements for each financial year. Under that law the directors have elected to prepare the financial statements in accordance with United Kingdom Generally Accepted Accounting Practice (United Kingdom Accounting Standards and applicable law). Under company law the directors must not approve the financial statements unless they are satisfied that they give a true and fair view of the state of affairs of the company and of the profit or loss of the company for that period.
>
> In preparing these financial statements, the directors are required to:
>
> - select suitable accounting policies and then apply them consistently;
> - make judgments and estimates that are reasonable and prudent;
> - state whether applicable UK Accounting Standards have been followed, subject to any material departures disclosed and explained in the financial statements *[not applicable for companies subject to the small companies regime and medium sized companies]*; and
> - prepare the financial statements on the going concern basis unless it is inappropriate to presume that the company will continue in business *[included where no separate statement on going concern is made by the directors].*
>
> The directors are responsible for keeping adequate accounting records that are sufficient to show and explain the company's transactions and disclose with reasonable accuracy at any time the financial position of the company and enable them to ensure that the financial statements comply with the CA 2006. They are also responsible for safeguarding the assets of the company and hence for taking reasonable steps for the prevention and detection of fraud and other irregularities.
>
> *[Where the financial statements are published on the internet] [The directors are responsible for the maintenance and integrity of the corporate and financial information included on the company's website. Legislation in the United Kingdom governing the preparation and dissemination of financial statements may differ from legislation in other jurisdictions.] [Author's note - not illustrated in APB Bulletin 2010/2].*

6.8.4 Directors' statement – disclosure of information to auditors

For audited companies, the directors' report must contain a statement that so far as each of the directors, at the time the report is approved, is aware:

- there is no relevant audit information of which the company's auditor is unaware; and
- the directors have taken all steps that they each ought to have taken to make themselves aware of any relevant audit information and to establish that the company's auditor is aware of that
s. 418(2) information.

Example 6.5

Directors' statement as to disclosure of information to auditors (Directors' report)

Each of the directors confirms that:

- so far as the director is aware, there is no relevant audit information of which the company's auditors are unaware; and
- the director has taken all the steps that he/she ought to have taken as a director in order to make himself/herself aware of any relevant audit information and to establish that the company's auditors are aware of that information.

This confirmation is given and should be interpreted in accordance with the provisions of s. 418 of the CA 2006.

In practice the directors' statements provided in accordance with APB Bulletin 2010/2 (Revised) Appendix 17 and CA 2006 s. 418(2) (**Examples 6.4** and **6.5**) may be combined into one statement.

6.9 Small dormant companies

Dormant companies which are exempt from audit (as explained in **7.2** (**Chapter 7**) may file 'small company' abbreviated accounts (an abbreviated balance sheet and notes), without an auditor's report, provided the balance sheet contains a statement by the directors in accordance with s. 475(2) (see Example accounts in **Chapter 13**).

6.10 Disclosure of directors' remuneration – small companies

CA 2006 s. 412 provides for regulations to be made about the disclosure of directors' remuneration. These are contained in *The Small Companies and Groups (Accounts and Directors' Report) Regulations 2008* (SI 2008/409).

For small companies, as defined, the only details in respect of directors' remuneration and benefits that are required are as set out in Sch. 3 of SI 2008/409 and summarised in **Table 6.7** below.

Schedule 3 of SI 2008/409 ('Information about Directors' Benefits: Remuneration (Companies Act or IAS accounts)') is set out in **Appendix B**.

Table 6.7 Small companies – directors' remuneration

A small company is required to disclose the overall total amounts of:	
• directors' remuneration in respect of qualifying services (paid to or receivable by directors) (see **Appendix B** for the definition of remuneration Sch 3.7);	Sch 3.1
• money and the value of net assets received or receivable under long term incentive schemes in respect of qualifying services;	
• company contributions to pension schemes;	
• compensation to directors or past directors for loss of office (CA 2006 s. 215);	Sch 3.2
• sums paid to third parties in respect of directors' services.	Sch 3.3
Disclosure is also required of the number of directors (if any) to whom retirement benefits are accruing in respect of qualifying services for:	Sch 3.1
• money purchase schemes; and	
• defined benefit schemes.	

CA 2006 s. 413 provides for the disclosure of directors' benefits: advances, credit and guarantees.

In the case of a company that does not prepare group accounts, details of:

- advances and credits granted by the company to its directors; and
- guarantees of any kind entered into by the company on behalf of its directors,

s. 413 must be shown in the notes to the company's individual accounts.

6.11 Disclosure of auditor's remuneration – small audited companies

Requirements for the disclosure of auditors' remuneration in respect of small and medium-sized companies are provided by *The Companies (Disclosure of Auditor Remuneration and Liability Limitation Agreements) Regulations 2008* (SI 2008/489) as amended by *The Companies (Disclosure of Auditor Remuneration and Liability Limitation Agreements) (Amendment) Regulations 2011* (SI 2011/2198).

Remuneration receivable by a small company's auditor for auditing the accounts must be disclosed in a note to the annual accounts. Remuneration includes benefits in kind and the nature and estimated money-value of those benefits must also be disclosed.

SI 2008/489 reg 4(1)–(3) Where more than one person has been appointed as a company's auditor in respect of any financial period, separate disclosure is required in respect of the remuneration of each such person.

SI 2008/489 reg 4(4) For a medium-sized company, disclosure of remuneration may be required in respect of assurance services (other than auditing), tax advisory services, and other services.

SI 2008/489 reg 6 A small eligible parent company preparing audited group accounts must disclose consolidated auditor's remuneration information on the basis of SI 2008/489 reg 6, in which case the parent company's individual accounts need not disclose auditor's remuneration.

Chapter 7 Dormant companies

7.1 Introduction

For the purposes of the Companies Act, a company is 'dormant' during any period in which it has no significant accounting transaction ('significant accounting transaction' is explained below in **7.2**). *s. 1169(1)*

Dormant companies (as defined) qualify automatically for exemption from audit provided ten per cent of the members do not request an audit, as explained in **7.3** below.

Dormant companies which are exempt from audit may file abbreviated accounts under the small companies regime (an abbreviated balance sheet and notes), without an auditor's report, provided the balance sheet contains a statement by the directors in accordance with CA 2006 s. 475(3). (See Example accounts in **Chapter 12** and abbreviated accounts in **Chapter 8**.)

Conditions for audit exemption are subject to:

- the requirement for a statement to be contained in the balance sheet (see **7.5**);
- the right of members to require audit (see **7.3**); and
- companies excluded from dormant companies exemption (see **7.4**).

Dormant subsidiary companies meeting certain requirements may be exempt from preparing and filing individual accounts (see **7.7**).

7.2 Definition of 'dormant company'

A dormant company is a company which (during any period) has no 'significant accounting transaction'.

A 'significant accounting transaction' means a transaction which is required by CA 2006 s. 386 to be entered in the company's accounting records, *other than* transactions:

- consisting of penalties or payments to the Registrar of Companies for:
  - (a) change of name fee;
  - (b) re-registration fee (*on the re-registration of a company's status, e.g. to public company*);
  - (c) penalty for failure to deliver accounts (*under s. 453*);
  - (d) annual return registration fee; or
- arising from the taking of shares in the company by a subscriber to the memorandum, on the formation of the company. *s. 1169(2)*

7.3 Conditions for exemption from audit

A company is exempt from the requirements for audit of its accounts in respect of a financial year if:

- it has been dormant since its formation; or
- it has been dormant since the end of the previous financial year. *s. 480*

Further, to be exempt the company must also:

- be entitled to prepare its individual accounts in accordance with the small companies regime (see s. 381-384), or would be so entitled but for having been a public company or a member of an ineligible group; and
- not be required to prepare group accounts for that year.

There are circumstances where small companies which are part of a group are not entitled to the audit exemption. However, where a company is both a subsidiary undertaking and dormant throughout the whole of the period or periods during the financial year when it is a group company,
s. 479 (3) it is entitled to the audit exemption.

CA 2006 s. 476 states that members of a company that would otherwise be entitled to exemption from audit may require it to obtain an audit of its accounts for a financial year by giving notice under the section. The notice must be given by members representing not less than:

- 10 per cent in total of the nominal value of the company's issued share capital (or any class of it); or
- 10 per cent in number of the members of the company (for a company not having a share
s. 476 capital).

The notice may not be given before the financial year to which it relates and must be given not later than one month before the end of that year.

A dormant company is not entitled to audit exemption unless its balance sheet contains a statement or statements under CA 2006 s. 475(2) as explained in **7.5** below.

A dormant company is not exempt from audit (and an audit of the accounts is, therefore, necessary) if there is a specific requirement in the company's articles of association to appoint auditors.

7.4 Companies excluded from dormant companies' exemption

A company is not entitled to the exemption from audit (conferred by CA 2006 s. 480) if:

(a) it was at any time within the financial year one of the following:
- an authorised insurance company;
- a banking company;
- an e-money issuer;
SI 2007 - a MiFID investment firm;
No. 2932 - a UCITS management company; or

s. 481 (b) the company carries on insurance market activity.

7.5 Directors' statements – entitlement to exemption

A dormant company is not entitled to audit exemption unless its balance sheet contains a state-
s. 480(3) ment or statements by the directors to the effect that:

- the company is entitled to exemption from audit by virtue of CA 2006 s. 480 (dormant compa-
s. 475(1-2) nies);
- the members have not required the company to obtain an audit of its accounts for the year in
s. 475(3) question in accordance with CA 2006 s. 476; and
- the directors acknowledge their responsibilities for complying with the requirements of the CA
s. 475(3) 2006 with respect to accounting records and the preparation of accounts.

The statements required to entitle audit exemption as above must appear on the balance sheet above the signature required to approve the accounts under CA 2006 s. 414. *s. 475(4)*

7.6 Dormant company acting as agent

Where the directors of a dormant company take advantage of audit exemption (conferred by CA 2006 s. 480) and the company has during the financial year acted as an agent for any person, the accounts (small company individual accounts and abbreviated accounts) are required to disclose that fact (SI 2008/409 Schedule 1.63) in the notes to the accounts. *Sch 1.63*

7.7 Dormant subsidiary company exemption from preparing or filing accounts

The *Companies and Limited Liability Partnerships (Accounts and Audit Exemptions and Change of Accounting Framework) Regulations 2012* (SI 2012/2301) have introduced CA 2006 s. 394A which provides that for accounting periods ended on or after 1 October 2012, a dormant subsidiary company is exempt from the requirement to prepare and file accounts if it fulfils the following conditions:

(a) its parent undertaking is established under the law of an EEA state;
(b) the company's shareholders unanimously agree to the exemption in respect of the financial year in question;
(c) the parent gives a statutory guarantee of all the outstanding liabilities to which the subsidiary is subject at the end of the financial year in accordance with CA 2006 s. 394C;
(d) the company is included in the consolidated accounts drawn up for that year or to an earlier date in that year by the parent undertaking, which must be prepared in accordance with Directive 83/349/EEC (the Seventh Company Law Directive) or International Accounting Standards;
(e) the use of the exemption by the subsidiary must be disclosed in the notes in the consolidated accounts drawn up by the parent;
(f) the following documents must be filed by the directors of the subsidiary at Companies House on or before the date that they were due to file the subsidiary's accounts:
   (i) written notice of the agreement in (b);
   (ii) a statement by the parent that it guarantees the subsidiary company under the particular section of the Act; *s. 394A, s. 448A*
   (iii) a copy of the consolidated annual report and accounts referred to in (d) and the auditor's report on those accounts; *s. 448A*
(g) the company is not quoted within s. 385(2) of the Companies Act;
(h) it is not an authorised insurance company, a banking company, an e-Money issuer, a MiFID investment firm or a UCITS management company, or carries on insurance market activity; and *s. 394B,*
(i) it is not a trade union or an employer's association. *s. 448B*

An annual return will still be required to be filed at Companies House.

Chapter 8 Abbreviated accounts

8.1 Introduction

A company classified as small or medium-sized and preparing UK GAAP (but not IAS) accounts (known as 'Companies Act accounts') is permitted to deliver 'abbreviated accounts' in place of full statutory accounts ('individual accounts') to the Registrar of Companies.

Abbreviated accounts are accounts prepared in accordance with: *SI 2008/409 Sch 4*

Small company

(a) SI 2008/409 Schedule 4 (Part 1) – abbreviated balance sheet; and
(b) SI 2008/409 Schedule 4 (Part 2) – notes to the accounts.

Medium-sized company

SI 2008/410 Schedule 1 and Regulation 4 – there are minimal disclosure exemptions within medium-sized company profit and loss account.

8.2 Contents of abbreviated accounts

Abbreviated accounts are not required to give a true and fair view; they are a form of accounts containing less information and disclosure than the full individual annual accounts for shareholders and comprise:

Small company – 'an abbreviated balance sheet', being an abbreviated version of the full balance sheet and certain notes. *SI 2008/409 Sch 4*

Medium-sized company – full statutory accounts (to accord with SI 2008/410) *except* that the analysis of turnover set out in Sch 1 para 68 may be omitted and some items within the profit and loss account may be combined. *SI 2008/410 reg. 4*

A summary of the options available for filing small company accounts with the Registrar of Companies is set out in **8.3**. Abbreviated accounts will usually comprise the elements shown in **Table 8.2**.

Abbreviated accounts, in practice, can be prepared on the basis of minimal or selective amendments from full annual accounts prepared under SI 2008/409 Sch 1, remembering that abbreviated accounts must be copies of those elements of the company's (full shareholders') annual accounts and reports that are required under SI 2008/409 Sch 4 (see **8.3** below).

8.3 Filing abbreviated accounts

The filing requirements for abbreviated accounts are set out in CA 2006 s. 444(3) (small companies) and CA 2006 s. 445 (3) (medium-sized companies).

A small company preparing Companies Act accounts (i.e. accounts under UK GAAP not IAS) is required to send a copy of its full annual accounts and directors' report to its members. It must also deliver to the Registrar of Companies one of the following:

- Full annual accounts – full individual or group annual accounts prepared in accordance with CA 2006 and SI 2008/409; or
- Abbreviated accounts – prepared in accordance with SI 2008/409 Regulation 6 and Schedule 4; or
- Abbreviated or full accounts but excluding the profit and loss account and the directors' report.

There is no provision for 'abbreviated group accounts' within CA 2006 and therefore small or medium-sized groups are unable to file abbreviated accounts prepared on a consolidated basis. Abbreviated accounts are not available for filing where IAS accounts are prepared.

Eligible small companies that are subject to the small companies regime are able to choose whether or not to file a profit and loss account or directors' report. **Table 8.1** below summarises the options available.

Table 8.1 Filing accounts on public record – summary of options available for small companies

FILING OPTION	**Full annual accounts**	**Full balance sheet only**	**Abbreviated accounts**
	UK GAAP and IAS companies	***UK GAAP and IAS companies***	***UK GAAP companies only***
Copy full balance sheet	Yes	Yes	n/a
Balance sheet statement	Yes (s. 414)	Yes (s. 444(5))	Yes (SI 2008/409 Sch 4 para 1(2))
Copy full P&L account	Yes	No – n/a	Optional
Copy Directors' report	Yes	No – n/a	Optional
Auditor's report *(if applicable)*			
– under s. 495	Yes – *if accounts audited*	Yes (full s. 495 auditor's report)* *– if full accounts audited*	No – n/a
– statement under s. 496 (where directors' report filed)	Yes – *if accounts audited*	Yes – if the directors' report is filed	No – n/a
Prescribed notes *(including accounting policies)*	Yes	Yes	Yes – *Per SI 2008/409 (including Sch 4)*
Special Auditor's report *(if applicable) – under s. 449*	n/a	n/a	Yes
Approval, signature and balance sheet statement – *under s. 450* (abbreviated accounts)	No – n/a	No – n/a	Yes

Where accounts delivered are audited but are neither abbreviated accounts nor full annual accounts, the auditor's report delivered with them is the full report under CA 2006 s. 495 notwithstanding that the accounts themselves may be restricted in content, for example to simply a balance sheet. (This is indicated in **Table 8.1** by *.) In these circumstances, APB in its Bulletin 2008/4 (April 2008) suggests (at Bulletin Paragraph 12) that the auditor's report should be accompanied by a textual explanation on the following lines:

Although the company is only required to file a balance sheet, the CA 2006 requires the accompanying auditor's report to be a copy of our report to the members on the company's full annual accounts and directors' report. Readers are cautioned that the profit and loss account and certain other primary statements and the directors' report, referred to in the copy of our auditor's report, are not required to be filed with the Registrar of Companies.

Table 8.2 sets out the normal contents of abbreviated accounts for small or medium-sized companies.

Table 8.2 Abbreviated accounts

	Small company SI 2008/409 Sch. 4	*Medium-sized company* SI 2008/410 Sch. 1
Directors' report	No report	Full report
Profit and loss account	No profit and loss account	Profit and loss account must disclose 'turnover' but may combine certain items *(SI 2008/410 reg. 4(3)(a))*
Balance sheet	Abbreviated balance sheet – SI 2008/409 Sch. 4 format	Full balance sheet – SI 2008/410 Sch. 1 format
Cash flow and other primary statements	Not required	Full statements required, if applicable
Notes	Limited information only SI 2008/409 Sch. 4 disclosures	Full notes, including disclosure of turnover (but omitting turnover analysis) *(SI 2008/410 reg. 4(2) and 4(3))*
	No information on directors' or employees' remuneration	
	No disclosure of auditor's remuneration	
Auditor's report	Special report (if applicable)	Special report

If abbreviated accounts are delivered to the Registrar of Companies, and the company is not exempt from audit (or the directors have not taken advantage of any such exemption), the accounts must be delivered together with a copy of the special auditor's report required by s. 449.

The decision whether or not to take advantage of the exemptions to prepare abbreviated accounts will be a commercial one. Full statutory accounts have to be prepared in any case for members; the directors of small or medium-sized companies will have regard to:

- the additional costs involved in the preparation of an additional set of accounts;
- the financial information omitted in abbreviated accounts; and
- the sensitivity or confidentiality of financial information required for public disclosure.

A decision can only be reached after a comparison is made of full and limited disclosure and after the relative costs and benefits have been considered. Many small companies choose to produce abbreviated accounts.

8.4 Abbreviated balance sheet

The balance sheet format and contents in abbreviated accounts of a small company are set out in regulations under SI 2008/409 Sch 4.

A small company may deliver to the Registrar of Companies a copy of the balance sheet showing the items listed in either of the balance sheet formats set out in the Regulations, in the order and under the headings and sub-headings given in the format adopted, but in other respects corresponding to the full balance sheet of the company.

Sch 4.1(1)

The abbreviated balance sheet formats provided by SI 2008/409 Schedule 4 are set out in **Table 8.3**.

Table 8.3 Form and content of abbreviated accounts of small companies delivered to the Registrar of Companies (SI 2008/409 Sch. 4)

Balance sheet formats

	Format 1		*Format 2*
			ASSETS
A.	Called up share capital not paid	A.	Called up share capital not paid
B.	Fixed assets	B.	Fixed assets
	I Intangible assets		I Intangible assets
	II Tangible assets		II Tangible assets
	III Investments		III Investments
C.	Current assets	C.	Current assets
	I Stocks		I Stocks
	II Debtors		II Debtors
	III Investments		III Investments
	IV Cash at bank and in hand		IV Cash at bank and in hand
D.	Prepayments and accrued income	D.	Prepayments and accrued income
E.	Creditors: amounts falling due within one year		LIABILITIES
F.	Net current assets (liabilities)	A.	Capital and reserves
G.	Total assets less current liabilities		I Called up share capital
H.	Creditors: amounts falling due after more than one year		II Share premium account
			III Revaluation reserve
I.	Provisions for liabilities		IV Other reserves
			V Profit and loss account
J.	Accruals and deferred income	B.	Provisions for liabilities
K.	Capitals and reserves	C.	Creditors
	I Called up share capital	D.	Accruals and deferred income
	II Share premium account		
	III Revaluation reserve		
	IV Other reserves		
	V Profit and loss account		

Debtors (both formats) – *the aggregate amount of debtors falling due after more than one year must be shown separately unless it is disclosed in the notes to the accounts.*

Creditors (format 2) – *the aggregate amount of creditors falling due after more than one year must be shown separately unless it is disclosed in the notes to the accounts.*

8.5 Notes to abbreviated accounts

Any information required for the purposes of the abbreviated accounts of a small company must (if not given in the accounts themselves) be given by way of a note to the accounts. *SI 2008/409 Sch. 4.2*

The information required to be given by way of a note is set out in **Table 8.4**.

SI 2008/409 Sch. 4 is reproduced in **Appendix B**.

Table 8.4 Notes to abbreviated accounts of a small company

	SI 2008/409 Sch 4 paragraph
Accounting policies	3
Share capital and debentures	4(1)
Particulars of share allotments	4(2) - 5
Fixed assets [for letter or Roman number format headings only]	6
Financial fixed assets	7
Debtors: amounts falling due after more than one year (aggregate)	Formats footnote (1)
Creditors: amounts falling due within one year or after more than one year for each category of creditors (Format 2)	Formats footnote (2)
Particulars of creditors:	
Debts falling due after five years	8(1)
Secured debts	8(2)
Basis of translation of foreign currencies	9
	SI 2008/409 Sch 2 paragraph
Subsidiary undertakings	1–3/11
Other significant (20% or more) undertakings	5–7/11
Membership of certain qualifying undertakings (being a partnership or unlimited company)	8
Parent undertakings and ultimate parent company	9–10
	CA 2006 section
Directors' benefits: advances, credits and guarantees	413

8.6 Approval and signing of abbreviated accounts

CA 2006 s. 450 sets out the provisions for the approval and signing of abbreviated accounts.

Abbreviated accounts must be approved by the board of directors and signed on behalf of the board by a director of the company. The signature must be on the balance sheet. *s. 450(1)–(2)*

The balance sheet must contain in a prominent position above the signature, a statement to the effect that it is prepared in accordance with the provisions of the Companies Act applicable (as the case may be) to companies subject to the small companies regime or to medium-sized companies. *s. 450(3)*

The requirement for a small company can be illustrated as follows:

> 'These [abbreviated] accounts have been prepared in accordance with the special provisions of section 444(3) of the CA 2006 applicable to companies subject to the small companies regime.'

It is recommended that the director's signature should be in black ink and the name of the director who signs the balance sheet should be printed below or beside the signature.

s. 450(4)–(5) There are provisions dealing with penalties if abbreviated accounts are approved that do not comply with the statutory requirements of the CA 2006.

Small companies' accounts that are subject to audit exemption are also required to have additional statements as explained in **Chapter 11** and illustrated in **Example 11.1**.

8.7 Parent companies

There is no statutory provision to file abbreviated group accounts. A parent company which files its own abbreviated individual accounts includes within those accounts considerable disclosure relating to subsidiaries and other significant holdings in undertakings (see **Chapter 9** and **Appendix A part 6**).

A parent company wishing to produce group accounts will need to prepare these as statutory accounts in addition to its own statutory individual abbreviated accounts.

8.8 Special auditor's report (CA 2006 s. 449)

Abbreviated accounts prepared by an audit-exempt company are not required to contain an auditor's report (but see the requirement for directors' statement in **8.6**).

Where the directors of a company deliver abbreviated accounts to the Registrar of Companies and the company is not exempt from audit (or the directors have not taken advantage of any such exemption), they must also deliver to the Registrar of Companies a copy of a special report of the company's auditor stating that in his opinion:

- the company is entitled to deliver abbreviated accounts in accordance with the relevant section: s. 444(3) (small companies) or 445(3) (medium-sized companies) (as appropriate); and
- the abbreviated accounts to be delivered are properly prepared in accordance with regulations under SI 2008/409 Sch 4 (small companies) or regulations under SI 2008/410 Sch 1 (medium-sized companies).

s. 449(3) Where produced, a special auditor's report is not required to include the full auditor's report on the full statutory accounts given under s. 495, except where:

- the s. 495 report was qualified; or
- the s. 495 report contained a statement under s. 498(2)(a) or (b) (accounts, records or returns inadequate or accounts not agreeing with records or returns) or s. 498(3) (failure to obtain necessary information and explanations).

For auditors of companies which are not audit-exempt, but which do prepare abbreviated accounts, APB guidance has been provided in APB Bulletin 2008/4 *The special auditor's report on abbreviated accounts in the United Kingdom* (April 2008). This is reflected in the example reports on abbreviated accounts in **Chapter 13**.

In Bulletin 2008/4, the APB recommends that, where the auditor's report on the full accounts is unqualified but contains an explanatory paragraph regarding a fundamental uncertainty (for example, concerning the going concern basis), the special auditor's report should also include the explanatory paragraph, within a section entitled 'Other information'. The auditor should include whatever information is considered important for a proper understanding of the report.

The legislation does not envisage a qualified opinion in the special auditor's report; if the auditor cannot give the positive statements of opinion required as above, the directors are not entitled to deliver abbreviated accounts.

8.9 Medium-sized companies

8.9.1 Annual accounts – medium-sized companies

The directors of a company that *qualifies* as a medium-sized company in relation to a financial year (see s. 465 to 467) *must* deliver to the Registrar of Companies a copy of:

- the company's annual accounts;
- the directors' report; and
- the auditor's report on the accounts and directors' report (as applicable).

8.9.2 Medium-sized company abbreviated accounts

Where a medium-sized company prepares Companies Act accounts, the directors *may* deliver to the Registrar of Companies 'abbreviated accounts', these being a copy of the company's annual accounts for the financial year that includes a profit and loss account in which items are combined in accordance with regulations under *The Large and Medium-sized Companies and Groups (Accounts and Reports) Regulations 2008* (SI 2008/410), and where any items whose omission is authorised by the regulations are omitted.

Where the medium-sized company chooses to submit abbreviated accounts to the Registrar of Companies, the company must submit:

- a copy of the abbreviated accounts drawn up in accordance with the SI 2008/410 Regulations;
- a copy of the Directors' Report; and
- a special auditor's report required by CA 2006 s. 449.

8.9.3 Medium-sized company – abbreviated profit and loss account

A medium-sized company may prepare abbreviated accounts in which the profit and loss account includes items that are combined. The items which can be combined and included as one item in each format of the profit and loss account are set out in **Table 8.5** *SI 2008/410 reg.4(3)*

Table 8.5 Profit and loss account items (SI 2008/410 Regulation 4(3))

Format 1	*Format 2*	*Format 3*	*Format 4*
2 Cost of sales		A1 Cost of sales	
	2 Change in stocks of finished goods and work-in-progress		A1 Reduction in stocks of finished goods and work-in-progress
			A2 (a) Raw materials and consumables (b) Other external charges
			B2 Increase in stocks of finished goods and work-in-progress
3 Gross profit or loss			
	3 Own work capitalised		B3 Own work capitalised
6 Other operating income	4 Other operating income	B2 Other operating income	B4 Other operating income
	5 (a) Raw materials and consumables (b) Other external charges		

References are to item numbers in the statutory formats of ***SI 2008/410 Sch. 1***

8.10 Small company abbreviated accounts checklist

Appendix F contains a checklist to assist in determining the availability and proper preparation of small company abbreviated accounts.

Chapter 9 Small groups

9.1 Small companies – option to prepare group accounts

If at the end of a financial year a company subject to the small companies regime is a parent company, the directors, as well as preparing individual accounts for the year, *may* prepare group accounts for the year. On this basis, a small parent company (as defined) is not, therefore, required to prepare group accounts.

All other parent companies (being companies that are ineligible or excluded from the small companies regime under CA 2006 s. 384) *must* prepare group accounts for the year *unless* the company is otherwise exempt from that requirement under exemptions set out in CA 2006 s. 399(3).

Notwithstanding the above, a small parent company may prepare group accounts for its own management accounting purposes and not submit them to the Registrar of Companies but file instead its own individual statutory accounts with appropriate disclosures. If group accounts are not prepared because of the group accounts exemption entitlement, the company may, if it wishes, file abbreviated accounts provided it qualifies as a small (or medium-sized) company.

A medium-sized parent company is not exempt from the requirement to prepare group accounts.

9.2 Qualifying conditions – group accounts exemptions

CA 2006 s. 383(4) and 466(4) set out the conditions to be met by a group for the parent company to qualify as 'small' or 'medium-sized' as appropriate.

A parent company qualifies as a small company in relation to a financial year only if the group headed by it qualifies as a small group. *s. 383(1)*

The size classification of a parent company is determined with regard to the aggregate qualifying criteria of the group taken as a whole (parent company and subsidiary undertakings), irrespective of the actual size qualification of the parent company itself.

A group qualifies as small in relation to the parent company's first financial year if the qualifying conditions are met in that year. In subsequent years, a group qualifies as small if the qualifying conditions:

- are met in that year and the preceding financial year;
- are met in that year and the group qualified as small in relation to the preceding financial year; or
- were met in the preceding financial year and the group qualified as small in relation to that year. *s. 383(2) (3)*

A group meets the qualifying conditions (and is, therefore, exempt from producing group (consolidated) accounts as a small group) if it does not exceed more than one of the following criteria on one or other of the following two bases: *s. 383(4)–(7)*

Criteria	**(The bases may be mixed)** *Net basis*	*Gross basis*
Small group (CA 2006 s. 383 (4))		
Turnover	£6.5 million	£7.8 million
Balance sheet total	£3.26 million	£3.9 million
Average number of employees (on a monthly basis)	50	50
Medium-sized group (CA 2006 s. 466 (4))		
Turnover	£25.9 million	£31.1 million
Balance sheet total	£12.9 million	£15.5 million
Average number of employees (on a monthly basis)	250	250

Criteria amended (increased) by SI 2008/393

It is important to note that the 'net' and 'gross' bases may be mixed in determining whether the criteria have been met. For example, if a group has a turnover of £8 million (gross) and £6 million (net), a balance sheet total of £3.8 million (gross) and £3.5 million (net) and 60 employees, on the size criteria the group would qualify as a small group. Although it exceeds the employee number threshold, it does not exceed the net turnover threshold or gross balance sheet threshold.

The aggregate figures are ascertained by aggregating the relevant figures from individual statutory accounts (determined in accordance with CA 2006 s. 382) for each member of the group.

The alternative bases for turnover and balance sheet totals (as qualifying conditions for exemption) are:

- *'Net' basis* – Aggregate figures for turnover and balance sheet totals after any set-offs and consolidation adjustments made for the elimination of group transactions in accordance with CA 2006 s. 404 and the regulations thereunder (Companies Act group accounts) or international accounting standards (IAS group accounts); and
- *'Gross' basis* – Aggregate figures for turnover and balance sheet totals without such set-offs and consolidation adjustments.

CA 2006 under SI 2008/409 Sch 6 consolidation adjustments include:

- elimination of intra-group transactions and assets and liabilities;
- elimination of intra-group unrealised profits or losses; and
- adjustments to effect uniform accounting policies within the group.

9.3 Medium-sized companies – group accounts

To be considered a small group the parent company within the group must be a small company. Therefore even if the gross income and balance sheet totals of a group are below the small group thresholds, if the parent is a medium-sized company (being companies that are ineligible or excluded from the small companies regime under CA 2006 s. 384) group accounts must be prepared *unless* the company is otherwise exempt from that requirement under exemptions set out in CA 2006 s. 399(3).

The exemptions available are under:

- CA 2006 s. 400 (company included in EEA accounts of larger group);
- CA 2006 s. 401 (company included in non-EEA accounts of larger group); and
- CA 2006 s. 402 (company none of whose subsidiary undertakings need be included in the consolidation).

CA 2006 s. 400–402 contain a number of requirements which must be met before a medium-sized company can take advantage of the exemptions provided by these sections. These sections of

CA 2006 should be referred to before a conclusion is reached as to whether a company may take these exemptions.

A medium-sized parent company to which these exemptions apply can nevertheless still choose to prepare group accounts (CA 2006 s. 399(4)).

9.4 Preparing small group accounts

9.4.1 Companies Act small group accounts

Where the directors of a parent company which is subject to the small companies regime and has prepared Companies Act individual accounts chooses to prepare Companies Act group accounts under CA 2006 s. 398 (Option to prepare group accounts), those group accounts must comply with the provisions of:

- SI 2008/409 Schedule 6 (Part 1) – Form and content of Companies Act group accounts (consolidated balance sheet and consolidated profit and loss account, and additional information to be provided by way of notes to the accounts);
- SI 2008/409 Schedule 6 (Part 2) – Information about related undertakings to be given in notes to the company's accounts. Information about related undertakings may be omitted from the notes to the accounts in certain circumstances where the related undertaking is established under the law of a country outside the United Kingdom, or carries on business outside the United Kingdom. The disclosures set out in **9.5** relating to Joint Ventures and Parent undertakings drawing up accounts of a large group are required regardless of whether the related undertaking is established under the law of a country outside the United Kingdom, or carries on business outside the United Kingdom; and
- SI 2008/409 Schedule 3 – Information about directors' benefits: remuneration to be given in notes to the company's accounts. *SI 2008/ 409 reg. 10(2)*

The group accounts of a small company are treated as having complied with any provision of Schedule 6 (Part 1) (Form and content of Companies Act group accounts) of *The Small Companies and Groups (Accounts and Directors' Report) Regulations 2008* (SI 2008/409) if they comply instead with the corresponding (additional) provisions of Schedule 6 (Part 1) of *The Large and Medium-Sized Companies and Groups (Accounts and Reports) Regulations 2008* (SI 2008/410).

9.4.2 Small groups and the FRSSE

A small group voluntarily preparing group accounts may take advantage of the provisions and exemptions afforded by the FRSSE (effective April 2008) (see **10.5**) but must have regard to the legal requirements reflected in the FRSSE and CA 2006 under SI 2008/409 Sch. 6 (see **9.4.1** (above)). When considering SI 2008/409 Sch. 6, any references in that Schedule to compliance with the provisions of 'Part 1 of Schedule 6' are to be construed as references to the legal requirements reflected in the FRSSE. As a consequence, where a small reporting entity is preparing consolidated financial statements, it should regard as standard the accounting practices and disclosure requirements set out in:

FRS 2	*Accounting for subsidiary undertakings*	
FRS 6	*Acquisitions and mergers*	
FRS 7	*Fair values in acquisition accounting*	
and, as they apply in respect of consolidated accounts:		
FRS 5	*Reporting the substance of transactions*	
FRS 9	*Associates and joint ventures*	
FRS 28	*Corresponding amounts*	
FRS 10	*Goodwill and intangible assets*	
FRS 11	*Impairment of fixed assets and goodwill*	(Only in respect of purchased goodwill on consolidation)

Where the reporting entity is part of a group that prepares publicly available consolidated accounts, it is entitled under the FRSSE to the exemptions provided by FRS 8 paragraph 3(a) and (c), being:

- disclosure of transactions or balances between group entities that have been eliminated on consolidation; and
- disclosure of transactions entered into between two or more members of a group, provided that any subsidiary undertaking which is a party to the transaction is wholly owned by a member of that group.

Where group accounts are prepared, the balance sheet should contain in a prominent position, above the director's approval signature, a statement that they are prepared in accordance with the provisions applicable to companies subject to the small companies' regime (see **Chapter 6** at **6.8**).

9.4.3 Small group accounts – balance sheet format heading ('Investments')

SI 2008/409 Sch 6.1(2)

Where small group accounts are prepared, Schedule 6 ('Group Accounts') of SI 2008/409 amends the balance sheet format headings for 'Investments'.

For item B.III in each of the balance sheet formats, the sub-headings of 'Investments' are modified as follows:

'B. III. Investments
1. Shares in group undertakings
2. Interests in associated undertakings
3. Other participating interests
4. Loans to group undertakings and undertakings in which a participating interest is held
5. Other investments other than loans
6. Others.'

9.5 'Related undertakings' disclosures

If group accounts are prepared the disclosures required regarding related undertakings are given in Part 2 of Sch 6 of SI 2008/409. As set out in the table below, 'related undertakings' may include parent, subsidiary and associated undertakings, joint ventures and other undertakings in which the company has an interest. If group accounts are not prepared the disclosures required regarding related undertakings are given in Part 1 of Sch 2 of SI 2008/409.

The table below sets out the disclosures which are required in either case.

Definitions are in **Appendix A(6)**.

	Small group accounts prepared **SI 2008/409 Sch 6 Part 2**	**Small group accounts not prepared** **SI 2008/409 Sch 2 Part 1**
SUBSIDIARY UNDERTAKINGS If at the end of the financial year the company has subsidiary undertakings, the name of each subsidiary undertaking must be stated. There must also be stated with respect to each subsidiary undertaking the country in which it is incorporated, if it is incorporated outside the United Kingdom or if it is unincorporated, the address of its principal place of business.	Sch 6 Part 2 Paras 22(1) -22(3)	Sch 2 Part 1 Paras 1(1) - 1(3)

It must also be stated whether the subsidiary undertaking is included in the consolidation and, if it is not, the reasons for excluding it from consolidation must be given.	Sch 6 Part 2 Para 22(4)	
It must be stated with respect to each subsidiary undertaking by virtue of which of the conditions specified in CA 2006 s. 1162(2) or (4) it is a subsidiary undertaking of its immediate parent undertaking. (This information need not be given if the relevant condition is that specified in CA 2006 s. 1162(2)(a) (holding of a majority of the voting rights) and the immediate parent undertaking holds the same proportion of the shares in the undertaking as it holds voting rights.)	Sch 6 Part 2 Para 22(5)	
HOLDINGS IN SUBSIDIARY UNDERTAKINGS With respect to the shares of a subsidiary undertaking held (a) by the parent company and (b) by the group, the identity of each class of shares and the proportion of the nominal value of the shares of that class held by the company and group respectively must be disclosed.	Sch 6 Part 2 Paras 23(1) - (2)	Sch 2 Part 1 Paras 2(1) - 2(2)
FINANCIAL INFORMATION ABOUT SUBSIDIARY UNDERTAKINGS The aggregate amount of capital and reserves as at the end of its relevant financial year** and the profit or loss for that year, must be disclosed in respect of each subsidiary undertaking. This information is not required:	Sch 6 Part 2 Para 24(1)	Sch 2 Part 1 Para 3(1)
• if the company would (if it were not subject to the small companies regime) be exempt by virtue of CA 2006 s. 400 or s. 401 (parent company included in accounts of larger group) from the requirement to prepare group accounts; or		Sch 2 Part 1 Para 3(2)
• if the company's investment in the subsidiary undertaking is included in the company's accounts by way of the equity method of valuation; or	Sch 6 Part 2 Para 24(2)	Sch 2 Part 1 Para 3(3)
• if the subsidiary undertaking is not required by any provision of CA 2006 to deliver a copy of its balance sheet for its relevant financial year and does not otherwise publish that balance sheet in the United Kingdom or elsewhere, and the company's holding is less than 50% of the nominal value of the shares in the undertaking; or • if it is not material. ** **"relevant financial year"** of a subsidiary undertaking is that year if its financial year ends with that of the company and if not, its financial year ending last before the end of the company's financial year.	Sch 6 Part 2 Para 24(2) Sch 6 Part 2 Para 24(3) Sch 6 Part 2 Para 24(4)	Sch 2 Part 1 Para 3(4) Sch 2 Part 1 Para 3(5) Sch 2 Part 1 Para 3(6)

SHARES OF COMPANY HELD BY SUBSIDIARY UNDERTAKINGS		
The number, description and amount of the shares in the company held by or on behalf of its subsidiary undertakings must be disclosed.	Sch 6 Part 2 Para 25(1)	Sch 2 Part 1 Para 4(1)
This information is not required if the subsidiary undertaking is concerned as personal representative or, subject as follows, as trustee. Unless the company, or any subsidiary undertaking of the company, is beneficially interested under the trust, otherwise than by way of security only for the purposes of a transaction entered into by it in the ordinary course of a business which includes the lending of money.	Sch 6 Part 2 Para 25(2)-(3)	Sch 2 Part 1 Para 4(3)
JOINT VENTURES		
The following information must be given in relation to joint ventures: • the name of the undertaking; • the address of the principal place of business of the undertaking; • the factors on which joint management of the undertaking is based; and • the proportion of the capital of the undertaking held by undertakings included in the consolidation.	Sch 6 Part 2 Para 26(1)	
If the financial year end of the joint venture is not the same as the reporting company the financial year end of the joint venture prior to the reporting company's year end must be stated.	Sch 6 Part 2 Para 26(2)	
ASSOCIATED UNDERTAKINGS		
If an undertaking included in the consolidation has an interest in an associated undertaking the name of each associated undertaking must be stated. There must also be stated with respect to each associated undertaking the country in which it is incorporated, if it is incorporated outside the United Kingdom or if it is unincorporated, the address of its principal place of business.	Sch 6 Part 2 Para 27(1)-(3)	
The identity of each class of shares held in the associated undertaking by the parent company and the group and the proportion of the nominal value of the shares of that class represented by those shares must be disclosed. The disclosure should show the parent company and group holdings separately.	Sch 6 Part 2 Para 27(4)-(5)	
SIGNIFICANT HOLDINGS IN UNDERTAKINGS OTHER THAN SUBSIDIARY UNDERTAKINGS		
Where group accounts are prepared, the following information must be given where at the end of the financial year the company has a significant holding in an undertaking which is not a subsidiary undertaking, joint venture or associated undertaking of the company.	Sch 6 Part 2 Para 28(1)	
OR		
Where group accounts are not prepared, the following information must be given where at the end of the financial year the company has a significant holding in an undertaking which is not a subsidiary undertaking of the company.		Sch 2 Part 1 Para 5(1)

(A holding is significant for this purpose if it amounts to 20% or more of the nominal value of any class of shares in the undertaking, or the amount of the holding (as stated or included in the company's accounts) exceeds 20% of the amount (as so stated) of the company's assets).	Sch 6 Part 2 Para 28(2)	Sch 2 Part 1 Para 5(2)
• The name of the undertaking must be stated. • There must also be stated with respect to each undertaking the country in which it is incorporated, if it is incorporated outside the United Kingdom or if it is unincorporated, the address of its principal place of business. • The identity of each class of shares and the proportion of the nominal value of the shares of that class held by the company in the undertaking must be disclosed. • The aggregate amount of the capital and reserves of the undertaking as at the end of its relevant financial year, and its profit or loss for that year must also be disclosed. ***	Sch 6 Part 2 Para 29(1) Sch 6 Part 2 Para 29(2) Sch 6 Part 2 Para 29(4) Sch 6 Part 2 Para 30(1)	Sch 2 Part 1 Para 6(1) Sch 2 Part 1 Para 6(2) Sch 2 Part 1 Para 6(3) Sch 2 Part 1 Para 7(1)
*** This information is not required if: • the company would (if it were not subject to the small companies regime) be exempt by virtue of CA 2006 s. 400 or s. 401 (parent company included in accounts of larger group) from the requirement to prepare group accounts; and • the company's investment in all undertakings in which it has a significant holding is included in the company's accounts by way of the equity method of valuation; or		Sch 2 Part 1 Para 7(2)
• the subsidiary undertaking is not required by any provision of CA 2006 to deliver a copy of its balance sheet for its relevant financial year and does not otherwise publish that balance sheet in the United Kingdom or elsewhere, and the company's holding is less than 50% of the nominal value of the shares in the undertaking; or • it is not material.	Sch 6 Part 2 Para 30(2) Sch 6 Part 2 Para 30(3)	Sch 2 Part 1 Para 7(3) Sch 2 Part 1 Para 7(4)
Where group accounts are prepared, the following information must be given where at the end of the financial year the group has a significant holding in an undertaking which is not a subsidiary undertaking of the parent company, joint venture or associated undertaking of the company. (A holding is significant for this purpose if it amounts to 20% or more of the nominal value of any class of shares in the undertaking, or the amount of the holding (as stated or included in the group accounts) exceeds 20% of the amount (as so stated) of the group's assets). • The name of the undertaking must be stated.	Sch 6 Part 2 Para 31(1) Sch 6 Part 2 Para 31(2) Sch 6 Part 2 Para 32(1)	

• There must also be stated with respect to each undertaking the country in which it is incorporated, if it is incorporated outside the United Kingdom, or, if it is unincorporated, the address of its principal place of business.	Sch 6 Part 2 Para 32(2)	
• The identity of each class of shares and the proportion of the nominal value of the shares of that class held by the company in the undertaking must be disclosed.	Sch 6 Part 2 Para 32(4)	
• The aggregate amount of the capital and reserves of the undertaking as at the end of its relevant financial year, and its profit or loss for that year must also be disclosed. ***	Sch 6 Part 2 Para 33(1)	
*** This information is not required:-		
• if the subsidiary undertaking is not required by any provision of CA 2006 to deliver a copy of its balance sheet for its relevant financial year and does not otherwise publish that balance sheet in the United Kingdom or elsewhere, and the company's holding is less than 50% of the nominal value of the shares in the undertaking; or	Sch 6 Part 2 Para 33(2)	
• if it is not material.	Sch 6 Part 2 Para 33(3)	
MEMBERSHIP OF CERTAIN UNDERTAKINGS		
The following information must be given where at the end of the financial year the reporting company (or group) is a member of a qualifying undertaking.	Sch 6 Part 2 Para 34	Sch 2 Part 1 Para 8
(A 'qualifying undertaking' is defined as either: a qualifying partnership; or an unlimited company each of whose members is: (i) a limited company; or (ii) another unlimited company each of whose members is a limited company; or (iii) a Scottish partnership each of whose members is a limited company, and references in this paragraph to a limited company, another unlimited company or a Scottish partnership include a comparable undertaking incorporated in or formed under the law of a country or territory outside the United Kingdom.)	Sch 6 Part 2 Para 34(6)	Sch 2 Part 1 Para 8(6)
• The name and legal form of the undertaking; and	Sch 6 Part 2 Para 34(2)	Sch 2 Part 1 Para 8(2)
• The address of the undertaking's registered office (whether in or outside the United Kingdom) or, if it does not have such an office, its head office (whether in or outside the United Kingdom).	Sch 6 Part 2 Para 34(4)	Sch 2 Part 1 Para 8(4)
(This information is not required if it is not material.)		
Where the undertaking is a qualifying partnership there must also be stated either that a copy of the latest accounts of the undertaking has been or is to be appended to the copy of the company's accounts sent to the Registrar of Companies under CA 2006 s. 444, or the name of at least one body corporate (which may be the company) in whose group accounts the undertaking has been or is to be dealt with on a consolidated basis.	Sch 6 Part 2 Para 34(3)	Sch 2 Part 1 Para 8(3)

(The name of at least one body corporate need not be given if the notes to the company's accounts disclose that advantage has been taken of the exemption conferred by regulation 7 of the Partnerships (Accounts) Regulations 2008.)	Sch 6 Part 2 Para 34(5)	Sch 2 Part 1 Para 8(5)
PARENT UNDERTAKING DRAWING UP ACCOUNTS FOR LARGER GROUP	Sch 6 Part 2 Para 35	Sch 2 Part 1 Para 9
Where the reporting company is a subsidiary undertaking, the name of the parent undertaking must be given, and if the undertaking is incorporated outside the United Kingdom, the country in which it is incorporated, or if it is unincorporated, the address of its principal place of business.	Sch 6 Part 2 Para 35(2)-3(3)	Sch 2 Part 1 Para 9(2)-(3)
This disclosure is required with respect to the parent undertaking of the largest group of undertakings for which group accounts are drawn up and of which the company is a member, and the smallest such group of undertakings.	Sch 6 Part 2 Para 35(1)	Sch 2 Part 1 Para 9(1)
If copies of the group accounts referred to above are available to the public, there must also be stated the address from which copies of the accounts can be obtained.	Sch 6 Part 2 Para 35(4)	Sch 2 Part 1 Para 9(4)
IDENTIFICATION OF ULTIMATE PARENT COMPANY	Sch 6 Part 2 Para 36	Sch 2 Part 1 Para 10
If any company is regarded by the directors as being the reporting company's ultimate parent company. The name of that ultimate parent company must be disclosed.	Sch 6 Part 2 Para 36(1)-(2)	Sch 2 Part 1 Para 10(1)-(2)
If the ultimate parent company is incorporated outside the United Kingdom, the country in which it is incorporated must be stated (if known to the directors).	Sch 6 Part 2 Para 36(3)	Sch 2 Part 1 Para 10(3)

9.6 Group accounts filing

There is no statutory provision to prepare and submit abbreviated group accounts.

A small group is required to file at Companies House either:

- individual accounts of the parent company, if no group accounts are filed where the group qualifies as exempt; or
- consolidated (small or medium-sized company) accounts of the group.

Companies Act group accounts delivered to the Registrar of Companies under CA 2006 s.444 need not give the information otherwise required (in the full Companies Act group accounts) concerning:

- directors' benefits: remuneration – in accordance with SI 2008/409 Sch. 3; or
- shares of company held by subsidiary undertakings) in accordance with SI 2008/ 409 Sch. 6 paragraph 25.

SI 2008/409 reg. 11

9.7 Entitlement to group exemption – auditor's report

If the directors of a company have prepared accounts and reports in accordance with the small companies regime and in the auditor's opinion they were not entitled so to do, the auditor must

state that fact in the auditor's report; the auditor is therefore required to refer to the exemption and make a statement of non-entitlement only if in his opinion the directors were not entitled to the
s. 498(5) exemption.

9.8 Group companies – availability of audit exemption

If a company is a member of a small group then the company may be able to take advantage of the audit exemption for small companies. Furthermore, a new audit exemption was introduced for accounting periods ended on or after 1 October 2012 for subsidiary companies of any size meeting certain additional requirements.

Audit exemption, including the requirements of each type of exemption available to group companies, is covered in **Chapter 11**.

Chapter 10 Essentials of the FRSSE – the Financial Reporting Standard for Smaller Entities

10.1 Development of the FRSSE

10.1.1 Introduction

The Financial Reporting Standard for Smaller Entities (FRSSE) is the Financial Reporting Standard which brings together, in one document, all accounting requirements applicable to smaller entities. The FRSSE prescribes the basis for preparing and presenting the accounts of small entities (as defined in the standard – basically on the same criteria as 'small companies') and incorporates all relevant companies legislation and accounting standards.

A small company may choose not to adopt the FRSSE, in which case all accounting standards (UK or international) and UITF Consensus Abstracts apply in full where appropriate or not otherwise specifically exempted.

A small company preparing true and fair view accounts which chooses to adopt the FRSSE is exempt from all other accounting standards (FRSs and SSAPs) and UITF Abstracts (except those relevant to the production of consolidated accounts, that is FRSs 2, 5, 6, 7, 9, 10, 11 and 28). (FRS 10 and, as directed by FRS 10, FRS 11 need be applied only in respect of purchased goodwill arising on consolidation.)

The FRSSE was originally issued in 1997. The ASB has subsequently revised the FRSSE on four occasions when there have been sufficient accounting developments to incorporate. For accounts produced under the CA 2006 regime (see **10.1.2**), the applicable version of the FRSSE is the FRSSE (effective April 2008). Unless another version of the FRSSE is specifically referred to, all references to the FRSSE in this book are to the April 2008 version.

In one self-contained document, the FRSSE presents definitions, accounting treatments and measurement criteria that are consistent with existing accounting standards but in a simplified version. Some disclosure requirements are also simplified or excluded. In the absence of specific guidance within the FRSSE, accepted accounting practice should be interpreted and adopted having regard to FRSs, SSAPs and UITF Abstracts generally. Industry – or sector – specific SORPs may indicate the circumstances in which the current FRSSE is to be adopted.

The FRSSE is not available to and does not apply to:

- large or medium-sized companies, groups or other entities;
- public companies;
- companies preparing IAS accounts (individual or group);
- companies preparing accounts (individual or group) under fair value accounting rules (SI 2008/409 Sch. 1 Section D);
- authorised insurance companies, banking companies, e-money issuers, MiFID investment firms, UCITS management companies or companies that carry on insurance market activity;
- persons (other than small companies) who have permission under Part 4 of FSMA 2000 (in the UK) to carry on a regulated activity *(or, notwithstanding the definition of a small company in the*

legislation, companies authorised under the Investment Intermediaries Act 1995 (in the Republic of Ireland)); and
- members of an ineligible group. *(A group is ineligible if any of its members is: a public company; a body corporate (other than a company) whose shares are admitted to trading on a regulated market in an EEA State; a person (other than a small company) who has permission under Part 4 of FSMA 2000 to carry on a regulated activity; a small company that is an authorised insurance company, a banking company, an e-money issuer, a MiFID investment firm or a UCITS management company; or a person who carries on insurance market activity.)*

A 'small' subsidiary which is a member of a 'large' or 'medium-sized' group (which is not otherwise excluded) is entitled to choose to adopt the FRSSE if it so wishes.

A small company which chooses to adopt the FRSSE should disclose which version of the FRSSE it is adopting. The disclosure may be included with the accounts note of accounting policies or in the statement required by the Companies Act on the balance sheet. For example, the statement could read as follows:

> 'These accounts have been prepared in accordance with provisions applicable to companies subject to the small companies regime as set out within Part 15 of the CA 2006 and with the Financial Reporting Standard for Smaller Entities (effective April 2008).'

If abbreviated accounts are also prepared, the statement referring to the Financial Reporting Standard for Smaller Entities (effective April 2008) should be included with the note of accounting policies so that it is reproduced within the abbreviated accounts.

10.1.2 The 'FRSSE (effective April 2008)' – CA 2006

The Financial Reporting Standard for Smaller Entities (effective April 2008) updated and superseded the previous FRSSE to incorporate company law changes, primarily CA 2006. The FRSSE is regarded as standard for financial statements relating to accounting periods ***beginning on or after 6 April 2008***.

The recently issued FRS 100 *Application of Financial Reporting Requirements* made a number of consequential amendments to the FRSSE and these are explained in **Chapter 15** (**15.6**)

The FRC has indicated that in light of proposals from the European Commission made in October 2011 regarding small company reporting, the FRSSE is likely to be retained and a revised FRSSE issued. See **Chapter 15** for further details on the developments relating to financial reporting in the UK and the possible impacts on the FRSSE.

10.2 Essentials of the 'FRSSE (effective April 2008)'

10.2.1 Contents of chapter

This chapter provides the essential elements and requirements of the FRSSE by summarising its main contents and making cross references to the FRSSE itself. The full text of the FRSSE is available from the FRC website at:

www.frc.org.uk/FRC-Documents/ASB/FRSSE-(effective-April-2008).aspx

This book does not contain a facsimile of the FRSSE; a FRSSE compliance checklist is at **Appendix E**.

The FRSSE in the context of accounting standards generally and in particular the requirement for small company accounts to give a true and fair view is explained in **10.2.2** and **10.2.3**.

Further commentary on a variety of aspects of the FRSSE covers:

- cash flow statements (**10.4** and **Table 10.3**);
- small groups (**10.5**);
- FRS 3 and the FRSSE (**10.6**);
- reporting the substance of transactions (**10.7**);
- 'related party' requirements (**10.8**);
- loans and transactions with directors (**10.9**);
- pensions and retirement benefits (**10.10**);
- foreign currency accounting (**10.11**);
- provisions and discounting (**10.12**);
- revenue recognition (**10.13**); and
- share based payments (**10.14**).

10.2.2 Small companies – true and fair view

Accounts are required under CA 2006 s. 393 to give a true and fair view within the accounting framework set out in the CA 2006.

Accounts drawn up in compliance with the FRSSE incorporating the requirements of SI 2008/409 Sch. 1 are deemed to be 'true and fair' as required under the small companies regime of the CA 2006. To achieve a true and fair view, regard must be had to the actual substance of any transaction or arrangement and adequate explanation made (e.g. in the notes to the accounts) of the treatment adopted.

Where there is doubt whether applying provisions of the FRSSE would be sufficient to give a true and fair view, adequate explanation shall be given in the notes to the transaction or arrangement concerned and the treatment adopted in order for the true and fair view requirement to be met.

10.2.3 Accounting standards and the FRSSE

While the principles of accounting standards explained in **Chapter 4** apply to companies generally, small companies can have regard to the single FRSSE covering all relevant accounting standards in one standalone document.

The FRSSE is designed to provide smaller entities (not just companies) with a single accounting standard that is focused on their particular circumstances. The FRSSE applies to all smaller entities (as defined) which prepare true and fair view accounts and which choose to adopt the FRSSE. Accounts complying with the SORP of a particular industry or sector should not, however, be prepared in accordance with the FRSSE, other than in the circumstances which are specified in the SORP.

With certain exceptions (for example small groups) exemption is granted from other accounting standards and UITF Abstracts. Nevertheless, in the absence of guidance on a particular accounting practice within the FRSSE itself, the ASB stated that the preparers and auditors of accounts of small entities should have regard to SSAPs, FRSs and UITF Abstracts, not as mandatory documents, but as a means of establishing current accepted accounting practice.

Table 10.1 shows the effect for a small company of adopting the FRSSE. Small reporting entities applying the FRSSE are exempt from FRSs or UITF consensus interpretations issued subsequent to the latest version.

Table 10.1 The FRSSE and FRSs 1 to 30

	Small company adopting the FRSSE	***Small company not adopting the FRSSE (and applying FRSs as applicable)***
FRS 1 *Cash flow statements*	FRSSE encourages, but does not require, a cash flow statement See **10.4** and **Table 10.3**	Cash flow statement not required for small entities
FRS 2 *Accounting for subsidiary undertakings*	Not addressed by the FRSSE, except cross-referred to it if group accounts are prepared	FRS 2 applies in full for small parent preparing consolidated financial statements
FRS 3 *Reporting financial performance*	Only key elements included in FRSSE See **10.6**	FRS 3 applies in full
FRS 4 *Capital Instruments*	Only basic elements (classification of capital instruments, finance cost allocation, carrying amount of borrowings, etc.) included in FRSSE	FRS 4 applies in full (but see FRS 25) See **Appendix A (4)** (and FRS 25)
FRS 5 *Reporting the substance of transactions*	Only basic principles included in FRSSE	FRS 5 applies in full See **10.7**
FRS 6 *Acquisitions and mergers*	Not addressed by the FRSSE, except cross-referred to it if group accounts are prepared	FRS 6 applies in full for small parent preparing consolidated financial statements
FRS 7 *Fair values in acquisition accounting*	Not addressed by the FRSSE, except cross-referred to it if group accounts are prepared	FRS 7 applies in full for small parent preparing consolidated financial statements
FRS 8 *Related party disclosures*	FRSSE adopts basic principles of FRS 8 but only those related party transactions material to the reporting entity require disclosure See **10.8**	FRS 8 applies in full, requiring full disclosure of transactions and balances and additional judgment of materiality in relation to the related parties and the reporting entity
FRS 9 *Associates and joint ventures*	Not addressed by the FRSSE, except cross-referred to it if group accounts are prepared	Applies in group accounts, where prepared
FRS 10 *Goodwill and intangible assets*	FRSSE includes basic measurement requirements but most presentation and disclosure requirements are omitted Annual impairment reviews avoided	Applies in full, involving: (a) annual impairment reviews required for asset lives of over 20 years; and (b) recognition and revaluation provisions of intangible assets (including internally developed intangible assets) with a market value
FRS 11 *Impairment of fixed assets and goodwill*	Only key principles included in FRSSE	Applies in full, involving: (a) full note disclosures; (b) calculation of 'value in use'; and (c) monitoring of cash flows for five years following an impairment review involving 'value in use'

Table 10.1 The FRSSE and FRSs 1 to 30 (cont'd)

FRS 12 *Provisions, contingent liabilities and contingent assets*	FRSSE includes basic principles but most disclosure requirements are omitted Detailed rules for discounting omitted	Applies in full, involving: (a) reference to risk in measuring a provision; (b) detailed rules for discount rates; and (c) full note disclosures
FRS 13 *Derivatives and other financial instruments: disclosures*	Not applicable	Not applicable
FRS 15 *Tangible fixed assets*	FRSSE includes basic principles consistent with FRS 15 but most detailed disclosure requirements are omitted	Applies in full, involving: (a) detailed bases of valuation; (b) annual reviews of impairment and residual values for certain assets; (c) renewals accounting; and (d) detailed disclosure requirements
FRS 16 *Current tax*	FRSSE includes main requirements of FRS 16 involving recognition of dividends: (a) excluding attributable tax credits or underlying tax; and (b) including withholding taxes	Applies in full
FRS 17 (IAS 19) *Retirement benefits*	FRSSE follows FRS 17 and adopts the basic principles for defined contribution schemes	Applies in full For defined benefit schemes extensive disclosure requirements with value of any surplus or deficit for financial statements based on actuarial approach
FRS 18 *Accounting policies*	FRSSE adopts the basic principles of FRS 18 involving accounting policies that are relevant, reliable, comparable and understandable	Applies in full involving more detailed disclosures of: (a) true and fair view override departures; (b) significant appropriate estimation techniques; (c) non-adoption of going concern basis; and (d) provisions of any SORP
FRS 19 *Deferred tax*	FRSSE follows FRS 19 Discounting not required Disclosure of 'material components' of charge only required	Applies in full involving: (a) full provision for deferred tax; (b) deferred tax recognised on 'incremental liability' approach (i.e. when it meets the definition of an asset or liability in its own right); and (c) discounting permissible for deferred tax assets and liabilities
FRS 20 (IFRS 2) *Share-based payment*	Not applicable (FRSSE includes simplified disclosures)	Applies in full covering accounting treatment and disclosures for share-based payment transactions (shares and share options)
FRS 21 (IAS 10) *Events after the balance sheet date*	Not applicable (but main principles of FRS 21 adopted by FRSSE)	Applies in full
FRS 22 (IAS 33) *Earnings per share*	Not applicable	Voluntary but not mandatory

Table 10.1 The FRSSE and FRSs 1 to 30 (cont'd)

FRS 23 (IAS 21) *The effects of changes in foreign exchange rates*	Not applicable	Applies in full with effect from application of FRS 26
FRS 24 (IAS 29) *Financial reporting in hyperinflationary economies*	Not applicable	Applies in full with effect from application of FRS 26
FRS 25 (IAS 32) *Financial instruments: disclosure and presentation*	Not applicable	Applies in full (Presentation) [with effect from application of FRS 26 (Disclosure)]
FRS 26 (IAS 39) *Financial instruments: measurement*	Not applicable	Applies in full covering fair value accounting treatment and disclosures for financial instruments and hedge accounting
FRS 27 *Life Assurance*	Not applicable	The small companies regime does not apply to authorised insurance companies, therefore not considered applicable
FRS 28 *Corresponding amounts*	Key principles apply	Applies in full
FRS 29 (IFRS 7) *Financial instruments: disclosures*	Not applicable	Applies in full
FRS 30 *Heritage assets*	Not applicable – FRSSE exempt	Applies in full where applicable

10.3 The FRSSE in outline

Table 10.2 presents a basic outline summary of the areas covered by the FRSSE. References to 'FRSSE paragraphs' are to paragraphs of the FRSSE (effective April 2008).

Table 10.2 The FRSSE in outline

	FRSSE paragraphs
General	
Objective	1
Scope	1.1
Requirement to prepare financial statements	2.1
True and fair view	2.2 – 2.5
Accounting principles and policies	2.6 – 2.11
Going concern	2.12
Prudence.	2.13
Accruals	2.14
Prior period adjustments	2.15
Formats of accounts – general rules	2.16 – 2.26
Balance sheet format	2.27
Profit and loss account formats	2.28 – 2.29
Approval and signing of accounts	2.30 – 2.34
Delivery of accounts to registrar	2.35 – 2.36
Exemptions from audit	2.37 – 2.38
Liability limitation agreement	2.39

Table 10.2 The FRSSE in outline (cont'd)

Profit and loss account	3.1 – 3.8
Revenue recognition	4.1 – 4.15
Statement of total recognised gains and losses	5.1
Fixed assets and goodwill	6.1 – 6.57
Leases (HP and leasing)	7.1 – 7.18
Current assets	8.1 – 8.16
Taxation	9.1 – 9.15
Pensions	10.1 – 10.4
Provisions, contingent liabilities and contingent assets	11.1 – 11.11
Financial instruments	12.1 – 12.15
Foreign currency translation	13.1 – 13.12
Post balance sheet events	14.1 – 14.4
Related party disclosures	15.1 – 15.24
Consolidated financial statements	16.1 – 16.8
Directors' remuneration	17.1 – 17.3
The directors' report	18.1 – 18.16

10.4 Cash flow statements

The FRSSE does not include a requirement for a cash flow statement, since small entities are already exempt from the requirements of FRS 1. Nevertheless, within a non-mandatory 'voluntary disclosures' section of the FRSSE, the ASB 'strongly encourages' smaller entities to present a simplified cash flow statement using the indirect method.

The indirect method starts with operating profit (normally profit before income from shares in group undertakings) and adjusts it for non-cash charges and credits to reconcile it with cash generated from operations. Other sources and applications of cash are shown to arrive at total cash generated (or utilised) in the period.

Disclosures are recommended to include the following:

- cash, being 'cash at bank and in hand' less overdrafts repayable on demand – reconciled to the balance sheet;
- cash flows, being net of any attributable VAT or other sales tax, unless the tax is irrecoverable; and
- material transactions not resulting in movements of cash, which shall be disclosed by way of note where necessary for a proper understanding of the underlying transactions.

The form of cash flow statement indicated as voluntary disclosure by the FRSSE is set out in **Table 10.3**. This example has been derived from the example contained in the FRSSE (effective April 2008) (Appendix III).

Table 10.3 Small company cash flow statement for the year ended 30 April 2013

		2013		*2012*
	£'000	*£'000*	*£'000*	*£'000*
CASH GENERATED FROM OPERATIONS				
Operating (loss)/profit	**(10,000)**		**4,400**	
Reconciliation to cash generated from operations:				
Depreciation	245		240	
Increase in stocks	(194)		(270)	
Decrease in trade debtors	2,440		19,090	
(Decrease)/increase in trade creditors	(4,678)		1,240	
Increase in other creditors	3,127		100	
		9,060		24,800
CASH FROM OTHER SOURCES				
Interest received	150		100	
Issues of shares for cash	5,500		–	
New long-term bank borrowings	4,500		–	
Proceeds from sale of tangible fixed assets	50		940	
		10,200		1,040
APPLICATION OF CASH				
Interest paid	(3,000)		(1,000)	
Tax paid	(2,220)		(2,100)	
Dividends paid	–		(10,000)	
Purchase of fixed assets	(1,500)		(5,600)	
Repayment of amounts borrowed	(3,000)		–	
		(9,720)		(18,700)
NET (DECREASE) INCREASE IN CASH		**(8,580)**		**7,140**
Cash at bank and in hand less overdrafts at beginning of year		(4,321)		(11,461)
CASH AT BANK AND IN HAND LESS OVERDRAFTS AT END OF YEAR		**(12,901)**		**(4,321)**
Consisting of:				
Cash at bank and in hand		500		1,909
Overdrafts included in 'bank loans and overdrafts falling due within one year'		(13,401)		(6,230)
		(12,901)		**(4,321)**

Major non-cash transactions: finance leases
During the year, the company entered into finance lease arrangements in respect of assets with a total capital value at the inception of the leases of £2,850 (2012 – Nil).

10.5 Small groups

A small eligible parent company (as defined – see **9.2**) is not required to prepare group accounts. If at the end of a financial year a company subject to the small companies regime is a parent company, the directors, as well as preparing individual accounts for the year, *may* prepare group accounts for the year – but they are not required to do so.

Those small groups that voluntarily prepare group accounts may nevertheless take advantage of the provisions in FRSSE (effective April 2008). Entities preparing group accounts must have regard to the legal requirements reflected in the FRSSE and Schedule 6 of SI 2008/409 under the CA 2006 (see **9.4**).

Where the reporting entity is part of a group that prepares publicly available consolidated accounts, it is entitled under the FRSSE to the exemptions from disclosure provided by FRS 8 paragraph 3(a) and (c), being:

- in consolidated accounts, transactions or balances between group entities that have been eliminated on consolidation; and
- transactions entered into between two or more members of a group, provided that any subsidiary undertaking which is a party to the transaction is wholly owned by a member of that group.

10.6 FRS 3 and the FRSSE

Table 10.4 indicates how the requirements of FRS 3 have been reflected in the FRSSE .

Table 10.4 FRS 3 and the FRSSE

FRS 3 para	FRSSE para	
13	5.1	Primary statement of total recognised gains and losses (no separate statement required if gains and losses all recognised in profit and loss account).
19–20	3.5–3.6	Exceptional items: include as charge or credit within statutory headings (with separate disclosure if prominence required for true and fair view).
19		No reference to continuing or discontinued operations in the FRSSE.
21	3.7	Profit or loss on disposal accounted for in period of disposal (net sales proceeds less net carrying amount).
22		Extraordinary items are only mentioned in the FRSSE to note that they are extremely rare, and that they should be shown separately after the profit or loss on ordinary activities after taxation.
29	2.15	Prior period adjustments.
23	9.3	Disclosure of special circumstances affecting overall tax charge (but no specific requirement to disclose tax on exceptional items).
5,2,7-8	C	Definitions of 'exceptional items', 'ordinary activities', 'prior period adjustments' and 'total recognised gains and losses'.

10.7 Reporting the substance of transactions

In order to ensure that accounts show a true and fair view, the FRSSE requires that any arrangement, transaction or series of transactions into which a company has entered should be accounted for not merely in accordance with their legal form but with their substance, that is, their true commercial effect. While this basic principle of FRS 5 is reflected in the FRSSE, the requirements of the FRS are not generally covered in detail, other than setting out requirements for consignment stock and debt factoring.

10.8 Related party transactions

The FRSSE requires the disclosure of:

- information on related party transactions;
- the name of the controlling party (if any) and ultimate controlling party (if different), whether or not any transactions between the parties have taken place;
- personal guarantees given by directors in respect of borrowings by the reporting entity; and
- transactions with directors.

Material related party transactions that require disclosure are those where the reporting entity:

- purchases, sells or transfers goods and other assets or liabilities; or
- renders or receives services; or
- provides or receives finance or financial support (irrespective of whether a price is charged) to, from or on behalf of a related party.

The materiality of a related party transaction shall be judged in terms of its significance to the reporting entity (and not in relation to the other related party as is required by FRS 8 even where (for example) that related party is an individual).

Aggregated disclosures are allowed subject to certain restrictions.

Table 10.5 Related parties – FRSSE definition

Two or more parties are related parties when at any time during the financial period:

- one party has direct or indirect control of the other party; or
- the parties are subject to common control from the same source; or
- one party has significant influence over the financial and operating policies of the other party, to an extent that the other party is inhibited from pursuing its own separate interests.

For the avoidance of doubt, the FRSSE definition states that related parties of the reporting entity include the following:

- parent undertakings, subsidiary and fellow subsidiary undertakings;
- associates and joint ventures;
- investors with significant influence and their **close families**; and
- **directors** of the reporting entity and of its parent undertakings and their **close families**.

The disclosures should include:

- the names of the transacting related parties;
- a description of the relationship between the parties;
- a description of the transactions;
- the amounts involved;
- any other elements of the transactions necessary for an understanding of the financial statements;
- the amounts due to or from related parties at the balance sheet date and provisions for doubtful debts due from such parties at that date; and
- amounts written off in the period in respect of debts due to or from related parties.

No disclosure is required in consolidated accounts of intra-group transactions and balances eliminated on consolidation. A parent undertaking is not required to provide related party disclosures in its own accounts when those accounts are presented with consolidated accounts of the group.

Transactions with related parties may be disclosed on an aggregated basis (aggregation of similar transactions by type of related party) unless disclosure of an individual transaction, or connected transactions, is necessary for an understanding of the impact of the transactions on the accounts of the reporting entity or is required by law.

Disclosure is not required of:

- pension contributions paid to a pension fund; nor
- emoluments in respect of services as an employee of the reporting entity.

Nor is disclosure required of the relationship and transactions between the reporting entity and the following parties simply as a result of their role as:

- providers of finance in the course of their business in that regard;
- utility companies;

- government departments and their sponsored bodies; or
- a customer, supplier, franchiser, distributor or general agent.

When the reporting entity is controlled by another party, there must be disclosure of the related party relationship, the name of the controlling party and, if different, that of the ultimate controlling party. If the controlling party or ultimate controlling party of the reporting entity is not known, that fact should be disclosed. (These disclosures are irrespective of whether any transactions have taken place between the controlling parties and the reporting entity.)

10.9 Loans and transactions with directors

When preparing accounts and having determined the legality of a loan, the directors of a small company need to consider the extent of disclosure. It is important to recognise the distinction that, notwithstanding that a transaction (other than a loan) may be legal, it may still require disclosure in the accounts.

CA 2006 s. 197(1) ('Loans to directors: requirement of members' approval') makes a general prohibition on loans to directors, together with related guarantees or provision of security for loans without the approval of the members of the company. However, for small loans CA 2006 s. 207(1) ('Loans: exceptions for minor and business transactions') provides that such approval is not required if the aggregate value of the transaction (together with other relevant transactions or arrangements) does not exceed £10,000.

Expenditure on company business is permitted under CA 2006 s. 204 ('Loans: exception for expenditure on company business') for anything done by a company to provide a director of the company or of its holding company (or a person connected with any such director) with funds to meet expenditure incurred for the company or to enable the proper performance of the director's duties as an officer of the company, provided the aggregate of the value of the transaction (and the value of any other relevant transactions or arrangement) does not exceed £50,000.

The 'value of a transaction or arrangement' referred to above is defined in detail (and some complexity) in CA 2006 s. 211.

Factors determining disclosure may include:

- CA 2006 requirements – s. 197 ('Loans to directors: requirement of members' approval') et seq;
- FRS 8 *Related Party Disclosures* or, for small companies adopting it, the FRSSE; and
- requirements of the company's memorandum and articles of association.

The requirements of the FRSSE covering transactions with directors, now referred to as 'Directors' benefits: advances, credit and guarantees', are based on CA 2006 s. 413 and are summarised below.

CA 2006 s. 413 provides for the provision of information about 'Directors' benefits: advances, credit and guarantees'. The following details must, where appropriate, be shown in the notes to accounts (individual or group accounts):

- advances and credits granted to directors; and
- guarantees of any kind entered into on behalf of directors.

For group accounts, 'directors' are 'parent company directors' and advances, credit and guarantees relate to those granted by the parent company or by any of its subsidiary undertakings to the directors of the parent company. 'Directors' include a person who was a director of the company (or parent company) at any time in the financial year to which the accounts relate.

The details required in the disclosure of an advance or credit are: its amount; an indication of the interest rate; its main conditions; and any amounts repaid. There is no definition of an advance or a credit in CA 2006.

The details required in the disclosure of a guarantee entered into on behalf of a director are: its main terms; the amount of the maximum liability that may be incurred by the company (or its subsidiary); and any amount paid and any liability incurred by the company (or its subsidiary) for the purpose of fulfilling the guarantee (including any loss incurred by reason of enforcement of the guarantee).

10.9.1 Practical guidance – related party and director disclosures

Loan to a director

During the year an advance was made to [Director] of £xx. The loan was interest free, unsecured and repayable on demand. £xx remained outstanding at the year end.

	Disclosure under FRS 8	Disclosure under FRSSE (alone)	Disclosure under CA 2006 s. 413	Disclosure in abbreviated accounts
If material to the director only	Disclose	None	Disclose	Disclose
If material to the company only	Disclose	Disclose	Disclose	Disclose
If material to the company and director	Disclose	Disclose	Disclose	Disclose
If material to neither company nor director	None	None	Disclose – there is no de minimis under s. 413	Disclose

In the case that the balance due from the director arose due to a number of smaller transactions (e.g. on company credit card), the disclosure is still required. CA 2006 s. 413 requires every individual transaction to be disclosed; however it is widely accepted that a common sense approach can be applied with disclosure aggregating similar transactions (see ICAEW guidance below). Such a disclosure might read:

During the year a number of advances were made to [Director] totalling £xx. This amount was interest free, unsecured and repayable on demand. £xx remained outstanding at the year end.

Sale/other transaction with a director

During the year, goods were sold to [Director] for £xx. The market value of the goods was £xx and the sale was/was not on an arms-length basis.

	Disclosure under FRS 8	Disclosure under FRSSE (alone)	Disclosure under CA 2006 s. 413	Disclosure in abbreviated accounts
If material to the director only	Disclose	None	As this is not a loan (assuming the sale was not on credit), no disclosure is required under s. 413	None
If material to the company only	Disclose	Disclose	None (as above)	None
If material to the company and director	Disclose	Disclose	None (as above)	None
If material to neither company nor director	None	None	None (as above)	None

Loan to a connected person (not a director) (e.g. close family of a director)

An advance was made to [connected person] during the period of £xx. The loan was interest free, unsecured and repayable on demand. £xx remained outstanding at the year end.

	Disclosure under FRS 8	Disclosure under FRSSE (alone)	Disclosure under CA 2006 s. 413	Disclosure in abbreviated accounts
If material to the person only	Disclose	None	None	None
If material to the company only	Disclose	Disclose	None	None
If material to the company and person	Disclose	Disclose	None	None
If material to neither company nor person	None	None	None	None

ICAEW guidance concerning disclosure under CA 2006 *s. 413*

In May 2010 the Audit and Assurance Faculty of the ICAEW included an article in its 'Audit and Beyond' publication with the aim of giving guidance on how s. 413 can practically be applied (**nb**: this is included as guidance only and is not considered to be an exact interpretation of the law).

In relation to aggregating advances and credits, the article suggests, although recognising that this may not be in line with the exact letter of the section, that there may be merit in the view that advances or credits could be aggregated rather than being shown individually as the original EU directive from which s. 413 is derived does not require the disclosure of every individual amount. However, the priority in any decisions made regarding the appropriateness of disclosures is the requirement on the directors to prepare financial statements which give a true and fair view of the company.

The article sets out a seven point approach to preparing the disclosure note for the financial statements which is aimed to make it easier for companies to justify what has been disclosed and what has not.

1. Create a chronological record of transactions between the company and the director to establish whether there were any 'advances' (i.e. whether the account was overdrawn at any time).
2. Identify opening and closing debit balances and the maximum amounts outstanding (the account may be overdrawn on more than one occasion and be rectified in between times).
3. Identify individually material advances in the overdrawn periods and list them separately (loans exceeding £10,000 in aggregate require prior approval by the members).
4. Identify any other individually material advances (e.g. where the director used company money for personal purposes) and consider whether these need reporting separately.
5. Aggregate the remaining advances.
6. Identify amounts repaid by the director, listing material amounts individually and separately.
7. Compile the note, adding details of interest, security etc.

10.10 Pensions and retirement benefits

10.10.1 Accounting for retirement benefits

The FRSSE incorporates aspects of FRS 17 'Retirement Benefits', modified and simplified where appropriate for accounting and disclosure in the accounts of smaller entities.

Two types of pension schemes are defined within the FRSSE. A 'Defined contribution scheme' is a pension or other retirement benefit scheme into which an employer pays regular contributions, fixed as an amount or as a percentage of pay. The employer has no legal or constructive obligation to pay further contributions in the event of the scheme having insufficient assets to pay all employee benefits relating to employee service in the current and prior periods. Any scheme other than a defined contribution scheme is defined as a 'Defined benefit scheme', the rules of which define benefits independently of the contributions payable (and the benefits are not directly related to scheme investments).

Even though comparatively few smaller entities use defined benefit retirement schemes, implementation of the accounting rules concerning these schemes in the accounts of the employer company is onerous and warrants careful consideration. Actuarial advice will be required.

The requirements for accounting for retirement benefits under the FRSSE are in essence as follows:

Defined contribution schemes – scheme contributions payable for the period included within operating profit in the profit and loss account for the period. The notes must include details of the nature of the scheme (i.e. that it is a defined contribution scheme, the cost for the year and any outstanding or prepaid contributions at the balance sheet date).

Defined benefit schemes – scheme assets and liabilities are measured:

- scheme assets – at fair value; and
- scheme liabilities – on an actuarial basis using the projected unit method, with the resulting net asset or liability recognised in the balance sheet.

Example 10.1 contains example pension scheme disclosures, reproduced (and adapted) from an appendix in the FRSSE.

Example 10.1 Example pension scheme disclosures

Defined contribution pension scheme

The company operates a defined contribution pension scheme. The assets of the scheme are held separately from those of the company in an independently administered fund. The pension cost charge represents contributions payable by the company to the fund and amounted to £50,000 (2012 – £45,000). Contributions totalling £2,500 (2012 – £1,500) were payable to the fund at the year end and are included in creditors.

Defined benefit pension scheme
(NOTE [Example FRSSE (effective April 2008)]):

The company operates a pension scheme providing benefits based on final pensionable pay. The assets of the scheme are held separately from those of the company, being invested with insurance companies.

The contributions are determined by a qualified actuary on the basis of triennial valuations using the projected unit method. The most recent valuation was as at 31 December 2011 which has been updated to reflect conditions at the balance sheet date. The assumptions that have the most significant effect on the results of the valuation are those relating to the rate of return on investments and the rate of increase in salaries and pensions. It was assumed that the investment returns would be 6 per cent per year, that salary increases would average 4 per cent per year and that present and future pensions would increase at the rate of 3 per cent per year.

The pension charge for the year was £46,000 (2012 £25,000). This included £12,000 (2012 £nil) in respect of past service costs. The contributions of the company and employees will remain at 10 per cent and 5 per cent of earnings respectively.

The defined benefit scheme is closed to new members and so under the projected unit method the current service cost would be expected to increase over time as members of the scheme approach retirement.

Value of scheme assets and liabilities	2013	2012
	£	£
Market value of assets	1,488,000	962,000
Present value of scheme liabilities	(1,009,000)	(758,000)
Pension scheme surplus/(deficit)	479,000	204,000
Related deferred tax asset/(liability)	(144,000)	(61,000)
Net pension scheme asset/(liability)	335,000	143,000

Movements in year	2013	2012
	£	£
Pension scheme surplus/(deficit) at beginning of year	204,000	92,000
Current service cost	(34,000)	(25,000)
Cash contribution	25,000	35,000
Past service costs	(12,000)	–
Other finance income	20,000	11,000
Actuarial gain	276,000	91,000
Pension scheme surplus/(deficit) at end of year	479,000	204,000

10.11 Foreign currency accounting

Each asset, liability, revenue or cost arising from a transaction denominated in a foreign currency should be translated into the local currency at the exchange rate in operation on the date on which the transaction occurred; if the rates do not fluctuate significantly, an average rate for a period may be used as an approximation. Where the transaction is to be settled at a contracted rate, that rate should be used.

Where a trading transaction is covered by a related or matching forward contract, the rate of exchange specified in that contract may be used.

Except for the treatment of foreign equity investments financed by foreign currency borrowings, no subsequent translations should normally be made once *non-monetary* assets have been translated and recorded.

At each balance sheet date, *monetary assets and liabilities* denominated in a foreign currency shall be translated by using the closing exchange rate or, where appropriate, the rates of exchange fixed under the terms of the relevant transactions. Where there are related or matching forward contracts in respect of trading transactions, the rates of exchange specified in those contracts may be used. SSAP 20 *Foreign currency translation* defines monetary assets and liabilities as including cash and bank balances, loans and amounts receivable and payable.

All exchange gains or losses on settled transactions and unsettled monetary items should be reported as part of the profit or loss for the year from ordinary activities.

Where a company has used foreign currency borrowings to finance, or to provide a hedge against, its foreign equity investments and the conditions set out in the FRSSE (para 13.6) apply, the equity investments may be denominated in the appropriate foreign currencies and the carrying amounts translated at the end of each accounting period at closing rates for inclusion in the investing company's financial statements. Where investments are treated in this way, any exchange differences arising should be taken to reserves and the exchange gains or losses on the foreign currency borrowings should then be offset, as a reserve movement, against these exchange differences.

Increasingly UK companies are being used as trading vehicles in other parts of the world. Companies preparing their accounts in accordance with the FRSSE will do so in a currency other than sterling in appropriate circumstances. The FRSSE itself does not describe the appropriate circumstances and therefore reference is required to SSAP 20 and FRS 23 *The Effects of changes in foreign exchange rates*. Such 'foreign currency' accounts are acceptable to the Registrar of Companies.

FRS 23 provides guidance on how a company should identify its functional currency and it is this currency that a company should use to measure its results and financial position and therefore in which its accounts should be prepared. Paragraph 8 of FRS 23 describes the functional currency as the currency of the primary economic environment in which the entity operates. The 'primary economic environment' is normally the economic environment in which the company 'primarily generates and expends cash'. Paragraphs 9 and 10 of FRS 23 go on to say:

9 *An entity considers the following factors in determining its functional currency:*

(a) the currency:

- *(i) that mainly influences sales prices for goods and services (this will often be the currency in which sales prices for its goods and services are denominated and settled); and*
- *(ii) of the country whose competitive forces and regulations mainly determine the sales prices of its goods and services;*

(b) the currency that mainly influences labour, material and other costs of providing goods or services (this will often be the currency in which such costs are denominated and settled).

10 *The following factors may also provide evidence of an entity's functional currency:*

(a) the currency in which funds from financing activities (ie issuing debt and equity instruments) are generated;

(b) the currency in which receipts from operating activities are usually retained.

Having decided that its functional currency is not sterling, the directors of a company should prepare the accounts of the company in the appropriate foreign currency and **12.4** provides an example of such accounts.

Where accounts are prepared in a foreign currency, these must disclose the foreign currency's exchange rate to sterling at the balance sheet date in the notes to the accounts.

10.12 Provisions and discounting

A provision (for a liability of uncertain amount or timing) should be the best estimate of the expenditure required to settle the obligation at the balance sheet date.

Where the effect of the time value of money is material, a provision shall be determined by discounting the amount to the present value of the expenditures expected to be required to settle the obligation. Discounting is also required in circumstances where it is necessary to show a true and fair view. The FRSSE requires the unwinding of the discount to be disclosed as 'other finance costs' adjacent to interest.

10.13 Revenue recognition

Application Note G to FRS 5 provides guidance on the principles of revenue recognition and the treatment of turnover. The Application Note codifies existing practice and sets out a consistent treatment of revenue transactions ('exchange transactions' between seller and customer). The guidance explains how, when and whether to recognise revenue, in a variety of circumstances.

The FRSSE incorporates the essential principles of revenue recognition promoted by Application Note G to FRS 5, incorporating the guidance contained in UITF 40 (see **Appendix A(8)**).

Entities adopting the FRSSE must comply with the principles of UITF 40 (despite a statement of exemption within the UITF) as a result of requirements of HM Revenue & Customs (HMRC). All entities should apply UITF 40 (where applicable) for accounting periods ending on or after 22 June 2005.

Companies are required by law to calculate their taxable profits in accordance with generally accepted accounting practice (UK GAAP or IAS), subject to any specific tax law overrides. HMRC expects that all entities will adopt the most appropriate accounting policies consistent with current practice. It is clear that non-FRSSE entities should apply UITF 40 for accounting periods ending on or after 22 June 2005 and, in the light of this and the requirement in the FRSSE that entities which follow the FRSSE should have regard to full standards as a means of establishing current practice, it is believed that entities which follow the FRSSE should have regard to UITF 40 in preparing their accounts.

Revenue recognition is covered in more detail in **Appendix A(8).**

10.14 Share-based payments

Share-based payment arrangements (such as employee share option schemes or SAYE arrangements) are relatively uncommon for smaller entities. FRS 20 incorporated into UK accounting the requirements of the international standard IFRS 2. The FRSSE includes requirements for share-based payment arrangements but with major simplifications.

A share-based payment transaction is defined as 'a transaction in which the entity acquires goods or services by incurring a liability to transfer cash or other assets to the supplier of those goods or services for amounts that are based on the price (or value) of the entity's shares or other equity instruments of the entity'.

An entity which undertakes share-based payment arrangements (including transactions with employees or others providing similar services), where liability is based on the price of the entity's shares or other equity instruments, shall account for them as either:

- cash-settled share-based payment (to be accounted for as an expense at the best estimate of the expenditure required to settle the liability); or
- equity-settled share-based payment (to be reported on a disclosure basis only).

10.15 Going concern and the FRSSE

As explained in **Chapter 3**, accounts must be prepared on the presumption of the business as a going concern, unless there is an intention to cease trading or liquidate the company. This applies to all accounts whether or not the company is small or is entitled to audit exemption or files abbreviated accounts.

10.15.1 Going concern: directors' responsibilities

All directors (including directors of smaller companies) are required by the CA 2006 to decide if it is appropriate to prepare annual accounts on a going concern basis.

The FRSSE provides that accounts must not be prepared on a going concern basis if the directors determine that they intend to liquidate or cease trading, or that they have no realistic alternative but to do so. The FRSSE requires directors to:

- assess the ability of the company to continue as a going concern;
- disclose in accounts any material uncertainties indicated by the assessment; and
- disclose the period covered by the assessment (where the period covers less than one year from the date of approval of the annual accounts).

Assessment of the going concern basis of accounting involves the directors making judgments, at a particular time, about future events which are inherently uncertain. The directors must have reasonable grounds for concluding that it is realistic for the company to continue as a going concern for at least twelve months from date of approval of the financial statements.

In order to satisfy themselves, the directors may need to:

- prepare a budget, trading estimate, cash flow forecast or a similar analysis;
- base analysis on reasoned assumptions, identifying possible adverse outcomes; and
- document any underlying assumptions and their conclusions.

10.15.2 FRC guidance

In October 2009 the FRC published *Going Concern and Liquidity Risk: Guidance for Directors of UK Companies 2009* which brought together the requirements of company law, accounting standards and the UK listing rules. The guidance applied to accounting periods ending on or after 31 December 2009.

The FRC guidance aims to help all directors (including those of smaller companies) by summarising the criteria necessary to support the 'going concern basis' and identifying basic procedures needed to support conclusions. As set out in **Table 10.6**, the guidance is based on three principles covering:

- the process which directors should follow when assessing going concern;
- the period covered by the assessment; and
- the disclosures on going concern and liquidity risk.

The principles contained should be applied by directors of all companies when preparing annual (and half yearly) financial statements. Directors are encouraged to focus on the principles and to apply them in a manner proportionate to the nature of their particular business.

Table 10.6 ***Going Concern and Liquidity Risk: Guidance for Directors of UK Companies 2009 (October 2009) – the three principles***
Assessing going concern:
Directors should make and document a rigorous assessment of whether the company is a going concern when preparing annual and half yearly financial statements. The process carried out by the directors should be proportionate in nature and depth depending upon the size, level of financial risk and complexity of the company and its operations.
The review period:
Directors should consider all available information about the future when concluding whether the company is a going concern at the date they approve the financial statements.
Their review should usually cover a period of at least twelve months from the date of approval of annual and half yearly financial statements.
Disclosures:
Directors should make balanced, proportionate and clear disclosures about going concern for the financial statements to give a true and fair view. Directors should disclose if the period that they have reviewed is less than twelve months from the date of approval of annual and half yearly financial statements and explain their justification for limiting their review period.

The extent of forecasting procedures required, as outlined in **10.15.1**, may vary considerably according to particular circumstances. A company with substantial cash balances and a committed order book is very different from one with significant borrowings and uncertainties about future sales. As the FRC guidance explains, 'the extent of the directors' review process will depend upon the size and nature of the company and the complexity of its business. Small companies tend to be dependent upon a single provider of finance, have only one business activity and a limited number of creditors including the tax authorities. As a result the extent of the process and procedures for a small company are likely to be much simpler than that for medium and large companies. However, it is still important that the assessment is carried out and documented and addresses, to the extent necessary, the directors' plans to manage the company's borrowing requirements, the timing of cash flows and the company's exposure to contingent liabilities'. Recent FRC guidance linked with the Sharman Inquiry has suggested that 'sensitivity analysis on key aspects of their financial performance (for example, sales projections or cash collections) is likely to be needed even for smaller companies'.

The assessment performed by the directors will lead to one of the following three conclusions.

- No material uncertainties related to events or conditions that may cast significant doubt about the ability of the company to continue as a going concern have been identified by the directors.
- Material uncertainties related to the events and conditions that may cast significant doubt about the ability of the company to continue as a going concern have been identified by the directors, but the going concern basis remains appropriate.
- The going concern basis is not appropriate as the company has no realistic alternative but to cease trading or to go into liquidation, or the directors intend to cease trading or place the company into liquidation.

10.15.3 Going concern: accounts disclosures

In practice it has been very rare for accounts to be prepared on a basis other than as a 'going concern'. Specific reference to 'going concern' within company accounts has generally not been necessary because it is a fundamental presumption unless indicated otherwise.

In the current and recent economic environment it is clear from its guidance that the Financial Reporting Council (FRC) 'does expect that many accounts may benefit from a short note explaining how credit market and other economic difficulties have an impact, if any, on the company's particular circumstances'.

Many more small company accounts may, as a result, contain notes considering the implications of future trading assessments on the adoption the 'going concern' basis of accounting. See example presentation in **Chapter 12**.

In the current economic climate, predicting future trading trends may be difficult. Doubts about the ability of a company to remain as a going concern do not necessarily mean that the company is, or is likely to become, insolvent. For accounts disclosure purposes, as a rule of thumb disclosure would usually be appropriate where there are 'significant doubts' about future trading or there are 'material uncertainties of such significance' about the ability to continue to trade. Any disclosure should set out the facts and circumstances in a manner that is proportionate to the nature of the company.

The FRC guidance *Going Concern and Liquidity Risk: Guidance for Directors of UK Companies 2009* (**10.15.2**) provides example disclosures as set out in **Example 10.2**.

Example 10.2 Going Concern and Liquidity Risk: Guidance for Directors of UK Companies 2009 (October 2009) – Appendix I

Examples of going concern disclosures for small companies
Disclosures should be specific to the individual circumstances of each company.

No material uncertainties that may cast significant doubt about the ability of the company to continue as a going concern have been identified by the directors.

Example 1 – A small company that has adopted the FRSSE and anticipates reduced sales next year
There has been a significant reduction in requests for estimates for new decorating work and the directors expect sales to reduce significantly next year. However, costs are expected to reduce accordingly and the company should be able to operate within its overdraft. The directors are not aware of any reason why the overdraft facility might be withdrawn. As a result they have adopted the going concern basis of accounting.

Material uncertainty that casts significant doubt about the ability of the company to continue as a going concern has been identified by the directors.

Example 2 – A small company that has adopted the FRSSE and has experienced difficulties in securing future work
The company has orders for work for the next two months. However, despite significant efforts, it has so far proved impossible to obtain additional sales orders. If new orders are not forthcoming, the directors will need to close the factory and make the employees redundant.
The directors have concluded that a material uncertainty exists that casts significant doubt upon the company's ability to continue as a going concern and that, therefore, the company may be unable to realise its assets and discharge its liabilities in the normal course of business. However, given the continuing efforts to secure new orders, the directors continue to adopt the going concern basis of accounting.

Any specific disclosure about going concern contained within a company's annual accounts should also be included in any abbreviated accounts filed at Companies House. This is illustrated in the example abbreviated accounts (Note 8) in **Chapter 12**.

In March 2011, the Sharman Panel of Inquiry into Going Concern and Liquidity Risks was commissioned to identify what lessons can be learned from the recent financial crisis which may be of relevance to both auditors and companies in relation to going concern and liquidity risks and to make recommendations of measures and provide guidance to improve the reporting of these matters.

In January 2013, the FRC issued a consultation paper following the final recommendations of the panel of the Inquiry (published in June 2012) and referred to in **10.15.2** (above). The paper does not recommend any additional disclosures for small companies.

10.16 FRSSE disclosure checklist

Appendix E contains an accounts disclosure checklist covering all of the requirements of FRSSE (effective April 2008).

Chapter 11 Determining small company audit exemption

11.1 Introduction

Made in September 2012, the *Companies and Limited Liability Partnerships (Accounts and Audit Exemptions and Change of Accounting Framework) Regulations* 2012 (SI 2012/2301) amended the CA 2006 to align small company audit thresholds with accounting thresholds. They also exempt certain subsidiary companies from audit. The revised legislation applies to accounting periods ended on or after 1 October 2012.

There are four categories of company for which exemption from statutory audit is available under the CA 2006:

- small companies (s. 477);
- subsidiary companies (s. 479A);
- dormant companies (s. 480); and
- non profit-making companies subject to public sector audit (s. 482) (special rules apply to these companies – details of these are outside the scope of this book).

The audit exemption available for small companies is not available if the company is part of a non-small group. There are also a number of other restrictions and requirements for each exemption as set out in detail below.

In considering if the company is to take advantage of these exemptions, the members and directors should also consider if an audit is beneficial or required for other reasons, such as providing peace of mind, to assist in obtaining financing, to meet banking terms or as a requirement of the Articles of Association or a shareholders' agreement.

11.2 Small companies – conditions for exemption from audit

A company is exempt from the requirements for the audit of its accounts in respect of a financial year if it qualifies as a small company. However if the company is a member of a group then further conditions in CA 2006 s. 479 apply (see **11.4**).

Whether a company qualifies as a small company is determined in accordance with CA 2006 ss. 382(1)–(6), as set out in **Chapter 5** at **5.2**.

The company must also:

- not be one of the categories of companies excluded from small companies exemption (s. 478) (see **11.3**); and
- not have received notice requiring it to obtain an audit from ten per cent or more of members (s. 476) (see **11.6**).

The directors must also make the statements required by s. 475 (2) and (3) of the CA 2006 before the signature on the balance sheet, as set out in **11.8**.

The audit requirements for charitable companies are now governed by the provisions of charity legislation rather than company law.

11.3 Companies excluded from small companies' audit exemption

A non-group company is not entitled to the small companies audit exemption conferred by CA 2006 s. 477 if it was at any time within the financial year in question:

- a public company;
- a company that is an authorised insurance company, a banking company, an e-money issuer, a MiFID investment firm or a UCITS management company, or carries on insurance market activity; or
- a special register body (as defined under the Trade Union and Labour Relations (Consolidation) Act 1992) or an employers' association (as defined under the Industrial Relations (Northern Ireland) Order 1992).

s. 478

11.4 Group companies – availability of small audit exemption

A company which meets the definition of a small company and is also a group company (being a parent company or a subsidiary undertaking) is only entitled to audit exemption if the following conditions are met:

- the group (of which it is part) qualifies as a small group determined in accordance with section 383 in relation to the financial year (during any part of which it was a group company); and
- the group was not at any time in the year an 'ineligible' group (as defined by CA 2006 s. 384(2) and (3)).

A dormant subsidiary undertaking being a group company and dormant during the financial year for the whole period it was a group company is also entitled to audit exemption. (This exemption applies to all sizes of groups with dormant subsidiaries.) *s. 479(3)*

CA 2006 s. 479(4) defines a 'group' in relation to a group company as that company together with all its associated undertakings. *s. 479(4)*

11.5 Subsidiaries of EEA companies – audit exemption

In accordance with CA 2006 s. 479A, a subsidiary company (irrespective of its size) is exempt from audit if it fulfils all of the following conditions:

(a) its parent undertaking is established under the law of an EEA state;
(b) all of the subsidiary company's shareholders agree the exemption in respect of the financial year in question;
(c) the parent gives a guarantee (under s. 479C) of all the outstanding liabilities to which the subsidiary is subject at the end of the financial year until they are satisfied in full;
(d) the company is included in the consolidated accounts drawn up by the parent undertaking. These accounts must be prepared in accordance with Directive 83/349/EEC (the Seventh Company Law Directive) or international accounting standards;
(e) the consolidated accounts drawn up by the parent must disclose the use of the exemption by the subsidiary;
(f) the directors of the subsidiary must file the following documents at Companies House on or before the date that they file the subsidiary's accounts:

   (i) written notice of the agreement in (b);
   (ii) a written statement by the parent of the guarantee in (c); and
   (iii) a copy of the consolidated annual report and accounts referred to in (d) and the auditor's report on those accounts;

(g) the company is not quoted (as defined by s. 385);
(h) the company is not an authorised insurance company, a banking company, an e-money issuer, a MiFID investment firm or a UCITS management company, or carries on insurance market activity; and
(i) the company is not a special register body (as defined under the Trade Union and Labour Relations (Consolidation) Act 1992) or an employers' association (as defined under the Industrial Relations (Northern Ireland) Order 1992).

The directors of the subsidiary company must make the statements required by s. 475(2) and (3) of the CA 2006 before the signature on the balance sheet, as set out in **11.8**.

The decision of the parent company to provide the guarantee referred to in (d) above must consider if the guarantee provided exposes the parent company to significant liabilities (actual and contingent).

If the company is a subsidiary of a company which prepares a consolidated annual report and accounts that is not in English, it is believed that these group accounts will need to be translated prior to filing at Companies House.

Often the purpose of the subsidiary structure is to limit the liability of the parent company. If the subsidiary has minority shareholders, or may be sold in the future, this may complicate matters further. In many cases legal advice should be obtained before the parent company enters into any such guarantee.

Furthermore, the parent company should consider if there is a significant cost saving in taking advantage of the exemption as the figures included in the company's accounts may have to be audited as part of the group's audit.

11.6 Right to require an audit

The members of a company that would otherwise be entitled to exemption from audit (under CA 2006 s. 475(1)(a) (small or dormant companies)) may by notice require it to obtain an audit of its accounts for a financial year. *s. 476(1)*

Any member or members holding not less than ten per cent in aggregate in the nominal value of the company's issued share capital of a company (or any class of it) or (if the company does not have share capital) not less than ten per cent in number of the members of the company may require an audit of the company's accounts. *s. 476(2)*

To obtain an audit of the company's accounts, the member or members must deposit a notice in writing at the company's registered office during the financial year but not later than one month before the end of the year. The company is then not entitled to audit exemption for the year to which the notice relates. *s. 476(3)*

There is no requirement for a company to advise members of their rights to require an audit (or the manner in which it may be exercised) nor, for example, of their rights to audit when the accounting year end is changed.

11.7 Audit or assurance reports on accounts of small companies

Many accounts of small companies may be prepared without any form of audit or assurance report being attached – simply because none is statutorily required. **Table 11.1** sets out the position.

Where a company is entitled to audit exemption, the directors may nevertheless wish (or be required by banking terms) to have the assurance of a non-statutory or 'contractual' audit (voluntarily obtained on terms of engagement instructed by the directors) or the comfort of an accountants' report on the proper compilation of the accounts.

Reports on accounts prepared for unaudited companies are illustrated in **Chapter 13**. The special auditor's report under s. 449 is reflected in the examples in **Chapter 13** (**Examples 13.2** and **13.3**).

Table 11.1 Audit or assurance reports for small companies

Type of accounts	*Type of assurance report*
Audit exemption – s. 477	
Small company accounts – audit exemption	No audit or other report required
Abbreviated accounts – audit exemption	No audit or other report required
Audit – s. 475	
Small company accounts – audited *(if statutorily required)*	Auditor's report – s. 495
Small company accounts – audited *(at members' request – s. 476)*	Auditor's report – s. 495
Abbreviated accounts – audited	Special auditor's report – s. 449
Audit – Contractual (Agreed upon procedures)	
Small company accounts – audited *(voluntarily at company's option)*	Auditor's report – in accordance with *directors' instructions (for example, determined by banking covenants)*
Full accounts – audited *(voluntarily at company's option)*	
Accountants' report – Contractual (Compilation/agreed upon procedures)	
Full small company or abbreviated accounts	Accountants' report – in accordance with *directors' instructions*

11.8 Audit exemption – Directors' statement

A company's annual accounts for a financial year must be audited unless the company is exempt from audit under CA 2006 s. 477 (small companies), s. 479A (subsidiary companies), s. 480 (dormant companies), or s. 482 (non-profit-making companies subject to public sector audit). *s. 475*

The balance sheet of a small or subsidiary or dormant company taking advantage of the audit exemption must contain a statement by the directors to the effect that:

- the company is exempt from audit under CA 2006 s. 477 (small companies), s. 479A (subsidiary companies) or s. 480 (dormant companies);
- the members have not required the company to obtain an audit of its accounts for the year in question in accordance with CA 2006 s. 476; and
- the directors acknowledge their responsibilities for complying with the requirements of CA 2006 with respect to accounting records and the preparation of accounts. *s. 475(2)–(3)*

The directors' statement required by CA 2006 s. 475 must appear on the balance sheet above the signature required by CA 2006 s. 414.

Where the directors of a company subject to the small companies regime deliver to the Registrar of Companies IAS accounts, or Companies Act accounts that are not abbreviated accounts, and do not deliver a copy of the company's profit and loss account or a copy of the directors' report, the copy of the balance sheet delivered to the Registrar of Companies must contain in a prominent position a statement that the company's annual accounts and reports have been delivered in accordance with the provisions applicable to companies subject to the small companies regime. *s. 444(5)*

Examples of a form of directors' statement covering the above requirements are illustrated in **Example 11.1** the wording of which is derived from the example on the Companies House website. *s. 475*

Example 11.1 Small company audit exemption directors' statements: balance sheet

For the financial year ended [31 May 2013], the company was entitled to exemption from audit under [s. 477 of the CA 2006 relating to small companies, s. 479A of the CA 2006 relating to subsidiary companies or s. 480 of the CA 2006 relating to dormant companies] [*as the case may be*]. *[Note 1]*

The directors:

- confirm that the members have not required the company to obtain an audit of its accounts for the year in question in accordance with s. 476; and
- acknowledge their responsibilities for complying with the requirements of the CA 2006 with respect to accounting records and the preparation of accounts.

The [company's annual accounts and report] [abbreviated accounts] have been prepared in accordance with the provisions applicable to companies subject to the small companies regime. [*Note 2*]

Notes: [Words in italics are explanatory only]

The above statements are applicable as follows:

(1) applicable, where audit exemption applies, in
(a) small company (SI 2008/409) balance sheets (individual and group);
(b) Sch 1 (SI 2008/409) balance sheets;
(c) abbreviated balance sheets;

(2) applicable where the company's annual accounts and reports have been delivered in accordance with the provisions applicable to companies subject to the small companies regime and where small company accounts (on the basis of Sch 4 (SI 2008/409)) are adopted, for both audited or audit exempt accounts; also applicable where abbreviated accounts are prepared, for both audited or audit-exempt accounts.

The responsibilities to keep adequate accounting records (under s. 386) and the requirements determining the contents of individual company accounts (under s. 394) are explained more fully in **Chapter 3** at **3.10** and **3.2** respectively. The obligation for directors of a company not to approve accounts unless they are satisfied that they give a true and fair view (of the company's assets, liabilities, financial position and profit or loss) is explained in **Chapter 3** at **3.3**.

Part III Example accounts and reports

Chapter 12 Example accounts

The example accounts set out in this chapter are entirely fictional.

The example accounts do not represent a comprehensive checklist of the statutory disclosure requirements nor do they purport to be definitive or exhaustive. The intention is to illustrate the more common situations. Other presentations may be equally acceptable, provided that they adhere to the rules set out in the CA 2006, supporting statutory regulations and relevant financial reporting and accounting standards.

Depending on the circumstances, the accounts may contain:

- no accountants' report (in the case of audit exemption);
- an appropriate auditor's report (where an audit is required); or
- an independent accountants' report.

These alternative reports are illustrated in **Chapter 13**.

In the example accounts, tinted or boxed items indicate the following:

- **grey tint** – text that may be omitted or is relevant, as the case may be, only in the circumstances where the FRSSE is adopted;
- **other boxed items** – text that is optional or may be omitted according to the circumstances.

Text in *italics* in the example accounts represents commentary and explanation or alternative presentation.

12.1 Accounts of Small Company Limited

The illustrative example accounts of Small Company Limited illustrate the unaudited accounts of a small company (as defined in **Chapter 5**) producing accounts under the provisions of the CA 2006 for a financial period beginning on or after 6 April 2008; the example year end is 30 June 2013.

Pages 1–12 of the example accounts comprise the unaudited 'Companies Act individual accounts' of the company (a small company) prepared in accordance with CA 2006, **and taking full advantage of special provisions with respect to the preparation of annual accounts of small companies in accordance with Sch 1 of SI 2008/409**.

In practice, a small company is entitled to exceed the basic minimum disclosure as is considered desirable or in order to give a true and fair view.

Both the profit and loss account and the balance sheet are presented in Format 1.

The company has also chosen to adopt the FRSSE (effective April 2008).

The company is audit-exempt.

Pages 13–15 of the example accounts, indicated as 'For management information only', do not form part of the statutory accounts but are illustrative of a detailed profit and loss account, together with summaries, that might be prepared for management accounting purposes. These would not normally be submitted to the Registrar of Companies.

Increasingly, accounts of small UK companies are being prepared in a foreign currency – principally in Euros (€) or US dollars ($). The circumstances which permit this treatment are explained further in **10.11** and an example of a small company's accounts prepared in € is given later in this chapter and is explained at **12.4**.

12.2 Abbreviated accounts of Small Company Limited

The example abbreviated accounts comprise the 'Companies Act abbreviated accounts' of the company prepared for filing with the Registrar of Companies in accordance with CA 2006 s. 444, including a balance sheet complying with Part 1 of Sch 4 of SI 2008/409.

The accounts are based upon the 'Companies Act individual accounts' above of the small company.

Abbreviated accounts will include as appropriate.

- ***Directors' balance sheet statement*** under CA 2006 (**SI 2008/409 Sch 4.1(2)**) – company subject to the small companies regime.
- ***Directors' balance sheet statement*** under CA 2006 **Section 475 –** audit-exempt small company under CA 2006 s. 477.

These are illustrated immediately above the director's signature on the abbreviated balance sheet in the example abbreviated accounts below.

- ***'Special' independent auditor's report*** under CA 2006 **Section 495** (for audited small company only) – see examples in **Chapter 13** at **13.4**.

SI 2008/409 Sch 4 paragraph 1(2) is reproduced in **Appendix B**.

12.3 Unaudited accounts of Dormant Small Company Limited

The example dormant company accounts illustrate the unaudited accounts of a dormant small company.

12.4 Accounts of Overseas Trader Small Company Limited

As explained in **Chapter 10** at **10.11**, a company should prepare its accounts in the appropriate functional currency. This may not be sterling.

The illustrative example accounts of Overseas Trader Small Company Limited illustrate the unaudited accounts of a small company (as defined in **Chapter 5**) producing accounts under the provisions of the CA 2006 for a financial period beginning on or after 6 April 2008; the example year end is 31 December 2012.

They have been prepared in Euros (€) as the directors will have decided that the company's functional currency is € and not £. This they will have done by reference to the guidance for determining a company's functional currency which is contained in FRS 23.

Additionally, the company has chosen to adopt the FRSSE (effective April 2008) and is audit-exempt.

12.5 Auditor's reports

The illustrative example accounts of Small Company Limited illustrate the accounts of an unaudited (audit exempt) small company. The example accounts therefore exclude an illustrative audit report. **Chapter 13** provides examples of audit reports appropriate where a small company is subject to audit.

Registered number:
04091884
England and Wales
(See important note below)

SMALL COMPANY LIMITED
ANNUAL REPORT AND UNAUDITED ACCOUNTS
30 JUNE 2013

Annual report and unaudited accounts – *These comprise: (a) the directors' report ('annual report'); and (b) the company's annual accounts ('Companies Act individual accounts') together with notes to the accounts.*

Advantage has been taken of the special provisions available under CA 2006 ss. 381–384 and Schedule 1 of SI 2008/409 as a small company.

Registered number – *In accordance with the Registrar's Rules 2009,* ***one*** *of the following documents* ***must*** *contain the name and registered number of the company: copy of Balance sheet or Abbreviated accounts and (where applicable) copy of Profit and loss account, Directors' report, Directors' remuneration report and auditor's report (See* ***Chapter 14*** *for Registrar's Rules 2009). Any document delivered to the Registrar of Companies must state in a prominent position the registered number of the company to which it relates (CA 2006 s. 1068(3)(c)). For filing purposes, it is not sufficient to state the registered number only on the cover page of annual accounts.*

SMALL COMPANY LIMITED

Directors	Julie Collins – Chairman Peter Smith – Managing director William Gallagher Elizabeth Black
Secretary	William Gallagher
Registered office	2 Appletree Place London SE1 2AP
Registered number	04091884 England and Wales
[*Auditor*]	[*True & Fairview LLP* *Chartered Accountants* *17 Queen's Place* *London EC4P 3BC*]

ANNUAL REPORT AND UNAUDITED ACCOUNTS – 30 JUNE 2013

Directors and advisers, etc. *– Although it is common practice to give the information on this page, there is no requirement to do so, and the page may be omitted and the information combined into the body of the report.*

Company Secretary *– A private company is not required to have a secretary. CA 2006 s.270(1)*

SMALL COMPANY LIMITED
REPORT OF THE DIRECTORS

Page [1]

Registered number 04091884 England and Wales

The directors present their annual report with the unaudited accounts of the company for the year ended 30 June 2013.

Principal activity
The principal activity of the company in the year under review was the manufacture and distribution of office equipment and components.

The company's subsidiary company, Sub Consultants Limited, provides consultancy and office design advisory services.

Directors
The directors in office in the year were as follows:

Elizabeth Black (appointed 16 February 2013)
Julie Collins
William Gallagher
Peter Smith
James Patterson (resigned 16 February 2013)

Political and charitable contributions
During the year the company made a political contribution of £2,500 to the New Conservative Party and various charitable contributions totalling £3,000.

The above report has been prepared in accordance with the provisions applicable to companies subject to the small companies regime as set out in Part 15 of the Companies Act 2006. *CA 2006 s. 419(2)*

Signed on behalf of *[/by order of]* the board of directors *CA 2006 s. 419(1)*

W. Gallagher
....

William Gallagher
Director [*or Secretary*]

Approved by the board: 9 November 2013

Directors' responsibilities statements *– A small company eligible for audit exemption is required to provide a statutory statement in accordance with CA 2006 s. 475 to appear on the balance sheet above the director's signature of approval (see statement illustrated on* ***Example accounts page [3]****). A small company subject to audit will need to prepare a more detailed statement appearing generally within the directors' report or as a separate statement (See* **Example 6.1** *in* **Chapter 6** *at* **6.8.3***).*

The APB ISA (UK and Ireland) 700 (Revised) 'The auditor's report on financial statements' necessitates the financial statements or accompanying information (for example, the directors' report) to include an adequate statement of directors' responsibilities (see **Chapter 13***). The auditor's report must include reference to the respective responsibilities of the auditor and directors. An independent accountants' report on unaudited (audit-exempt) accounts should, on the same basis, include a statement that the directors are responsible for the preparation of the accounts.*

Reappointment of auditors or accountants *– There is no requirement to disclose the appointment or reappointment of auditors (if relevant) or accountants. Similarly, no reference to 'independent accountants' need be made.*

Page [2]

SMALL COMPANY LIMITED
PROFIT AND LOSS ACCOUNT
FOR THE YEAR ENDED 30 JUNE 2013

	Notes	*2013*	*2012*
		£	£
Turnover – Continuing operations	2	1,098,495	795,250
Cost of sales		(541,722)	(322,690)
Gross profit		556,773	472,560
Distribution costs		(185,724)	(155,040)
Administrative expenses		(160,933)	(138,900)
Operating profit – Continuing operations	3	210,116	178,620
Income from fixed asset investments		9,845	2,010
Interest payable and similar charges		(17,300)	(9,600)
[Non-equity] preference dividend – paid		(1,350)	(1,350)
Profit on ordinary activities before taxation		201,311	169,680
Taxation – UK corporation tax	4	(42,275)	(39,388)
Profit for the financial year after taxation		£ 159,036	£ 130,292

Alternative disclosures *(Not required if FRSSE adopted).*

Continuing operations
All of the company's activities [operations] in the above two financial years derived from continuing operations. [or:]
Turnover and operating profit derive wholly from continuing operations.

Total recognised gains and losses
The company has no recognised gains or losses other than the profit or loss for the period [above two financial years] and therefore no separate statement of total recognised gains and losses has been presented.

The above statements are only to be used where applicable.

***Statement of total recognised gains and losses** – this could be presented on this page beneath the profit and loss account or on a separate page* (see **Example accounts page [4]**).

***Taxation** – the full format heading is 'Tax on profit or loss on ordinary activities'. 'Taxation' will include current and deferred tax, the material components of both of which should be disclosed separately in the notes. For a deferred tax charge (or credit), the main components will be timing adjustments (originating and reversing) and tax rate adjustments (increasing or reducing the opening liability).*

Dividends – see **Appendix A(9)** for comment on the presentation of dividends (both equity and preference [non-equity] dividends).

SMALL COMPANY LIMITED
BALANCE SHEET – 30 JUNE 2013

Page [3]

	Notes	*2013* £	*2012* £
Fixed assets			
Intangible assets	6	15,800	8,523
Tangible assets	7	392,600	295,620
Investments	8	1,000	1,000
		409,400	305,143
Current assets			
Stocks		167,455	102,349
Debtors	9	181,653	99,679
Cash at bank and in hand		10,620	8,450
		359,728	210,478
Creditors: amounts falling due within one year	10	(276,451)	(193,976)
Net current assets		83,277	16,502
Total assets less current liabilities		492,677	321,645
Creditors: amounts falling due after more than one year	11	(41,969)	(15,473)
Net assets		£450,708	£306,172
Capital and reserves:			
Called up share capital	12	45,000	45,000
Share premium account		10,000	10,000
Profit and loss account	13	395,708	251,172
Shareholders' funds	14	£450,708	£306,172

These accounts have been prepared in accordance with the provisions applicable to companies subject to the small companies regime as set out in Part 15 of the Companies Act 2006 *[and with the Financial Reporting Standard for Smaller Entities (effective April 2008)]*.

For the financial year ended 30 June 2013 the company was entitled to exemption from audit under section 477 of the Companies Act 2006; and no notice has been deposited under section 476.

The directors acknowledge their responsibilities for ensuring that the company keeps accounting records which comply with s. 386 [of the Act] and for preparing accounts which give a true and fair view of the state of affairs of the company as at the end of the financial year and of its profit or loss for the financial year in accordance with the requirements of sections 394 and 395 and which otherwise comply with the requirements of the Companies Act 2006 relating to accounts, so far as applicable to the company.

[or [alternative]: The directors acknowledge their responsibilities for complying with the requirements of the Companies Act 2006 with respect to accounting records and the preparation of accounts. [s. 475(3)]

Signed on behalf of
the board of directors

W. Gallagher

....

William Gallagher
Director

Approved by the board: 9 November 2013

Directors' statements *– The statements above the director's signature represent the statements required by (a) CA 2006 s. 414 (Small company accounts prepared in accordance with the special provisions) applicable to companies subject to the small companies regime), (b) the FRSSE, and (c) CA 2006 ss. 475 and 477 (Small company audit exempt accounts only). See footnote to* ***Example accounts Page [1]*** *('Directors' responsibilities statements').*

Approval of accounts *– A company's annual accounts must be approved by the board of directors and be signed on behalf of the board by a director of the company (CA 2006 s. 414).*

SMALL COMPANY LIMITED
STATEMENT OF TOTAL RECOGNISED GAINS AND LOSSES
FOR THE YEAR ENDED 30 JUNE 2013

Page [4]

	2013 £	2012 £
Profit for the financial year after taxation	159,036	130,292
Unrealised surplus on revaluation of property	—	—
Total recognised gains relating to the year	£159,036	£130,292

Note of historical cost profits and losses
The difference between the results as disclosed in the profit and loss account and the result on an unmodified historical cost basis is not material.

Statement of total recognised gains and losses *(this example is just included for illustrative purposes only to show the format of the statement if one was required) – This statement, showing the total of recognised gains and losses and its components, should be presented as a primary statement with the same prominence as the other primary statements (i.e. profit and loss account and balance sheet). The gains and losses are those recognised in the period insofar as they are attributable to shareholders. The statement could be presented on the* **Example accounts page [2]** *beneath the profit and loss account.*

Where the 'profit (loss) for the financial year after taxation' represents the entire total recognised gains or losses relating to the year (where, for example, there are no other unrealised surpluses or losses), a separate 'statement of total recognised gains and losses' is not required.

However, unless the company adopts the FRSSE, the profit and loss account on **page [2]** *should include a statement along the following lines, immediately below the profit and loss account:*

Example wording – 'The company has no recognised gains and losses other than those included above and therefore no separate statement of total recognised gains and losses has been presented.'

Note of historical cost profits and losses *– Where there is a material difference between the result disclosed in the profit and loss account and the result on an unmodified basis (for example, where a company charges a significant amount of depreciation on a revalued fixed asset), this difference should be disclosed in a note. Such a note of historical cost profits and losses should be presented immediately following the profit and loss account or the statement of total recognised gains and losses and normally forms a reconciliation from the result disclosed in the profit and loss account to the result on an unmodified basis.*

SMALL COMPANY LIMITED
NOTES TO THE UNAUDITED ACCOUNTS – 30 JUNE 2013 **Page [5]**

1 Accounting policies

Basis of accounting
The accounts have been prepared under the historical cost convention [and in accordance with the Financial Reporting Standard for Smaller Entities (effective April 2008)].

Going concern basis of accounting
The accounts have been prepared on the assumption that the company is able to carry on business as a going concern, which the directors consider appropriate having regard to the circumstances outlined in Note 18 to the accounts.

Going concern basis of accounting ***(alternative if company has net liabilities)***
At the balance sheet date, the company's liabilities exceeded its assets. The company has received assurance from the directors that they will continue to give financial support to the company for twelve months from the date of signing these financial statements.

On this basis, the directors consider it appropriate to prepare the accounts on a going concern basis. However, should the financial support mentioned above not be forthcoming, the going concern basis used in preparing the company's accounts may be invalid and adjustments would have to be made to reduce the value of assets to their realisable amount and to provide for any further liabilities which might arise. The accounts do not include any adjustment to the company's assets or liabilities that might be necessary should this basis not continue to be appropriate.

Consolidation
The company is a parent company subject to the small companies regime. The company and its subsidiary comprise a small group. The company is therefore not required to and has not chosen to prepare group accounts.

Cash flow
The accounts do not include a cash flow statement because the company, as a small reporting entity, is exempt from the requirement to prepare such a statement [under Financial Reporting Standard 1 *Cash flow statements*/Financial Reporting Standard for Smaller Entities (effective April 2008)].

Turnover
Turnover represents net invoiced sales of goods, excluding VAT [*having regard to the fulfilment of contractual obligations*].

Tangible fixed assets
Depreciation is provided, at the following annual rates in order to write off each asset over its estimated useful life:

Freehold buildings	–	2% on cost
Plant and machinery	–	15% on cost

No depreciation is provided on freehold land.

Intangible fixed assets
Intangible fixed assets (including purchased goodwill and patents) are amortised at rates calculated to write off the assets on a straight line basis over their estimated useful economic lives. Impairment of intangible assets is reviewed where circumstances indicate that the carrying value of an asset may not be fully recoverable.

Stocks
Stocks and work-in-progress are valued at the lower of cost and net realisable value, after making due allowance for obsolete and slow-moving items. Cost includes all direct expenditure and an appropriate proportion of fixed and variable overheads.

Deferred taxation
Deferred tax arises as a result of including items of income and expenditure in taxation computations in periods different from those in which they are included in the company's accounts. Deferred tax is provided in full on timing differences which result in an obligation to pay more (or a right to pay less) tax at a future date, at the tax rates that are expected to apply when the timing differences reverse, based on current tax rates and laws.

Deferred tax is not provided on timing differences arising from the revaluation of fixed assets where there is no commitment to sell the asset.

Deferred tax assets are recognised to the extent that it is regarded as more likely than not that they will be recovered. Deferred tax assets and liabilities are not discounted.

Research and development
Expenditure on research and development is written off in the year in which it is incurred.

Foreign currencies
Monetary assets and liabilities in foreign currencies are translated into sterling at the rates of exchange ruling at the balance sheet date. Transactions in foreign currencies are translated into sterling at the rate of exchange ruling at the date of the transaction. Exchange differences are taken into account in arriving at the operating profit.

SMALL COMPANY LIMITED **Page [6]**
NOTES TO THE UNAUDITED ACCOUNTS – 30 JUNE 2013

Leased assets
Rentals applicable to operating leases where substantially all of the benefits and risks of ownership remain with the lessor are charged to the profit and loss account on a straight line basis over the lease term.

Assets held under finance leases and hire purchase contracts are capitalised and depreciated over their useful lives. The corresponding lease or hire purchase obligation is treated in the balance sheet as a liability. The interest element of rental obligations is charged to the profit and loss account over the period of the lease at a constant proportion of the outstanding balance of capital repayments.

Pension costs
Contributions in respect of the company's defined contribution pension scheme are charged to the profit and loss account for the year in which they are payable to the scheme. Differences between contributions payable and contributions actually paid in the year are shown as either accruals or prepayments at the year end.

Long term contracts
The amount recoverable on each long term contract is based on stage of completion, by calculating costs incurred to date as a percentage of total costs, less any provision for known or anticipated losses and progress payments received and receivable.

Where the outcome of incomplete contracts can be assessed with reasonable certainty, the attributable profit is recognised in the profit and loss account as an appropriate proportion of the estimated profit for that contract. The amount by which turnover is in excess of progress payments received and receivable is classified as amounts recoverable on contracts and separately disclosed in debtors. In assessing amounts recoverable, the directors provide for the cost of potential claims based on experience.

Disclosure of accounting policies – *The FRSSE requires the disclosure of each material accounting policy and also any changes in accounting policies or estimation techniques.*

Although not specifically stated within the FRSSE, in the absence of any specifically disclosed statement of accounting policy, the presumption is that the accounting principles set out in the FRSSE have been observed in the preparation of the accounts.

Although the disclosure of certain accounting policies is indicated above (by boxing) as not required by the FRSSE, disclosure will nevertheless be appropriate either to show a true and fair view or because the policies are considered to be 'material' in presenting the accounts.

There is a general presumption that the company is a 'going concern', to be determined for a period of not less than one year from the date of approval of the accounts.

Deferred tax – *The FRSSE requires deferred tax where appropriate to be provided on the 'full provision' basis. On the previously adopted 'partial provision' basis, provision was made in respect of material timing differences only when there was a reasonable probability that a liability would arise in the foreseeable future.*

SMALL COMPANY LIMITED
NOTES TO THE UNAUDITED ACCOUNTS – 30 JUNE 2013 **Page [7]**

2 Turnover

Turnover attributable to geographical markets outside the United Kingdom amounted to 21% (2012 – 19%).

3 Operating profit

The operating profit is stated after charging:

	2013	*2012*
	£	£
Depreciation of tangible fixed assets	60,512	57,315
Amortisation of intangible fixed assets	983	811
Operating lease charges	3,800	3,200
[Auditors' remuneration]	4,700	4,350
Pension costs	11,400	5,500
Directors' remuneration	61,050	47,595

Two directors (2012 – 2) are members of money purchase pension schemes.

4 Taxation

	2013	*2012*
	£	£
Domestic current year tax		
UK corporation tax at 20% (2012: 20%)	43,417	40,058
Adjustment for prior years	(1,142)	(670)
Current tax charge	£42,275	£39,388

5 Dividends

	2013	*2012*
	£	£
[Non-equity] preference dividend – paid	1,350	1,350
Dividend on ordinary shares – paid	14,500	6,000
(32.22p per share; 2012, 13.33p per share)		
	£15,850	£7,350

***Directors' remuneration** – A small company's individual accounts must give the overall aggregate total of:*

(a) directors' remuneration (for qualifying services as director or management of the company or any subsidiary);

(b) amounts received or receivable under long-term incentive schemes;

(c) company contributions to pension schemes (SI 2008/409 Sch 3.1);

(d) compensation to directors or past directors for loss of office; and

*(e) sums paid to third parties in respect of directors' services (see **Chapter 6** at **6.11**).* **SI 2008/409 Schedule 3.**

Disclosure is also required of the number of directors (if any) to whom retirement benefits are accruing in respect of qualifying services under:

(a) money purchase schemes; and

(b) defined benefit schemes. (SI 2008/409 Sch 3.1(2))

SMALL COMPANY LIMITED
NOTES TO THE UNAUDITED ACCOUNTS – 30 JUNE 2013

***Auditor's remuneration – small companies* (CA 2006 s. 494)**

Not applicable to audit-exempt small companies, included for illustrative purposes as would be required disclosure if the accounts were audited: The notes to the annual accounts of a small or medium-sized company (as defined) must disclose the amount of any remuneration receivable by the company's auditors for the auditing of the accounts, including the nature and estimated money-value of benefits in kind.

6 Intangible fixed assets

	Goodwill £	*Other Intangible assets* £	*Total* £
Cost			
At 1 July 2012	5,000	9,564	14,564
Additions	–	8,260	8,260
At 30 June 2013	5,000	17,824	22,824
Amortisation			
At 1 July 2012	2,500	3,541	6,041
Charge for the year	500	483	983
At 30 June 2013	3,000	4,024	7,024
Net book values			
At 30 June 2013	£2,000	£13,800	£15,800
At 30 June 2012	£2,500	£6,023	£8,523

7 Tangible fixed assets

	Land and buildings £	*Plant and machinery* £	*Total* £
Cost			
At 1 July 2012	358,600	337,400	696,000
Additions	20,000	145,893	165,893
Disposals	(2,500)	(34,213)	(36,713)
At 30 June 2013	376,100	449,080	825,180
Depreciation			
At 1 July 2012	88,380	312,000	400,380
On disposals	–	(28,312)	(28,312)
Charge for year	6,400	54,112	60,512
At 30 June 2013	94,780	337,800	432,580
Net book values			
At 30 June 2013	£281,320	£111,280	£392,600
At 30 June 2012	£270,220	£25,400	£295,620

SMALL COMPANY LIMITED **Page [9]**
NOTES TO THE UNAUDITED ACCOUNTS – 30 JUNE 2013

7 Tangible fixed assets (*continued*)

The net book value of plant and machinery includes £14,000 (2012 – Nil) in respect of assets held under finance leases. The amount of depreciation in respect of such assets amounted to £3,550 for the year (2012 – Nil).

8 Investments

	Subsidiary undertaking	*Total*
Cost		
at 1 July 2012 and 30 June 2013	£1,000	£1,000

Subsidiary undertaking
The company's investment in its subsidiary company represents the cost of acquisition of the whole of the ordinary share capital of Sub Consultants Limited, which provides consultancy and advisory services.

At 30 June 2013, the aggregate of the share capital and reserves of Sub Consultants Limited amounted to £34,900 and the profit for the year to that date was £2,280.

9 Debtors

	2013 £	*2012* £
Trade debtors	140,903	75,260
Other debtors	40,750	24,419
	£181,653	£99,679

Other debtors include an amount of £1,050 (2012 – Nil) falling due after more than one year.

10 Creditors: amounts falling due within one year

	2013 £	*2012* £
Bank loans and overdrafts (secured)	49,260	34,790
Obligations under finance leases	10,000	–
Trade creditors	175,318	129,240
Other creditors	23,173	20,477
Taxation and social security	18,700	9,469
	£276,451	£193,976

SMALL COMPANY LIMITED
NOTES TO THE UNAUDITED ACCOUNTS – 30 JUNE 2013 **Page [10]**

11 Creditors: amounts falling due after more than one year

	2013	*2012*
	£	£
Bank loans and overdraft	25,000	–
Obligations under finance leases	5,000	–
Other creditors	1,969	5,473
Preference shares – 13.5% preference shares of £1 each	10,000	10,000
	£41,969	£15,473

Debt due after more than one year		
repayable between one and five years	20,000	–
repayable in five years or more	5,000	–
Preference shares	10,000	10,000
	£35,000	£10,000

The secured bank loan, the aggregate total of which amounts to £30,000, is repayable in annual instalments of £5,000 commencing 31 December 2013.

Preference shares represent non-equity interests stated at par value. Dividends are payable annually at 13.5% net of tax credit and are cumulative. The shares are redeemable (at par value) on 30 April 2019; have a priority over ordinary shares, in the event of an earlier winding-up (to the extent of their par value and the arrears (if any) of dividends); and have no vote, provided dividends are not in arrears.

Creditors: amounts falling due after more than one year (Note 11)
Preference shares *– Preference shares providing for mandatory redemption at a fixed or determinable future date or for fixed or determinable amounts are classified as 'financial liabilities' in accordance with the FRSSE (effective April 2008). 'Financial instruments' are 'financial liabilities', 'financial assets' or 'equity instruments' depending on the substance of the underlying contractual arrangement (see* ***Appendix A(4)****).*

SMALL COMPANY LIMITED **Page [11]**
NOTES TO THE UNAUDITED ACCOUNTS – 30 JUNE 2013

12 Called up share capital

	2013	*2012*
	£	£
Allotted, called up and fully paid		
45,000 ordinary shares of £1 each	45,000	45,000

13 Profit and loss account

	2013	*2012*
	£	£
Retained profit at 1 July 2012	251,172	126,880
Profit for the financial year after taxation	159,036	130,292
[Equity] dividends paid	(14,500)	(6,000)
Retained profit at 30 June 2013	£395,708	£251,172

14 Shareholders' funds

Reconciliation of movements on shareholders' funds

	2013	*2012*
	£	£
Profit for the financial year after taxation	159,036	130,292
Dividends paid	(14,500)	(6,000)
	144,536	124,292
New share capital subscribed	–	5,000
Net additions to shareholders' funds	144,536	129,292
Opening shareholders' funds at 1 July 2012	306,172	176,880
Closing shareholders' funds at 30 June 2013	£450,708	£306,172

15 Contingent liability

A writ for damages amounting to £50,000 has been served on the company, alleging supply of faulty goods. The directors have obtained legal advice and are contesting the claim, which they consider is without foundation. No provision has been made in these accounts in respect of the claim.

SMALL COMPANY LIMITED
NOTES TO THE UNAUDITED ACCOUNTS – 30 JUNE 2013

Page [12]

16 Commitments

Capital commitments

At 30 June 2013, capital expenditure commitments were as follows:

	2013	*2012*
Contracted but not provided for in the accounts	£9,000	£—

Lease commitments – operating leases

At 30 June 2013, the company had annual commitments of £3,240 (2012 – £3,140) under non-cancellable operating leases which expire within two to five years.

Other financial commitments

At 30 June 2013, the company had entered into a joint venture agreement to commence in late 2013, the initial contribution to which will be £30,000.

17 Related party transactions

Transactions with related parties

During the year, sales of £140,456 were made to Smith Trading Limited. The sales were on an arm's length basis. Normal credit terms applied and the amount was paid within 30 days of the sale. Smith Trading Limited is a related party by virtue of being controlled by Deirdre Smith, wife of Peter Smith, Director.

Dividends paid to directors

Ordinary dividends paid to directors in their capacity as shareholders during the year included £7,753 to Peter Smith (2012 – £3,208) and £5,428 to Julie Collins (2012 – £2,246).

Advance to director

During the year William Gallagher was granted an unsecured short-term loan of £9,000 to facilitate the purchase of a house.

The loan is repayable on 31 December 2013. Interest, at the rate of 6% per annum, is payable upon repayment.

Controlling party

During the two years ended 30 June 2013, Peter Smith, a director, together with members of his close family, controlled the company by virtue of a controlling interest (directly or indirectly) of 61.2% of the issued ordinary share capital.

18 Post balance sheet events

On 5 August 2013 the company acquired the goodwill and net assets of Automated Office Technology Products for a consideration of £30,000 which has been financed by a secured bank loan, repayable over five years.

19 Future trading and the current economic environment

Subsequent to the year end, the company has experienced a significant reduction in business activity, resulting in significantly lower sales. However, costs are anticipated to reduce correspondingly and, whilst the company is dependent upon the continuation of existing banking and trading facilities, it should be able to operate within its overdraft. Despite serious doubts about future trading conditions, the directors are not aware of any reason why overdraft or other facilities will not be extended. As a result they have adopted the going concern basis of accounting.

FOR MANAGEMENT INFORMATION ONLY
Page [13]

SMALL COMPANY LIMITED
DETAILED PROFIT AND LOSS ACCOUNT
FOR THE YEAR ENDED 30 JUNE 2013

	2013		2012	
	£	£	£	£
Sales		1,098,495		795,250
Cost of sales				
Stocks 1 July 2012	102,349		120,451	
Purchases	295,202		144,314	
	397,551		264,765	
Less: stocks 30 June 2013	(167,455)		(102,349)	
	230,096		162,416	
Production wages	195,322		99,356	
Depreciation and amortisation	46,372		43,363	
Hire of plant and machinery (operating leases)	3,200		2,500	
Other production expenses (including research and development)	66,732		15,055	
	311,626		160,274	
Cost of sales		541,722		322,690
Gross profit		556,773		472,560
Distribution costs				
Distribution				
Carriage	35,264		27,569	
Motor expenses	21,743		18,406	
Lorry and warehouse	11,654		5,483	
Depreciation	4,202		4,485	
	72,863		55,943	
Selling and marketing				
Salaries	47,388		45,953	
Directors' remuneration	20,000		10,000	
Advertising	10,400		16,222	
Travel and motor expenses	24,377		18,823	
Entertaining	10,696		8,099	
	112,861		99,097	
	185,724		155,040	
Totals carried forward	185,724	556,773	155,040	472,560

This page does not form part of the statutory accounts.

FOR MANAGEMENT INFORMATION ONLY
Page [14]

SMALL COMPANY LIMITED
DETAILED PROFIT AND LOSS ACCOUNT
FOR THE YEAR ENDED 30 JUNE 2013
(continued)

	2013		*2012*	
	£	£	£	£
Totals brought forward	185,724	556,773	155,040	472,560
Administrative expenses				
Establishment expenses				
Rent and rates	31,740		29,687	
Light, heat and power	8,300		6,920	
Insurance	7,900		6,591	
Repairs	5,021		3,617	
Depreciation	6,025		5,669	
	58,986		52,484	
Administration costs				
Salaries and payroll	21,311		19,841	
Directors' remuneration	40,800		37,345	
Pension costs	11,400		5,500	
Postage and telephone	4,321		3,110	
Printing and stationery	3,030		2,415	
Depreciation	4,896		4,609	
General administration	6,279		5,968	
Accountancy [and Audit]	3,500		3,150	
Legal and professional	500		–	
Bank charges	300		256	
Bad debts	5,610		4,222	
	101,947		86,416	
	160,933		138,900	
		346,657		293,940
Operating profit		210,116		178,620
Income from investments		9,845		2,010
Interest payable				
Bank loan	(10,200)		–	
Bank overdraft	(5,600)		(9,600)	
Finance lease charges	(1,500)		–	
		(17,300)		(9,600)
Preference dividend		(1,350)		(1,350)
Profit on ordinary activities before taxation		£201,311		£169,680

This page does not form part of the statutory accounts.

FOR MANAGEMENT INFORMATION ONLY
Page [15]

SMALL COMPANY LIMITED
PROFIT AND LOSS ACCOUNT SUMMARIES
FOR THE YEAR ENDED 30 JUNE 2013

Summaries of items disclosed in the statutory profit and loss account

	2013	*2012*
	£	£
Depreciation and amortisation		
Production – cost of sales	45,389	42,552
Amortisation – cost of sales	983	811
	46,372	43,363
Distribution	4,202	4,485
Establishment expenses	6,025	5,669
Administration costs	4,896	4,609
	£61,495	£58,126
Staff costs*		
Production wages	195,322	99,356
Selling and marketing salaries	47,388	45,953
Administration salaries	21,311	19,841
Directors' remuneration	60,800	47,345
Pension costs	11,400	5,500
	£336,221	£217,995

* *Not disclosed in small company annual accounts.*

This page does not form part of the statutory accounts.

Registered number:
04091884
England and Wales
(See important note below)

SMALL COMPANY LIMITED
ABBREVIATED [UNAUDITED] ACCOUNTS
30 JUNE 2013

Abbreviated accounts and audit exemption

*Audit exemption is available for some companies subject to the small companies regime. See **Chapter 11** at **11.2** for the detailed definition. No auditors' report or accountants' report is statutorily required to be attached to the accounts.*

*A company which is entitled to take advantage of audit exemption in preparing Companies Act individual accounts may prepare abbreviated accounts for filing with the Registrar of Companies. This is explained in **Chapter 8** and **Table 8.1**.*

*Abbreviated accounts delivered to the Registrar of Companies (other than those of audit-exempt or dormant companies) must otherwise be accompanied by a special report of the auditors under CA 2006 section 449. See **Chapter 8** at **8.8**.*

***Abbreviated accounts (small company)** – These comprise: (a) unaudited abbreviated balance sheet (SI 2008/409 Sch 4) (with directors' statements); (b) notes to the abbreviated accounts and (c) special auditor's report – but only where appropriate.*

***Registered number** – Any document delivered to the Registrar of Companies must state in a prominent position the registered number of the company to which it relates (CA 2006 s. 1068(3)(c)). In accordance with the Registrar's Rules 2009, **one** of the following documents **must** contain the name and registered number of the company: copy of Balance sheet or Abbreviated accounts and (where applicable) copy of Profit and loss account, Directors' report, Directors' remuneration report and auditor's report (see **Chapter 14** for Registrar's Rules 2009).*

SMALL COMPANY LIMITED
ABBREVIATED BALANCE SHEET – 30 JUNE 2013

Page [1]

Registered number 04091884 England and Wales

	Notes	2013 £	2012 £
Fixed assets	2		
Intangible assets		15,800	8,523
Tangible assets		392,600	295,620
Investments		1,000	1,000
		409,400	305,143
Current assets			
Stocks		167,455	102,349
Debtors	3	181,653	99,679
Cash at bank and in hand		10,620	8,450
		359,728	210,478
Creditors: amounts falling due within one year	4	(276,451)	(193,976)
Net current assets		83,277	16,502
Total assets less current liabilities		492,677	321,645
Creditors: amounts falling due after more than one year	4	(11,969)	(15,473)
Net assets		£450,708	£306,172
Capital and reserves			
Called up share capital	6	45,000	45,000
Share premium account		10,000	10,000
Profit and loss account		395,708	251,172
Shareholders' funds		£450,708	£306,172

These abbreviated accounts have been prepared in accordance with provisions applicable to companies subject to the small companies regime as set out in Part 15 of the Companies Act 2006 [and with the Financial Reporting Standard for Smaller Entities (effective April 2008)].

[Audit exemption only – ss. 475 and 477]
For the financial year ended 30 June 2013 the company was entitled to exemption from audit under s. 477 [*small company exemption*] of the Companies Act 2006 and no notice has been deposited under s. 476 [*member or members requesting an audit*].

The directors acknowledge their responsibilities for ensuring that the company keeps accounting records which comply with s. 386 [of the Act] and for preparing accounts which give a true and fair view of the state of affairs of the company as at the end of the financial year and of its profit or loss for the financial year in accordance with the requirements of sections 394–395 and which otherwise comply with the requirements of the Companies Act 2006 relating to accounts, so far as applicable to the company.

[*or (alternative): The directors acknowledge their responsibilities for complying with the requirements of the Companies Act 2006 with respect to accounting records and the preparation of accounts.*] [s.475 (3)]

Signed on behalf of
the board of directors

W. Gallagher

....

William Gallagher
Director
Approved by the board: 9 November 2013

SMALL COMPANY LIMITED **Page [2]**
NOTES TO THE ABBREVIATED ACCOUNTS – 30 JUNE 2013

1 Accounting policies

Basis of accounting
The accounts have been prepared under the historical cost convention [and in accordance with the Financial Reporting Standard for Smaller Entities (effective April 2008)].

Going concern basis of accounting
The accounts have been prepared on the assumption that the company is able to carry on business as a going concern, which the directors consider appropriate having regard to the circumstances outlined in Note 8 to the abbreviated accounts.

Going concern basis of accounting ***(alternative if company has net liabilities)***
At the balance sheet date, the company's liabilities exceeded its assets. The company has received assurance from the directors that they will continue to give financial support to the company for twelve months from the date of signing these financial statements.

On this basis, the directors consider it appropriate to prepare the accounts on a going concern basis. However, should the financial support mentioned above not be forthcoming, the going concern basis used in preparing the company's accounts may be invalid and adjustments would have to be made to reduce the value of assets to their realisable amount and to provide for any further liabilities which might arise. The accounts do not include any adjustment to the company's assets or liabilities that might be necessary should this basis not continue to be appropriate.

Consolidation
The company is a parent company subject to the small companies regime. The company and its subsidiary comprise a small group. The company is therefore not required to and has not chosen to prepare group accounts.

Turnover
Turnover represents net invoiced sales of goods, excluding VAT *[having regard to the fulfilment of contractual obligations]*.

Tangible fixed assets
Depreciation is provided, at the following annual rates in order to write off each asset over its estimated useful life:

Freehold buildings – 2% on cost
Plant and machinery – 15% on cost

No depreciation is provided on freehold land.

Intangible fixed assets
Intangible fixed assets (including purchased goodwill and patents) are amortised at rates calculated to write off the assets on a straight basis over their estimated useful economic lives. Impairment of intangible assets is reviewed where circumstances indicate that the carrying value of an asset may not be fully recoverable.

Stocks
Stocks and work-in-progress are valued at the lower of cost and net realisable value, after making due allowance for obsolete and slow-moving items. Cost includes all direct expenditure and an appropriate proportion of fixed and variable overheads.

Deferred taxation
Deferred tax arises as a result of including items of income and expenditure in taxation computations in periods different from those in which they are included in the company's accounts. Deferred tax is provided in full on timing differences which result in an obligation to pay more (or a right to pay less) tax at a future date, at the tax rates that are expected to apply when the timing differences reverse, based on current tax rates and laws.

Deferred tax is not provided on timing differences arising from the revaluation of fixed assets where there is no commitment to sell the asset.

Deferred tax assets are recognised to the extent that it is regarded as more likely than not that they will be recovered. Deferred tax assets and liabilities are not discounted.

Research and development
Expenditure on research and development is written off in the year in which it is incurred.

Foreign currencies
Monetary assets and liabilities in foreign currencies are translated into sterling at the rates of exchange ruling at the balance sheet date. Transactions in foreign currencies are translated into sterling at the rate of exchange ruling at the date of the transaction. Exchange differences are taken into account in arriving at the operating profit.

Leased assets
Rentals applicable to operating leases where substantially all of the benefits and risks of ownership remain with the lessor are charged to the profit and loss account on a straight line basis over the lease term.

Assets held under finance leases and hire purchase contracts are capitalised and depreciated over their useful lives. The corresponding lease or hire purchase obligation is treated in the balance sheet as a liability. The interest element of rental obligations is charged to the profit and loss account over the period of the lease at a constant proportion of the outstanding balance of capital repayments.

Pension costs
Contributions in respect of the company's defined contribution pension scheme are charged to the profit and loss account for the year in which they are payable to the scheme. Differences between contributions payable and contributions actually paid in the year are shown as either accruals or prepayments at the year end.

Long term contracts
The amount recoverable on each long term contract is based on stage of completion, by calculating costs incurred to date as a percentage of total costs, less any provision for known or anticipated losses and progress payments received and receivable.

Where the outcome of incomplete contracts can be assessed with reasonable certainty the attributable profit is recognised in the profit and loss account as an appropriate proportion of the estimated profit for that contract. The amount by which turnover is in excess of progress payments received and receivable is classified as amounts recoverable on contracts and separately disclosed in debtors. In assessing amounts recoverable the directors provide for the cost of potential claims based on experience.

Disclosure of accounting policies – *See comment on Small Company Limited Annual Report and Accounts,* **example accounts page [6]**. *See also SI 2008/409 Schedule 4.3* (**Appendix B**).

SMALL COMPANY LIMITED **Page [3]**
NOTES TO THE ABBREVIATED ACCOUNTS – 30 JUNE 2013

2 Fixed assets

	Intangible assets	*Tangible fixed assets*	*Investments*	*Total*
	£	£	£	£
Cost				
At 1 July 2012	14,564	696,000	1,000	711,564
Additions	8,260	165,893	–	174,153
Disposals	–	(36,713)	–	(36,713)
At 30 June 2013	22,824	825,180	1,000	849,004
Depreciation				
At 1 July 2012	6,041	400,380	–	406,421
On disposals	–	(28,312)	–	(28,312)
Charge for year	983	60,512	–	61,495
At 30 June 2013	7,024	432,580	–	439,604
Net book values				
At 30 June 2013	£15,800	£392,600	£1,000	£409,400
At 30 June 2012	£8,523	£295,620	£1,000	£305,143

Investments
At 30 June 2013 investments comprise an investment in a subsidiary undertaking. The company's investment in its subsidiary company of £1,000 represents the cost of acquisition of the whole of the ordinary share capital of Sub Consultants Ltd which provides consultancy and advisory services. At 30 June 2013, the aggregate amount of the share capital and reserves of Sub Consultants Limited amounted to £34,900 and the profit for the year to that date was £2,280.

3 Debtors

Debtors include an amount of £1,050 (2012 – Nil) falling due after more than one year.

SMALL COMPANY LIMITED **Page [4]**
NOTES TO THE ABBREVIATED ACCOUNTS – 30 JUNE 2013

4 Creditors

Creditors include the following:

	2013 £	*2012* £
Bank loan not wholly repayable within five years		
repayable within five years	25,000	–
repayable after five years	5,000	–
	30,000	–
Bank overdraft	44,260	34,790
	£74,260	£34,790

The bank loan and overdraft are secured.

5 Contingent liability

A writ for damages amounting to £50,000 has been served on the company, alleging supply of faulty goods. The directors have obtained legal advice and are contesting the claim, which they consider is without foundation. No provision has been made in these accounts in respect of the claim.

6 Called up share capital

	2013 £	*2012* £
Allotted, called up and fully paid		
45,000 ordinary shares of £1 each	£45,000	£45,000

7 Transactions with directors

Advance to director
During the year William Gallagher was granted a short-term loan of £10,000 to facilitate the purchase of a house.

The loan is repayable on 31 December 2013. Interest, at the rate of 6% per annum, is payable upon repayment.

8 Future trading and the current economic environment

Subsequent to the financial year end, the company has experienced a significant reduction in business activity, resulting in significantly lower sales. However, costs are anticipated to reduce correspondingly and, whilst the company is dependent upon the continuation of existing banking and trading facilities, it should be able to operate within its overdraft. Despite serious doubts about future trading conditions, the directors are not aware of any reason why overdraft or other facilities will not be extended. As a result they have adopted the going concern basis of accounting.

Transactions with directors
Information about directors' benefits: advances, credit and guarantees CA 2006 s. 413 (see ***10.9****).*

Registered number:
017081896
England and Wales
(See important note below)

DORMANT SMALL COMPANY LIMITED
ANNUAL REPORT AND UNAUDITED ACCOUNTS
YEAR ENDED 30 JUNE 2013

Dormant company definition – A dormant company is a company which (during any period) has no 'significant accounting transaction' and meets the criteria set out in **Chapter 7** at **7.3** and **7.4**.

Unaudited dormant company accounts – *These accounts illustrate the accounts of a company which has been dormant (within the meaning of section 1169(1)) of the* CA 2006*) throughout the financial year and which is exempt from the provisions relating to the audit of accounts (section 480).* See **Chapter 7**.

There is little benefit in preparing abbreviated dormant company accounts other than the omission of the directors' report and the profit and loss account. Abbreviated accounts will omit the boxed text but need to include the directors' statement.

Disclosure: *The form and content of small dormant company accounts must have regard to SI 2008/409 Schs 1 and 4* (see **Appendix B**). *See also checklist items 10 and 11 in* **Appendix F**.

Registered number – *Any document delivered to the Registrar of Companies must state in a prominent position the registered number of the company to which it relates (CA 2006 s. 1068(3) (c)).*

In accordance with the Registrar's Rules 2009, ***one*** *of the following documents* ***must*** *contain the name and registered number of the company: copy of Balance sheet or Abbreviated accounts and (where applicable) copy of Profit and loss account, Directors' report, Directors' remuneration report and auditor's report (see* ***Chapter 14*** *for Registrar's Rules 2009).*

DORMANT SMALL COMPANY LIMITED

Registered number 017081896 **England and Wales**

Report of the directors
Not required in abbreviated accounts

The directors present their annual report with the unaudited accounts of the company for the year ended 30 June 2013. The company is dormant and has not traded during the year. [The company has, however, acted as agent during the year.]

Julie Collins and William Gallagher were the directors of the company throughout the year.

Signed on behalf of the board of directors by

W. Gallagher

....
William Gallagher
Director/Secretary

Approved by the board: 9 November 2013

Profit and loss account for the year ended 30 June 2013
The company has not traded during the year or the preceding financial year. During these years, the company received no income and incurred no expenditure and therefore made neither profit nor loss.

BALANCE SHEET – 30 JUNE 2013

	2013 £	*2012* £
Current assets		
Debtors		
Amounts owed by group undertakings – (Ultimate parent company – Small Company Limited)	100	100
Total assets less current liabilities	£100	£100
Capital and reserves		
Called up share capital		
Allotted and fully paid 100 ordinary shares of £1	100	100
Shareholders' funds	£100	£100

For the financial year ended 30 June 2013 the company was entitled to exemption from audit under section 480 of the Companies Act 2006 (as a dormant company) and no notice requiring an audit has been deposited under section 476 [*member or members requesting an audit*].

The directors acknowledge their responsibilities for complying with the requirements of the Companies Act 2006 with respect to accounting records and the preparation of accounts. [*s. 475(3)*]

[or (alternative): The directors acknowledge their responsibilities for ensuring that the company keeps accounting records which comply with section 386 [of the Act] and for preparing accounts which give a true and fair view of the state of affairs of the company as at the end of the financial year and of its profit or loss for the financial year in accordance with the requirements of sections 394 and 395 and which otherwise comply with the requirements of the Companies Act 2006 relating to accounts, so far as applicable to the company.]

Signed on behalf of the board of directors by

W. Gallagher

....
William Gallagher
Director

Approved by the board: 9 November 2013

Note to the accounts – Agency arrangements – *see next page.*

DORMANT SMALL COMPANY LIMITED
NOTES TO THE ACCOUNTS – 30 JUNE 2013

Note to the accounts – Agency arrangements
Audit-exempt dormant company

The company was dormant and has not traded during the year. It has, however, acted in certain transactions as agent, for which it received no income.

Registered
No. 03333333
(England and Wales)

OVERSEAS TRADER SMALL COMPANY LIMITED
ANNUAL REPORT AND UNAUDITED ACCOUNTS
31 DECEMBER 2012

OVERSEAS TRADER SMALL COMPANY LIMITED

Directors	W Peter M Dennis
Secretary	M Anthony
Registered office	7 McGregor Avenue Birmingham B1A 1AA
Registered number	03333333 (England and Wales)

ANNUAL REPORT AND UNAUDITED ACCOUNTS – 31 DECEMBER 2012

Contents

OVERSEAS TRADER SMALL COMPANY LIMITED **Page [1]**
REPORT OF THE DIRECTORS

Registered number 03333333 England and Wales

The directors present their report with the unaudited accounts of the company for the year ended 31 December 2012.

Principal activities
The principal activity of the company is advertising.

Directors
The following directors have held office since 1 January 2012:

W Peter
M Dennis

This report has been prepared in accordance with the provisions applicable to companies subject to the small companies regime as set out within Part 15 of the Companies Act 2006.

By order of the Board

M Anthony
....

M Anthony
Secretary

Date 26 May 2013.....................

OVERSEAS TRADER SMALL COMPANY LIMITED
PROFIT AND LOSS ACCOUNT
YEAR ENDED 31 DECEMBER 2012

Page [2]

	Notes	2012	2011
		€	€
Turnover	2	1,925,165	3,651,772
Cost of sales		(656,779)	(1,179,522)
Gross profit		1,268,386	2,472,250
Distribution costs		(90,256)	(169,720)
Administrative expenses		(264,619)	(1,923,638)
Operating profit	3	913,511	378,892
Other interest receivable and similar income	4	18,758	1,654
Profit on ordinary activities before taxation		932,269	380,546
Taxation	5	(244,195)	(69,333)
Profit for the year	12	€ 688,074	€ 311,213

OVERSEAS TRADER SMALL COMPANY LIMITED **Page [3]**
BALANCE SHEET 31 DECEMBER 2012

	Notes	2012	2012	2011	2011
		€	€	€	€
Fixed assets					
Tangible assets	8		9,170		21,652
Current assets					
Debtors	9	212,454		49,398	
Cash at bank and in hand		2,095,553		1,330,627	
		2,308,007		1,380,025	
Creditors: amounts falling due within one year	10	(724,120)		(398,624)	
Net current assets			1,583,887		981,401
Total assets less current liabilities			€ 1,593,057		€ 1,003,053
Capital and reserves					
Called up share capital	11		3		3
Profit and loss account	12		1,593,054		1,003,050
Shareholders' funds			€ 1,593,057		€ 1,003,053

These accounts have been prepared in accordance with the provisions applicable to companies subject to the small companies regime as set out within Part 15 of the Companies Act 2006 and with the Financial Reporting Standard for Smaller Entities (effective April 2008).

For the financial year ended 31 December 2012 the company was entitled to exemption from audit under section 477 Companies Act 2006 and no notice has been deposited under section 476.

The directors acknowledge their responsibilities for ensuring that the company keeps accounting records which comply with section 386 of the Act and for preparing accounts which give a true and fair view of the state of affairs of the company as at the end of the financial year and of its profit or loss for the financial year in accordance with the requirements of sections 394 and 395 and which otherwise comply with the requirements of the Companies Act 2006 relating to accounts, so far as applicable to the company.

Approved by the Board ....

W Peter
....
W Peter
Director

26 May 2013

OVERSEAS TRADER SMALL COMPANY LIMITED
NOTES TO THE ACCOUNTS – 31 DECEMBER 2012

1 Accounting policies

Basis of accounting
The accounts have been prepared under the historical cost convention and in accordance with the Financial Reporting Standard for Smaller Entities (effective April 2008).

Turnover
Turnover represents amounts receivable for goods and services net of VAT and trade discounts.

Tangible fixed assets and depreciation
Tangible fixed assets are stated at cost less depreciation. Depreciation is provided at rates calculated to write off the cost less estimated residual value of each asset over its expected useful life, as follows:

- Leasehold land and buildings — Over the period of the lease
- Fixtures, fittings & equipment — 25% written down allowance

Deferred taxation
Deferred taxation is provided in full on timing differences which result in an obligation at the balance sheet date to pay more tax, or a right to pay less tax, at a future date, at rates expected to apply when they crystallise based on current tax rates and law. Timing differences arise from the inclusion of items of income and expenditure in taxation computations different from those in which they are included in the accounts.

Deferred tax assets are recognised to the extent that it is regarded as more likely than not that they will be recovered. Deferred tax assets and liabilities are not discounted.

Foreign currency translation
The accounts are prepared in Euros. The rate of exchange used to translate sterling balances into Euros at 31 December 2012 was £0.81737 = €1. Monetary assets and liabilities denominated in non-Euro currencies are translated into Euros at the rates of exchange ruling at the balance sheet date. Transactions in non-Euro currencies are recorded at the rate of exchange ruling at the date of the transaction. All differences are taken to the profit and loss account.

2 Turnover
In the year to 31 December 2012, 100% (2011 – 100%) of the company's turnover was to markets outside the United Kingdom.

3 Operating profit

	2012	2011
	€	€
This is stated after charging:		
Depreciation of tangible assets	12,482	4,298
Directors' remuneration	49,035	47,177
Operating lease charges	4,205	3,609

4 Other interest receivable and similar income

	2012	2011
	€	€
Bank interest	18,758	1,654
	€ 18,758	€ 1,654

OVERSEAS TRADER SMALL COMPANY LIMITED
NOTES TO THE ACCOUNTS – 31 DECEMBER 2012 **Page [5]**

5 Taxation

	2012	2011
	€	€
Domestic current tax year		
U.K. corporation tax on profits in the year	245,156	69,333
Adjustment for prior years	(961)	—
	€ 244,195	€ 69,333

6 Dividends

	2012	2011
	€	€
Ordinary paid	€ 98,070	€ 93,349

7 Deferred tax

	2012	2011
The amounts unprovided are as follows:	€	€
Accelerated capital allowances at 20% (2011 – 20%)	1,500	1,034
	€ 1,500	€ 1,034

8 Tangible fixed assets

	Land and buildings leasehold	Fixtures, fittings & equipment	Total
	€	€	€
Cost			
At 1 January 2012 & at 31 December 2012	23,464	22,059	45,523
Depreciation			
At 1 January 2012	3,910	19,961	23,871
Charge for the year	12,182	300	12,482
At 31 December 2012	16,092	20,261	36,353
Net book value			
At 31 December 2012	€ 7,372	€ 1,798	€ 9,170
At 31 December 2011	€19,554	€ 2,098	€ 21,652

OVERSEAS TRADER SMALL COMPANY LIMITED
NOTES TO THE ACCOUNTS – 31 DECEMBER 2012 **Page [6]**

9 Debtors

	2012	2011
	€	€
Trade debtors	209,809	32,900
Other debtors	2,645	16,498
	€ 212,454	€ 49,398

10 Creditors: amounts falling due within one year

	2012	2011
	€	€
Trade creditors	86,490	135,683
Taxation and social security	255,099	69,333
Other creditors	382,531	193,608
	€ 724,120	€ 398,624

11 Share capital

	2012	2011
Allotted, called up and fully paid	€	€
2 Ordinary Shares of £1 each	€ 3	€ 3

12 Statement of movements on profit and loss account

	Profit and loss account
	€
Balance at 1 January 2012	1,003,050
Retained profit for the year	688,074
Dividends paid	(98,070)
Balance at 31 December 2012	€ 1,593,054

13 Transactions with directors

Dividends of €98,070 (2011 - €93,349) were paid to the director shareholders during the year, split equally between the directors.

14 Control

During the two years ended 31 December 2012, the company was under the control of W Peter and M Dennis, who own one share each.

Chapter 13 Small company audit and assurance reports

13.1 Auditor's reports

This chapter comments on, and provides examples of, audit reports where a small company is subject to audit, either as required by statute or where the directors have requested a Companies Act audit. Audit reports must also be prepared having regard to International Standards on Auditing – ISAs (UK and Ireland).

No statutory report is required from an auditor where a small company is entitled to (and takes advantage of) audit exemption (CA 2006 s. 477); see **Chapter 11**.

Where an audit report is included, the directors are not required to make certain statements about their responsibilities on the face of the balance sheet. Instead, a more detailed statement of directors' responsibilities is required by the International Standards on Auditing and should appear either as a separate statement or as part of the directors' report. See **6.8.3**.

13.1.1 Audit – Part 16 of CA 2006

Audit is covered in Part 16 of CA 2006, which contains provisions (s. 475-539) concerning the requirement for audited accounts and the auditor's report.

13.1.2 Elements of an auditor's report

An auditor's report must include an introduction identifying the annual accounts and the financial reporting framework under which they are prepared, together with a description of the scope of the audit identifying the auditing standards adopted.

In essence, under CA 2006 s. 495, the auditor is required to report his opinion on these elements.

1. *True and fair view* – whether the annual accounts show a 'true and fair view' (having regard to the directors' statutory duty under CA 2006 s. 393(1)).
2. *Relevant reporting framework* – whether the accounts have been prepared in accordance with the relevant financial reporting framework.
3. *Appropriate legislation* – whether the accounts have been prepared in accordance with CA 2006 (Part 15) or IAS (IAS Regulation Article 4), if applicable.

The auditor's report must be either 'unqualified or qualified' and contain reference to any emphasis of matters which the auditor may wish to include without qualifying the report.

13.1.3 Auditor's report – CA 2006 s. 495

The form of report to be adopted with respect to Companies Act accounts is determined by CA 2006 and by the International Standards on Auditing as applicable within the UK. Following the adoption of International Standards on Auditing (ISAs), an auditor's report on accounts is required to follow ISA (UK and Ireland) 700 *The Auditor's Report on Financial Statements.* Example reports are issued by the Auditing Practices Board (APB) – see **Example 13.1**.

CA 2006 s. 495 (Auditor's report on company's annual accounts) is reproduced in full in **Table 13.1**.

Table 13.1 Auditor's report on annual accounts CA 2006 s. 495

495 Auditor's report on company's annual accounts

(1) A company's auditor must make a report to the company's members on all annual accounts of the company of which copies are, during his tenure of office—
  (a) in the case of a private company, to be sent out to members under section 423;
  (b) in the case of a public company, to be laid before the company in general meeting under section 437.

(2) The auditor's report must include—
  (a) an introduction identifying the annual accounts that are the subject of the audit and the financial reporting framework that has been applied in their preparation, and
  (b) a description of the scope of the audit identifying the auditing standards in accordance with which the audit was conducted.

(3) The report must state clearly whether, in the auditor's opinion, the annual accounts—
  (a) give a true and fair view—
    (i) in the case of an individual balance sheet, of the state of affairs of the company as at the end of the financial year;
    (ii) in the case of an individual profit and loss account, of the profit or loss of the company for the financial year;
    (iii) in the case of group accounts, of the state of affairs as at the end of the financial year and of the profit or loss for the financial year of the undertakings included in the consolidation as a whole, so far as concerns members of the company;
  (b) have been properly prepared in accordance with the relevant financial reporting framework; and
  (c) have been prepared in accordance with the requirements of this Act (and, where applicable, Article 4 of the IAS Regulation).

Expressions used in this subsection that are defined for the purposes of Part 15 (see section 474) have the same meaning as in that Part.

(4) The auditor's report—
  (a) must be either unqualified or qualified; and
  (b) must include a reference to any matters to which the auditor wishes to draw attention by way of emphasis without qualifying the report.

13.1.4 Signature of auditor's report

The auditor's report must state the name of the auditor and be signed and dated. However, where the auditor is a firm, the report delivered to the members must be signed by the 'senior statutory auditor' in his own name, for and on behalf of the auditor. (CA 2006 s. 504)

Although the set of the financial statements filed with the Registrar of Companies must contain the signatures of the directors who have signed the financial statements on behalf of the board of directors (where the paper accounts are being filed), a physical signature is not required on the auditor's report. In practice many auditors still prefer that the set submitted to the Registrar of Companies contains a signature. Where the auditor is a firm, the set filed with the Registrar of Companies can be signed in the name of the firm rather that in the name of the senior statutory auditor, although the name of the senior statutory auditor should be included.

The Registrar of Companies has requested that all signatures with the report and accounts should be in black ink.

13.2 ISA (UK and Ireland) 700 (Revised) The Auditor's Report on Financial Statements

13.2.1 ISAs (UK and Ireland) and the auditor's report

The report of an auditor is required to follow ISA (UK and Ireland) 700 *(Revised) The Auditor's Report on Financial Statements*.

ISA (UK and Ireland) 700, although generally prescriptive as to the form and content of the auditor's report, does not preclude some flexibility when using the format and wording of the example reports prescribed by the Statement. The use of the term 'accounts', for example, in preference to 'financial statements' accords with the CA 2006 and is essentially a question of personal choice, permissible provided the term is adequately defined (see example accounts in **Chapter 12** on the index page preceding **page 1**).

The APB* issued from time to time a Bulletin providing illustrative examples of auditor's reports. The APB Bulletin 2010/02 (Revised), *Compendium of Illustrative Auditor's Reports on United Kingdom Private Sector Financial Statements for periods ended on or after 15 December 2010 (Revised)* is the most recent bulletin and was issued in March 2012 and is applicable for periods ended on or after 23 March 2011.

ISA (UK and Ireland) 700, *The Auditor's Report on Financial Statements*, facilitates, but does not mandate, a more concise auditor's report. This may be achieved by permitting the description of the scope of an audit and the auditor's reporting responsibilities to be made either within the body of the auditor's report (as was previously the norm) or by cross reference to the APB website (where a relevant statement of scope is maintained) or by cross reference to a 'Statement of the Scope of an Audit' that is included elsewhere within the Annual Report.

If it is decided to include the description of the scope of an audit within the auditor's report, the Bulletin suggests the description should be presented as follows:

> *'An audit involves obtaining evidence about the amounts and disclosures in the financial statements sufficient to give reasonable assurance that the financial statements are free from material misstatement, whether caused by fraud or error. This includes an assessment of: whether the accounting policies are appropriate to the [describe nature of entity] circumstances and have been consistently applied and adequately disclosed; the reasonableness of significant accounting estimates made by [describe those charged with governance]; and the overall presentation of the financial statements. In addition, we read all the financial and non-financial information in the [describe the annual report] to identify material inconsistencies with the audited financial statements [and to identify any information that is apparently materially incorrect based on, or materially inconsistent with, the knowledge acquired by us in the course of performing the audit]. If we become aware of any apparent material misstatements or inconsistencies we consider the implications for our report.'*
>
> *[The phrase in brackets has been added following the revision of ISA 720 in October 2012.]*

If cross reference is made to the APB website, the relevant website address is: www.frc.org.uk/apb/scope/private.cfm

*Note that the APB was disbanded in July 2012. The function of the APB is now performed by the FRC's Audit and Assurance Council.

13.3 Example Auditor's Report of a small company

Example 13.1 is extracted from APB Bulletin 2010/2 Revised (March 2012) (at Appendix 1 Example 1) and illustrates an 'unqualified' report with no 'emphasis of matter' paragraph of a small company where the audit is performed in accordance with International Standards on Auditing (UK and Ireland) issued by the APB. The example assumes:

- the company qualifies as a 'small company' and adopts the FRSSE;
- the company does not prepare group financial statements;
- the company prepares a directors' report but no other 'surround information' (for example chairman's report, corporate governance statement or other financial commentary);
- the company adopts UK GAAP (and not IAS); and
- the auditor does not take advantage of ES PASE (APB Ethical Standard – *Provisions Available for Small Entities (Revised)* (December 2010)) (except in circumstances where the report includes the text indicated by grey tinting).

Amendments in the example made (by the author), for completeness and illustrative purposes, are presented in **[bold text]**.

Example 13.1

INDEPENDENT AUDITOR'S REPORT TO THE MEMBERS *[Author's note (1)]* **OF [SMALL COMPANY] LIMITED**

We have audited the financial statements of **[Small Company Limited]** for the year ended **[31 December 2012]** which comprise the [specify the titles of the primary statements such as Profit and Loss Account, the Balance Sheet, the Cash Flow Statement, the Statement of Total Recognised Gains and Losses, the Reconciliation of Movements in Shareholders' Funds] and the related notes. The financial reporting framework that has been applied in their preparation is applicable law and the Financial Reporting Standard for Smaller Entities (effective April 2008) (United Kingdom Generally Accepted Accounting Practice applicable to Smaller Entities).

This report is made solely to the company's members, as a body, in accordance with Chapter 3 of Part 16 of the Companies Act 2006. Our audit work has been undertaken so that we might state to the company's members those matters that we are required to state to them in an auditor's report and for no other purpose. To the fullest extent permitted by law, we do not accept or assume responsibility to anyone other than the company and the company's members as a body, for our audit work, for this report, or for the opinions we have formed. *[Author's note (2)]*

Respective responsibilities of directors and auditor
As explained more fully in the Directors' Responsibilities Statement **[set out on page xx]**, the directors are responsible for the preparation of the financial statements and for being satisfied that they give a true and fair view. Our responsibility is to audit and express an opinion on the financial statements in accordance with applicable law and International Standards on Auditing (UK and Ireland). Those standards require us to comply with the Auditing Practices Board's [(APB's)] Ethical Standards for Auditors. [, including 'APB Ethical Standard – Provisions Available for Small Entities (Revised)', in the circumstances set out in note [X] to the financial statements]. *[Author's note (3)]*

Scope of the audit of the financial statements

Either:

A description of the scope of an audit of financial statements is [provided on the APB's website at www.frc.org.uk/apb/scope/private.cfm] / [set out [on page **X**] of the Annual Report].

Example 13.1 (cont'd)

Or:

An audit involves obtaining evidence about the amounts and disclosures in the financial statements sufficient to give reasonable assurance that the financial statements are free from material misstatement, whether caused by fraud or error. This includes an assessment of : whether the accounting policies are appropriate to the **company's** circumstances and have been consistently applied and adequately disclosed ; the reasonableness of significant accounting estimates made by **the directors** ; and the overall presentation of the financial statements. In addition, we read all the financial and non-financial information in the **directors' report** to identify material inconsistencies with the audited financial statements *and to identify any information that is apparently materially incorrect based on, or materially inconsistent with, the knowledge acquired by us in the course of performing the audit.* If we become aware of any apparent misstatements or inconsistencies we consider the implications for our report.

[Author's note (4)]

Opinion on financial statements

In our opinion the financial statements:

- give a true and fair view of the state of the company's affairs as at **31 December 2012** and of its profit [loss] for the year then ended;
- have been properly prepared in accordance with United Kingdom Generally Accepted Accounting Practice applicable to Smaller Entities; and
- have been prepared in accordance with the requirements of the Companies Act 2006.

Opinion on other matter prescribed by the Companies Act 2006
In our opinion the information given in the Directors' Report for the financial year for which the financial statements are prepared is consistent with the financial statements.

Matters on which we are required to report by exception
We have nothing to report in respect of the following matters where the Companies Act 2006 requires us to report to you if, in our opinion:

- adequate accounting records have not been kept, or returns adequate for our audit have not been received from branches not visited by us; or
- the financial statements are not in agreement with the accounting records and returns; or
- certain disclosures of directors' remuneration specified by law are not made; or
- we have not received all the information and explanations we require for our audit; or
- the directors were not entitled to [prepare the financial statements in accordance with the small companies regime] [and] [take advantage of the small companies' exemption in preparing the directors' report].

Lucy Caldwell *[Author's note (5)]*

....

Lucy Caldwell (Senior Statutory Auditor)
for and on behalf of
TRUE & FAIRVIEW LLP,
Statutory Auditor

17 Queens Place,
LONDON EC4P 3BC

23 April 2013

Author's notes and commentary to **Example 13.1**

(1) ***Report to the members*** – *The statutory auditor's report is made to the members of the company (CA 2006 s. 495). No statutory report is required where a small company is otherwise entitled to audit exemption (CA 2006 section 477). A non-statutory audit report for an audit exempt company would be addressed to the directors of the company, in accordance with whose instructions the audit is conducted.*

(2) ***Duty of care to third parties*** – *the ICAEW recommends that auditors include additional wording in audit reports in order to clarify auditors' responsibilities to third parties – that is, other than to the members (or the directors, as the case may be) as a body. (Audit 1/03 – The Audit Report and The Auditors' Duty of Care to Third Parties.) (January 2003, most recent update January 2010.) (See **13.5**.)*

(3) ***APB Ethical Standard – Provisions Available for Small Entities (Revised)*** *(ES PASE) – Paragraph 24 of ES PASE requires disclosure in the auditor's report where the audit firm has taken advantage of an exemption provided by ES PASE. The Appendix to ES PASE provides illustrative disclosures of relevant circumstances where the audit firm has taken advantage of an exemption (for example, where auditors have assisted in the preparation of accounts or provided tax advice). The words in square brackets in the above example should be deleted if the relief and exemptions provided by ES PASE are not utilised.*
www.frc.org.uk/Our-Work/Codes-Standards/Audit-and-assurance/Standards-and-guidance/Standards-and-guidance-for-auditors/Ethical-standards-for-auditors.aspx

An example note illustrated within the APB ES PASE Appendix provides that 'In common with many other businesses of our size and nature we use our auditors to prepare and submit returns to the tax authorities and assist with the preparation of the financial statements'.

(4) ***Description of the scope of an audit of financial statements*** – *ISA (UK and Ireland) 700 (Revised October 2012) requires that an auditor's report should either: cross refer to a Statement of the scope of an audit maintained on the APB's (now FRC's) website; or cross refer to such a scope statement that is included elsewhere within the Annual Report; or include a prescribed description of the scope of an audit.*

The prescribed description of the scope of an audit (as illustrated in **Example 13.1***) is set out in ISA (UK and Ireland) 700 (Revised) and APB Bulletin 2010/2 (revised) Auditor's Reports on Financial Statements in the United Kingdom. Paragraph 2 to the APB Bulletin sets out the description of the 'Scope of an audit' that may be cross referenced from an auditor's report.*

(5) ***Signature and dating of auditor's report*** – *CA 2006 s. 503 and* ISA (UK and Ireland) 700 *The Auditor's Report on Financial Statements paras 23-26.*

13.4 Special Auditor's Report – abbreviated accounts

Two examples below illustrate statutory reports on abbreviated accounts relating to a small company that has not taken advantage of audit exemption. The reports below are not appropriate (or required) if the company is exempt from audit (CA 2006 s. 477 small company or s. 480 dormant company).

The examples of special auditor's reports on abbreviated accounts comprise:

- **(Example 13.2)** – small company abbreviated accounts (advantage not taken (or available) of audit exemption);
- **(Example 13.3)** – small company abbreviated accounts (qualified full audit opinion – advantage not taken (or available) of audit exemption).

The example reports illustrated within the abbreviated accounts assume that the accounts are not published on a website.

APB Bulletin 2008/4 (April 2008) *The special auditor's report on abbreviated accounts in the United Kingdom* provides guidance for auditors regarding the filing obligations of small (and medium-sized) companies under the CA 2006, and in particular, provides guidance concerning the 'Special Auditor's Report on Abbreviated Accounts' (CA 2006 s. 449). **Examples 13.2** and **13.3** reflect the guidance in APB Bulletin 2008/4.

Example 13.2

INDEPENDENT AUDITOR'S REPORT TO [SMALL COMPANY LIMITED] UNDER SECTION 449 OF THE COMPANIES ACT 2006

We have examined the abbreviated accounts set out on pages [x] to [x], together with the financial statements of the [Small Company Limited] for the year ended 31 December 2012 prepared under section 396 of the Companies Act 2006.

This report is made solely to the company, in accordance with section 449 of the Companies Act 2006. Our work has been undertaken so that we might state to the company those matters we are required to state to it in a special auditors' report and for no other purpose. To the fullest extent permitted by law, we do not accept or assume responsibility to anyone other than the company, for our work, for this report, or for the opinions we have formed.

Respective responsibilities of directors and auditor
The directors are responsible for preparing the abbreviated accounts in accordance with section 444 of the Companies Act 2006. It is our responsibility to form an independent opinion as to whether the company is entitled to deliver abbreviated accounts to the Registrar of Companies and whether the abbreviated accounts have been properly prepared in accordance with the regulations made under that section and to report our opinion to you.

We conducted our work in accordance with Bulletin 2008/4 issued by the Auditing Practices Board. In accordance with that Bulletin we have carried out the procedures we consider necessary to confirm, by reference to the financial statements, that the company is entitled to deliver abbreviated accounts and that the abbreviated accounts to be delivered are properly prepared. *The scope of our work for the purpose of this report did not include examining or dealing with events after the date of our report on the full statutory accounts.*

Opinion
In our opinion the company is entitled to deliver abbreviated accounts prepared in accordance with section 444(3) of the Companies Act 2006, and the abbreviated accounts [on pages [x] to [x]] have been properly prepared in accordance with the regulations made under that section.

Lucy Caldwell. *s. 503 CA 2006*

....
Lucy Caldwell (Senior Statutory Auditor)
for and on behalf of
TRUE & FAIRVIEW LLP
Statutory Auditors

17 Queens Place,
LONDON EC4P 3BC 23 April 2013

Note 1 ***Duty of care to third parties*** – additional wording as recommended by ICAEW (Audit 1/03 – The Audit Report and The Auditors' Duty of Care to Third Parties) (January 2003 as updated January 2010). (See **13.5**.)

Note 2 ***Events after the date of the report*** – Text in *italics* in the penultimate paragraph above is only appropriate where the special report is dated **after** the signing of the auditor's report on the full annual accounts.

Example 13.3

INDEPENDENT AUDITOR'S REPORT TO SMALL COMPANY LIMITED UNDER SECTION 449 OF THE COMPANIES ACT 2006 [*QUALIFIED FULL AUDIT OPINION*]

We have examined the abbreviated accounts set out on pages [x] to [x], together with the [full statutory] financial statements of the company for the year ended 31 December 2012 prepared under section 396 of the Companies Act 2006.

> This report is made solely to the company, in accordance with section 449 of the Companies Act 2006. Our work has been undertaken so that we might state to the company those matters we are required to state to it in a special auditors' report and for no other purpose. To the fullest extent permitted by law, we do not accept or assume responsibility to anyone other than the company, for our work, for this report, or for the opinions we have formed.

Respective responsibilities of directors and auditors

The directors are responsible for preparing the abbreviated accounts in accordance with section 444 of the Companies Act 2006. It is our responsibility to form an independent opinion as to whether the company is entitled to deliver abbreviated accounts to the Registrar of Companies and whether the abbreviated accounts have been properly prepared in accordance with the regulations made under that section and to report our opinion to you.

We conducted our work in accordance with Bulletin 2008/4 issued by the Auditing Practices Board. In accordance with that Bulletin we have carried out the procedures we consider necessary to confirm, by reference to the financial statements, that the company is entitled to deliver abbreviated accounts and that the abbreviated accounts to be delivered are properly prepared. *The scope of our work for the purpose of this report did not include examining or dealing with events after the date of our report on the full statutory financial statements.*

Opinion

In our opinion the company is entitled to deliver abbreviated accounts prepared in accordance with section 444(3) of the Companies Act 2006, and the abbreviated accounts [on pages [x] to [x]] have been properly prepared in accordance with the regulations made under that section.

Other information

On 14 March 2013 we reported as auditor to the members of the company on the financial statements prepared under section 396 of the Companies Act 2006 and our report was as follows [/included the following statement/paragraph]:

[Full wording of qualified audit report under section 495 Companies Act 2006 or Statements under section 498(2) [Inadequate accounting records] or section 498(3) [Failure to obtain necessary information] or Explanatory comment contained in Unqualified Audit Report under section 495 Companies Act 2006 concerning fundamental uncertainty to be set out in full]:

s. 5.3 CA 2006

Lucy Caldwell.

....

Lucy Caldwell (Senior Statutory Auditor)
for and on behalf of
TRUE & FAIRVIEW LLP
Statutory Auditors

17 Queens Place,
LONDON EC4P 3BC

23 April 2013

Example of explanatory paragraph to be included under 'Other information'
Going concern. In forming our opinion, we have considered the adequacy of disclosures made in note 1 of the accounts concerning the uncertainty as to the continuation and renewal of the company's bank overdraft facility. In view of the significance of this uncertainty we consider that it should be drawn to your attention, but our opinion is not qualified in this respect.

Qualified full audit opinion – The special auditor's report (where necessary) in connection with abbreviated accounts is not required to reproduce the full text of the auditor's report on the annual accounts, except (as illustrated above) in the circumstances of a qualification or explanatory paragraph regarding a fundamental uncertainty. This is explained further in **8.9**.

13.5 Audit and assurance: non-statutory reports

Many small companies, although no longer required to have a statutory audit, may nevertheless choose to have one carried out.

Where a company takes advantage of exemption from *statutory* audit, the directors may wish to have some form of independent review of the accounts, being either:

- ***an audit*** – a non-statutory or 'contractual' audit (voluntarily obtained on terms decided by the directors), or
- ***an independent assurance report*** – an accountants' report covering both the proper compilation of the accounts and the directors' 'true and fair view' assertion. These reports are discussed in **13.6** (and illustrated in **Example 13.4**); or
- ***a compilation report*** – an accountants' report on the proper compilation of the accounts. Reports on accounts prepared for unaudited companies are discussed in **13.7** (and illustrated in **Example 13.5**).

13.6 Independent assurance reports

Guidance on performing limited assurance reports (reviews) on financial statements of companies that are exempt from audit was published by the ICAEW in an Interim Technical Release (Audit and Assurance Faculty) AAF 03/06 *The ICAEW Assurance Service on Unaudited Financial Statements*. The Technical Release contains a number of examples illustrating report situations, depending on the parties to the engagement terms. The objectives of the independent assurance report would be to provide comfort to the directors and to enhance the credibility of the accounts with third parties, including members and the Registrar of Companies.

This technical release is currently being revised to bring it in line with International Standard for Review Engagements (ISRE) 2400 (revised 2012). The new technical release is expected early in 2013.

Further guidance was issued as part of the ICAEW's Assurance Sourcebook, published in July 2012, which was written to be consistent with guidance in AAF 03/06.

Example 13.4 reproduces one of the example Independent Assurance Reports from AAF 03/06.

Example 13.4 Example Independent Assurance Report
ICAEW Interim Technical Release (Audit and Assurance Faculty) – AAF 03/06 (August 2006)
Example Reports Appendix E (Reporting to Directors)

CHARTERED ACCOUNTANTS' INDEPENDENT ASSURANCE REPORT ON THE UNAUDITED FINANCIAL STATEMENTS OF [NAME OF ENTITY]

TO THE BOARD OF DIRECTORS OF [NAME OF ENTITY] ('THE COMPANY')

We have performed certain procedures in respect of the Company's unaudited financial statements for the year [/period] ended [date] as set out on pages [x] to [x], made enquiries of the Company's directors and assessed accounting policies adopted by the directors, in order to gather sufficient evidence for our conclusion in this report.

This report is made solely to the Company's directors, as a body, in accordance with the terms of our engagement letter dated [date]. It has been released to the directors on the basis that this report shall not be copied, referred to or disclosed in whole (save for the directors' own internal purposes or as may be required by law or by a competent regulator) or in part, without our prior written consent. Our work has been undertaken so that we might state to the directors those matters that we have agreed to state to them in this report and for no other purpose. To the fullest extent permitted by law, we do not accept or assume responsibility to anyone other than the Company and the Company's directors, as a body for our work, for this report or for the conclusions we have formed.

Respective responsibilities
You have confirmed that you have met your duty as set out in the directors' statement on page [x]. You consider that the Company is exempt from the statutory requirement for an audit for the year [/period]. Our responsibility is to form and express an independent conclusion, based on the work carried out, to you on the financial statements.

Scope
We conducted our engagement in accordance with the Institute of Chartered Accountants in England and Wales Interim Technical Release AAF 03/06. Our work was based primarily upon enquiry, analytical procedures and assessing accounting policies in accordance with Generally Accepted Accounting Practice in the UK [/the Financial Reporting Standard for Smaller Entities]. If we considered it to be necessary, we also performed limited examination of evidence relevant to certain balances and disclosures in the financial statements where we became aware of matters that might indicate a risk of material misstatement in the financial statements.

The terms of our engagement exclude any requirement to carry out a comprehensive assessment of the risks of material misstatement, a consideration of fraud, laws, regulations and internal controls, and we have not done so. We are not required to, and we do not, express an audit opinion on these financial statements.

Conclusion
Based on our work, nothing has come to our attention to refute the directors' confirmation that in accordance with the [Companies Act 2006] the financial statements give a true and fair view of the state of the Company's affairs as at [date] and of its profit [/loss] for the year [/period] then ended and have been properly prepared in accordance with Generally Accepted Accounting Practice in the UK [/the Financial Reporting Standard for Smaller Entities].

....
Name of firm
Chartered Accountants

[Location]

[Date]

13.7 Compilation: reports on accounts prepared for unaudited companies – ICAEW Technical Release Audit 02/10

Notwithstanding that a company is able to take advantage of audit exemption in preparing its annual accounts, the company may nevertheless wish to have the comfort of some form of report from independent (but non-statutory) reporting accountants. Any report attached to the accounts of the company where no statutory report is required should be addressed to the directors, since the accountants are acting as agents of the directors.

A Technical Release, issued by the Audit and Assurance Faculty of the Institute of Chartered Accountants in England and Wales in November 2010 (Audit 02/10 *Chartered Accountants' Reports on Compilation of Financial Statements of Incorporated Entities*), gives general guidance on the form and content of reports where accountants 'compile' (being the generally acknowledged term for 'prepare') accounts on behalf of client companies.

The example accountants' report (a non-statutory (or contractual) report) contained in the Technical Release issued in November 2010 is reproduced in **Example 13.5**.

The example is essentially appropriate in circumstances where the directors wish the accountants to assist them in meeting the directors' statutory obligation under the Companies Act, to prepare annual accounts showing a true and fair view. Where the accounts compiled by an accountant constitute abbreviated accounts, the form of report in **Example 13.5** may also be used to support the abbreviated accounts. Optional paragraphs (or text to be completed as appropriate) are indicated by [square brackets].

The use of the report remains voluntary – there is no requirement for companies to use professional accountants to help compile accounts or to obtain an accounts compilation report.

Where accounts are compiled by a professional accountant and an accountants' report is prepared on the lines of **Example 13.5**, the Technical Release 02/10 stresses the importance of agreeing terms of engagement between the directors and the reporting accountants. The Technical Release provides example terms.

Example 13.5 Chartered Accountants' Report on the Compilation of Financial Statements of Incorporated Entities (AAF 02/10)

Chartered Accountant's/Accountants' report to the board of directors on the preparation of the unaudited statutory accounts of XYZ Limited for the year [/period] ended ...

In order to assist you to fulfil your duties under the Companies Act 2006, we have prepared for your approval the accounts of XYZ Limited for the year [/period] ended [date] [as set out on pages x-x/which comprise [insert statements]] from the company's accounting records and from information and explanations you have given us.

As a practising member [/member firm of] of the Institute of Chartered Accountants in England and Wales (ICAEW), we are subject to its ethical and other professional requirements which are detailed at www.icaew.com/membershandbook.

[This report is made solely to the Board of Directors of XYZ Limited, as a body, in accordance with the terms of our engagement letter dated [date].] Our work has been undertaken [solely to prepare for your approval the accounts of XYZ Limited and state those matters that we have agreed to state to them/the Board of Directors of XYZ Limited, as a body, in this report] in accordance with AAF 2/10 as detailed at www.icaew.com/compilation. [To the fullest extent permitted by law, we do not accept or assume responsibility to anyone other than XYZ Limited and its Board of Directors as a body for our work or for this report.]

[It is your duty to ensure that XYZ Limited has kept adequate accounting records and to prepare statutory accounts that give a true and fair view of the assets, liabilities, financial position and profit[/loss] of XYZ Limited. You consider that XYZ Limited is exempt from the statutory audit requirement for the year [/period].]

Example 13.5 Chartered Accountants' Report on the Compilation of Financial Statements of Incorporated Entities (AAF 02/10) (cont'd)

[We have not been instructed to carry out an audit or a review of the accounts of XYZ Limited. For this reason, we have not verified the accuracy or completeness of the accounting records or information and explanations you have given to us and we do not, therefore, express any opinion on the statutory accounts.]

[Explanatory paragraph: e.g. records destroyed by fire.] *Explanatory paragraph may be positioned in other places in the report depending on the nature of the matter described.*

Signature. . . . . *(The report is signed in the name of the professional accountant or, where appropriate, in the name of the accounting firm.)*

Typed name of professional accountant

Chartered Accountants

Address

Date . . . .

Part IV Filing accounts and the future of UK GAAP

Chapter 14 Accounts filing for small companies

14.1 Introduction

This book does not aim to cover the finer details of the filing requirements for the accounts of small companies but this chapter gives guidance on filing with both the Registrar of Companies and HMRC and explains some of the current filing methods which are introducing changes to the process which has existed for many years of paper filing of accounts with the Registrar and tax authorities.

In general, accounts of small companies need to be filed:

- with the Registrar of Companies within the filing deadline (see below); and
- with HMRC with the company's tax return (if the company is required to file a tax return) not more than 12 months following the end of the year to which they relate.

One recent development in filing accounts with the Registrar of Companies is that electronic filing of accounts is permitted and the number of accounts being submitted electronically is growing. This chapter sets out the various options for a company in relation to filing accounts electronically.

14.2 Filing deadlines

In general, private companies are required to file accounts with the Registrar of Companies within nine months from the end of the accounting period (accounting reference date or ARD).

When filing the company's first accounts, the deadline for delivery is 21 months after the date of incorporation. The deadline remains the same even if this company extends its first accounting period to the maximum of 18 months. It is calculated to the exact corresponding date in the 21st month following the incorporation. For example, a company incorporated on 29 January 2013 has until midnight on 29 October 2014 to submit its first accounts.

When the accounting period is extended, other than for the first accounts, the filing deadline remains as nine months after the end of the period. However, when a private company shortens the accounting period, the filing deadline for that period is the longer of the following:

- nine months after the new ARD; or
- three months after the date of the notice of the ARD change being delivered to the Registrar.

Companies submitting their accounts after the filing deadline has passed will incur a late filing penalty of at least £150. The penalty increases in line with the period of late submission. The maximum penalty for a private company which submits accounts six months after the normal filing deadline is £1,500. However, if the company files its accounts late two years in a row, the penalty in the second year is doubled.

14.3 Filing accounts with the Registrar of Companies

The Registrar of Companies is given authority under the CA 2006 to make rules governing the filing of documents at Companies House. These 'Registrar's Rules' are secondary legislation, made under section 1117 of the Act, and include the form, delivery and method of authentication for documents (including accounts) to be delivered to the Registrar.

The rules specify differing filing requirements for hard copy and electronic filings. For example, although the Companies Act requirement for an original signature to be included on the accounts that are filed was repealed as from 1 October 2009, signatures are still required by the Registrar's Rules to be included on balance sheets filed in paper form.

Furthermore, Companies House has recently reviewed its policy on filing documents with *original* signatures and has concluded that the Registrar of Companies will 'accept in good faith that documents presented for filing which have automatically generated signatures have been properly approved by the signatory'. And that 'documents will no longer be rejected simply because the signature does not appear to be original'.

www.companieshouse.gov.uk/about/policyDocuments/documentSignatures.shtml

A detailed list of the Registrar's Rules, including when amendments came into force, is available at:

www.companieshouse.gov.uk/about/policyDocuments/registrarsRules/infoRegistrarsRules.shtml

The most significant recent change came into force on 30 November 2012 when Volume 1 of the Registrar's Rules 2009 (Documents delivered in electronic form) was revoked and the new *Registrar's (Electronic Form) Rules 2012 - Volume 1* came into force. Most recently, on 8 February 2013 a new WebFiling template for audit exempt abbreviated accounts has been added to Volume 1.

The rules contained in Volumes 2, 3, 4 and 5 of the Registrar's Rules 2009 (as amended) remain in force.

Table 14.1 The Registrar's Rules

The Registrar's Rules consist of the following five volumes:
Registrar's (Electronic Form) Rules 2012 Volume 1 – Documents delivered in electronic form;
Registrar's Rules 2009 Volume 2 – Documents delivered in paper form;
Registrar's Rules 2009 Volume 3 – Documents (or parts thereof) delivered on a CD-ROM or DVD-ROM;
Registrar's Rules 2009 Volume 4 – Informal correction of a document delivered to the registrar;
Registrar's Rules 2009 Volume 5 – Authentication of a certificate sent by the Registrar by electronic means.

14.3.1 Filing accounts in paper form

Of particular relevance to the filing of accounts on paper at Companies House are the following rules relating to registered number, signatures and the form and content of documents.

Table 14.2 Filing accounts at Companies House

The Registrar's (requirements for paper documents) Rules 2009

Registered number

Paragraph 22(3) of Volume 2 of the amended Registrar's Rules 2009 lists the documents (delivered on paper) which must contain the name and registered number of the company to which the document relates (but only one of the documents filed must show this information).
Only one of the following documents filed must contain the name and registered number of the company:

- copy of balance sheet or abbreviated accounts;
- (where applicable): copy of profit and loss account; copy of directors' report; or directors' remuneration report;
- copy of auditor's report.

The company name or registered number required as above must be in black typescript or handwritten in black ink in a 'prominent position' in the document filed; this does **not**, however, include, for example, the cover of an annual accounts package.

Table 14.2 Filing accounts at Companies House (cont'd)

***Signature** – the following documents (filed in paper form) must be signed by a director:*

- copy of balance sheet;
- abbreviated accounts; or
- annual accounts.

The signature must be applied to the document in a prominent position, **at the end of the balance sheet**.

Form and content of documents:

Generally, paper documents sent to Companies House must state in a prominent position the registered name and number of the company. Paper documents must be:

- on A4 size, plain white paper with a matt finish *(note – Companies House does usually accept accounts on US letter sized paper and off-white paper as long as the document can be scanned legibly to A4)*;
- **black**, clear and legible text, of uniform density; and
- clear and legible bold letters and numbers.

Documents should not be poor lettering or photocopies, carbon copies, or produced from a dot matrix printer *(note – as this may cause problems scanning the documents).*

14.3.1.1 Common reasons for accounts rejections at Companies House

In 2010, Companies House published a document listing the most common reasons why paper accounts had been rejected, which were:

- incorrect statements to the accounts, e.g. referring to the wrong Act (this was more common in 2010 due to the recent change from CA 1985 to CA 2006);
- filing accounts with the same date as previously filed accounts (see amended accounts below);
- signatory name missing on the balance sheet;
- balance sheet signature missing;
- audit exemption statements missing or incorrect; and
- accounting reference date (ARD)/made up date absent or incorrect.

www.companieshouse.gov.uk/about/pdf/commonAccountsRejections.pdf

In response to this, the ICAEW issued a document entitled 'Rejected Accounts' which gives guidance on preventing accounts being rejected by the Registrar:

www.icaew.com/en/technical/financial-reporting/other-reporting-issues/other-uk-regulation/briefing-on-companies-house-rejected-accounts-173847

If such accounts are submitted close to the filing deadline and the corrected accounts cannot be returned before the filing deadline expires, an automatic late filing penalty will be issued. There used to be a grace period of 14 days for accounts that were rejected near the deadline, however this ceased to exist on 1 October 2009.

14.3.2 Filing accounts in electronic form

There are four ways to file accounts electronically at Companies House.

- WebFiling;
- Filing of iXBRL accounts:
  - joint filing with HMRC;
  - electronic filing using enabled accounts production software;
  - electronic filing of iXBRL accounts using enabled company secretarial software or a third party web-based service.

14.3.2.1 WebFiling accounts

Companies House's WebFiling service allows the filing of a number of documents electronically, including (with some restrictions):

- dormant company accounts (DCA) AA02;
- audit exempt abbreviated accounts; and
- audit exempt full accounts.

Audited companies, Community Interest Companies (CIC) and Limited Liability Partnerships (LLP) cannot file annual accounts using the WebFiling service.

The Dormant Company Accounts (DCA) AA02 and the Audit Exempt Abbreviated Accounts are online WebFilings where the information is completed on screen.

Audit Exempt Full Accounts (and the Joint Filing Accounts for joint filing with HMRC – see below) are downloadable templates that are filled in then uploaded to Companies House.

Electronic filing is particularly useful if accounts are filed near to the filing deadline when there is invariably a risk of incurring penalties for late filing in the event that Companies House does not receive the document in time.

Table 14.3 sets out the process for the filing of accounts at Companies House via the WebFiling service.

Table 14.3 WebFiling

Paragraph 6 of Volume 1 of the Registrar's (Electronic Form) Rules 2012

- pre-registration of filing company's details with the Registrar;
- access to the internet;
- use of a security code and registered email address;
- use of a company authentication code.

Accounts delivered to the Registrar of Companies via WebFiling must be in the form of the template supplied for that purpose by the Registrar of Companies as part of the WebFiling facility.
Information must be input into the data input fields on the locally saved PDF copy of the template.
Paragraph 9(3) of Volume 1 of the Registrar's (Electronic Form) Rules 2012

- WebFiled accounts must be in form and substance copies of the actual annual accounts and reports or abbreviated or dormant accounts prepared for the company.

To use WebFiling the company must first register for this service on the Companies House website. WebFiling requires two codes for the submission of data for an individual company:

- a password to access the service (password is linked to the presenter's email address); and
- the Company's Authentication Code (CAC) which is the electronic equivalent of a company's officer's signature (CAC is linked to the company number).

The CAC must be requested via Companies House WebFiling page and it is sent by post to the company's registered office address.

Audit exempt full accounts filing via the WebFiling service uses a PDF template that registered users download and complete offline. A key feature of the template is that it contains in-built checks and help text which assists with avoiding the omission of key information and making calculation errors in the balance sheet and notes.

Once downloaded, the template prompts the user to make choices that define the content of the accounts. The accounts can then be completed offline over a period of time and saved drafts can then, for example, be emailed to colleagues or clients before submitting the final version to Companies House using a company 'authentication code'. The completed template is then saved on the computer as a locked copy of the accounts filed with Companies House.

These accounts are delivered to Companies House by:

- selecting the 'submit' or 'send' button found at the end of the locally saved electronic copy of the template;
- supplying the company's registered number and CAC when prompted; and
- supplying the presenter's email address when prompted.

The Dormant Company Accounts (DCA) AA02 and the audit exempt abbreviated accounts templates that cannot be downloaded must be completed online while the user is logged onto the WebFiling service. It is important to remember that the presenter of a company's accounts must act under the specific authority of that company's directors in delivering the accounts to the Registrar.

A document delivered using WebFiling is considered as received when it is given an envelope number by the Registrar.

14.3.2.2 Joint Filing of accounts with HMRC

The joint filing service which submits iXBRL tagged accounts online to both HMRC and to Companies House can be accessed through the HMRC Online Services page (linked also from the Companies House and gov.uk websites) to download the joint filing accounts template.

A Government Gateway user ID and password is required to access HMRC Online Services and additionally the Company's Authentication Code (CAC) must be entered into the template.

As with the WebFiling, online joint iXBRL filing templates are designed primarily for small audit exempt companies with relatively straightforward financial information.

The intelligent PDF accounts template enables the accounts data to be entered offline and to be saved or printed during completion. It has built-in checks which ensure that the calculations are correct and it also takes into account different filing deadlines thereby enabling timely submissions to both HMRC and Companies House.

The user can select whether they wish to submit full or abbreviated accounts to Companies House. The submission is done directly from the template (not via WebFiling).

If abbreviated accounts are sent to Companies House, this data is extracted from the full accounts data and the full accounts data is held within the template awaiting submission to HMRC.

When HMRC filing is due the full accounts data can be filed; this can be done months after filing accounts with Companies House.

14.3.2.3 Electronic filing of iXBRL accounts at Companies House

If the accounts production software being used produces UK GAAP accounts in iXBRL format then these can be filed directly with Companies Hose electronically.

The accounts can be filed either directly from the accounts production software (if the software includes this feature), or can be uploaded via an enabled company secretarial software package or third party web-based service.

Companies House maintains a list of suitable software packages at:

www.companieshouse.gov.uk/toolsToHelp/accountsSoftware.shtml

The software filing service enables the submission of the following:

- audit exempt full accounts;
- small abbreviated accounts;
- dormant company accounts; and
- audited individual full accounts with a standard auditor's report.

To file accounts using software a company will need a Companies House online filing presenter account (applied for via the Companies House website).

14.4 Filing amended accounts

If it is found that a set of accounts submitted to Companies House is defective (i.e. containing errors or not compliant with a requirement of the Companies Act), then the directors may submit amending financial statements to the Registrar of Companies. This may be because the company has realised that the accounts are defective or because the Registrar has written to the directors to request that they either give a satisfactory explanation for the accounts or prepare revised accounts.

The rules relating to revised accounts are set out in Part 15 of the CA 2006 (s. 454-459) and *The Companies (Revision of Defective Accounts and Reports) Regulations 2008* (SI 2008/373):

www.legislation.gov.uk/uksi/2008/373/contents/made

Revised accounts sent to Companies House must be marked as 'amending'. It is recommended that the 'amending' is very clearly marked (to prevent rejection by Companies House for being made up to the same date as a set of accounts that has previously been filed). The highlighting should not obscure any part of the accounts, however, as they could then be rejected if they do not scan legibly.

The amending accounts must contain the following statements (in a prominent position):

- the revised accounts replace the original accounts for the financial year (specifying it);
- the revised accounts are now the statutory accounts for that year; and
- the revised accounts have been prepared as at the date of the original accounts, and not as at the date of the revision and accordingly do not deal with events between those dates.

The accounts must also contain details (in a prominent position) of:

- the way in which the original accounts did not comply with the requirements of the CA 2006; and *SI 2008/373 part 2 Reg 4*
- any significant amendments made as a result of correcting the defects.

If the original accounts were audited, the amending accounts must contain an audit report on the revised accounts. This report differs from the original report and includes statements of whether:

- in the auditor's opinion, the revised accounts have been properly prepared in accordance with the CA 2006;
- the revised accounts give a true and fair view to the individual balance sheet and profit and loss (consolidated in the case of group accounts), seen *as at the date the original accounts were approved*; and
- the original accounts failed to comply with the requirements of the CA 2006 in the respects identified by the directors. *SI 2008/373 part 2 Reg 5*

Where a revised directors' report is prepared, the report must also state whether, in the auditor's opinion, the information given in that revised report is consistent with the accounts for the financial year.

If the previous set of accounts was not audited, but the revised set is found not to be exempt from audit, the company must also deliver an auditor's report to Companies House within 28 days after the date of revision of the accounts.

The original (defective) accounts will remain on the public record. Removing incorrect documents from the public record requires a court order (unless Companies House, in error, accepted an item which should have been rejected).

Companies House provides further guidance at:

www.companieshouse.gov.uk/infoAndGuide/faq/amendingAccounts.shtml

14.5 Filing accounts with HMRC

A UK Corporation Tax Return for a small limited company (preparing Companies Act or IAS individual accounts) includes form CT600, the accounts and the tax computation together with any accompanying information as required. This must be submitted to HMRC electronically. The accounts forming part of the return must be in iXBRL format (see **14.6** below).

iXBRL tagging of UK statutory financial statements has been required for tax purposes since 2011. It has been mandatory for organisations since accounting periods ending after 31 March 2010 and filing their tax return after 31 March 2011.

If the company chooses to file abbreviated accounts at Companies House, the full statutory accounts must be filed as part of the tax return.

A dormant company will not have to deliver a return unless it is sent a statutory notice to do so. In most cases, if HMRC has been notified that a company is dormant, no notice to deliver a return will be issued.

Overseas companies resident in the UK must deliver the accounts required by a notice to deliver a return in iXBRL. Also a company not resident in the UK, but carrying on a trade in the UK through a permanent establishment, branch or agency in the UK, must deliver any trading and profit and loss account and any balance sheet of the UK establishment, branch or agency required as part of its return in iXBRL format.

14.6 Electronic tagging of accounts (iXBRL)

In March 2006 a review was carried out of HMRC's online services. One of the recommendations of the review, which was supported by government, was that HMRC and Companies House should work together to provide a joint filing facility. In support of these recommendations, Companies House has encouraged online filing wherever possible.

Inline Extensible Business Reporting Language (iXBRL) is an electronic format for embedding XBRL 'tags' into financial statements. XBRL itself is an open and global standard for exchanging business information.

The accounts tagged under iXBRL are still in a format which can be read 'manually' (as opposed to by a computer only): this is what the 'inline' refers to – the tags applied are hidden behind the scenes, in line with the normal text.

Embedding tags into an annual report and accounts document can by performed in a variety of ways:

- using an accounts preparation package which has the tagging facility built in;
- using tagging software to apply the tags to accounts created in a word-processed document; or
- engaging a third party tagging firm or accountant to create the iXBRL file from the word processed document file ('managed tagging').

HMRC maintains a list of approved providers of software and managed tagging providers at:

www.hmrc.gov.uk/efiling/ctsoft_dev.htm

HMRC has produced taxonomies (a dictionary of tags) for UK GAAP and IFRS which set out the available tags to be used in a set of financial statements. The items listed in the taxonomies must be tagged if they are present in any given set of accounts and computations. The tags will be applied to both financial and narrative information.

HMRC has made provision for transitional arrangements which allows companies to use a Minimum Tagging List (for UK GAAP of around 1,200 tags) rather than the Full Taxonomy during the transition period, although companies may adopt full tagging immediately. Full tagging was expected to be mandatory from April 2013. However, in May 2012 HMRC indicated that, following consultation, they now have no plans to move to full tagging.

14.7 Planned changes in accounts filing

As part of the journey towards Companies House's aim of becoming a fully electronic registry, in 2010 Companies House announced that it expected all incorporations and filings of annual returns, accounts and the main company changes would be digital-only (electronic) by March 2013 for the standard company types.

Although mandatory electronic filing at Companies House has been put on hold until the government's moratorium on new regulation for small businesses has ended in 2014, the number of accounts being filed electronically has grown rapidly over the recent past.

The Companies House register is not yet fully electronic, but a significant proportion (almost 60% in December 2012) of the accounts submitted are being filed electronically.

It can only be anticipated that this proportion will increase 'voluntarily' and will, indeed, become a requirement over the coming years.

Chapter 15 The future of UK accounting and financial reporting

15.1 Introduction

For a number of years the Accounting Standards Board (ASB) (and now the FRC) has been working to align the accounting standards used in the UK (UK GAAP) with International Financial Reporting Standards (IFRS). To date IFRS is only mandatory for UK quoted companies although some UK Accounting Standards have been revised to be more consistent with the equivalent IFRS or International Accounting Standard. The outcome of this process will have a significant effect on the application by companies of UK GAAP over the course of the next two to three years.

15.2 Future of UK financial reporting timeline

The table below sets out the recent events in the revision of the financial reporting framework in the UK.

Table 15.1 Development of UK Financial Reporting Framework timeline

August 2009	ASB started the consultation process on the next major element of the convergence process when it issued a Policy Proposal – *The Future of UK GAAP.*
February 2010	The consultation period for the proposals included in *The Future of UK GAAP* ended.
July 2010	Following the review of the responses received during the consultation period by the ASB, in liaison with key stakeholders and UK Department for Business, Innovation and Skills (BIS), the ASB presented some of its key findings.
October 2010	The Future of Financial Reporting in the UK and Republic of Ireland: FRED 43 *Application of Financial Reporting Standards* and FRED 44 *Financial Reporting Standard for Medium-sized Entities* (FRSME) were issued. The proposed date for the introduction of the revised financial reporting framework for the UK and the Republic of Ireland was accounting periods starting on or after 1 July 2013.
March 2011	The Future of Financial Reporting in the UK and Republic of Ireland: FRED 45 *Financial Reporting Standards for Public Benefit Entities* (FRSPBE) was issued.
April 2011	Consultation period ended for FRED 43 and FRED 44.
July 2011	Consultation period ended for FRED 45.
Autumn 2011	Tentative decisions issued by the ASB as elements of the consultation responses received were reviewed and considered. (EU issued proposals in October 2011 which included a specific regime for small companies.)

Table 15.1 Development of UK Financial Reporting Framework timeline (cont'd)	
January 2012	Following the review of the consultation responses and building on the tentative decisions issued in Autumn 2011, the ASB issued: FRED 46 *Application of Financial Reporting Requirements* (draft FRS 100); FRED 47 *Reduced Disclosure Framework* (draft FRS 101); FRED 48 *The Financial Reporting Standard applicable in the UK and Republic of Ireland* (draft FRS 102). FREDs 46 to 48 replaced FREDs 43 to 45. There was no longer proposed to be a separate standard for Public Benefit Entities (PBE). The additional considerations for PBEs set out in the draft FRSPBE, subject to amendments as a result of the consultation, were included in FRED 48. The proposed date for the introduction of the revised financial reporting framework for the UK and the Republic of Ireland set out in FRED 46 was set for accounting periods starting on or after 1 January 2015 although early adoption will be permitted.
July 2012	On 2 July 2012, the FRC replaced the ASB as the prescribed body for issuing standards. As part of the transitional provisions anything done by the ASB or in the process of being done by the ASB in relation to accounting standards is treated as being done by, or continued by the FRC.
October 2012	The FRC published an Exposure Draft: Amendment to FRED 48 (draft FRS 102) *The Financial Reporting Standard applicable in the UK and Republic of Ireland.*
November 2012	The FRC issued FRS 100 *Application of Financial Reporting Requirements* and FRS 101 *Reduced Disclosure Framework.*
Spring 2013 (expected date)	Issue of FRS 102 *The Financial Reporting Standard applicable in the UK and Republic of Ireland.* FRS 102 was approved by the FRC Board on 5 March 2013.

15.3 The New Financial Reporting Framework

The new financial reporting framework for the UK and Ireland is as set out in FRS 100 *Application of Financial Reporting Requirements* which was issued in November 2012.

The framework replaces all FRSs, Statements of Standard Accounting Practice and Urgent Issues Task Force Abstracts with a single FRS – FRS 102 (FRED 48). This FRS is an adaptation of the IFRS for SMEs. FRS 102 is expected in March 2013.

FRS 100 introduces a reduced disclosure framework for the financial reporting by certain qualifying entities* (FRS 101 for those companies applying EU-adopted IFRS and within FRS 102 for those companies applying that standard).

In a slightly amended form, the new financial reporting framework retains the FRSSE; however the FRSSE will be updated if changes are made to EU Directives relating to financial reporting requirements for small companies.

Under the new framework, an entity will either apply the FRSSE, FRS 102 (with or without reduced disclosures) or IFRS (with or without reduced disclosures). The entities that will be able to adopt each set of requirements are set out in table **15.2**.

Table 15.2 New Financial Reporting Framework from FRS 100

	IFRS	Reduced disclosures (FRS 101)	FRS 102	Reduced disclosures (FRS 102)	FRSSE
Small unlisted entities					
Group or individual entity	Optional	Not available	Optional	Not available	Optional
Large or medium sized unlisted entities					
Group consolidated	Optional	Not available	Optional	Not available	Not available
Parent or subsidiary*	Optional	Available	Optional	Available	Not available
Individual entity	Optional	Not available	Optional	Not available	Not available
Listed entities					
Group consolidated	Required	Not available	Not available	Not available	Not available
Parent or subsidiary*	Optional	Available	Optional	Available	Not available
Individual entity	Optional	Not available	Optional	Not available	Not available

* A qualifying entity is a member of a group that prepares publicly available financial statements, which are intended to give a true and fair view, in which that member is consolidated.

Typically a small unlisted company will choose to continue to apply the FRSSE as updated to be in line with the revised EU Directives.

15.4 Implementation date and early adoption

The new financial reporting framework contained in FRS 100 will be mandatory for accounting periods starting on or after 1 January 2015 and, although it is yet to be published, it is expected that FRS 102 will have the same implementation date. Therefore if an entity has a December year end, the first accounting period for which the new standards will be mandatory will be the year ending 31 December 2015. However, it is important to note that on first application, the comparative figures for the prior year will have to be restated to reflect any required changes in accounting policies. Therefore effectively the organisation would be required to account for the transactions of the year to 31 December 2014 under both the current UK GAAP and the new financial reporting framework. Such an entity will also need to consider whether there would be implications for the opening reserves position at 1 January 2014.

Some restatement may be straightforward enough to do retrospectively but for other areas it may be appropriate to amend how the accounting records are kept so the reporting under both frameworks can be achieved with the minimal level of disruption.

Early adoption will be permitted for accounting periods ending on or after 31 December 2012. Subsidiaries of listed companies which, like their parent groups, may currently be applying EU-adopted IFRS basis because of group reporting obligations, might consider early adoption of FRS 101 to reduce disclosures in their own accounts. The impact of FRS 101 and this reduced disclosure framework for such companies is not covered in detail in this book.

However, if the entity is subject to a SORP (Statement of Recommended Practice) which is being revised as a result of the changes in UK GAAP, the new financial reporting framework and the revised SORP must be introduced at the same time.

15.5 What will the format of the financial statements be under FRS 102?

With reference to the latest draft version of FRS 102, a set of financial statements will include the following:

- a **Statement of Financial Position** as at the reporting date; and either:
  - a single **Statement of Comprehensive Income** for the reporting period displaying all items of income and expense recognised during the period including those items recognised in determining profit and loss and items of other comprehensive income; or
  - a separate **Income Statement** and a separate **Statement of Comprehensive Income**;
- a **Statement of Changes in Equity** for the reporting period**;
- a **Statement of Cash flows** for the reporting period; and
- **Notes** comprising a summary of significant accounting policies and other explanatory information.

** if the only changes to equity during the period for which financial statements are presented arise from profit or loss, payment of dividends, corrections of prior period errors and changes in accounting policies, the entity may present a single statement of income and retained earnings in place of the statement of comprehensive income and statement of changes in equity.

The draft of FRS 102 is not prescriptive regarding the title of primary statements. Therefore there would be no requirement to change from 'profit and loss account' and 'balance sheet' if companies preferred these titles.

The line by line differences between current UK GAAP and the proposals which will appear in FRS 102 are not covered in this book.

15.6 The effect on the FRSSE

The FRC has confirmed that the FRSSE will be retained for the foreseeable future. FRS 100 makes a number of 'consequential amendments' to the FRSSE as follows:

1. In the current FRSSE there are a number of references to specific UK Financial Reporting Standards or UITF Abstracts. As all of these will be withdrawn with effect from accounting periods beginning on or after 1 January 2015, the references have been updated to refer to FRS 101 or FRS 102. Currently when applying the FRSSE, if the treatment of a particular transaction is not given in the FRSSE the preparer of the accounts should refer to full UK GAAP for guidance on the appropriate treatment. The same principle will apply going forward (i.e. the preparer will refer to FRS 101 or FRS 102 for guidance). If an entity which applies the FRSSE has adopted an accounting policy for a particular area based on current full UK GAAP there will not be a requirement to revise the accounting policy when the new financial reporting framework is introduced in the UK. It will only be when a type of transaction occurs in the entity for the first time which is not covered by its existing accounting policies that it would be required to refer to FRS 101 or FRS 102 for guidance.
2. The presumed life of goodwill and intangible assets is revised to a presumed five years from the current 20 when an entity is unable to make a reliable estimate of the useful life. (If, for example, an entity is currently using an estimated life of ten years, if there is a justification for the ten years the entity would not be required to reduce the life to five years).
3. Clarification is provided regarding the annual consideration of whether there is any indication that an asset is impaired. (This does not introduce any new requirements as the annual consideration was required under the previous FRSSE).
4. The definitions of related parties are amended to be consistent with those within FRS 102.

15.7 Further changes that may affect financial reporting for smaller entities

15.7.1 Micro companies

Micro companies were defined by the EC in March 2012 in the Amendments to Directive 78/660/ EEC (4th Directive) (www.europarl.europa.eu/sides/getDoc.do?pubRef=-//EP//TEXT+TA+P7-TA-2011-0563+0+DOC+XML+V0//EN&language=EN) as those not exceeding two out of the following three thresholds:

- Turnover €700,000
- Gross assets €350,000
- Employees 10

The EU has now formally approved exemptions which could be available to some of these micro companies.

Now it remains for the UK government to decide whether (and if so, when and how) to bring these exemptions into UK law.

These exemptions which may become available are shown below:

- The micro company would only need to prepare an abridged balance sheet and abridged profit or loss account (with limited disclosure notes) for its members.
- The only disclosures required would be where the company:
  - has acquired its own shares;
  - has outstanding commitments; or
  - has advanced loans to directors.
- The micro company would also be allowed to not recognise any accruals, accrued income, deferred income or prepayments, provided that these do not relate to 'the cost of raw materials and consumables, value adjustments, staff costs and tax'. (Note that cash accounting would not be permitted under these exemptions.)

The annual accounts drawn up in accordance with these exemptions will be regarded as being 'true and fair'.

Furthermore, the abridged profit and loss account would not need to be filed with Companies House.

15.7.2 EC proposals for small companies

A separate EC proposal from October 2011 (http://eur-lex.europa.eu/LexUriServ/LexUriServ.do?uri=CELEX:52011PC0684:EN:NOT) on revisions to the Fourth and Seventh Directives, if passed by the EC, will simplify the disclosures that all small companies are required to make (not just those for micro companies). The proposed updates would be mandatory for all member states (unlike the optional adoption of the reduced micro entity framework).

The small company threshold limits would also be increased to:

- Turnover €10m (currently €8.8m)
- Gross assets €5m (currently €4.4m)
- Employees 50 (currently 50)

(The size limits would be translated into sterling when the law is enacted.)

The most significant part of these proposals is that the law would prevent EU countries from mandating additional disclosures for small companies over and above those specified under EU law. The proposal explains that this 'maximum harmonisation' 'will ensure that companies of the same size benefit from a level playing field across the EU'.

Small company accounts will need to contain the following information. EU countries are not allowed to require anything else beyond:

- abridged balance sheet; and
- abridged profit and loss account

And notes on:

- accounting policies;
- guarantees, commitments, contingencies and arrangements that are not recognised in the balance sheet;
- post-balance sheet events not recognised in the balance sheet;
- long-term and secured debts; and
- related party transactions.

Items such as the directors' report and any other additional notes would not be required. The only disclosure that would still be required would be on the purchase of an entity's own shares.

The proposals are currently being debated within the EC and it is expected that there will be a clearer indication of when, and in what form, the proposals might be enacted by the end of 2013.

A full copy of the proposals can be found at:
http://eur-lex.europa.eu/LexUriServ/LexUriServ.do?uri=CELEX:52011PC0684:EN:NOT

15.7.3 Impact on the FRSSE

It is estimated that a large proportion of entities that currently apply the FRSSE would be classified as 'micro entities' and therefore there is an open question at present as to what would happen with the FRSSE if the UK adopts the exemptions for micros. Would it be worthwhile to maintain a separate accounting standard for smaller entities when it would apply to a significantly smaller number of UK entities? Is there therefore a possibility that 'small', but not 'micro', entities, would instead have to adopt a revised version of FRS 102?

By increasing the limits, the current EC proposals discussed above, would increase the number of companies classified as small in the UK and would also prevent additional disclosures for small entities. In which case a separate standard for small entities may still be beneficial.

If the proposal is approved, however, the FRSSE in its current form will no longer be consistent with UK law and will need to be withdrawn. A revised standard for small entities would need to be developed, should the FRSSE be continued.

Although making additional disclosures mandatory for small UK companies would be prevented by the EC, the draft Directive does not appear to prevent EC countries from specifying recognition and measurement requirements and therefore some of the requirements of the FRSSE could remain in place. In addition, the removal of disclosure requirements could push the FRC to make the new FRSSE more prescriptive on accounting treatments to ensure consistency.

Once the EC proposals are final, it is likely that the FRC will conduct a consultation process into the future of the FRSSE.

Appendices

Appendix A Guidelines and definitions

This appendix gives brief guidelines on statutory definitions, interpretation and analysis. Comment is not necessarily comprehensive but aims to cover those headings or terms that tend to present difficulty in practice for smaller companies. The text contains references to statute and accounting standards from where further guidance may be available.

Definitions are provided by accounting standards, including the FRSSE, as well as the legislation. Although the various Companies Acts have provided a measure of standardisation for company accounts (for example, in the form of prescriptive formats and codification of accounting rules and principles), legislation often only provides limited guidance in terms of definition or interpretation.

Most of the problems that arise in practice concern interpretation of statutory intent. Over the years, accounting standards have increasingly provided a measure of guidance and interpretation. Nevertheless, difficulties often concern topics such as: presentation, analysis of expenses, categorisation or composition of statutory headings, or simply accounts presentation.

Where there are no definitions or rules laid down by the Companies Act or provided by accounting standards (including IAS), it is necessary to:

- refer to definitions in accounting standards (FRSSE, FRSs and SSAPs);
- determine a reasonable interpretation of the requirement;
- ensure the proposed interpretation is sensible and appropriate to the business; and
- adopt the interpretation consistently from year to year.

1 Accounts

Definitions of statutory terms concerning a company's accounts, prepared to show a 'true and fair view', are set out below.

1.1 Annual report

The annual 'directors' report' of a company. *s. 415*

The directors of a company must prepare a directors' report for each financial year of the company. For a financial year in which the company is a parent company (and the directors of the company prepare group accounts), the directors' report must be a consolidated report (a 'group directors' report') relating to the undertakings included in the consolidation.

For small companies, an exemption is available from filing the directors' report with the Registrar of Companies.

1.2 Annual accounts *s. 471*

Individual accounts – the accounts of a company prepared by the directors, for each financial year: *s. 394*

- comprising a balance sheet (as at the last day of the year), a profit and loss account, and notes to the accounts; *s. 396*
- showing a 'true and fair view'; and *s. 393*
- complying with the provisions of CA 2006 and SI 2008/409 Sch 1 (small companies) (as to form, content and additional note information). *s. 396*

Individual accounts must be prepared in accordance with the appropriate framework and accordingly
s. 395 may be prepared:

- in accordance with CA 2006 s. 396 ('Companies Act individual accounts'); or
- in accordance with international accounting standards ('IAS individual accounts').

Group accounts – the accounts prepared, in addition to 'individual accounts', by the directors of a
s. 404(1) parent company:

- comprising consolidated accounts (consolidated balance sheet and consolidated profit and loss account of the parent and its 'subsidiary undertakings' and related notes); and
- showing a 'true and fair view' of the consolidated undertakings as a whole (so far as concerns members of the parent company).

s. 403 Group accounts must (with exceptions) be prepared either:

- in accordance with SI 2008/409 Sch 6 (Small companies) or SI 2008/410 Sch 6 (Large and medium-sized companies) ('Companies Act group accounts'); or
- in accordance with international accounting standards or if required by Article 4 of the IAS Regulation ('IAS group accounts').

Group accounts exemptions – the following exemptions from preparing group accounts are available:

- eligible small groups (CA 2006 s. 383) – see **Chapter 9**;
- parent companies included in accounts of larger EEA group (CA 2006 s. 400);
- parent companies included in accounts of larger non-EEA group (CA 2006 s. 401); and
- if all subsidiary undertakings excluded from consolidation (CA 2006 s. 402).

Entitlement to exemptions in all cases is determined upon conditions – see **Chapter 9**.

IAS accounts – accounts ('IAS individual accounts' or 'IAS group accounts') prepared in accordance with international accounting standards adopted by the EU (EC Regulation No. 1606/2002).

Annual accounts of small companies – the individual or group accounts of small companies, as defined, prepared in accordance with the special provisions for small companies set out in CA 2006
s. 471 and SI 2008/409 Schedules 1 and 6.

A company's 'annual accounts', in relation to a financial year, means the company's individual accounts for that year (CA 2006 s. 394) and any group accounts prepared by the company for that year (CA 2006 s. 398–399). CA 2006 s. 408 provides an option to omit an individual parent company's profit and loss account from annual accounts where the company prepares group accounts.

In the case of an unquoted company, its 'annual report and accounts' for a financial year are:

- its annual accounts;
- the directors' report; and
- the auditor's report on those accounts and on the consistency of the directors' report with those accounts (unless the company is exempt from audit).

Individual profit and loss account of parent company – the profit and loss account of a parent
s. 408 company:

- prepared in addition to, but omitted from, 'group accounts'; and
- omitting the supplemental information required by CA 2006 s. 411 (information about employee numbers and costs).

The fact of omission and the amount of the parent company's profit or loss for the year must be disclosed in group accounts, and the individual profit and loss account of the parent company must still be approved by the board of directors (in accordance with CA 2006 s. 414(1)).

Notes to the accounts – notes forming part of the annual accounts (or annexed thereto), giving information required by any provision of CA 2006 or international accounting standards. *s. 472*

Income and expenditure account – the equivalent of a profit and loss account in the case of the undertaking not trading for profit. *s. 474(2)*

1.3 Statutory accounts

The accounts that must be prepared for members and/or filed with the Registrar of Companies. These will be either:

- annual accounts, together with the directors' report and also (if required) auditor's report; or *s. 444*
- abbreviated accounts, prepared in accordance with CA 2006 s. 444(3) or s. 445(3), together with (if appropriate) special auditor's report, and directors' statement.

(As explained in **Chapter 8**, some companies can file abbreviated accounts with the Registrar of Companies. This set will be prepared in addition to the full accounts prepared for members.)

1.4 Abbreviated accounts

The accounts prepared in accordance with special provisions for small (or medium-sized) companies, as the case may be – see **Chapter 8**.

For small-sized companies the copies of accounts and reports delivered to the Registrar of Companies must be copies of the company's annual accounts and reports, except that where the company prepares Companies Act accounts the directors may deliver to the Registrar of Companies 'abbreviated accounts', these being a copy of a balance sheet drawn up in accordance with regulations made by the Secretary of State; items as may be specified by the regulations may also be omitted from the copy profit and loss account delivered to the Registrar of Companies. The relevant regulations are SI 2008/409 for small companies. *s. 444(3)*

Where a medium-sized company prepares Companies Act accounts, the directors may deliver to the Registrar of Companies 'abbreviated accounts', these being a copy of the company's annual accounts for the financial year but where the profit and loss account includes items combined in accordance with regulations made by the Secretary of State, and where items as authorised by the regulations are omitted. The relevant regulations are SI 2008/410 for medium-sized companies. *s. 445(3)*

1.5 Company accounts – charities

The accounts of a charity that is a company must be either:

- 'Companies Act individual accounts'; or *s. 394*
- 'Companies Act group accounts'. *s. 398*

An incorporated charity is not able to prepare accounts in accordance with IAS.

The format of accounts of a charity that is a company is set out in the Statement of Recommended Practice 'Accounting and Reporting by Charities (revised 2005)'.

2 Profit and loss account

Profit and loss account Formats 1 and 3 headings include 'Cost of sales', 'Distribution costs' and 'Administrative expenses'. Allocation of costs and overheads often requires careful consideration, but, in practice, it has been found that expenses not conveniently or accurately falling under one of these statutory headings can be attributed to additional, more appropriate, headings. For example, a service or retail organisation may consider most of its overhead expenditure to be of a general nature rather than specifically 'distribution' or 'administrative'. Whilst the statutory format headings form the basic framework for the allocation of costs, the nature of the particular business will often suggest that a more informative (and, perhaps, more detailed) approach can be adopted.

2.1 Turnover

'The amounts derived from the provision of goods and services falling within the company's ordinary activities, after deduction of trade discounts, value added tax and any other taxes based on the amounts so derived.' *s. 474(1)*

Commission or rental income, for example, where forming part of the principal activity of the company, would be included in turnover. The heading 'Turnover' could in such cases be amended to a more appropriate title (e.g. 'Commission income' or 'Income from investment properties') in view of the 'special nature of the company's business'. SI 2008/408. *Sch 1.4(1)*

Turnover (or 'sales') is defined by FRS 5 as the revenue resulting from exchange transactions under which a seller supplies to customers the goods and services that it is in business to provide, as part of its 'operating activities'. Sales of fixed assets are not normally revenue transactions giving rise to 'turnover'. *FRS 5*

Application Note G to FRS 5 and UITF 40 provide guidance on the principles of revenue recognition and the treatment of turnover (see **8** (below)).

2.2 Costs in formats 1 and 3

Costs and overheads may be attributed to the headings 'Cost of sales', 'Distribution costs' and 'Administrative expenses'. There is no statutory interpretation of these items.

2.3 Other operating income

'Other operating income' will include all other income not arising from turnover or the company's principal activities, except income dealt with elsewhere in the formats (e.g. dividends or interest, etc. receivable). It might include: commissions, rental income, profit on disposal of fixed assets or foreign currency trading gains.

2.4 Own work capitalised (Formats 2 and 4)

The gross amount of items capitalised in the construction of a company's own tangible fixed assets, including direct labour, materials and overheads.

2.5 Other external charges (Formats 2 and 4)

'Other external charges' may include other production-related costs, other costs related directly to generating turnover, or subcontractors' costs and costs of self-employed consultants.

2.6 Other operating charges (Formats 2 and 4)

'Other operating charges' may include other overhead expenses (including audit and professional fees), other charges relating to ordinary activities or foreign currency trading losses.

In practice, the two headings 'Other external charges' and 'Other operating charges' have often been interpreted as alternatives. However defined, they should be used consistently.

2.7 Staff costs

CA 2006 s. 411 ('Information about employee numbers and costs') applies to companies other than those subject to the small companies regime.

'Staff costs' are wages and salaries, social security costs and other pension costs paid or payable to, or incurred by, the company on behalf of persons employed under contracts of service, i.e. employees of the company (including directors who are employees). This heading will not include subcontractors' costs or consultants, etc.

Social security costs: company (employers') contributions to any compulsory state, social security, National Insurance, or pension scheme, fund or arrangement.

Other pension costs: all other costs incurred by a company towards employee pensions (for example, company pension scheme).

The disclosure of the average number of employees within appropriate categories is to be determined by the directors 'having regard to the manner in which the company's activities are organised'. The number of employees included in this disclosure should be correlated with the amount disclosed for 'staff costs'.

2.8 Income from shares in group undertakings

Dividends received and receivable:

- parent company – from subsidiary undertakings;
- fellow subsidiary – from fellow group undertakings; and
- consolidated P&L account – from non-consolidated subsidiaries.

(In group accounts) the group's shares of earnings of non-consolidated (equity accounted) subsidiaries.

2.9 Income from participating interests

Individual company – income (e.g. dividends received and receivable) from shares in associated companies (FRS 9), share of profits from partnerships, unincorporated associations.

Consolidated P&L account – group share of pre-tax profit (or loss) of associated companies.

2.10 Auditor's remuneration

Audit fee and related expenses charged in the accounts, including estimated money value of any benefits in kind, should be disclosed. *s. 494*

Companies (Disclosure of Auditor Remuneration and Liability Limitation Agreements) Regulations 2008 (SI 2008/389) reg 4 as amended by SI 2011/2198 sets out the disclosure requirements concerning the remuneration of auditors of small and medium-sized companies.

SI 2008/489, reg 4(1–2) A small or medium-sized company must disclose in a note to the annual accounts the amount of any remuneration receivable by the company's auditor for the auditing of those accounts. Where the remuneration includes benefits in kind, the nature and estimated money-value of those benefits must also be disclosed in a note.

SI 2008/489, reg 4(3) Separate disclosure is required for separate firms of auditors, for example where there is a change of auditor during the year.

Remuneration paid to an auditor for non-audit work must also be disclosed by companies other than small and medium sized companies – see SI 2008/489 as amended by *The Companies (Disclosure of Auditor Remuneration and Liability Limitation Agreements)(Amendment) Regulations 2011* (SI 2011/2198).

2.11 Interest payable and similar charges

The following might be included under this profit and loss account heading:

- Bank loan and overdraft interest, interest on other loans, interest on finance leases, hire-purchase interest, commitment fees, factoring charges, group interest (less interest capitalised).
- Dividends payable in respect of certain shares (for example, preference shares) treated as financial liabilities under FRS 25 (see 4 (below)).
- Foreign currency losses arising from financing. (Gains of a similar nature may be included under 'Other interest receivable and similar income'.)

The following definitions (2.12–2.19) are based on the definitions contained in FRS 3 *Reporting financial performance.*

2.12 Ordinary activities

Any activities which are undertaken by a reporting entity as part of its business and such related activities in which the reporting entity engages in furtherance of, incidental to, or arising from, these activities.

Ordinary activities include the effects on the reporting entity of any event in the various environments in which it operates, including the political, regulatory, economic and geographical environments, irrespective of the frequency or unusual nature of the events.

2.13 Continuing operations

Operations other than 'discontinued operations'.

2.14 Acquisitions

Operations of the reporting entity that are acquired in the period.

2.15 Discontinued operations

Operations of the reporting entity that are sold or terminated and that satisfy *all* of the following conditions:

- the sale or termination is completed either in the period or before the earlier of three months after the commencement of the subsequent period and the date on which the financial statements are approved;
- if a termination, the former activities have ceased permanently;

- the sale or termination has a material effect on the nature and focus of the reporting entity's operations and represents a material reduction in its operating facilities resulting either from its withdrawal from a particular market (whether class of business or geographical) or from a material reduction in turnover in the reporting entity's continuing markets; and
- the assets, liabilities, results of operations and activities are clearly distinguishable, physically, operationally and for financial reporting purposes.

2.16 Exceptional items

Material items which derive from events or transactions that fall within the ordinary activities of the reporting entity and which individually or, if of a similar type, in aggregate, need to be disclosed by virtue of their size or incidence if the financial statements are to give a true and fair view.

Exceptional items should be attributed to continuing or discontinued operations and should be disclosed with adequate description of the nature of the item.

Other than the three specific examples noted below, exceptional items should not be aggregated on the face of the profit and loss account but should each be included within its natural statutory format heading or relevant FRS 3 heading.

The following exceptional items should be disclosed separately on the face of the profit and loss account:

- profits and losses on the sale or termination of an operation;
- costs of a fundamental reorganisation or restructuring having a material effect on the nature and focus of the reporting entity's operations; and
- profits and losses on the disposal of fixed assets.

These 'super exceptional' items should be shown after operating profit and before interest, and included under the appropriate heading of continuing or discontinued operations.

2.17 Extraordinary items

Material items possessing a high degree of abnormality which arise from events or transactions that fall outside the ordinary activities of the reporting entity and which are not expected to recur. They do not include exceptional items nor do they include prior period items merely because they relate to a prior period.

Extraordinary items are extremely rare. Although it remains a statutory format heading (see **6.6** and **Table 6.5**), the extraordinary item has effectively been abolished by accounting standards.

2.18 Prior period adjustments

Material adjustments applicable to prior periods arising from changes in accounting policies or from the correction of fundamental errors. Fundamental errors in a prior periods' accounts are of such significance as to destroy the true and fair view and hence the validity of those accounts. Normal recurring adjustments or corrections of accounting estimates made in prior periods are not to be accounted for as prior period adjustments. Prior period adjustments should be accounted for by restating comparative figures and adjusting the opening balance of reserves.

2.19 Total recognised gains and losses

The total of all gains and losses of the reporting entity that are recognised in a period and are attributable to shareholders.

3 Balance sheet

Commentary on selected balance sheet headings, including guidelines on the analysis of debtors and creditors, is set out below.

3.1 Fixed assets

'Fixed assets' include assets and property which cannot easily be converted into cash (i.e. not current assets). This includes tangible fixed assets, investments and intangible assets such as goodwill.

Assets awaiting disposal: A fixed asset intended for disposal at the balance sheet date and not intended for use on a continuing basis in the company's activities may be reclassified as a 'current asset'. (This does not apply to assets which it is intended to replace in the normal course of business).

'Development costs' may be capitalised in 'special [undefined] circumstances'. Otherwise, 'costs of research' must not be treated as an asset.

'Preliminary expenses' and 'expenses of, and commission on, any issue of shares or debentures' may not be treated as assets. SI 2008/409. *Sch 1.3(2)*

3.2 Goodwill

'Amounts representing goodwill shall only be included to the extent that goodwill was acquired for valuable consideration' (SI 2008/409 Sch 1 – balance sheet format Note 2). Any goodwill valued and created by the company itself, therefore, cannot be capitalised and included in a company's balance sheet.

Acquired goodwill should be systematically depreciated over a period (chosen by the directors) not exceeding the useful economic life of the goodwill. The period of write-off and the reasons for choosing that period must be disclosed. SI 2008/409. *Sch 1.22*

The above considerations do not apply to goodwill arising on consolidation.

3.3 Tangible fixed assets

The SI 2008/409 Schedule 1 balance sheet format heading B II 2 for small companies is 'plant and machinery etc.'

Otherwise, in practice, there is some latitude in the formats generally with headings: for example, 'equipment' would not generally be included in 'plant and machinery' but may be aggregated with 'motor vehicles'. Strict interpretation would not allow, for example, 'plant and machinery' to be changed to 'plant and equipment', particularly in a company where the main activity is manufacturing. However, in a situation where 'equipment' is immaterial, this might acceptably be aggregated with plant and machinery under a heading 'plant, machinery and equipment'. Additional headings may be given but doing so increases the amount of disclosure required.

'Payments on account' and 'Assets in course of construction' have to be shown separately from other items but individually may be aggregated.

3.4 Current assets

Assets that can reasonably be expected to be converted into cash within one year in the normal course of business. Current assets include cash, debtors, stock, short term investments, prepaid expenses and other liquid assets that can be readily converted to cash.

3.5 Stock

A company's merchandise, raw materials, and finished and unfinished products which have not yet been sold. These are considered current assets since they can be converted into cash quite easily.

Stock is generally valued at the lower of cost and net realisable value. The basis of arriving at the cost of 'stock' must be a reasonable approximation to actual cost (appropriate, in the opinion of the directors, to the circumstances of the company), e.g. FIFO (first in, first out), weighted average or other similar method. SI 2008/409. *Sch 1.28*

3.6 Analysis of debtors and creditors

The guidelines below indicate how certain of the 'debtors' and 'creditors' headings are made up. *Materiality* should be considered in any attempt to distinguish between the various categories, as excessive accuracy or refinement may not be necessary.

Amounts owing by group or any associated undertakings should be separately identified and disclosed.

Amounts falling due after more than one year should be separately analysed for each of the headings.

Debtors

Trade debtors

Will generally comprise:

- sales ledger balances (amounts invoiced to customers);
- purchase ledger debit balances;
- sales invoices/credit notes accrued; less
- provision for bad debts or credits for returns, cash discounts, etc.

Prepayments and accrued income

Will include:

- prepaid items;
- accrued income; and
- deferred tax assets (unless separately disclosed).

Other debtors

Debtors other than the above and debtors not otherwise separately disclosed; for example:

- debtors arising from non-trading activities;
- loans and advances; and
- proceeds due from sale of fixed assets.

Creditors

Trade creditors

Trade creditors are liabilities to pay for goods or services that have been received or supplied and that have been invoiced or formally agreed with the supplier. They will generally comprise: *FRS 12*

- purchase ledger (or equivalent) balances;
- sales ledger credit balances; and
- trade invoices (for purchases) accrued.

Generally, 'trade creditor' items will meet both of the following requirements:

- *expenditure has been incurred as part of the normal business activities of the company* (*e.g. purchase of goods, overhead expenditure, capital expenditure, etc.*); *and*
- *an invoice has been received dated as at or before the year end; late invoices* (*i.e. received after year end but dated before it*) *would normally be included in this heading.*

Taxation and social security

Includes liabilities for VAT, NIC, PAYE and excise duties.

Current corporation tax is normally separately identified under a heading such as 'Corporation tax'.

Accruals

Accruals are liabilities to pay for goods or services that have been received or supplied before the year end, but that have not been paid for, invoiced or formally agreed with the supplier. Examples
FRS 12 include:

- estimated accruals where invoice not received;
- capital expenditure accruals;
- bonuses, accrued remuneration; and
- accrued holiday pay *(not commonly used in UK GAAP accounts).*

Generally, 'accruals' items will meet both of the following requirements:

- *expenditure has been incurred before year end but the related invoice is not dated until after year end* (*or due payment date is after year end if no invoice will be received*) (*compare 'trade creditors'*); *and*
- *the amount and payment date of the item can be determined with reasonable certainty.*

Other creditors

Creditors, other than above including:

- short-term loans; and
- loans from directors (where not shown elsewhere).

Dividends payable

Unpaid final dividends approved by the members but unpaid are normally shown under a separate heading.

3.7 Cash at bank and in hand; bank loans and overdrafts

The heading 'Cash at bank and in hand' comprises the amounts as recorded in the company's accounting records, not those as shown necessarily in the bank statements.

Bank balances and bank overdrafts, etc. should not be offset to show a net balance *unless* there is a legal right of set-off.

Cash is defined in FRS 1 (revised 1996) *Cash flow statements* as 'cash in hand and deposits repayable on demand with any qualifying financial institution, less overdrafts from any qualifying financial institution repayable on demand. Deposits are repayable on demand if they can be withdrawn at any time without notice and without penalty or if a maturity or period of notice of not more than 24 hours or one working day has been agreed. Cash includes cash in hand and deposits denominated in foreign currencies'.

3.8 Provisions for liabilities

A 'provision' is a liability of uncertain timing or amount, to be settled by the transfer of economic benefits. FRS 12

'Liabilities include any amount retained as reasonably necessary for the purpose of providing for any liability, the nature of which is clearly defined and that is either likely to be incurred, or certain to be incurred but uncertain as to amount or as to the date on which it will arise.' s. 682

3.9 Contingent assets and liabilities

A contingent asset is a possible asset that arises from past events and whose existence will be confirmed only by the occurrence of one or more uncertain future events not wholly within the entity's control.

Contingent assets are not included as assets in the balance sheet, but may be disclosed by way of note.

A contingent liability is:

- a possible obligation that arises from past events and whose existence will be confirmed only by the occurrence of one or more uncertain future events not wholly within the entity's control; or
- a present obligation that arises from past events but is not recognised because:
  - it is not probable that a transfer of economic benefits will be required to settle the obligation; or
  - the amount of the obligation cannot be measured with sufficient reliability.

Contingent liabilities are not recognised on the balance sheet as liabilities but should be disclosed by way of note.

3.10 Taxation

The two balance sheet format headings for 'Other creditors' including taxation and social security (Creditors) and Taxation, including deferred taxation (within 'Provision for liabilities') may be contrasted as follows.

'Other creditors' including taxation and social security must be analysed between:

- taxation and social security – including corporation tax, VAT, ACT payable on proposed dividends, PAYE and social security payable, and excise duties; and
- other creditors – including any other sundry creditors (but not proposed dividends, the recognition of which are prohibited [FRS 21]).

'Provision for liabilities' will include any provision for deferred taxation (separately disclosed).

4 Financial instruments

FRS 4 *Capital instruments* dealt with the classification, presentation and disclosure of capital instruments. For accounting periods beginning on or after 1 January 2005, FRS 4 has generally been superseded by FRS 25 (IAS 32) *Financial Instruments: Presentation* (other than for entities adopting the FRSSE).

Many of the situations envisaged by FRS 25 (and FRS 4) may not be encountered by small companies and are not covered in the FRSSE.

Basically, every financial instrument or constituent part under FRS 25 is recognised as a 'financial asset', a 'financial liability' or an 'equity instrument'. The definitions set out here (in **4.1–4.5**) are based on those contained in FRS 25 or FRSSE (effective April 2008).

As a result of FRS 25, certain shares (such as Preference shares) that were previously accounted for as 'share capital' are classified as 'financial liabilities'. A preference share will be a financial liability where it provides for redemption for a fixed (or determinable) amount, being either (a) mandatory redemption, or (b) with the right to redemption at or after a particular date. While no longer presented as 'share capital', the legal form, status and terms of such preference shares would remain unaffected.

4.1 Financial instrument

A financial instrument is any contract that gives rise to a financial asset of one entity and a financial liability or equity instrument of another entity.

4.2 Financial asset

A financial asset is any asset that is:

- ***cash;***
- ***an equity instrument of another entity;***
- ***a contractual right to receive cash or another financial asset from another entity*** or to exchange financial assets or financial liabilities with another entity under conditions that are potentially favourable to the entity; or
- ***a contract that will or may be settled in the entity's own equity instruments*** and is either (a) a *non-derivative* for which the entity is or may be obliged to receive a variable number of the entity's own equity instruments; or (b) *a derivative* that will or may be settled other than by the exchange of a fixed amount of cash or another financial asset for a fixed number of the entity's own equity instruments. For this purpose the entity's own equity instruments do not include instruments that are themselves contracts for the future receipt or delivery of the entity's own equity instruments.

4.3 Financial liability

A financial liability is any liability that is:

- ***a contractual obligation*** to deliver cash or another financial asset to another entity or to exchange financial assets or financial liabilities with another entity under conditions that are potentially unfavourable to the entity; or
- ***a contract that will or may be settled in the entity's own equity instruments*** and is either (a) a *non-derivative* for which the entity is or may be obliged to deliver a variable number of the entity's own equity instruments; or (b) *a derivative* that will or may be settled other than by the exchange of a fixed amount of cash or another financial asset for a fixed number of the entity's own equity instruments. For this purpose the entity's own equity instruments do not include instruments that are themselves contracts for the future receipt or delivery of the entity's own equity instruments.

4.4 Equity instrument

An equity instrument is any contract that evidences a residual interest in the assets of an entity after deducting all of its liabilities.

4.5 Equity instrument granted

The right (conditional or unconditional) to an equity instrument of the entity conferred by the entity on another party, under a share-based payment arrangement.

4.6 Fair value

Fair value is the amount for which an asset could be exchanged, or a liability settled, between knowledgeable, willing parties in an arm's length transaction.

4.7 Derivative or Derivative Financial Instrument

A 'derivative financial instrument' is a financial instrument that derives its price or rate from some underlying item (for example equities, bonds, commodities, interest rates, exchange rates, and stock market or other indices). Derivative financial instruments include futures, options, forward contracts, interest rate and currency swaps, interest rate caps, collars and floors, forward interest rate agreements, commitments to purchase shares or bonds, note issuance facilities and letters of credit.

5 Alternative bases of accounting

CA 2006 permits two bases of accounting – historical cost accounting rules and alternative accounting rules. A company may choose whichever basis it wishes to follow and may use different bases within the same set of accounts; it is common practice, for example, to prepare accounts on a historical cost basis, but to revalue properties or investments.

Companies may, therefore, prepare accounts:

- on the pure historical cost convention;
- on the historical cost convention modified to include certain assets at valuation; or
- on the current cost convention.

Alternative methods of valuation permitted under the 'alternative accounting rules' and as set out in SI 2008/409 are illustrated in **Table A**.

Table A Alternative methods of valuation

Fixed assets	(Sch 1.17–22)	
Primary method of valuation	***Alternative method of valuation ('Alternative accounting rules')***	
Historical cost of purchase or production, less any provision for depreciation or diminution in value		
Intangible fixed assets, other than goodwill	Current cost	(Sch 1.32(1))
Tangible fixed assets	Market value (as at the date of their last valuation)	

Table A Alternative methods of valuation (cont'd)

	or	
	Current cost	(Sch 1.32(2))
Investments (fixed assets)	Market value (as at the date of their last valuation)	
	or	
	Directors' valuation (or any basis which the directors consider to be appropriate in the circumstances; the method of valuation and the reasons for adopting it must be disclosed)	(Sch 1.32(3))
Current assets		(Sch 1.23–24)
Primary method of valuation	***Alternative method of valuation ('Alternative accounting rules')***	
Cost (purchase price or production cost – other than distribution costs) or net realisable value, if lower		
Investments (current assets)	Current cost	(Sch 1.32(4))
Stocks	Current cost	(Sch 1.32(5))

5.1 Purchase price

SI 2008/409 Sch 1.27

Includes any consideration, whether in cash or otherwise, and also any incidental expenses.

5.2 Production cost

SI 2008/409 Sch 1.27

The price of raw materials and consumables together with costs directly attributable to the production of the asset; a reasonable proportion of indirect costs (relating to the period of production); and interest on capital borrowed to finance the production of the asset (to the extent that it is accrued during the period of production).

5.3 Revaluation reserve

SI 2008/409 Sch 1.35

This is the amount arising from a revaluation of fixed assets. The difference between the amount of any item determined according to one of the alternative accounting rules and the amount at which it would be determined on the historical cost accounting rules should be debited or credited, as applicable, to a 'revaluation reserve'.

6 Groups – parent and subsidiary undertakings

The principal definitions for accounting purposes for a parent company and its subsidiaries, which cover 'undertakings' and not just 'bodies corporate', are set out below.

s. 474

A group comprises a parent undertaking and its subsidiary undertakings.

A company is a 'subsidiary' of another company, its 'holding company', if that other company:

- holds a majority of the voting rights in it; or
- is a member of it and has the right to appoint or remove a majority of its board of directors; or
- is a member of it and controls alone, pursuant to an agreement with other members, a majority of the voting rights in it; or
- if it is a 'subsidiary' of a company that is itself a subsidiary of that other company. *s. 1159(1)*

A company is a 'wholly-owned subsidiary' of another company if it has no members except that other and that other's wholly-owned subsidiaries or persons acting on behalf of that other company or its wholly-owned subsidiaries. *s. 1159(2)*

An undertaking is a 'parent undertaking' in relation to another undertaking (*'a subsidiary undertaking'*) *if*:

- it holds a majority of the voting rights in the undertaking; or
- it is a member of the undertaking and has the right to appoint or remove a majority of its board of directors; or
- it has the right to exercise a dominant influence over the undertaking:
  - by virtue of provisions contained in the undertaking's articles;
  - by virtue of a control contract; or
- it is a member of the undertaking and controls alone, pursuant to an agreement with other shareholders or members, a majority of the voting rights in the undertaking. *s. 1162(2)*

An undertaking is treated as a member of another undertaking:

- if any of its subsidiary undertakings is a member of that undertaking; or
- if any shares in that other undertaking are held by a person acting on behalf of the undertaking or any of its subsidiary undertakings. *s. 1162(3)*

An undertaking is also a parent undertaking in relation to another undertaking (a subsidiary undertaking) if:

- it has the power to exercise, or actually exercises, a dominant influence or control over it; or
- it and the subsidiary undertaking are managed on a unified basis. *s. 1162(4)*

An 'undertaking' means: *s. 1161(1)*

- a body corporate or partnership; or
- an unincorporated association carrying on a trade or business, with or without a view to profit.

'Fellow subsidiary undertakings' are undertakings which are subsidiary undertakings of the same parent undertaking but are not parent undertakings or subsidiary undertakings of each other. *s. 1161(4)*

'Group undertaking' means an undertaking which is: *s. 1161(5)*

- a parent undertaking or subsidiary undertaking of that undertaking; or
- a subsidiary undertaking of any parent undertaking of that undertaking.

A *'participating interest'* is an interest in an undertaking (other than one which is a group undertaking) which is held on a long-term basis (generally, an equity interest in excess of 20 per cent) for the purpose of securing a contribution to activities by the exercise of control or influence arising from that interest. *FRS 2*

An interest in shares includes:

- an interest which is convertible into an interest in shares; and
- an option to acquire shares or any such interest. SI 2008/409 Sch 8(8), FRS 9

An interest held on behalf of an undertaking shall be treated as held by it.

In the statutory balance sheet and profit and loss formats 'participating interest' does not include an interest in a group undertaking.

An 'associated undertaking' means an undertaking in which an undertaking, included in the consolidation, has a participating interest and over whose operating and financial policy it exercises a significant influence, and which is not:

- a subsidiary undertaking of the parent company; or
- a joint venture.

SI 2008/409, Sch 6.19 Where an undertaking holds 20 per cent or more of the voting rights in another undertaking, it is presumed to exercise such 'significant influence' over it unless the contrary is shown.

SI 2008/409, Sch 6.18 *A 'joint venture'* may be dealt with in group accounts by the method of proportional consolidation. A 'joint venture' is an undertaking, which (not being a body corporate or subsidiary undertaking of the parent company) is managed jointly by two or more undertakings, one of which is included in a consolidation.

References to 'shares' are references to:

- allotted shares (for an undertaking with a share capital);
- rights to share in the capital of the undertaking (for an undertaking with capital but no share capital); or
- interests:
  (a) conferring any right to share in the profits or liability to contribute to the losses of the undertaking; or
  (b) giving rise to an obligation to contribute to the debts or expenses of the undertaking in the event of a winding-up (undertaking without capital).

s. 1161(2), FRS 9

7 The substance of transactions

7.1 Determining the substance of transactions

FRS 5 *Reporting the substance of transactions* requires that accounts should represent faithfully the commercial effects of the transactions and other events they purport to represent.

The scope of FRS 5 extends to the transactions of an entity, subject only to certain specific exclusions, where the financial statements are intended to give a true and fair view of the entity's financial position and profit or loss for a period. Where transactions are straightforward and their substance and commercial effect are readily apparent, applying established accounting practices will usually be sufficient to ensure that such transactions are appropriately reported in the accounts. FRS 5 affects mainly those more complex transactions whose substance may not be readily apparent.

Under CA 2006, SI 2008/409 Sch 1.9 specifies that the directors of a company must, in determining how amounts are presented within items in the profit and loss account and balance sheet, have regard to the substance of the reported transaction or arrangement, in accordance with generally accepted accounting principles or practice.

7.2 Principle of 'substance over form'

Transactions should be accounted for in accordance with their substance and not merely their legal form, since the latter may not fully indicate the commercial effect of the arrangements entered into. FRS 5 was introduced to address the issue of 'off balance sheet financing' where complex arrangements were developed, the result of which was (invariably deliberately) that the legal form as reported in the accounts was not in accordance with the commercial effect of the arrangement. The most widely recognised effect was the omission of liabilities from the balance sheet.

A reporting entity's accounts should report the substance of the transactions into which it has entered. In determining the substance of a transaction, all its aspects and implications should be identified and greater weight given to those more likely to have a commercial effect in practice. A series of transactions that achieves or is designed to achieve an overall commercial effect should be viewed as a whole.

Some arrangements within groups give as much effective control over another entity as if that entity were a subsidiary. A 'quasi-subsidiary' of a reporting entity is a company, trust, partnership or other vehicle that, although not fulfilling the definition of a subsidiary, is directly or indirectly controlled by the reporting entity and gives rise to benefits for that entity which are in substance no different from those that would arise were the vehicle a subsidiary. Quasi-subsidiaries should therefore be included in statutory group accounts.

Examples of complex transactions are given in the Application Notes included in FRS 5. Those transactions may be summarised as follows.

1. *Consignment stock* – Consignment stock is stock held by one party but legally owned by another, on terms that give the stockholder the right to sell the stock in the normal course of its business or, at its option, to return it unsold to the legal owner.
2. *Sale and repurchase agreements* – Sale and repurchase agreements are arrangements under which assets are sold by one party to another on terms that provide for the seller to repurchase the asset in certain circumstances.
3. *Factoring of debts* – Factoring of debts takes a variety of forms of obtaining finance, sales ledger administration services or protection from bad debts.
4. *Securitised assets* – Securitisation is a means by which providers of finance fund a specific block of assets rather than the general business of a company. Securitised assets have included household mortgages, credit card balances, hire purchase loans and trade debts and such non-monetary assets as property and stocks.
5. *Loan transfers* – The transfer of interest-bearing loans to an entity other than a special purpose vehicle.
6. *PFI (Public Finance Initiative) and similar contracts* – Under a PFI contract, a service such as the operation of hospital, prison, road or bridge is awarded by a public sector body to a private sector operator.

8 Revenue recognition

8.1 Basic principles of revenue recognition

In addition to the Application Notes set out above, Application Note G to FRS 5 provides guidance on the principles of revenue recognition and the treatment of turnover. The Application Note codifies existing practice and sets out a consistent treatment of revenue transactions ('exchange transactions' between seller and customer). The guidance explains how, when and whether to recognise revenue, in a variety of circumstances.

Turnover (or 'sales') is the revenue resulting from exchange transactions under which a seller supplies to customers the goods and services that it is in business to provide, as part of its 'operating activities'. Sales of fixed assets are not normally revenue transactions giving rise to 'turnover'.

In essence, revenue is recognised on the performance of a transaction when a seller:

- fulfils its contractual obligation to a customer through the supply of goods and services; and
- obtains the right to consideration (payment) in exchange for performance of the transaction.

This means that revenue must be accounted for generally at the point of delivery ('fulfilling a contractual obligation') rather than, for example, when an order is taken.

Payments in advance from a customer give rise to a liability (rather than revenue) until such time as the transaction is completed ('performed'), with the seller fulfilling their contractual obligation. In the case of partial performance of an obligation, revenue is recognised to the appropriate extent of such partial performance. Stage payments may, or may not, represent 'partial performance' under a contractual arrangement and will only equate to partial performance where the timing of payments coincide with the extent of partial performance.

Revenue is measured at 'fair value' of the right to consideration (amount receivable), which is normally the price specified in the contractual arrangement net of discounts, value added tax and similar sales taxes. Occasionally, the fair value at the time of the transaction may also reflect the time value of money (for example, an interest free period) or allow for possible debtor default (credit risk), but any such adjustments made subsequently should not be included in revenue but expensed within costs and overheads.

'Fair value' is defined in Application Note G as 'the amount at which goods or services could be exchanged in an arm's length transaction between informed and willing parties, other than in a forced or liquidation sale'.

8.2 Revenue recognition: areas of specific guidance

Revenue recognition is generally straightforward. However, for a number of instances where there has been inappropriate or inconsistent accounting treatment, Application Note G provides specific guidance. Further, UITF 40 *Revenue recognition and service contracts* has subsequently endeavoured to clarify the accounting for service contracts (see **8.3**).

Areas of specific guidance given in FRS 5 Application Note G, mainly concerning transactions giving rise to turnover, cover:

- long-term contractual performance;
- separation and linking of contractual arrangements;
- bill and hold arrangements;
- sales with rights of return; and
- presentation of turnover as principal or agent.

The requirements for accounting and disclosure of stocks and long-term contracts provided by SSAP 9 are not amended by FRS 5 Application Note G nor by UITF 40. Long term contractual performance results in the seller recognising turnover as contract activity progresses, to the extent that the contract can be assessed with reasonable certainty. Recognition is determined by, and in accordance with, the stage of completion of the contractual obligations; proportion of costs incurred should be a determining factor of recognition only where the costs provide evidence of the extent of the seller's performance.

A contract for services should be accounted for as a long-term contract where contract activity falls into different accounting periods and (having regard to the aggregate effect of all such contracts within the accounts) it is concluded that the effect is material.

Separation and linking should reflect the commercial substance of an arrangement. Examples provided by the Application Note include sales of software and related maintenance services, inception (or non-refundable) fees, and vouchers (such as money off or 'points' schemes). The accounting treatment of such arrangements invariably depends upon the contractual detail and whether component parts of the arrangement can be separately and independently identified (for example, the sale of some packaged software and a subsequent support service). A retailer selling on a 'two-for-one' basis, for example, must only account for actual revenue taken (reflecting the discount given) and not the notional value of two items sold. Gift vouchers must only be recorded as revenue when exchanged for goods or services.

In 'bill and hold arrangements' (where goods are supplied and title transferred but physical delivery deferred to a later date), if the seller is determined to have a right to consideration and stock becomes an asset of the customer, then it follows that the seller should recognise turnover together with the related changes in assets or liabilities.

Turnover should exclude the sales value of estimated returns from the total sales value of the goods supplied to customers.

Turnover is generally assumed to be sales on the seller's own account. Where there is no disclosure of acting as 'Agent', there is a rebuttable presumption that the seller is acting as 'Principal'. Turnover should be accordingly reported as follows:

- principal – gross amount received or receivable; and
- agent – commission or such other income (excluding amounts payable to the Principal).

Application Note G 'encourages' a seller acting as agent to disclose (as additional non-statutory information) the gross value of sales throughput, together with a brief explanation of the relationship of turnover as agent to such gross value of sales. Although not statutorily required, such disclosure is therefore established as good practice.

8.3 Revenue recognition: contracts for services

UITF 40 *Revenue recognition and service contracts* was issued in March 2005 in order to clarify the accounting for service contracts and in particular service contracts that are not treated as long term contracts under SSAP 9 (see **8.2**)

Revenue on service contracts should be accrued as service activity takes place (to reflect the seller's partial performance of its contractual obligations). Revenue should reflect the accrual of the right to consideration as contract activity progresses by reference to value of the work performed. Distinguishable phases of a single contract may be accounted for as two or more separate transactions, provided the value of each phase can be reliably estimated.

A contract for services should be accounted for as a long-term contract where contract activity falls into different accounting periods and it is concluded that the effect is material, having regard to the aggregate effect of all such contracts on the financial statements.

Contracts for services should not be accounted for as long-term contracts unless they involve the provision of a single service or a number of services that constitute a single project.

Where the substance of a contract is that a right to consideration does not arise until the occurrence of a specified future event or outcome (a 'critical event'), revenue is not recognised until that event occurs. This only applies where:

- the right to consideration is conditional or contingent on the 'critical event'; or
- the occurrence of the 'critical event' is outside the control of the seller.

UITF 40 *Revenue recognition and service contracts* applies to all reporting entities, including those adopting the FRSSE (see **10.13**).

9 Dividends

9.1 Treatment of dividends

There is no requirement for companies to show paid and proposed dividends as separate items in the profit and loss account. Companies are required to state the following in accounts:

- amounts set aside or withdrawn (or proposed to be set aside or withdrawn) from reserves;
- aggregate of dividends paid in the financial year (other than those for which a liability existed at the immediately preceding balance sheet date);
- aggregate amount of dividends liable to be paid at the balance sheet date; and
- aggregate amount of dividends proposed before the date of approval of the accounts and not otherwise disclosed. *(SI 2008/409 Sch 1 para 43.)*

The FRSSE requires the following: 'Dividends relating to a financial instrument or a component that is a financial liability shall be recognised as expense in profit or loss. Distributions to holders of an equity instrument shall be debited by the entity directly to equity, net of any related income tax benefit. If an entity declares dividends after the balance sheet date, the dividends shall not be recognised as a liability at the balance sheet date'.

9.2 Classification of preference dividends

The FRSSE (in Appendix III) has provided some practical illustrative guidance on the features of preference shares to help in their classification for accounting purposes.

The FRSSE appendix explains that in determining whether preference shares are a 'financial liability' or an 'equity instrument', it is necessary to assess the particular rights attached to the shares. For example, preference shares may (a) carry fixed rights to dividends (cumulative or otherwise); (b) have the same voting rights as the ordinary shares; (c) place an obligation or discretion as to redemption on the issuer; and (d) rank above ordinary shares (and receive par value) in a winding up.

In a straightforward case, where the shares provide for redemption on a set date, they would be classified as 'financial liabilities' because under the rights attached to the shares at the set redemption date, the issuer has an obligation to redeem (that is, to transfer financial assets to the holder of the preference shares). Where the issuer is not obliged to redeem the preference shares, appropriate classification is determined by the other rights attaching to them, by assessing the substance of the contractual arrangements and by reference to the definitions of 'financial liabilities' and 'equity instruments'. Only when the distributions to the holders of the preference shares are at the discretion of the issuer would such shares be classified as 'equity instruments'.

As a result of the above, some preference shares will be shown as liabilities in the balance sheet rather than as part of share capital and reserves (in accordance with FRS 25 (IAS 32) and FRSSE). Dividends thereon are charged as an (interest) expense in the profit and loss account.

9.3 Presentation of dividends

The treatment of dividends will vary depending whether the dividends are paid or proposed and whether the dividends relate to equity or preference shares. Therefore, *depending on the facts*, the treatment will be either:

- charged as an (interest) expense;
- 'debited directly to equity' as a distribution to equity shareholders; or
- included as narrative within the note as a means of disclosure.

'Debited directly to equity' is currently taken to mean 'charged directly to, or as a movement on, reserves'.

Equity dividends will generally not be shown on the face of the profit and loss account and be presented wholly within the notes to the accounts as a movement on reserves ('Profit and loss account reserve') and/or within the reconciliation of shareholders' funds ('Statement of shareholders equity'), with a narrative note dealing with aggregate dividends liable to be paid at the balance sheet date and aggregate dividends proposed before the date of approval of the accounts.

Appendix B SI 2008/409 – The Small Companies and Groups (Accounts and Directors' Report) Regulations 2008

This appendix reproduces in full *The Small Companies and Groups (Accounts and Directors' Report) Regulations 2008* (SI 2008/409). These Regulations are also available at: www.legislation.gov.uk/uksi/2008/409/contents/made

In summary, as set out in the Contents below, the statutory instrument comprises:

Part 1 Introduction

Part 2 Form and content of individual accounts

Part 3 Directors' report

Part 4 Form and content of group accounts

Part 5 Interpretation

Schedule 1 – Companies Act individual accounts

Schedule 2 – Information about related undertakings where company not preparing group accounts (companies act or IAS individual accounts)

Schedule 3 – Information about directors' benefits: remuneration (Companies Act or IAS accounts)

Schedule 4 – Companies Act abbreviated accounts for delivery to registrar of companies

Schedule 5 – Matters to be dealt with in directors' report

Schedule 6 – Group accounts

Schedule 7 – Interpretation of term 'provisions'

Schedule 8 – General interpretation

Made - - - -	*19th February 2008*
Coming into force - -	*6th April 2008*

CONTENTS

The Secretary of State makes the following Regulations in exercise of the powers conferred by sections 396(3), 404(3), 409(1) to (3), 412(1) to (3), 416(4), 444(3)(a) and (b), 677(3)(a), 712(2)(b)(i), 836(1)(b)(i) and 1292(1)(a) and (c) of the CA 2006(**a**).

In accordance with sections 473(3) and 1290 of the CA 2006 a draft of this instrument was laid before Parliament and approved by a resolution of each House of Parliament.

PART 1

INTRODUCTION

Citation and interpretation

1.—(1) These Regulations may be cited as the Small Companies and Groups (Accounts and Directors' Report) Regulations 2008.

(2) In these Regulations "the 2006 Act" means the CA 2006.

Commencement and application

2.—(1) These Regulations come into force on 6th April 2008.

(2) They apply in relation to financial years beginning on or after 6th April 2008.

(a) 2006 c.46.

(3) They apply to companies which are subject to the small companies regime under Part 15 of the 2006 Act (see section 381 of that Act(**a**)).

PART 2

FORM AND CONTENT OF INDIVIDUAL ACCOUNTS

Companies Act individual accounts

3.—(1) Companies Act individual accounts under section 396 of the 2006 Act Companies Act: individual accounts) must comply with the provisions of Schedule 1 to these Regulations as to the form and content of the balance sheet and profit and loss account, and additional information to be provided by way of notes to the accounts.

(2) The profit and loss account of a company that falls within section 408 of the 2006 Act (individual profit and loss account where group accounts prepared)(**b**) need not contain the information specified in paragraphs 59 to 61 of Schedule 1 to these Regulations (information supplementing the profit and loss account).

(3) Accounts are treated as having complied with any provision of Schedule 1 to these Regulations if they comply instead with the corresponding provision of Schedule 1 to the Large and Medium-Sized Companies and Groups (Accounts and Reports) Regulations 2008(**c**).

Information about related undertakings (Companies Act or IAS individual accounts)

4.—(1) Companies Act or IAS individual accounts must comply with the provisions of Schedule 2 to these Regulations as to information about related undertakings to be given in notes to the company's accounts.

(2) Information otherwise required to be given by Schedule 2 to these Regulations need not be disclosed with respect to an undertaking that—

(a) is established under the law of a country outside the United Kingdom, or

(b) carries on business outside the United Kingdom,

if the conditions specified in section 409(4) of the 2006 Act are met (see section 409(5) of the 2006 Act for disclosure required where advantage taken of this exemption).

This paragraph does not apply in relation to the information required by paragraphs 4 and 8 of Schedule 2 to these Regulations.

Information about directors' benefits: remuneration (Companies Act or IAS individual accounts)

5. Companies Act or IAS individual accounts must comply with the provisions of Schedule 3 to these Regulations as to information about directors' remuneration to be given in notes to the company's accounts.

Accounts for delivery to registrar of companies (Companies Act individual accounts)

6.—(1) The directors of a company for which they are preparing Companies Act individual accounts may deliver to the registrar of companies under section 444 of the 2006 Act (filing obligations of companies subject to small companies regime) a copy of a balance sheet which complies with Schedule 4 to these Regulations rather than Schedule 1.

(a) Section 381 is amended by regulation 6(1) of S.I. 2008/393.
(b) Section 408 is amended by regulation 10 of S.I. 2008/393.
(c) S.I. 2008/410.

(2) Companies Act individual accounts delivered to the registrar need not give the information required by—

(a) paragraph 4 of Schedule 2 to these Regulations (shares of company held by subsidiary undertakings), or

(b) Schedule 3 to these Regulations (directors' benefits).

PART 3

DIRECTORS' REPORT

Directors' report

7. The report which the directors of a company are required to prepare under section 415 of the 2006 Act (duty to prepare directors' report) must disclose the matters specified in Schedule 5 to these Regulations.

PART 4

FORM AND CONTENT OF GROUP ACCOUNTS

Companies Act group accounts

8.—(1) Where the directors of a parent company which—

(a) is subject to the small companies regime, and

(b) has prepared Companies Act individual accounts in accordance with regulation 3,

prepare Companies Act group accounts under section 398 of the 2006 Act (option to prepare group accounts), those accounts must comply with the provisions of Part 1 of Schedule 6 to these Regulations as to the form and content of the consolidated balance sheet and consolidated profit and loss account, and additional information to be provided by way of notes to the accounts.

(2) Accounts are treated as having complied with any provision of Part 1 of Schedule 6 if they comply instead with the corresponding provision of Schedule 6 to the Large and Medium-Sized Companies and Groups (Accounts and Reports) Regulations 2008.

Information about directors' benefits: remuneration (Companies Act or IAS group accounts)

9. Companies Act or IAS group accounts must comply with the provisions of Schedule 3 to these Regulations as to information about directors' remuneration to be given in notes to the company's accounts.

Information about related undertakings (Companies Act or IAS group accounts)

10.—(1) Companies Act or IAS group accounts must comply with the provisions of Part 2 of Schedule 6 to these Regulations as to information about related undertakings to be given in notes to the company's accounts.

(2) Information otherwise required to be given by Part 2 of Schedule 6 need not be disclosed with respect to an undertaking that—

(a) is established under the law of a country outside the United Kingdom, or

(b) carries on business outside the United Kingdom,

if the conditions specified in section 409(4) of the 2006 Act are met (see section 409(5) of the 2006 Act for disclosure required where advantage taken of this exemption).

This paragraph does not apply in relation to the information required by paragraphs 26 and 35 of Schedule 6 to these Regulations.

Accounts for delivery to registrar of companies (Companies Act group accounts)

11. Companies Act group accounts delivered to the registrar of companies under section 444 of the 2006 Act need not give the information required by—

(a) Schedule 3 to these Regulations (directors' benefits), or

(b) paragraph 25 of Schedule 6 to these Regulations (shares of company held by subsidiary undertakings).

PART 5

INTERPRETATION

Definition of "provisions"

12. Schedule 7 to these Regulations defines "provisions" for the purpose of these Regulations and for the purposes of—

(a) section 677(3)(a) (Companies Act accounts: relevant provisions for purposes of financial assistance) in Part 18 of the 2006 Act,

(b) section 712(2)(b)(i) (Companies Act accounts: relevant provisions to determine available profits for redemption or purchase by private company out of capital) in that Part, and

(c) section 836(1)(b)(i) (Companies Act accounts: relevant provisions for distribution purposes) in Part 23 of that Act.

General interpretation

13. Schedule 8 to these Regulations contains general definitions for the purposes of these Regulations.

Gareth Thomas
Parliamentary Under Secretary of State for Trade and Consumer Affairs,
Department for Business, Enterprise and Regulatory Reform

19th February 2008

SCHEDULE 1

Regulation 3(1)

COMPANIES ACT INDIVIDUAL ACCOUNTS

PART 1

GENERAL RULES AND FORMATS

SECTION A

GENERAL RULES

1.—(1) Subject to the following provisions of this Schedule—

(a) every balance sheet of a company must show the items listed in either of the balance sheet formats in Section B of this Part, and

(b) every profit and loss account must show the items listed in any one of the profit and loss account formats in Section B.

(2) References in this Schedule to the items listed in any of the formats in Section B are to those items read together with any of the notes following the formats which apply to those items.

(3) The items must be shown in the order and under the headings and sub-headings given in the particular format used, but—

(a) the notes to the formats may permit alternative positions for any particular items, and

(b) the heading or sub-heading for any item does not have to be distinguished by any letter or number assigned to that item in the format used.

2.—(1) Where in accordance with paragraph 1 a company's balance sheet or profit and loss account for any financial year has been prepared by reference to one of the formats in Section B, the company's directors must use the same format in preparing Companies Act individual accounts for subsequent financial years, unless in their opinion there are special reasons for a change.

(2) Particulars of any such change must be given in a note to the accounts in which the new format is first used, and the reasons for the change must be explained.

3.—(1) Any item required to be shown in a company's balance sheet or profit and loss account may be shown in greater detail than required by the particular format used.

(2) The balance sheet or profit and loss account may include an item representing or covering the amount of any asset or liability, income or expenditure not otherwise covered by any of the items listed in the format used, save that none of the following may be treated as assets in any balance sheet—

(a) preliminary expenses,

(b) expenses of, and commission on, any issue of shares or debentures,

(c) costs of research.

4.—(1) Where the special nature of the company's business requires it, the company's directors must adapt the arrangement, headings and sub-headings otherwise required in respect of items given an Arabic number in the balance sheet or profit and loss account format used.

(2) The directors may combine items to which Arabic numbers are given in any of the formats set out in Section B if—

(a) their individual amounts are not material to assessing the state of affairs or profit or loss of the company for the financial year in question, or

(b) the combination facilitates that assessment.

(3) Where sub-paragraph (2)(b) applies, the individual amounts of any items which have been combined must be disclosed in a note to the accounts.

5.—(1) Subject to sub-paragraph (2), the directors must not include a heading or sub-heading corresponding to an item in the balance sheet or profit and loss account format used if there is no amount to be shown for that item for the financial year to which the balance sheet or profit and loss account relates.

(2) Where an amount can be shown for the item in question for the immediately preceding financial year that amount must be shown under the heading or sub-heading required by the format for that item.

6. Every profit and loss account must show the amount of a company's profit or loss on ordinary activities before taxation.

7.—(1) For every item shown in the balance sheet or profit and loss account the corresponding amount for the immediately preceding financial year must also be shown.

(2) Where that corresponding amount is not comparable with the amount to be shown for the item in question in respect of the financial year to which the balance sheet or profit and loss account relates, the former amount may be adjusted, and particulars of the non-comparability and of any adjustment must be disclosed in a note to the accounts.

8. Amounts in respect of items representing assets or income may not be set off against amounts in respect of items representing liabilities or expenditure (as the case may be), or vice versa.

9. The company's directors must, in determining how amounts are presented within items in the profit and loss account and balance sheet, have regard to the substance of the reported transaction or arrangement, in accordance with generally accepted accounting principles or practice.

SECTION B

*THE REQUIRED FORMATS FOR ACCOUNTS(**a**)*

Balance sheet formats

Format 1

A. Called up share capital not paid *(1)*

B. Fixed assets
- I. Intangible assets
  1. Goodwill *(2)*
  2. Other intangible assets *(3)*
- II. Tangible assets
  1. Land and buildings
  2. Plant and machinery etc.
- III. Investments
  1. Shares in group undertakings and participating interests
  2. Loans to group undertakings and undertakings in which the company has a participating interest
  3. Other investments other than loans
  4. Other investments *(4)*

(a) A number in brackets following any item is a reference to the note of that number in the notes following the formats.

C. Current assets
- I. Stocks
  1. Stocks
  2. Payments on account
- II. Debtors *(5)*
  1. Trade debtors
  2. Amounts owed by group undertakings and undertakings in which the company has a participating interest
  3. Other debtors *(1)*
- III. Investments
  1. Shares in group undertakings
  2. Other investments *(4)*
- IV. Cash at bank and in hand

D. Prepayments and accrued income *(6)*

E. Creditors: amounts falling due within one year
1. Bank loans and overdrafts
2. Trade creditors
3. Amounts owed to group undertakings and undertakings in which the company has a participating interest
4. Other creditors *(7)*

F. Net current assets (liabilities) *(8)*

G. Total assets less current liabilities

H. Creditors: amounts falling due after more than one year
1. Bank loans and overdrafts
2. Trade creditors
3. Amounts owed to group undertakings and undertakings in which the company has a participating interest
4. Other creditors *(7)*

I. Provisions for liabilities

J. Accruals and deferred income *(7)*

K. Capital and reserves
- I. Called up share capital *(9)*
- II. Share premium account
- III. Revaluation reserve
- IV. Other reserves
- V. Profit and loss account

Balance sheet formats

Format 2

ASSETS

A. Called up share capital not paid *(1)*

B. Fixed assets
- I. Intangible assets
  1. Goodwill *(2)*
  2. Other intangible assets *(3)*
- II. Tangible assets
  1. Land and buildings
  2. Plant and machinery etc.

- III. Investments
    1. Shares in group undertakings and participating interests
    2. Loans to group undertakings and undertakings in which the company has a participating interest
    3. Other investments other than loans
    4. Other investments *(4)*

C. Current assets
- I. Stocks
    1. Stocks
    2. Payments on account
- II. Debtors *(5)*
    1. Trade debtors
    2. Amounts owed by group undertakings and undertakings in which the company has a participating interest
    3. Other debtors *(1)*
- III. Investments
    1. Shares in group undertakings
    2. Other investments *(4)*
- IV. Cash at bank and in hand

D. Prepayments and accrued income *(6)*

LIABILITIES

A. Capital and reserves
- I. Called up share capital *(9)*
- II. Share premium account
- III. Revaluation reserve
- IV. Other reserves
- V. Profit and loss account

B. Provisions for liabilities

C. Creditors *(10)*
1. Bank loans and overdrafts
2. Trade creditors
3. Amounts owed to group undertakings and undertakings in which the company has a participating interest
4. Other creditors *(7)*

D. Accruals and deferred income *(7)*

Notes on the balance sheet formats

(1) Called up share capital not paid

(Formats 1 and 2, items A and C.II.3.)

This item may either be shown at item A or included under item C.II.3 in Format 1 or 2.

(2) Goodwill

(Formats 1 and 2, item B.I.1.)

Amounts representing goodwill must only be included to the extent that the goodwill was acquired for valuable consideration.

(3) Other intangible assets

(Formats 1 and 2, item B.I.2.)

Amounts in respect of concessions, patents, licences, trade marks and similar rights and assets must only be included in a company's balance sheet under this item if either—

(a) the assets were acquired for valuable consideration and are not required to be shown under goodwill, or

(b) the assets in question were created by the company itself.

(4) Others: Other investments

(Formats 1 and 2, items B.III.4 and C.III.2.)

Where amounts in respect of own shares held are included under either of these items, the nominal value of such shares must be shown separately.

(5) Debtors

(Formats 1 and 2, items C.II.1 to 3.)

The amount falling due after more than one year must be shown separately for each item included under debtors unless the aggregate amount of debtors falling due after more than one year is disclosed in the notes to the accounts.

(6) Prepayments and accrued income

(Formats 1 and 2, item D.)

This item may alternatively be included under item C.II.3 in Format 1 or 2.

(7) Other creditors

(Format 1, items E.4, H.4 and J and Format 2, items C.4 and D.)

There must be shown separately—

(a) the amount of any convertible loans, and

(b) the amount for creditors in respect of taxation and social security.

Payments received on account of orders must be included in so far as they are not shown as deductions from stocks.

In Format 1, accruals and deferred income may be shown under item J or included under item E.4 or H.4, or both (as the case may require). In Format 2, accruals and deferred income may be shown under item D or within item C.4 under Liabilities.

(8) Net current assets (liabilities)

(Format 1, item F.)

In determining the amount to be shown under this item any prepayments and accrued income must be taken into account wherever shown.

(9) Called up share capital

(Format 1, item K.I and Format 2, Liabilities item A.I.)

The amount of allotted share capital and the amount of called up share capital which has been paid up must be shown separately.

(10) Creditors

(Format 2, Liabilities items C.1 to 4.)

Amounts falling due within one year and after one year must be shown separately for each of these items and for the aggregate of all of these items unless the aggregate amount of creditors falling due within one year and the aggregate amount of creditors falling due after more than one year is disclosed in the notes to the accounts.

Profit and loss account formats

Format 1
(see note (14) below)

1. Turnover
2. Cost of sales *(11)*
3. Gross profit or loss
4. Distribution costs *(11)*
5. Administrative expenses *(11)*
6. Other operating income
7. Income from shares in group undertakings
8. Income from participating interests
9. Income from other fixed asset investments *(12)*
10. Other interest receivable and similar income *(12)*
11. Amounts written off investments
12. Interest payable and similar charges *(13)*
13. Tax on profit or loss on ordinary activities
14. Profit or loss on ordinary activities after taxation
15. Extraordinary income
16. Extraordinary charges
17. Extraordinary profit or loss
18. Tax on extraordinary profit or loss
19. Other taxes not shown under the above items
20. Profit or loss for the financial year

Profit and loss account formats

Format 2

1. Turnover
2. Change in stocks of finished goods and in work in progress
3. Own work capitalised
4. Other operating income
5. (a) Raw materials and consumables
   (b) Other external charges
6. Staff costs
   (a) wages and salaries
   (b) social security costs
   (c) other pension costs
7. (a) Depreciation and other amounts written off tangible and intangible fixed assets
   (b) Exceptional amounts written off current assets
8. Other operating charges
9. Income from shares in group undertakings
10. Income from participating interests
11. Income from other fixed asset investments *(12)*
12. Other interest receivable and similar income *(12)*
13. Amounts written off investments
14. Interest payable and similar charges *(13)*
15. Tax on profit or loss on ordinary activities
16. Profit or loss on ordinary activities after taxation
17. Extraordinary income
18. Extraordinary charges
19. Extraordinary profit or loss
20. Tax on extraordinary profit or loss
21. Other taxes not shown under the above items
22. Profit or loss for the financial year

Profit and loss account formats

Format 3
(see note (14) below)

A. Charges

1. Cost of sales *(11)*
2. Distribution costs *(11)*
3. Administrative expenses *(11)*
4. Amounts written off investments
5. Interest payable and similar charges *(13)*
6. Tax on profit or loss on ordinary activities
7. Profit or loss on ordinary activities after taxation
8. Extraordinary charges
9. Tax on extraordinary profit or loss
10. Other taxes not shown under the above items
11. Profit or loss for the financial year

B. Income

1. Turnover
2. Other operating income
3. Income from shares in group undertakings
4. Income from participating interests
5. Income from other fixed asset investments *(12)*
6. Other interest receivable and similar income *(12)*
7. Profit or loss on ordinary activities after taxation
8. Extraordinary income
9. Profit or loss for the financial year

Profit and loss account formats

Format 4

A. Charges

1. Reduction in stocks of finished goods and in work in progress

2. (a) Raw materials and consumables
   (b) Other external charges

3. Staff costs

   (a) wages and salaries
   (b) social security costs
   (c) other pension costs

4. (a) Depreciation and other amounts written off tangible and intangible fixed assets
   (b) Exceptional amounts written off current assets

5. Other operating charges

6. Amounts written off investments

7 Interest payable and similar charges *(13)*

8. Tax on profit or loss on ordinary activities

9. Profit or loss on ordinary activities after taxation

10. Extraordinary charges

11. Tax on extraordinary profit or loss

12. Other taxes not shown under the above items

13. Profit or loss for the financial year

B. Income

1. Turnover

2. Increase in stocks of finished goods and in work in progress

3. Own work capitalised

4. Other operating income

5. Income from shares in group undertakings

6. Income from participating interests

7. Income from other fixed asset investments *(12)*

8. Other interest receivable and similar income *(12)*

9. Profit or loss on ordinary activities after taxation

10. Extraordinary income

11. Profit or loss for the financial year

Notes on the profit and loss account formats

(11) Cost of sales: distribution costs: administrative expenses

(Format 1, items 2, 4 and 5 and Format 3, items A.1, 2 and 3.)

These items must be stated after taking into account any necessary provisions for depreciation or diminution in value of assets.

(12) Income from other fixed asset investments: other interest receivable and similar income

(Format 1, items 9 and 10; Format 2, items 11 and 12; Format 3, items B.5 and 6 and Format 4, items B.7 and 8.)

Income and interest derived from group undertakings must be shown separately from income and interest derived from other sources.

(13) Interest payable and similar charges

(Format 1, item 12; Format 2, item 14; Format 3, item A.5 and Format 4, item A.7.)

The amount payable to group undertakings must be shown separately.

(14) Formats 1 and 3

The amount of any provisions for depreciation and diminution in value of tangible and intangible fixed assets falling to be shown under items 7(a) and A.4(a) respectively in Formats 2 and 4 must be disclosed in a note to the accounts in any case where the profit and loss account is prepared using Format 1 or Format 3.

PART 2

ACCOUNTING PRINCIPLES AND RULES

SECTION A

ACCOUNTING PRINCIPLES

Preliminary

10.—(1) The amounts to be included in respect of all items shown in a company's accounts must be determined in accordance with the principles set out in this Section.

(2) But if it appears to the company's directors that there are special reasons for departing from any of those principles in preparing the company's accounts in respect of any financial year they may do so, in which case particulars of the departure, the reasons for it and its effect must be given in a note to the accounts.

Accounting principles

11. The company is presumed to be carrying on business as a going concern.

12. Accounting policies must be applied consistently within the same accounts and from one financial year to the next.

13. The amount of any item must be determined on a prudent basis, and in particular—

(a) only profits realised at the balance sheet date must be included in the profit and loss account, and

(b) all liabilities which have arisen in respect of the financial year to which the accounts relate or a previous financial year must be taken into account, including those which only become apparent between the balance sheet date and the date on which it is signed on behalf of the board of directors in accordance with section 414 of the 2006 Act (approval and signing of accounts).

14. All income and charges relating to the financial year to which the accounts relate must be taken into account, without regard to the date of receipt or payment.

15. In determining the aggregate amount of any item, the amount of each individual asset or liability that falls to be taken into account must be determined separately.

SECTION B

HISTORICAL COST ACCOUNTING RULES

Preliminary

16. Subject to Sections C and D of this Part of this Schedule, the amounts to be included in respect of all items shown in a company's accounts must be determined in accordance with the rules set out in this Section.

Fixed assets

General rules

17.—(1) The amount to be included in respect of any fixed asset must be its purchase price or production cost.

(2) This is subject to any provision for depreciation or diminution in value made in accordance with paragraphs 18 to 20.

Rules for depreciation and diminution in value

18. In the case of any fixed asset which has a limited useful economic life, the amount of—

(a) its purchase price or production cost, or

(b) where it is estimated that any such asset will have a residual value at the end of the period of its useful economic life, its purchase price or production cost less that estimated residual value,

must be reduced by provisions for depreciation calculated to write off that amount systematically over the period of the asset's useful economic life.

19.—(1) Where a fixed asset investment of a description falling to be included under item B.III of either of the balance sheet formats set out in Part 1 of this Schedule has diminished in value, provisions for diminution in value may be made in respect of it and the amount to be included in respect of it may be reduced accordingly.

(2) Provisions for diminution in value must be made in respect of any fixed asset which has diminished in value if the reduction in its value is expected to be permanent (whether its useful economic life is limited or not), and the amount to be included in respect of it must be reduced accordingly.

(3) Any provisions made under sub-paragraph (1) or (2) which are not shown in the profit and loss account must be disclosed (either separately or in aggregate) in a note to the accounts.

20.—(1) Where the reasons for which any provision was made in accordance with paragraph 19 have ceased to apply to any extent, that provision must be written back to the extent that it is no longer necessary.

(2) Any amounts written back in accordance with sub-paragraph (1) which are not shown in the profit and loss account must be disclosed (either separately or in aggregate) in a note to the accounts.

Development costs

21.—(1) Notwithstanding that an item in respect of "development costs" is included under "fixed assets" in the balance sheet formats set out in Part 1 of this Schedule, an amount may only be included in a company's balance sheet in respect of development costs in special circumstances.

(2) If any amount is included in a company's balance sheet in respect of development costs the following information must be given in a note to the accounts—

(a) the period over which the amount of those costs originally capitalised is being or is to be written off, and (b) the reasons for capitalising the development costs in question.

Goodwill

22.—(1) The application of paragraphs 17 to 20 in relation to goodwill (in any case where goodwill is treated as an asset) is subject to the following.

(2) Subject to sub-paragraph (3), the amount of the consideration for any goodwill acquired by a company must be reduced by provisions for depreciation calculated to write off that amount systematically over a period chosen by the directors of the company.

(3) The period chosen must not exceed the useful economic life of the goodwill in question.

(4) In any case where any goodwill acquired by a company is shown or included as an asset in the company's balance sheet there must be disclosed in a note to the accounts—

(a) the period chosen for writing off the consideration for that goodwill, and

(b) the reasons for choosing that period.

Current assets

23. Subject to paragraph 24, the amount to be included in respect of any current asset must be its purchase price or production cost.

24.—(1) If the net realisable value of any current asset is lower than its purchase price or production cost, the amount to be included in respect of that asset must be the net realisable value.

(2) Where the reasons for which any provision for diminution in value was made in accordance with sub-paragraph (1) have ceased to apply to any extent, that provision must be written back to the extent that it is no longer necessary.

Miscellaneous and supplementary provisions

Excess of money owed over value received as an asset item

25.—(1) Where the amount repayable on any debt owed by a company is greater than the value of the consideration received in the transaction giving rise to the debt, the amount of the difference may be treated as an asset.

(2) Where any such amount is so treated—

(a) it must be written off by reasonable amounts each year and must be completely written off before repayment of the debt, and

(b) if the current amount is not shown as a separate item in the company's balance sheet, it must be disclosed in a note to the accounts.

Assets included at a fixed amount

26.—(1) Subject to sub-paragraph (2), assets which fall to be included—

(a) amongst the fixed assets of a company under the item "tangible assets", or

(b) amongst the current assets of a company under the item "raw materials and consumables", may be included at a fixed quantity and value.

(2) Sub-paragraph (1) applies to assets of a kind which are constantly being replaced where—

(a) their overall value is not material to assessing the company's state of affairs, and

(b) their quantity, value and composition are not subject to material variation.

Determination of purchase price or production cost

27.—(1) The purchase price of an asset is to be determined by adding to the actual price paid any expenses incidental to its acquisition.

(2) The production cost of an asset is to be determined by adding to the purchase price of the raw materials and consumables used the amount of the costs incurred by the company which are directly attributable to the production of that asset.

(3) In addition, there may be included in the production cost of an asset—

(a) a reasonable proportion of the costs incurred by the company which are only indirectly attributable to the production of that asset, but only to the extent that they relate to the period of production, and

(b) interest on capital borrowed to finance the production of that asset, to the extent that it accrues in respect of the period of production,

provided, however, in a case within paragraph (b), that the inclusion of the interest in determining the cost of that asset and the amount of the interest so included is disclosed in a note to the accounts.

(4) In the case of current assets distribution costs may not be included in production costs.

28.—(1) The purchase price or production cost of—

(a) any assets which fall to be included under any item shown in a company's balance sheet under the general item "stocks", and

(b) any assets which are fungible assets (including investments),

may be determined by the application of any of the methods mentioned in sub-paragraph (2) in relation to any such assets of the same class, provided that the method chosen is one which appears to the directors to be appropriate in the circumstances of the company.

(2) Those methods are—

(a) the method known as "first in, first out" (FIFO),

(b) the method known as "last in, first out" (LIFO),

(c) a weighted average price, and

(d) any other method similar to any of the methods mentioned above.

(3) For the purposes of this paragraph, assets of any description must be regarded as fungible if assets of that description are substantially indistinguishable one from another.

Substitution of original stated amount where price or cost unknown

29.—(1) This paragraph applies where—

(a) there is no record of the purchase price or production cost of any asset of a company or of any price, expenses or costs relevant for determining its purchase price or production cost in accordance with paragraph 27, or

(b) any such record cannot be obtained without unreasonable expense or delay.

(2) In such a case, the purchase price or production cost of the asset must be taken, for the purposes of paragraphs 17 to 24, to be the value ascribed to it in the earliest available record of its value made on or after its acquisition or production by the company.

SECTION C

ALTERNATIVE ACCOUNTING RULES

Preliminary

30.—(1) The rules set out in Section B are referred to below in this Schedule as the historical cost accounting rules.

(2) Those rules, with the omission of paragraphs 16, 22 and 26 to 29, are referred to below in this Part of this Schedule as the depreciation rules; and references below in this Schedule to the historical cost accounting rules do not include the depreciation rules as they apply by virtue of paragraph 33.

31. Subject to paragraphs 33 to 35, the amounts to be included in respect of assets of any description mentioned in paragraph 32 may be determined on any basis so mentioned.

Alternative accounting rules

32.—(1) Intangible fixed assets, other than goodwill, may be included at their current cost.

(2) Tangible fixed assets may be included at a market value determined as at the date of their last valuation or at their current cost.

(3) Investments of any description falling to be included under item B III of either of the balance sheet formats set out Part 1 of this Schedule may be included either—

(a) at a market value determined as at the date of their last valuation, or

(b) at a value determined on any basis which appears to the directors to be appropriate in the circumstances of the company.

But in the latter case particulars of the method of valuation adopted and of the reasons for adopting it must be disclosed in a note to the accounts.

(4) Investments of any description falling to be included under item C III of either of the balance sheet formats set out in Part 1 of this Schedule may be included at their current cost.

(5) Stocks may be included at their current cost.

Application of the depreciation rules

33.—(1) Where the value of any asset of a company is determined on any basis mentioned in paragraph 32, that value must be, or (as the case may require) be the starting point for determining, the amount to be included in respect of that asset in the company's accounts, instead of its purchase price or production cost or any value previously so determined for that asset.

The depreciation rules apply accordingly in relation to any such asset with the substitution for any reference to its purchase price or production cost of a reference to the value most recently determined for that asset on any basis mentioned in paragraph 32.

(2) The amount of any provision for depreciation required in the case of any fixed asset by paragraphs 18 to 20 as they apply by virtue of sub-paragraph (1) is referred to below in this paragraph as the adjusted amount, and the amount of any provision which would be required by any of those paragraphs in the case of that asset according to the historical cost accounting rules is referred to as the historical cost amount.

(3) Where sub-paragraph (1) applies in the case of any fixed asset the amount of any provision for depreciation in respect of that asset—

(a) included in any item shown in the profit and loss account in respect of amounts written off assets of the description in question, or

(b) taken into account in stating any item so shown which is required by note (11) of the notes on the profit and loss account formats set out in Part 1 of this Schedule to be stated after taking into account any necessary provision for depreciation or diminution in value of assets included under it, may be the historical cost amount instead of the adjusted amount, provided that the amount of any difference between the two is shown separately in the profit and loss account or in a note to the accounts.

Additional information to be provided in case of departure from historical cost accounting rules

34.—(1) This paragraph applies where the amounts to be included in respect of assets covered by any items shown in a company's accounts have been determined on any basis mentioned in paragraph 32.

(2) The items affected and the basis of valuation adopted in determining the amounts of the assets in question in the case of each such item must be disclosed in a note to the accounts.

(3) In the case of each balance sheet item affected (except stocks) either—

(a) the comparable amounts determined according to the historical cost accounting rules, or

(b) the differences between those amounts and the corresponding amounts actually shown in the balance sheet in respect of that item,

must be shown separately in the balance sheet or in a note to the accounts.

(4) In sub-paragraph (3), references in relation to any item to the comparable amounts determined as there mentioned are references to—

(a) the aggregate amount which would be required to be shown in respect of that item if the amounts to be included in respect of all the assets covered by that item were determined according to the historical cost accounting rules, and

(b) the aggregate amount of the cumulative provisions for depreciation or diminution in value which would be permitted or required in determining those amounts according to those rules.

Revaluation reserve

35.—(1) With respect to any determination of the value of an asset of a company on any basis mentioned in paragraph 32, the amount of any profit or loss arising from that determination (after allowing, where appropriate, for any provisions for depreciation or diminution in value made otherwise than by reference to the value so determined and any adjustments of any such provisions made in the light of that determination) must be credited or (as the case may be) debited to a separate reserve ("the revaluation reserve").

(2) The amount of the revaluation reserve must be shown in the company's balance sheet under a separate sub-heading in the position given for the item "revaluation reserve" in Format 1 or 2 of the balance sheet formats set out in Part 1 of this Schedule, but need not be shown under that name.

(3) An amount may be transferred—

(a) from the revaluation reserve—

(i) to the profit and loss account, if the amount was previously charged to that account or represents realised profit, or

(ii) on capitalisation,

(b) to or from the revaluation reserve in respect of the taxation relating to any profit or loss credited or debited to the reserve.

The revaluation reserve must be reduced to the extent that the amounts transferred to it are no longer necessary for the purposes of the valuation method used.

(4) In sub-paragraph (3)(a)(ii) "capitalisation", in relation to an amount standing to the credit of the revaluation reserve, means applying it in wholly or partly paying up unissued shares in the company to be allotted to members of the company as fully or partly paid shares.

(5) The revaluation reserve must not be reduced except as mentioned in this paragraph.

(6) The treatment for taxation purposes of amounts credited or debited to the revaluation reserve must be disclosed in a note to the accounts.

SECTION D

FAIR VALUE ACCOUNTING

Inclusion of financial instruments at fair value

36.—(1) Subject to sub-paragraphs (2) to (5), financial instruments (including derivatives) may be included at fair value.

(2) Sub-paragraph (1) does not apply to financial instruments that constitute liabilities unless—

(a) they are held as part of a trading portfolio,

(b) they are derivatives, or

(c) they are financial instruments falling within sub-paragraph (4).

(3) Unless they are financial instruments falling within sub-paragraph (4), sub-paragraph (1) does not apply to—

(a) financial instruments (other than derivatives) held to maturity,

(b) loans and receivables originated by the company and not held for trading purposes,

(c) interests in subsidiary undertakings, associated undertakings and joint ventures,

(d) equity instruments issued by the company,

(e) contracts for contingent consideration in a business combination, or

(f) other financial instruments with such special characteristics that the instruments, according to generally accepted accounting principles or practice, should be accounted for differently from other financial instruments.

(4) Financial instruments that, under international accounting standards adopted by the European Commission on or before 5th September 2006 in accordance with the IAS Regulation, may be included in accounts at fair value, may be so included, provided that the disclosures required by such accounting standards are made.

(5) If the fair value of a financial instrument cannot be determined reliably in accordance with paragraph 37, sub-paragraph (1) does not apply to that financial instrument.

(6) In this paragraph—

"associated undertaking" has the meaning given by paragraph 19 of Schedule 6 to these Regulations;

"joint venture" has the meaning given by paragraph 18 of that Schedule.

Determination of fair value

37.—(1) The fair value of a financial instrument is its value determined in accordance with this paragraph.

(2) If a reliable market can readily be identified for the financial instrument, its fair value is to be determined by reference to its market value.

(3) If a reliable market cannot readily be identified for the financial instrument but can be identified for its components or for a similar instrument, its fair value is determined by reference to the market value of its components or of the similar instrument.

(4) If neither sub-paragraph (2) nor (3) applies, the fair value of the financial instrument is a value resulting from generally accepted valuation models and techniques.

(5) Any valuation models and techniques used for the purposes of sub-paragraph (4) must ensure a reasonable approximation of the market value.

Hedged items

38. A company may include any assets and liabilities, or identified portions of such assets or liabilities, that qualify as hedged items under a fair value hedge accounting system at the amount required under that system.

Other assets that may be included at fair value

39.—(1) This paragraph applies to—

(a) investment property, and

(b) living animals and plants, that, under international accounting standards, may be included in accounts at fair value.

(2) Such investment property and such living animals and plants may be included at fair value, provided that all such investment property or, as the case may be, all such living animals and plants are so included where their fair value can reliably be determined.

(3) In this paragraph, "fair value" means fair value determined in accordance with relevant international accounting standards.

Accounting for changes in value

40.—(1) This paragraph applies where a financial instrument is valued in accordance with paragraph 36 or 38 or an asset is valued in accordance with paragraph 39.

(2) Notwithstanding paragraph 13 in this Part of this Schedule, and subject to sub-paragraphs (3) and (4), a change in the value of the financial instrument or of the investment property or living animal or plant must be included in the profit and loss account.

(3) Where—

(a) the financial instrument accounted for is a hedging instrument under a hedge accounting system that allows some or all of the change in value not to be shown in the profit and loss account, or

(b) the change in value relates to an exchange difference arising on a monetary item that forms part of a company's net investment in a foreign entity,

the amount of the change in value must be credited to or (as the case may be) debited from a separate reserve ("the fair value reserve").

(4) Where the instrument accounted for—

(a) is an available for sale financial asset, and

(b) is not a derivative,

the change in value may be credited to or (as the case may be) debited from the fair value reserve.

The fair value reserve

41.—(1) The fair value reserve must be adjusted to the extent that the amounts shown in it are no longer necessary for the purposes of paragraph 40(3) or (4).

(2) The treatment for taxation purposes of amounts credited or debited to the fair value reserve must be disclosed in a note to the accounts.

PART 3

NOTES TO THE ACCOUNTS

Preliminary

42. Any information required in the case of any company by the following provisions of this Part of this Schedule must (if not given in the company's accounts) be given by way of a note to those accounts.

Reserves and dividends

43. There must be stated—

(a) any amount set aside or proposed to be set aside to, or withdrawn or proposed to be withdrawn from, reserves,

(b) the aggregate amount of dividends paid in the financial year (other than those for which a liability existed at the immediately preceding balance sheet date),

(c) the aggregate amount of dividends that the company is liable to pay at the balance sheet date, and

(d) the aggregate amount of dividends that are proposed before the date of approval of the accounts, and not otherwise disclosed under paragraph (b) or (c).

Disclosure of accounting policies

44. The accounting policies adopted by the company in determining the amounts to be included in respect of items shown in the balance sheet and in determining the profit or loss of the company must be stated (including such policies with respect to the depreciation and diminution in value of assets).

Information supplementing the balance sheet

45. Paragraphs 46 to 58 require information which either supplements the information given with respect to any particular items shown in the balance sheet or is otherwise relevant to assessing the company's state of affairs in the light of the information so given.

Share capital

46.—(1) Where shares of more than one class have been allotted, the number and aggregate nominal value of shares of each class allotted must be given.

(2) In the case of any part of the allotted share capital that consists of redeemable shares, the following information must be given—

(a) the earliest and latest dates on which the company has power to redeem those shares,

(b) whether those shares must be redeemed in any event or are liable to be redeemed at the option of the company or of the shareholder, and

(c) whether any (and, if so, what) premium is payable on redemption.

47. If the company has allotted any shares during the financial year, the following information must be given—

(a) the classes of shares allotted, and

(b) as respects each class of shares, the number allotted, their aggregate nominal value, and the consideration received by the company for the allotment.

Fixed assets

48.—(1) In respect of each item which is or would but for paragraph 4(2)(b) be shown under the general item "fixed assets" in the company's balance sheet the following information must be given—

(a) the appropriate amounts in respect of that item as at the date of the beginning of the financial year and as at the balance sheet date respectively,

(b) the effect on any amount shown in the balance sheet in respect of that item of—

(i) any revision of the amount in respect of any assets included under that item made during that year on any basis mentioned in paragraph 32,

(ii) acquisitions during that year of any assets,

(iii) disposals during that year of any assets, and

(iv) any transfers of assets of the company to and from that item during that year.

(2) The reference in sub-paragraph (1)(a) to the appropriate amounts in respect of any item as at any date there mentioned is a reference to amounts representing the aggregate amounts determined, as at that date, in respect of assets falling to be included under that item on either of the following bases, that is to say—

(a) on the basis of purchase price or production cost (determined in accordance with paragraphs 27 and 28), or

(b) on any basis mentioned in paragraph 32, (leaving out of account in either case any provisions for depreciation or diminution in value).

(3) In respect of each item within sub-paragraph (1) there must also be stated—

(a) the cumulative amount of provisions for depreciation or diminution in value of assets included under that item as at each date mentioned in sub-paragraph (1)(a),

(b) the amount of any such provisions made in respect of the financial year,

(c) the amount of any adjustments made in respect of any such provisions during that year in consequence of the disposal of any assets, and

(d) the amount of any other adjustments made in respect of any such provisions during that year.

49. Where any fixed assets of the company (other than listed investments) are included under any item shown in the company's balance sheet at an amount determined on any basis mentioned in paragraph 32, the following information must be given—

(a) the years (so far as they are known to the directors) in which the assets were severally valued and the several values, and

(b) in the case of assets that have been valued during the financial year, the names of the persons who valued them or particulars of their qualifications for doing so and (whichever is stated) the bases of valuation used by them.

Investments

50.—(1) In respect of the amount of each item which is or would but for paragraph 4(2)(b) be shown in the company's balance sheet under the general item "investments" (whether as fixed assets or as current assets) there must be stated how much of that amount is ascribable to listed investments.

(2) Where the amount of any listed investments is stated for any item in accordance with subparagraph (1), the following amounts must also be stated—

(a) the aggregate market value of those investments where it differs from the amount so stated, and

(b) both the market value and the stock exchange value of any investments of which the former value is, for the purposes of the accounts, taken as being higher than the latter.

Information about fair value of assets and liabilities

51.—(1) This paragraph applies where financial instruments have been valued in accordance with paragraph 36 or 38.

(2) There must be stated—

(a) the significant assumptions underlying the valuation models and techniques used where the fair value of the instruments has been determined in accordance with paragraph 37(4),

(b) for each category of financial instrument, the fair value of the instruments in that category and the changes in value—

(i) included in the profit and loss account, or

(ii) credited to or (as the case may be) debited from the fair value reserve, in respect of those instruments, and

(c) for each class of derivatives, the extent and nature of the instruments, including significant terms and conditions that may affect the amount, timing and certainty of future cash flows.

(3) Where any amount is transferred to or from the fair value reserve during the financial year, there must be stated in tabular form—

(a) the amount of the reserve as at the date of the beginning of the financial year and as at the balance sheet date respectively,

(b) the amount transferred to or from the reserve during that year, and

(c) the source and application respectively of the amounts so transferred.

52.—(1) This paragraph applies if—

(a) the company has financial fixed assets that could be included at fair value by virtue of paragraph 36,

(b) the amount at which those items are included under any item in the company's accounts is in excess of their fair value, and

(c) the company has not made provision for diminution in value of those assets in accordance with paragraph 19(1) of this Schedule.

(2) There must be stated—

(a) the amount at which either the individual assets or appropriate groupings of those individual assets are included in the company's accounts,

(b) the fair value of those assets or groupings, and

(c) the reasons for not making a provision for diminution in value of those assets, including the nature of the evidence that provides the basis for the belief that the amount at which they are stated in the accounts will be recovered.

Information where investment property and living animals and plants included at fair value

53.—(1) This paragraph applies where the amounts to be included in a company's accounts in respect of investment property or living animals and plants have been determined in accordance with paragraph 39.

(2) The balance sheet items affected and the basis of valuation adopted in determining the amounts of the assets in question in the case of each such item must be disclosed in a note to the accounts.

(3) In the case of investment property, for each balance sheet item affected there must be shown, either separately in the balance sheet or in a note to the accounts—

(a) the comparable amounts determined according to the historical cost accounting rules, or

(b) the differences between those amounts and the corresponding amounts actually shown in the balance sheet in respect of that item.

(4) In sub-paragraph (3), references in relation to any item to the comparable amounts determined in accordance with that sub-paragraph are to—

(a) the aggregate amount which would be required to be shown in respect of that item if the amounts to be included in respect of all the assets covered by that item were determined according to the historical cost accounting rules, and

(b) the aggregate amount of the cumulative provisions for depreciation or diminution in value which would be permitted or required in determining those amounts according to those rules.

Reserves and provisions

54.—(1) This paragraph applies where any amount is transferred—

(a) to or from any reserves, or

(b) to any provisions for liabilities, or

(c) from any provision for liabilities otherwise than for the purpose for which the provision was established,

and the reserves or provisions are or would but for paragraph 4(2)(b) be shown as separate items in the company's balance sheet.

(2) The following information must be given in respect of the aggregate of reserves or provisions included in the same item—

(a) the amount of the reserves or provisions as at the date of the beginning of the financial year and as at the balance sheet date respectively,

(b) any amounts transferred to or from the reserves or provisions during that year, and

(c) the source and application respectively of any amounts so transferred.

(3) Particulars must be given of each provision included in the item "other provisions" in the company's balance sheet in any case where the amount of that provision is material.

Details of indebtedness

55.—(1) For the aggregate of all items shown under "creditors" in the company's balance sheet there must be stated the aggregate of the following amounts—

(a) the amount of any debts included under "creditors" which are payable or repayable otherwise than by instalments and fall due for payment or repayment after the end of the period of five years beginning with the day next following the end of the financial year, and

(b) in the case of any debts so included which are payable or repayable by instalments, the amount of any instalments which fall due for payment after the end of that period.

(2) In respect of each item shown under "creditors" in the company's balance sheet there must be stated the aggregate amount of any debts included under that item in respect of which any security has been given by the company.

(3) References above in this paragraph to an item shown under "creditors" in the company's balance sheet include references, where amounts falling due to creditors within one year and after more than one year are distinguished in the balance sheet—

(a) in a case within sub-paragraph (1), to an item shown under the latter of those categories,

(b) in a case within sub-paragraph (2), to an item shown under either of those categories.

References to items shown under "creditors" include references to items which would but for paragraph 4(2)(b) be shown under that heading.

56. If any fixed cumulative dividends on the company's shares are in arrear, there must be stated—

(a) the amount of the arrears, and

(b) the period for which the dividends or, if there is more than one class, each class of them are in arrear.

Guarantees and other financial commitments

57.—(1) Particulars must be given of any charge on the assets of the company to secure the liabilities of any other person, including, where practicable, the amount secured.

(2) The following information must be given with respect to any other contingent liability not provided for—

(a) the amount or estimated amount of that liability,

(b) its legal nature, and

(c) whether any valuable security has been provided by the company in connection with that liability and if so, what.

(3) There must be stated, where practicable, the aggregate amount or estimated amount of contracts for capital expenditure, so far as not provided for.

(4) Particulars must be given of—

(a) any pension commitments included under any provision shown in the company's balance sheet, and

(b) any such commitments for which no provision has been made,

and where any such commitment relates wholly or partly to pensions payable to past directors of the company separate particulars must be given of that commitment so far as it relates to such pensions.

(5) Particulars must also be given of any other financial commitments that—

(a) have not been provided for, and

(b) are relevant to assessing the company's state of affairs.

(6) Commitments within any of sub-paragraphs (1) to (5) which are undertaken on behalf of or for the benefit of—

(a) any parent undertaking or fellow subsidiary undertaking, or

(b) any subsidiary undertaking of the company,

must be stated separately from the other commitments within that sub-paragraph, and commitments within paragraph (a) must also be stated separately from those within paragraph (b).

Miscellaneous matters

58. Particulars must be given of any case where the purchase price or production cost of any asset is for the first time determined under paragraph 29.

Information supplementing the profit and loss account

59. Paragraphs 60 and 61 require information which either supplements the information given with respect to any particular items shown in the profit and loss account or otherwise provides particulars of income or expenditure of the company or of circumstances affecting the items shown in the profit and loss account (see regulation 3(2) for exemption for companies falling within section 408 of the 2006 Act).

Particulars of turnover

60.—(1) If the company has supplied geographical markets outside the United Kingdom during the financial year in question, there must be stated the percentage of its turnover that, in the opinion of the directors, is attributable to those markets.

(2) In analysing for the purposes of this paragraph the source of turnover, the directors of the company must have regard to the manner in which the company's activities are organised.

Miscellaneous matters

61.—(1) Where any amount relating to any preceding financial year is included in any item in the profit and loss account, the effect must be stated.

(2) Particulars must be given of any extraordinary income or charges arising in the financial year.

(3) The effect must be stated of any transactions that are exceptional by virtue of size or incidence though they fall within the ordinary activities of the company.

Sums denominated in foreign currencies

62. Where sums originally denominated in foreign currencies have been brought into account under any items shown in the balance sheet or profit and loss account, the basis on which those sums have been translated into sterling (or the currency in which the accounts are drawn up) must be stated.

Dormant companies acting as agents

63. Where the directors of a company take advantage of the exemption conferred by section 480 of the 2006 Act (dormant companies: exemption from audit), and the company has during the financial year in question acted as an agent for any person, the fact that it has so acted must be stated.

SCHEDULE 2

Regulation 4

INFORMATION ABOUT RELATED UNDERTAKINGS WHERE COMPANY NOT PREPARING GROUP ACCOUNTS (COMPANIES ACT OR IAS INDIVIDUAL ACCOUNTS)

PART 1

REQUIRED DISCLOSURES

Subsidiary undertakings

1.—(1) The following information must be given where at the end of the financial year the company has subsidiary undertakings.

(2) The name of each subsidiary undertaking must be stated.

(3) There must be stated with respect to each subsidiary undertaking—

(a) if it is incorporated outside the United Kingdom, the country in which it is incorporated,

(b) if it is unincorporated, the address of its principal place of business.

Holdings in subsidiary undertakings

2.—(1) There must be stated in relation to shares of each class held by the company in a subsidiary undertaking—

(a) the identity of the class, and

(b) the proportion of the nominal value of the shares of that class represented by those shares.

(2) The shares held by or on behalf of the company itself must be distinguished from those attributed to the company which are held by or on behalf of a subsidiary undertaking.

Financial information about subsidiary undertakings

3.—(1) There must be disclosed with respect to each subsidiary undertaking—

(a) the aggregate amount of its capital and reserves as at the end of its relevant financial year, and

(b) its profit or loss for that year.

(2) That information need not be given if the company would (if it were not subject to the small companies regime) be exempt by virtue of section 400 or 401 of the 2006 Act (parent company included in accounts of larger group) from the requirement to prepare group accounts.

(3) That information need not be given if the company's investment in the subsidiary undertaking is included in the company's accounts by way of the equity method of valuation.

(4) That information need not be given if—

(a) the subsidiary undertaking is not required by any provision of the 2006 Act to deliver a copy of its balance sheet for its relevant financial year and does not otherwise publish that balance sheet in the United Kingdom or elsewhere, and

(b) the company's holding is less than 50% of the nominal value of the shares in the undertaking.

(5) Information otherwise required by this paragraph need not be given if it is not material.

(6) For the purposes of this paragraph the "relevant financial year" of a subsidiary undertaking is—

(a) if its financial year ends with that of the company, that year, and

(b) if not, its financial year ending last before the end of the company's financial year.

Shares of company held by subsidiary undertakings

4.—(1) The number, description and amount of the shares in the company held by or on behalf of its subsidiary undertakings must be disclosed.

(2) Sub-paragraph (1) does not apply in relation to shares in the case of which the subsidiary undertaking is concerned as personal representative or, subject as follows, as trustee.

(3) The exception for shares in relation to which the subsidiary undertaking is concerned as trustee does not apply if the company, or any subsidiary undertaking of the company, is beneficially interested under the trust, otherwise than by way of security only for the purposes of a transaction entered into by it in the ordinary course of a business which includes the lending of money.

(4) Part 2 of this Schedule has effect for the interpretation of the reference in sub-paragraph (3) to a beneficial interest under a trust.

Significant holdings in undertakings other than subsidiary undertakings

5.—(1) The information required by paragraphs 6 and 7 must be given where at the end of the financial year the company has a significant holding in an undertaking which is not a subsidiary undertaking of the company.

(2) A holding is significant for this purpose if—

(a) it amounts to 20% or more of the nominal value of any class of shares in the undertaking, or

(b) the amount of the holding (as stated or included in the company's accounts) exceeds 20% of the amount (as so stated) of the company's assets.

6.—(1) The name of the undertaking must be stated.

(2) There must be stated—

(a) if the undertaking is incorporated outside the United Kingdom, the country in which it is incorporated,

(b) if it is unincorporated, the address of its principal place of business.

(3) There must also be stated—

(a) the identity of each class of shares in the undertaking held by the company, and

(b) the proportion of the nominal value of the shares of that class represented by those shares.

7.—(1) There must also be stated—

(a) the aggregate amount of the capital and reserves of the undertaking as at the end of its relevant financial year, and

(b) its profit or loss for that year.

(2) That information need not be given if—

(a) the company would (if it were not subject to the small companies regime) be exempt by virtue of section 400 or 401 of the 2006 Act (parent company included in accounts of larger group) from the requirement to prepare group accounts, and

(b) the investment of the company in all undertakings in which it has such a holding as is mentioned in sub-paragraph (1) is shown, in aggregate, in the notes to the accounts by way of the equity method of valuation.

(3) That information need not be given in respect of an undertaking if—

(a) the undertaking is not required by any provision of the 2006 Act to deliver to the registrar a copy of its balance sheet for its relevant financial year and does not otherwise publish that balance sheet in the United Kingdom or elsewhere, and

(b) the company's holding is less than 50% of the nominal value of the shares in the undertaking.

(4) Information otherwise required by this paragraph need not be given if it is not material.

(5) For the purposes of this paragraph the "relevant financial year" of an undertaking is—

(a) if its financial year ends with that of the company, that year, and

(b) if not, its financial year ending last before the end of the company's financial year.

Membership of certain undertakings

8.—(1) The information required by this paragraph must be given where at the end of the financial year the company is a member of a qualifying undertaking.

(2) There must be stated—

(a) the name and legal form of the undertaking, and

(b) the address of the undertaking's registered office (whether in or outside the United Kingdom) or, if it does not have such an office, its head office (whether in or outside the United Kingdom).

(3) Where the undertaking is a qualifying partnership there must also be stated either—

(a) that a copy of the latest accounts of the undertaking has been or is to be appended to the copy of the company's accounts sent to the registrar under section 444 of the 2006 Act, or

(b) the name of at least one body corporate (which may be the company) in whose group accounts the undertaking has been or is to be dealt with on a consolidated basis.

(4) Information otherwise required by sub-paragraph (2) need not be given if it is not material.

(5) Information otherwise required by sub-paragraph (3)(b) need not be given if the notes to the company's accounts disclose that advantage has been taken of the exemption conferred by regulation 7 of the Partnerships and Unlimited Companies (Accounts) Regulations 1993(**a**).

(6) In this paragraph—

"dealt with on a consolidated basis", "member" and "qualifying partnership" have the same meanings as in the Partnerships and Unlimited Companies (Accounts) Regulations 1993;

"qualifying undertaking" means—

(a) a qualifying partnership, or

(b) an unlimited company each of whose members is—

(i) a limited company,

(ii) another unlimited company each of whose members is a limited company, or

(iii) a Scottish partnership each of whose members is a limited company,

and references in this paragraph to a limited company, another unlimited company or a Scottish partnership include a comparable undertaking incorporated in or formed under the law of a country or territory outside the United Kingdom.

Parent undertaking drawing up accounts for larger group

9.—(1) Where the company is a subsidiary undertaking, the following information must be given with respect to the parent undertaking of—

(a) the largest group of undertakings for which group accounts are drawn up and of which the company is a member, and

(b) the smallest such group of undertakings.

(**a**) S.I. 1993/1820.

(2) The name of the parent undertaking must be stated.

(3) There must be stated—

(a) if the undertaking is incorporated outside the United Kingdom, the country in which it is incorporated,

(b) if it is unincorporated, the address of its principal place of business.

(4) If copies of the group accounts referred to in sub-paragraph (1) are available to the public, there must also be stated the addresses from which copies of the accounts can be obtained.

Identification of ultimate parent company

10.—(1) Where the company is a subsidiary undertaking, the following information must be given with respect to the company (if any) regarded by the directors as being the company's ultimate parent company.

(2) The name of that company must be stated.

(3) If that company is incorporated outside the United Kingdom, the country in which it is incorporated must be stated (if known to the directors).

(4) In this paragraph "company" includes any body corporate.

Construction of references to shares held by company

11.—(1) References in this Part of this Schedule to shares held by a company are to be construed as follows.

(2) For the purposes of paragraphs 2 and 3 (information about subsidiary undertakings)—

(a) there must be attributed to the company any shares held by a subsidiary undertaking, or by a person acting on behalf of the company or a subsidiary undertaking; but

(b) there must be treated as not held by the company any shares held on behalf of a person other than the company or a subsidiary undertaking.

(3) For the purposes of paragraphs 5 to 7 (information about undertakings other than subsidiary undertakings)—

(a) there must be attributed to the company shares held on its behalf by any person; but

(b) there must be treated as not held by a company shares held on behalf of a person other than the company.

(4) For the purposes of any of those provisions, shares held by way of security must be treated as held by the person providing the security—

(a) where apart from the right to exercise them for the purpose of preserving the value of the security, or of realising it, the rights attached to the shares are exercisable only in accordance with his instructions, and

(b) where the shares are held in connection with the granting of loans as part of normal business activities and apart from the right to exercise them for the purpose of preserving the value of the security, or of realising it, the rights attached to the shares are exercisable only in his interests.

PART 2

INTERPRETATION OF REFERENCES TO "BENEFICIAL INTEREST"

Introduction

12.—(1) References in this Schedule to a beneficial interest are to be interpreted in accordance with the following provisions.

(2) This Part of this Schedule applies in relation to debentures as it applies in relation to shares.

Residual interests under pension and employees' share schemes

13.—(1) Where shares in an undertaking are held on trust for the purposes of a pension scheme or an employees' share scheme, there must be disregarded any residual interest of the undertaking or any of its subsidiary undertakings (the "residual beneficiary") that has not vested in possession.

(2) A "residual interest" means a right to receive any of the trust property in the event of—

(a) all the liabilities arising under the scheme having been satisfied or provided for, or

(b) the residual beneficiary ceasing to participate in the scheme, or

(c) the trust property at any time exceeding what is necessary for satisfying the liabilities arising or expected to arise under the scheme.

(3) In sub-paragraph (2)—

(a) references to a right include a right dependent on the exercise of a discretion vested by the scheme in the trustee or any other person, and

(b) references to liabilities arising under a scheme include liabilities that have resulted or may result from the exercise of any such discretion.

(4) For the purposes of this paragraph a residual interest vests in possession—

(a) in a case within sub-paragraph (2)(a), on the occurrence of the event there mentioned, whether or not the amount of the property receivable pursuant to the right mentioned in that sub-paragraph is then ascertained,

(b) in a case within sub-paragraph (2)(b) or (c), when the residual beneficiary becomes entitled to require the trustee to transfer to it any of the property receivable pursuant to that right.

Employer's charges and other rights of recovery

14.—(1) Where shares in an undertaking are held on trust there must be disregarded—

(a) if the trust is for the purposes of a pension scheme, any such rights as are mentioned in sub-paragraph (2),

(b) if the trust is for the purposes of an employees' share scheme, any such rights as are mentioned in paragraph (a) of that sub-paragraph,

being rights of the undertaking or any of its subsidiary undertakings.

(2) The rights referred to are—

(a) any charge or lien on, or set-off against, any benefit or other right or interest under the scheme for the purpose of enabling the employer or former employer of a member of the scheme to obtain the discharge of a monetary obligation due to him from the member,

(b) any right to receive from the trustee of the scheme, or as trustee of the scheme to retain, an amount that can be recovered or retained under section 61 of the Pension Schemes Act 1993(**a**) or section 57 of the Pension Schemes (Northern Ireland) Act 1993(**b**) (deduction of contributions equivalent premium from refund of scheme contributions) or otherwise, as reimbursement or partial reimbursement for any contributions equivalent premium paid in connection with the scheme under Chapter 3 of Part 3 of that Act.

Trustee's right to expenses, remuneration, indemnity etc.

15.—(1) Where an undertaking is a trustee, there must be disregarded any rights which the undertaking has in its capacity as trustee.

(a) 1993 c.48.
(b) 1993 c.49.

(2) This includes in particular—

(a) any right to recover its expenses or be remunerated out of the trust property, and

(b) any right to be indemnified out of that property for any liability incurred by reason of any act or omission of the undertaking in the performance of its duties as trustee.

Meaning of "pension scheme"

16.—(1) In this Part of this Schedule "pension scheme" means any scheme for the provision of benefits consisting of or including relevant benefits for or in respect of employees or former employees.

(2) For this purpose "relevant benefits" means any pension, lump sum, gratuity or other like benefit given or to be given on retirement or on death or in anticipation of retirement or, in connection with past service, after retirement or death.

Application of provisions to directors

17. In paragraphs 14(2) and 16, "employee" and "employer" are to be read as if a director of an undertaking were employed by it.

SCHEDULE 3

Regulations 5 and 9

INFORMATION ABOUT DIRECTORS' BENEFITS: REMUNERATION (COMPANIES ACT OR IAS ACCOUNTS)

PART 1

INFORMATION REQUIRED TO BE DISCLOSED

Total amount of directors' remuneration etc.

1.—(1) There must be shown the overall total of the following amounts—

(a) the amount of remuneration paid to or receivable by directors in respect of qualifying services;

(b) the amount of money paid to or receivable by directors, and the net value of assets (other than money, share options or shares) received or receivable by directors, under long term incentive schemes in respect of qualifying services; and

(c) the value of any company contributions—

(i) paid, or treated as paid, to a pension scheme in respect of directors' qualifying services, and

(ii) by reference to which the rate or amount of any money purchase benefits that may become payable will be calculated.

(2) There must be shown the number of directors (if any) to whom retirement benefits are accruing in respect of qualifying services—

(a) under money purchase schemes, and

(b) under defined benefit schemes.

Compensation to directors for loss of office

2.—(1) There must be shown the aggregate amount of any payments made to directors or past directors for loss of office.

(2) "Payment for loss of office" has the same meaning as in section 215 of the 2006 Act.

Sums paid to third parties in respect of directors' services

3.—(1) There must be shown the aggregate amount of any consideration paid to or receivable by third parties for making available the services of any person—

(a) as a director of the company, or

(b) while director of the company—

(i) as director of any of its subsidiary undertakings, or

(ii) otherwise in connection with the management of the affairs of the company or any of its subsidiary undertakings.

(2) In sub-paragraph (1)—

(a) the reference to consideration includes benefits otherwise than in cash, and

(b) in relation to such consideration the reference to its amount is to the estimated money value of the benefit.

The nature of any such consideration must be disclosed.

(3) For the purposes of this paragraph a "third party" means a person other than—

(a) the director himself or a person connected with him or body corporate controlled by him, or

(b) the company or any of its subsidiary undertakings.

PART 2

SUPPLEMENTARY PROVISIONS

General nature of obligations

4.—(1) This Schedule requires information to be given only so far as it is contained in the company's books and papers or the company has the right to obtain it from the persons concerned.

(2) For the purposes of this Schedule any information is treated as shown if it is capable of being readily ascertained from other information which is shown.

Provisions as to amounts to be shown

5.—(1) The following provisions apply with respect to the amounts to be shown under this Schedule.

(2) The amount in each case includes all relevant sums, whether paid by or receivable from the company, any of the company's subsidiary undertakings or any other person.

(3) References to amounts paid to or receivable by a person include amounts paid to or receivable by a person connected with him or a body corporate controlled by him (but not so as to require an amount to be counted twice).

(4) Except as otherwise provided, the amounts to be shown for any financial year are—

(a) the sums receivable in respect of that year (whenever paid) or,

(b) in the case of sums not receivable in respect of a period, the sums paid during that year.

(5) Sums paid by way of expenses allowance that are charged to United Kingdom income tax after the end of the relevant financial year must be shown in a note to the first accounts in which it is practicable to show them and must be distinguished from the amounts to be shown apart from this provision.

(6) Where it is necessary to do so for the purpose of making any distinction required in complying with this Schedule, the directors may apportion payments between the matters in respect of which they have been paid or are receivable in such manner as they think appropriate.

Exclusion of sums liable to be accounted for to company etc.

6.—(1) The amounts to be shown under this Schedule do not include any sums that are to be accounted for—

(a) to the company or any of its subsidiary undertakings, or

(b) by virtue of sections 219 and 222(3) of the 2006 Act (payments in connection with share transfers: duty to account), to persons who sold their shares as a result of the offer made.

(2) Where—

(a) any such sums are not shown in a note to the accounts for the relevant financial year on the ground that the person receiving them is liable to account for them, and

(b) the liability is afterwards wholly or partly released or is not enforced within a period of two years,

those sums, to the extent to which the liability is released or not enforced, must be shown in a note to the first accounts in which it is practicable to show them and must be distinguished from the amounts to be shown apart from this provision.

Meaning of "remuneration"

7.—(1) In this Schedule "remuneration" of a director includes—

(a) salary, fees and bonuses, sums paid by way of expenses allowance (so far as they are chargeable to United Kingdom income tax), and

(b) subject to sub-paragraph (2), the estimated money value of any other benefits received by him otherwise than in cash.

(2) The expression does not include—

(a) the value of any share options granted to a director or the amount of any gains made on the exercise of any such options,

(b) any company contributions paid, or treated as paid, in respect of him under any pension scheme or any benefits to which he is entitled under any such scheme, or

(c) any money or other assets paid to or received or receivable by him under any long term incentive scheme.

Meaning of "long term incentive scheme"

8.—(1) In this Schedule "long term incentive scheme" means an agreement or arrangement—

(a) under which money or other assets may become receivable by a director, and

(b) which includes one or more qualifying conditions with respect to service or performance which cannot be fulfilled within a single financial year.

(2) For this purpose the following must be disregarded—

(a) bonuses the amount of which falls to be determined by reference to service or performance within a single financial year;

(b) compensation for loss of office, payments for breach of contract and other termination payments; and

(c) retirement benefits.

Meaning of "shares" and "share option" and related expressions

9. In this Schedule—

(a) "shares" means shares (whether allotted or not) in the company, or any undertaking which is a group undertaking in relation to the company, and includes a share warrant as defined by section 779(1) of the 2006 Act; and

(b) "share option" means a right to acquire shares.

Meaning of "pension scheme" and related expressions

10.—(1) In this Schedule—

"pension scheme" means a retirement benefits scheme as defined by section 611 of the Income and Corporation Taxes Act 1988(**a**); and "retirement benefits" has the meaning given by section 612(1) of that Act.

(2) In this Schedule, "company contributions", in relation to a pension scheme and a director, means any payments (including insurance premiums) made, or treated as made, to the scheme in respect of the director by a person other than the director.

(3) In this Schedule, in relation to a director—

"defined benefits" means retirement benefits payable under a pension scheme that are not money purchase benefits;

"defined benefit scheme" means a pension scheme that is not a money purchase scheme;

"money purchase benefits" means retirement benefits payable under a pension scheme the rate or amount of which is calculated by reference to payments made, or treated as made, by the director or by any other person in respect of the director and which are not average salary benefits; and

"money purchase scheme" means a pension scheme under which all of the benefits that may become payable to or in respect of the director are money purchase benefits.

(**a**) 1988 c.1.

(4) Where a pension scheme provides for any benefits that may become payable to or in respect of any director to be whichever are the greater of—

(a) money purchase benefits as determined by or under the scheme; and

(b) defined benefits as so determined, the company may assume for the purposes of this paragraph that those benefits will be money purchase benefits, or defined benefits, according to whichever appears more likely at the end of the financial year.

(5) For the purpose of determining whether a pension scheme is a money purchase or defined benefit scheme, any death in service benefits provided for by the scheme are to be disregarded.

References to subsidiary undertakings

11.—(1) Any reference in this Schedule to a subsidiary undertaking of the company, in relation to a person who is or was, while a director of the company, a director also, by virtue of the company's nomination (direct or indirect) of any other undertaking, includes that undertaking, whether or not it is or was in fact a subsidiary undertaking of the company.

(2) Any reference to a subsidiary undertaking of the company—

(a) for the purposes of paragraph 1 (remuneration etc.) is to an undertaking which is a subsidiary undertaking at the time the services were rendered, and

(b) for the purposes of paragraph 2 (compensation for loss of office) is to a subsidiary undertaking immediately before the loss of office as director.

Other minor definitions

12.—(1) In this Schedule—
"net value", in relation to any assets received or receivable by a director, means value after deducting any money paid or other value given by the director in respect of those assets;
"qualifying services", in relation to any person, means his services as a director of the company, and his services while director of the company—

(a) as director of any of its subsidiary undertakings; or

(b) otherwise in connection with the management of the affairs of the company or any of its subsidiary undertakings.

(2) For the purposes of this Schedule, remuneration paid or receivable or share options granted in respect of a person's accepting office as a director are treated as emoluments paid or receivable or share options granted in respect of his services as a director.

SCHEDULE 4

Regulation 6(1)

COMPANIES ACT ABBREVIATED ACCOUNTS FOR DELIVERY TO REGISTRAR OF COMPANIES

PART 1

THE REQUIRED BALANCE SHEET FORMATS

1.—(1) A company may deliver to the registrar a copy of the balance sheet showing the items listed in either of the balance sheet formats set out below, in the order and under the headings and sub-headings given in the format adopted, but in other respects corresponding to the full balance sheet.

(2) The copy balance sheet must contain in a prominent position a statement that it has been prepared in accordance with the provisions applicable to companies subject to the small companies regime.

Balance sheet formats

Format 1

A. Called up share capital not paid

B. Fixed assets
  I. Intangible assets
  II. Tangible assets
  III. Investments

C. Current assets
  I. Stocks
  II. Debtors *(1)*
  III. Investments
  IV. Cash at bank and in hand

D. Prepayments and accrued income

E. Creditors: amounts falling due within one year

F. Net current assets (liabilities)

G. Total assets less current liabilities

H. Creditors: amounts falling due after more than one year

I. Provisions for liabilities

J. Accruals and deferred income

K. Capital and reserves
  I. Called up share capital
  II. Share premium account
  III. Revaluation reserve
  IV. Other reserves
  V. Profit and loss account

Balance sheet formats

Format 2

ASSETS

A. Called up share capital not paid

B. Fixed assets
- I. Intangible assets
- II. Tangible assets
- III. Investments

C. Current assets
- I. Stocks
- II. Debtors *(1)*
- III. Investments
- IV. Cash at bank and in hand

D. Prepayments and accrued income

LIABILITIES

A. Capital and reserves
- I. Called up share capital
- II. Share premium account
- III. Revaluation reserve
- IV. Other reserves
- V. Profit and loss account

B. Provisions for liabilities

C. Creditors *(2)*

D. Accruals and deferred income

Notes on the balance sheet formats

(1) Debtors

(Formats 1 and 2, items C.II.)

The aggregate amount of debtors falling due after more than one year must be shown separately, unless it is disclosed in the notes to the accounts.

(2) Creditors

(Format 2, Liabilities item C.)

The aggregate amount of creditors falling due within one year and of creditors falling due after more than one year must be shown separately, unless it is disclosed in the notes to the accounts.

PART 2

NOTES TO THE ACCOUNTS

Preliminary

2. Any information required in the case of any company by the following provisions of this Part of this Schedule must (if not given in the company's accounts) be given by way of a note to those accounts.

Disclosure of accounting policies

3. The accounting policies adopted by the company in determining the amounts to be included in respect of items shown in the balance sheet and in determining the profit or loss of the company must be stated (including such policies with respect to the depreciation and diminution in value of assets).

Information supplementing the balance sheet

Share capital and debentures

4.—(1) Where shares of more than one class have been allotted, the number and aggregate nominal value of shares of each class allotted must be given.

(2) In the case of any part of the allotted share capital that consists of redeemable shares, the following information must be given—

(a) the earliest and latest dates on which the company has power to redeem those shares,

(b) whether those shares must be redeemed in any event or are liable to be redeemed at the option of the company or of the shareholder, and

(c) whether any (and, if so, what) premium is payable on redemption.

5. If the company has allotted any shares during the financial year, the following information must be given—

(a) the classes of shares allotted, and

(b) as respects each class of shares, the number allotted, their aggregate nominal value, and the consideration received by the company for the allotment.

Fixed assets

6.—(1) In respect of each item to which a letter or Roman number is assigned under the general item "fixed assets" in the company's balance sheet the following information must be given—

(a) the appropriate amounts in respect of that item as at the date of the beginning of the financial year and as at the balance sheet date respectively,

(b) the effect on any amount shown in the balance sheet in respect of that item of—

(i) any revision of the amount in respect of any assets included under that item made during that year on any basis mentioned in paragraph 32 of Schedule 1 to these Regulations,

(ii) acquisitions during that year of any assets,

(iii) disposals during that year of any assets, and

(iv) any transfers of assets of the company to and from that item during that year.

(2) The reference in sub-paragraph (1)(a) to the appropriate amounts in respect of any item as at any date there mentioned is a reference to amounts representing the aggregate amounts determined, as at that date, in respect of assets falling to be included under that item on either of the following bases, that is to say—

(a) on the basis of purchase price or production cost (determined in accordance withparagraphs 27 and 28 of Schedule 1 to these Regulations), or

(b) on any basis mentioned in paragraph 32 of that Schedule,

(leaving out of account in either case any provisions for depreciation or diminution in value).

(3) In respect of each item within sub-paragraph (1) there must also be stated—

(a) the cumulative amount of provisions for depreciation or diminution in value of assets included under that item as at each date mentioned in sub-paragraph (1)(a),

(b) the amount of any such provisions made in respect of the financial year,

(c) the amount of any adjustments made in respect of any such provisions during that year in consequence of the disposal of any assets, and

(d) the amount of any other adjustments made in respect of any such provisions during that year.

Financial fixed assets

7.—(1) This paragraph applies if—

(a) the company has financial fixed assets that could be included at fair value by virtue of paragraph 36 of Schedule 1 to these Regulations,

(b) the amount at which those items are included under any item in the company's accounts is in excess of their fair value, and

(c) the company has not made provision for diminution in value of those assets in accordance with paragraph 19(1) of that Schedule.

(2) There must be stated—

(a) the amount at which either the individual assets or appropriate groupings of those individual assets are included in the company's accounts,

(b) the fair value of those assets or groupings, and

(c) the reasons for not making a provision for diminution in value of those assets, including the nature of the evidence that provides the basis for the belief that the amount at which they are stated in the accounts will be recovered.

Details of indebtedness

8.—(1) For the aggregate of all items shown under "creditors" in the company's balance sheet there must be stated the aggregate of the following amounts—

(a) the amount of any debts included under "creditors" which are payable or repayable otherwise than by instalments and fall due for payment or repayment after the end of the period of five years beginning with the day next following the end of the financial year, and

(b) in the case of any debts so included which are payable or repayable by instalments, the amount of any instalments which fall due for payment after the end of that period.

(2) In respect of each item shown under "creditors" in the company's balance sheet there must be stated the aggregate amount of any debts included under that item in respect of which any security has been given by the company.

Sums denominated in foreign currencies

9. Where sums originally denominated in foreign currencies have been brought into account under any items shown in the balance sheet or profit and loss account, the basis on which those sums have been translated into sterling (or the currency in which the accounts are drawn up) must be stated.

Dormant companies acting as agents

10. Where the directors of a company take advantage of the exemption conferred by section 480 of the 2006 Act (dormant companies: exemption from audit), and the company has during the financial year in question acted as an agent for any person, the fact that it has so acted must be stated.

SCHEDULE 5

Regulation 7

MATTERS TO BE DEALT WITH IN DIRECTORS' REPORT

Introduction

1. In addition to the information required by section 416 of the 2006 Act, the directors' report must contain the following information.

Political donations and expenditure

2.—(1) If—

(a) the company (not being the wholly-owned subsidiary of a company incorporated in the United Kingdom) has in the financial year—

(i) made any political donation to any political party or other political organisation,

(ii) made any political donation to any independent election candidate, or

(iii) incurred any political expenditure, and

(b) the amount of the donation or expenditure, or (as the case may be) the aggregate amount of all donations and expenditure falling within paragraph (a), exceeded £2000, the directors' report for the year must contain the following particulars.

(2) Those particulars are

(a) as respects donations falling within sub-paragraph (1)(a)(i) or (ii)—

(i) the name of each political party, other political organisation or independent election candidate to whom any such donation has been made, and

(ii) the total amount given to that party, organisation or candidate by way of such donations in the financial year; and

(b) as respects expenditure falling within sub-paragraph (1)(a)(iii), the total amount incurred by way of such expenditure in the financial year.

(3) If

(a) at the end of the financial year the company has subsidiaries which have, in that year, made any donations or incurred any such expenditure as is mentioned in sub-paragraph (1)(a), and

(b) it is not itself the wholly-owned subsidiary of a company incorporated in the United Kingdom,

the directors' report for the year is not, by virtue of sub-paragraph (1), required to contain the particulars specified in sub-paragraph (2).

But, if the total amount of any such donations or expenditure (or both) made or incurred in that year by the company and the subsidiaries between them exceeds £2000, the directors' report for the year must contain those particulars in relation to each body by whom any such donation or expenditure has been made or incurred.

(4) Any expression used in this paragraph which is also used in Part 14 of the 2006 Act (control of political donations and expenditure) has the same meaning as in that Part.

3.—(1) If the company (not being the wholly-owned subsidiary of a company incorporated in the United Kingdom) has in the financial year made any contribution to a non-EU political party, the directors' report for the year must contain—

(a) a statement of the amount of the contribution, or

(b) (if it has made two or more such contributions in the year) a statement of the total amount of the contributions.

(2) If—

(a) at the end of the financial year the company has subsidiaries which have, in that year, made any such contributions as are mentioned in sub-paragraph (1), and

(b) it is not itself the wholly-owned subsidiary of a company incorporated in the United Kingdom,

the directors' report for the year is not, by virtue of sub-paragraph (1), required to contain any such statement as is there mentioned, but it must instead contain a statement of the total amount of the contributions made in the year by the company and the subsidiaries between them.

(3) In this paragraph, "contribution", in relation to an organisation, means—

(a) any gift of money to the organisation (whether made directly or indirectly);

(b) any subscription or other fee paid for affiliation to, or membership of, the organisation; or

(c) any money spent (otherwise than by the organisation or a person acting on its behalf) in paying any expenses incurred directly or indirectly by the organisation.

(4) In this paragraph, "non-EU political party" means any political party which carries on, or proposes to carry on, its activities wholly outside the member States.

Charitable donations

4.—(1) If—

(a) the company (not being the wholly-owned subsidiary of a company incorporated in the United Kingdom) has in the financial year given money for charitable purposes, and

(b) the money given exceeded £2000 in amount,

the directors' report for the year must contain, in the case of each of the purposes for which money has been given, a statement of the amount of money given for that purpose.

(2) If—

(a) at the end of the financial year the company has subsidiaries which have, in that year, given money for charitable purposes, and

(b) it is not itself the wholly owned subsidiary of a company incorporated in the United Kingdom,

sub-paragraph (1) does not apply to the company.

But, if the amount given in that year for charitable purposes by the company and the subsidiaries between them exceeds £2000, the directors' report for the year must contain, in the case of each of the purposes for which money has been given by the company and the subsidiaries between them, a statement of the amount of money given for that purpose.

(3) Money given for charitable purposes to a person who, when it was given, was ordinarily resident outside the United Kingdom is to be left out of account for the purposes of this paragraph.

(4) For the purposes of this paragraph, "charitable purposes" means purposes which are exclusively charitable, and as respects Scotland a purpose is charitable if it is listed in section 7(2) of the Charities and Trustee Investment (Scotland) Act 2005(**a**).

Disclosure concerning employment etc. of disabled persons

5.—(1) This paragraph applies to the directors' report where the average number of persons employed by the company in each week during the financial year exceeded 250.

(2) That average number is the quotient derived by dividing, by the number of weeks in the financial year, the number derived by ascertaining, in relation to each of those weeks, the number of persons who, under contracts of service, were employed in the week (whether throughout it or not) by the company, and adding up the numbers ascertained.

(**a**) 2005 asp 10.

(3) The directors' report must in that case contain a statement describing such policy as the company has applied during the financial year—

(a) for giving full and fair consideration to applications for employment by the company made by disabled persons, having regard to their particular aptitudes and abilities,

(b) for continuing the employment of, and for arranging appropriate training for, employees of the company who have become disabled persons during the period when they were employed by the company, and

(c) otherwise for the training, career development and promotion of disabled persons employed by the company.

(4) In this paragraph—

(a) "employment" means employment other than employment to work wholly or mainly outside the United Kingdom, and "employed" and "employee" are to be construed accordingly; and

(b) "disabled person" means the same as in the Disability Discrimination Act 1995(**a**).

Disclosure required by company acquiring its own shares etc.

6.—(1) This paragraph applies where shares in a company—

(a) are purchased by the company or are acquired by it by forfeiture or surrender in lieu of forfeiture, or in pursuance of any of the following provisions (acquisition of own shares by company limited by shares)—

(i) section 143(3) of the Companies Act 1985(**b**),

(ii) Article 153(3) of the Companies (Northern Ireland) Order 1986(**c**), or

(iii) section 659 of the 2006 Act, or

(b) are acquired by another person in circumstances where paragraph (c) or (d) of any of the following provisions applies (acquisition by company's nominee, or by another with company financial assistance, the company having a beneficial interest)—

(i) section 146(1) of the Companies Act 1985(**d**),

(ii) Article 156(1) of the Companies (Northern Ireland) Order 1986(**e**), or

(iii) section 662(1) of the 2006 Act, or

(c) are made subject to a lien or other charge taken (whether expressly or otherwise) by the company and permitted by any of the following provisions (exceptions from general rule against a company having a lien or charge on its own shares)—

(i) section 150(2) or (4) of the Companies Act 1985(**f**),

(ii) Article 160(2) or (4) of the Companies (Northern Ireland) Order 1986(**g**), or

(iii) section 670(2) or (4) of the 2006 Act.

(a) 1995 c.50.
(b) Section 143 is prospectively repealed by the 2006 Act.
(c) Article 153 is prospectively repealed by the 2006 Act.
(d) Section 146(1)(aa) was inserted by section 102C(5) of 1986 c.53, as inserted by section 1(1) of 1997 c.41. Section 146 is prospectively repealed by the 2006 Act.
(e) Article 156(1)(aa) was inserted by section 102C(6) of 1986 c.53, as inserted by section 1(1) of 1997 c.41. Article 156 is prospectively repealed by the 2006 Act.
(f) Section 150 is prospectively repealed by the 2006 Act.
(g) Article 160 is prospectively repealed by the 2006 Act.

(2) The directors' report for a financial year must state—

(a) the number and nominal value of the shares so purchased, the aggregate amount of the consideration paid by the company for such shares and the reasons for their purchase;

(b) the number and nominal value of the shares so acquired by the company, acquired by another person in such circumstances and so charged respectively during the financial year;

(c) the maximum number and nominal value of shares which, having been so acquired by the company, acquired by another person in such circumstances or so charged (whether or not during that year) are held at any time by the company or that other person during that year;

(d) the number and nominal value of the shares so acquired by the company, acquired by another person in such circumstances or so charged (whether or not during that year) which are disposed of by the company or that other person or cancelled by the company during that year;

(e) where the number and nominal value of the shares of any particular description are stated in pursuance of any of the preceding sub-paragraphs, the percentage of the called-up share capital which shares of that description represent;

(f) where any of the shares have been so charged the amount of the charge in each case; and

(g) where any of the shares have been disposed of by the company or the person who acquired them in such circumstances for money or money's worth the amount or value of the consideration in each case.

SCHEDULE 6

Regulations 8(1) and 10

GROUP ACCOUNTS

PART 1

FORM AND CONTENT OF COMPANIES ACT GROUP ACCOUNTS

General rules

1.—(1) Subject to sub-paragraphs (1) and (2), group accounts must comply so far as practicable with the provisions of Schedule 1 to these Regulations (Companies Act individual accounts) as if the undertakings included in the consolidation ("the group") were a single company.

(2) For item B.III in each balance sheet format set out in that Schedule substitute—

"B. III. Investments

1. Shares in group undertakings
2. Interests in associated undertakings
3. Other participating interests
4. Loans to group undertakings and undertakings in which a participating interest is held
5. Other investments other than loans
6. Others".

(3) In the profit and loss account formats replace the items headed "Income from participating interests", that is—

(a) in Format 1, item 8,

(b) in Format 2, item 10,

(c) in Format 3, item B.4, and

(d) in Format 4, item B.6,

by two items: "Income from interests in associated undertakings" and "Income from other participating interests".

2.—(1) The consolidated balance sheet and profit and loss account must incorporate in full the information contained in the individual accounts of the undertakings included in the consolidation, subject to the adjustments authorised or required by the following provisions of this Schedule and to such other adjustments (if any) as may be appropriate in accordance with generally accepted accounting principles or practice.

(2) If the financial year of a subsidiary undertaking included in the consolidation does not end with that of the parent company, the group accounts must be made up—

(a) from the accounts of the subsidiary undertaking for its financial year last ending before the end of the parent company's financial year, provided that year ended no more than three months before that of the parent company, or

(b) from interim accounts prepared by the subsidiary undertaking as at the end of the parent company's financial year.

3.—(1) Where assets and liabilities to be included in the group accounts have been valued or otherwise determined by undertakings according to accounting rules differing from those used for the group accounts, the values or amounts must be adjusted so as to accord with the rules used for the group accounts.

(2) If it appears to the directors of the parent company that there are special reasons for departing from sub-paragraph (1) they may do so, but particulars of any such departure, the reasons for it and its effect must be given in a note to the accounts.

(3) The adjustments referred to in this paragraph need not be made if they are not material for the purpose of giving a true and fair view.

4. Any differences of accounting rules as between a parent company's individual accounts for a financial year and its group accounts must be disclosed in a note to the latter accounts and the reasons for the difference given.

5. Amounts that in the particular context of any provision of this Schedule are not material maybe disregarded for the purposes of that provision.

Elimination of group transactions

6.—(1) Debts and claims between undertakings included in the consolidation, and income and expenditure relating to transactions between such undertakings, must be eliminated in preparing the group accounts.

(2) Where profits and losses resulting from transactions between undertakings included in the consolidation are included in the book value of assets, they must be eliminated in preparing the group accounts.

(3) The elimination required by sub-paragraph (2) may be effected in proportion to the group's interest in the shares of the undertakings.

(4) Sub-paragraphs (1) and (2) need not be complied with if the amounts concerned are not material for the purpose of giving a true and fair view.

Acquisition and merger accounting

7.—(1) The following provisions apply where an undertaking becomes a subsidiary undertaking of the parent company.

(2) That event is referred to in those provisions as an "acquisition", and references to the "undertaking acquired" are to be construed accordingly.

8. An acquisition must be accounted for by the acquisition method of accounting unless the conditions for accounting for it as a merger are met and the merger method of accounting is adopted.

9.—(1) The acquisition method of accounting is as follows.

(2) The identifiable assets and liabilities of the undertaking acquired must be included in the consolidated balance sheet at their fair values as at the date of acquisition.

(3) The income and expenditure of the undertaking acquired must be brought into the group accounts only as from the date of the acquisition.

(4) There must be set off against the acquisition cost of the interest in the shares of the undertaking held by the parent company and its subsidiary undertakings the interest of the parent company and its subsidiary undertakings in the adjusted capital and reserves of the undertaking acquired.

(5) The resulting amount if positive must be treated as goodwill, and if negative as a negative consolidation difference.

10.—(1) The conditions for accounting for an acquisition as a merger are—

(a) that at least 90% of the nominal value of the relevant shares in the undertaking acquired (excluding any shares in the undertaking held as treasury shares) is held by or on behalf of the parent company and its subsidiary undertakings,

(b) that the proportion referred to in paragraph (a) was attained pursuant to an arrangement providing for the issue of equity shares by the parent company or one or more of its subsidiary undertakings,

(c) that the fair value of any consideration other than the issue of equity shares given pursuant to the arrangement by the parent company and its subsidiary undertakings did not exceed 10% of the nominal value of the equity shares issued, and

(d) that adoption of the merger method of accounting accords with generally accepted accounting principles or practice.

(2) The reference in sub-paragraph (1)(a) to the "relevant shares" in an undertaking acquired is to those carrying unrestricted rights to participate both in distributions and in the assets of the undertaking upon liquidation.

11.—(1) The merger method of accounting is as follows.

(2) The assets and liabilities of the undertaking acquired must be brought into the group accounts at the figures at which they stand in the undertaking's accounts, subject to any adjustment authorised or required by this Schedule.

(3) The income and expenditure of the undertaking acquired must be included in the group accounts for the entire financial year, including the period before the acquisition.

(4) The group accounts must show corresponding amounts relating to the previous financial year as if the undertaking acquired had been included in the consolidation throughout that year.

(5) There must be set off against the aggregate of—

(a) the appropriate amount in respect of qualifying shares issued by the parent company or its subsidiary undertakings in consideration for the acquisition of shares in the undertaking acquired, and

(b) the fair value of any other consideration for the acquisition of shares in the undertaking acquired, determined as at the date when those shares were acquired,

the nominal value of the issued share capital of the undertaking acquired held by the parent company and its subsidiary undertakings.

(6) The resulting amount must be shown as an adjustment to the consolidated reserves.

(7) In sub-paragraph (5)(a) "qualifying shares" means—

(a) shares in relation to which any of the following provisions applies (merger relief), and in respect of which the appropriate amount is the nominal value—

(i) section 131 of the Companies Act 1985(**a**),

(ii) Article 141 of the Companies (Northern Ireland) Order 1986(**b**), or

(iii) section 612 of the 2006 Act, or

(b) shares in relation to which any of the following provisions applies (group reconstruction relief), and in respect of which the appropriate amount is the nominal value together with any minimum premium value within the meaning of that section—

(i) section 132 of the Companies Act 1985(**c**),

(ii) Article 142 of the Companies (Northern Ireland) Order 1986(**d**), or

(iii) section 611 of the 2006 Act.

12.—(1) Where a group is acquired, paragraphs 9 to 11 apply with the following adaptations.

(2) References to shares of the undertaking acquired are to be construed as references to shares of the parent undertaking of the group.

(3) Other references to the undertaking acquired are to be construed as references to the group; and references to the assets and liabilities, income and expenditure and capital and reserves of the undertaking acquired must be construed as references to the assets and liabilities, income and expenditure and capital and reserves of the group after making the set-offs and other adjustments required by this Schedule in the case of group accounts.

(a) Section 131 is prospectively repealed by the 2006 Act.
(b) Article 141 is prospectively repealed by the 2006 Act.
(c) Section 132 is prospectively repealed by the 2006 Act.
(d) Article 142 is prospectively repealed by the 2006 Act.

13.—(1) The following information with respect to acquisitions taking place in the financial year must be given in a note to the accounts.

(2) There must be stated—

(a) the name of the undertaking acquired or, where a group was acquired, the name of the parent undertaking of that group, and

(b) whether the acquisition has been accounted for by the acquisition or the merger method of accounting;

and in relation to an acquisition which significantly affects the figures shown in the group accounts, the following further information must be given.

(3) The composition and fair value of the consideration for the acquisition given by the parent company and its subsidiary undertakings must be stated.

(4) Where the acquisition method of accounting has been adopted, the book values immediately prior to the acquisition, and the fair values at the date of acquisition, of each class of assets and liabilities of the undertaking or group acquired must be stated in tabular form, including a statement of the amount of any goodwill or negative consolidation difference arising on the acquisition, together with an explanation of any significant adjustments made.

(5) In ascertaining for the purposes of sub-paragraph (4) the profit or loss of a group, the book values and fair values of assets and liabilities of a group or the amount of the assets and liabilities of a group, the set-offs and other adjustments required by this Schedule in the case of group accounts must be made.

14.—(1) There must also be stated in a note to the accounts the cumulative amount of goodwill resulting from acquisitions in that and earlier financial years which has been written off otherwise than in the consolidated profit and loss account for that or any earlier financial year.

(2) That figure must be shown net of any goodwill attributable to subsidiary undertakings or businesses disposed of prior to the balance sheet date.

15. Where during the financial year there has been a disposal of an undertaking or group which significantly affects the figure shown in the group accounts, there must be stated in a note to the accounts—

(a) the name of that undertaking or, as the case may be, of the parent undertaking of that group, and

(b) the extent to which the profit or loss shown in the group accounts is attributable to profit or loss of that undertaking or group.

16. The information required by paragraph 13, 14 or 15 need not be disclosed with respect to an undertaking which—

(a) is established under the law of a country outside the United Kingdom, or

(b) carries on business outside the United Kingdom,

if in the opinion of the directors of the parent company the disclosure would be seriously prejudicial to the business of that undertaking or to the business of the parent company or any of its subsidiary undertakings and the Secretary of State agrees that the information should not be disclosed.

Minority interests

17.—(1) The formats set out in Schedule 1 to these Regulations have effect in relation to group accounts with the following additions.

(2) In the Balance Sheet Formats there must be shown, as a separate item and under an appropriate heading, the amount of capital and reserves attributable to shares in subsidiary undertakings included in the consolidation held by or on behalf of persons other than the parent company and its subsidiary undertakings.

(3) In the Profit and Loss Account Formats there must be shown, as a separate item and under an appropriate heading—

(a) the amount of any profit or loss on ordinary activities, and

(b) the amount of any profit or loss on extraordinary activities,

attributable to shares in subsidiary undertakings included in the consolidation held by or on behalf of persons other than the parent company and its subsidiary undertakings.

(4) For the purposes of paragraph 4 of Schedule 1 (power to adapt or combine items)—

(a) the additional item required by sub-paragraph (2) is treated as one to which a letter is assigned, and

(b) the additional items required by sub-paragraph (3)(a) and (b) are treated as ones to which an Arabic number is assigned.

Joint ventures

18.—(1) Where an undertaking included in the consolidation manages another undertaking jointly with one or more undertakings not included in the consolidation, that other undertaking ("the joint venture") may, if it is not—

(a) a body corporate, or

(b) a subsidiary undertaking of the parent company,

be dealt with in the group accounts by the method of proportional consolidation.

(2) The provisions of this Schedule relating to the preparation of consolidated accounts apply, with any necessary modifications, to proportional consolidation under this paragraph.

Associated undertakings

19.—(1) An "associated undertaking" means an undertaking in which an undertaking included in the consolidation has a participating interest and over whose operating and financial policy it exercises a significant influence, and which is not—

(a) a subsidiary undertaking of the parent company, or

(b) a joint venture dealt with in accordance with paragraph 18.

(2) Where an undertaking holds 20% or more of the voting rights in another undertaking, it is presumed to exercise such an influence over it unless the contrary is shown.

(3) The voting rights in an undertaking means the rights conferred on shareholders in respect of their shares or, in the case of an undertaking not having a share capital, on members, to vote at general meetings of the undertaking on all, or substantially all, matters.

(4) The provisions of paragraphs 5 to 11 of Schedule 7 to the 2006 Act (parent and subsidiary undertakings: rights to be taken into account and attribution of rights) apply in determining for the purposes of this paragraph whether an undertaking holds 20% or more of the voting rights in another undertaking.

20.—(1) The interest of an undertaking in an associated undertaking, and the amount of profit or loss attributable to such an interest, must be shown by the equity method of accounting (including dealing with any goodwill arising in accordance with paragraphs 17 to 20 and 22 of Schedule 1 to these Regulations).

(2) Where the associated undertaking is itself a parent undertaking, the net assets and profits or losses to be taken into account are those of the parent and its subsidiary undertakings (after making any consolidation adjustments).

(3) The equity method of accounting need not be applied if the amounts in question are not material for the purpose of giving a true and fair view.

PART 2

INFORMATION ABOUT RELATED UNDERTAKINGS WHERE COMPANY PREPARING GROUP ACCOUNTS (COMPANIES ACT OR IAS GROUP ACCOUNTS)

Introduction and interpretation

21. In this Part of this Schedule "the group" means the group consisting of the parent company and its subsidiary undertakings.

Subsidiary undertakings

22.—(1) The following information must be given with respect to the undertakings that are subsidiary undertakings of the parent company at the end of the financial year.

(2) The name of each undertaking must be stated.

(3) There must be stated—

(a) if the undertaking is incorporated outside the United Kingdom, the country in which it is incorporated,

(b) if it is unincorporated, the address of its principal place of business.

(4) It must also be stated whether the subsidiary undertaking is included in the consolidation and, if it is not, the reasons for excluding it from consolidation must be given.

(5) It must be stated with respect to each subsidiary undertaking by virtue of which of the conditions specified in section 1162(2) or (4) of the 2006 Act it is a subsidiary undertaking of its immediate parent undertaking.

That information need not be given if the relevant condition is that specified in subsection (2)(a) of that section (holding of a majority of the voting rights) and the immediate parent undertaking holds the same proportion of the shares in the undertaking as it holds voting rights.

Holdings in subsidiary undertakings

23.—(1) The following information must be given with respect to the shares of a subsidiary undertaking held—

(a) by the parent company, and

(b) by the group,

and the information under paragraphs (a) and (b) must (if different) be shown separately.

(2) There must be stated—

(a) the identity of each class of shares held, and

(b) the proportion of the nominal value of the shares of that class represented by those shares.

Financial information about subsidiary undertakings not included in the consolidation

24.—(1) There must be shown with respect to each subsidiary undertaking not included in the consolidation—

(a) the aggregate amount of its capital and reserves as at the end of its relevant financial year, and

(b) its profit or loss for that year.

(2) That information need not be given if the group's investment in the undertaking is included in the accounts by way of the equity method of valuation or if—

(a) the undertaking is not required by any provision of the 2006 Act to deliver a copy of its balance sheet for its relevant financial year and does not otherwise publish that balance sheet in the United Kingdom or elsewhere, and

(b) the holding of the group is less than 50% of the nominal value of the shares in the undertaking.

(3) Information otherwise required by this paragraph need not be given if it is not material.

(4) For the purposes of this paragraph the "relevant financial year" of a subsidiary undertaking is—

(a) if its financial year ends with that of the company, that year, and

(b) if not, its financial year ending last before the end of the company's financial year.

Shares of company held by subsidiary undertakings

25.—(1) The number, description and amount of the shares in the company held by or on behalf of its subsidiary undertakings must be disclosed.

(2) Sub-paragraph (1) does not apply in relation to shares in the case of which the subsidiary undertaking is concerned as personal representative or, subject as follows, as trustee.

(3) The exception for shares in relation to which the subsidiary undertaking is concerned as trustee does not apply if the company or any of its subsidiary undertakings is beneficially interested under the trust, otherwise than by way of security only for the purposes of a transaction entered into by it in the ordinary course of a business which includes the lending of money.

(4) Part 2 of Schedule 2 to these Regulations has effect for the interpretation of the reference in sub-paragraph (3) to a beneficial interest under a trust.

Joint ventures

26.—(1) The following information must be given where an undertaking is dealt with in the consolidated accounts by the method of proportional consolidation in accordance with paragraph 18 of this Schedule (joint ventures)—

(a) the name of the undertaking,

(b) the address of the principal place of business of the undertaking,

(c) the factors on which joint management of the undertaking is based, and

(d) the proportion of the capital of the undertaking held by undertakings included in the consolidation.

(2) Where the financial year of the undertaking did not end with that of the company, there must be stated the date on which a financial year of the undertaking last ended before that date.

Associated undertakings

27.—(1) The following information must be given where an undertaking included in the consolidation has an interest in an associated undertaking.

(2) The name of the associated undertaking must be stated.

(3) There must be stated—

(a) if the undertaking is incorporated outside the United Kingdom, the country in which it is incorporated,

(b) if it is unincorporated, the address of its principal place of business.

(4) The following information must be given with respect to the shares of the undertaking held—

(a) by the parent company, and

(b) by the group,

and the information under paragraphs (a) and (b) must be shown separately.

(5) There must be stated—

(a) the identity of each class of shares held, and

(b) the proportion of the nominal value of the shares of that class represented by those shares.

(6) In this paragraph "associated undertaking" has the meaning given by paragraph 19 of this Schedule; and the information required by this paragraph must be given notwithstanding that paragraph 20(3) of this Schedule (materiality) applies in relation to the accounts themselves.

Other significant holdings of parent company or group

28.—(1) The information required by paragraphs 29 and 30 must be given where at the end of the financial year the parent company has a significant holding in an undertaking which is not one of its subsidiary undertakings and does not fall within paragraph 26 (joint ventures) or paragraph 27 (associated undertakings).

(2) A holding is significant for this purpose if—

(a) it amounts to 20% or more of the nominal value of any class of shares in the undertaking, or

(b) the amount of the holding (as stated or included in the company's individual accounts) exceeds 20% of the amount of its assets (as so stated).

29.—(1) The name of the undertaking must be stated.

(2) There must be stated—

(a) if the undertaking is incorporated outside the United Kingdom, the country in which it is incorporated,

(b) if it is unincorporated, the address of its principal place of business.

(3) The following information must be given with respect to the shares of the undertaking held by the parent company.

(4) There must be stated—

(a) the identity of each class of shares held, and

(b) the proportion of the nominal value of the shares of that class represented by those shares.

30.—(1) There must also be stated—

(a) the aggregate amount of the capital and reserves of the undertaking as at the end of its relevant financial year, and

(b) its profit or loss for that year.

(2) That information need not be given in respect of an undertaking if—

(a) the undertaking is not required by any provision of the 2006 Act to deliver a copy of its balance sheet for its relevant financial year and does not otherwise publish that balance sheet in the United Kingdom or elsewhere, and

(b) the company's holding is less than 50% of the nominal value of the shares in the undertaking.

(3) Information otherwise required by this paragraph need not be given if it is not material.

(4) For the purposes of this paragraph the "relevant financial year" of an undertaking is—

(a) if its financial year ends with that of the company, that year, and

(b) if not, its financial year ending last before the end of the company's financial year.

31.—(1) The information required by paragraphs 32 and 33 must be given where at the end of the financial year the group has a significant holding in an undertaking which is not a subsidiary undertaking of the parent company and does not fall within paragraph 26 (joint ventures) or paragraph 27 (associated undertakings).

(2) A holding is significant for this purpose if—

(a) it amounts to 20% or more of the nominal value of any class of shares in the undertaking, or

(b) the amount of the holding (as stated or included in the group accounts) exceeds 20% of the amount of the group's assets (as so stated).

32.—(1) The name of the undertaking must be stated.

(2) There must be stated—

(a) if the undertaking is incorporated outside the United Kingdom, the country in which it is incorporated,

(b) if it is unincorporated, the address of its principal place of business.

(3) The following information must be given with respect to the shares of the undertaking held by the group.

(4) There must be stated—

(a) the identity of each class of shares held, and

(b) the proportion of the nominal value of the shares of that class represented by those shares.

33.—(1) There must also be stated—

(a) the aggregate amount of the capital and reserves of the undertaking as at the end of its relevant financial year, and

(b) its profit or loss for that year.

(2) That information need not be given if—

(a) the undertaking is not required by any provision of the 2006 Act to deliver a copy of its balance sheet for its relevant financial year and does not otherwise publish that balance sheet in the United Kingdom or elsewhere, and

(b) the holding of the group is less than 50% of the nominal value of the shares in the undertaking.

(3) Information otherwise required by this paragraph need not be given if it is not material.

(4) For the purposes of this paragraph the "relevant financial year" of an outside undertaking is—

(a) if its financial year ends with that of the parent company, that year, and

(b) if not, its financial year ending last before the end of the parent company's financial year.

Parent company's or group's membership of certain undertakings

34.—(1) The information required by this paragraph must be given where at the end of the financial year the parent company or group is a member of a qualifying undertaking.

(2) There must be stated

(a) the name and legal form of the undertaking, and

(b) the address of the undertaking's registered office (whether in or outside the United Kingdom) or, if it does not have such an office, its head office (whether in or outside the United Kingdom).

(3) Where the undertaking is a qualifying partnership there must also be stated either—

(a) that a copy of the latest accounts of the undertaking has been or is to be appended to the copy of the company's accounts sent to the registrar under section 444 of the 2006 Act, or

(b) the name of at least one body corporate (which may be the company) in whose group accounts the undertaking has been or is to be dealt with on a consolidated basis.

(4) Information otherwise required by sub-paragraph (2) need not be given if it is not material.

(5) Information otherwise required by sub-paragraph (3)(b) need not be given if the notes to the company's accounts disclose that advantage has been taken of the exemption conferred by regulation 7 of the Partnerships and Unlimited Companies (Accounts) Regulations 1993(**a**).

(6) In this paragraph—

"dealt with on a consolidated basis", "member" and "qualifying partnership" have the same meanings as in the Partnerships and Unlimited Companies (Accounts) Regulations 1993;

"qualifying undertaking" means—

(a) a qualifying partnership, or

(b) an unlimited company each of whose members is—

(i) a limited company,

(ii) another unlimited company each of whose members is a limited company, or

(iii) a Scottish partnership each of whose members is a limited company,

and references in this paragraph to a limited company, another unlimited company or a Scottish partnership include a comparable undertaking incorporated in or formed under the law of a country or territory outside the United Kingdom.

Parent undertaking drawing up accounts for larger group

35.—(1) Where the parent company is itself a subsidiary undertaking, the following information must be given with respect to that parent undertaking of the company which heads—

(a) the largest group of undertakings for which group accounts are drawn up and of which that company is a member, and

(b) the smallest such group of undertakings.

(2) The name of the parent undertaking must be stated.

(3) There must be stated—

(a) if the undertaking is incorporated outside the United Kingdom, the country in which it is incorporated,

(b) if it is unincorporated, the address of its principal place of business.

(4) If copies of the group accounts referred to in sub-paragraph (1) are available to the public, there must also be stated the addresses from which copies of the accounts can be obtained.

Identification of ultimate parent company

36.—(1) Where the parent company is itself a subsidiary undertaking, the following information must be given with respect to the company (if any) regarded by the directors as being that company's ultimate parent company.

(2) The name of that company must be stated.

(3) If that company is incorporated outside the United Kingdom, the country in which it is incorporated must be stated (if known to the directors).

(4) In this paragraph "company" includes any body corporate.

(a) S.I. 1993/1820.

Construction of references to shares held by parent company or group

37.—(1) References in this Part of this Schedule to shares held by the parent company or the group are to be construed as follows.

(2) For the purposes of paragraphs 23, 27(4) and (5) and 28 to 30 (information about holdings in subsidiary and other undertakings)—

(a) there must be attributed to the parent company shares held on its behalf by any person; but

(b) there must be treated as not held by the parent company shares held on behalf of a person other than the company.

(3) References to shares held by the group are to any shares held by or on behalf of the parent company or any of its subsidiary undertakings; but any shares held on behalf of a person other than the parent company or any of its subsidiary undertakings are not to be treated as held by the group.

(4) Shares held by way of security must be treated as held by the person providing the security—

(a) where apart from the right to exercise them for the purpose of preserving the value of the security, or of realising it, the rights attached to the shares are exercisable only in accordance with his instructions, and

(b) where the shares are held in connection with the granting of loans as part of normal business activities and apart from the right to exercise them for the purpose of preserving the value of the security, or of realising it, the rights attached to the shares are exercisable only in his interests.

SCHEDULE 7

Regulation 12

INTERPRETATION OF TERM "PROVISIONS"

PART 1

MEANING FOR PURPOSES OF THESE REGULATIONS

Definition of "Provisions"

1.—(1) In these Regulations, references to provisions for depreciation or diminution in value of assets are to any amount written off by way of providing for depreciation or diminution in value of assets.

(2) Any reference in the profit and loss account formats set out in Part 1 of Schedule 1 to these Regulations to the depreciation of, or amounts written off, assets of any description is to any provision for depreciation or diminution in value of assets of that description.

2. References in these Regulations to provisions for liabilities are to any amount retained as reasonably necessary for the purpose of providing for any liability the nature of which is clearly defined and which is either likely to be incurred, or certain to be incurred but uncertain as to amount or as to the date on which it will arise.

PART 2

MEANING FOR PURPOSES OF PARTS 18 AND 23 OF THE 2006 ACT

Financial assistance for purchase of own shares

3. The specified provisions for the purposes of section 677(3)(a) of the 2006 Act (Companies Act accounts: relevant provisions for purposes of financial assistance) are provisions for liabilities within paragraph 2 of this Schedule.

Redemption or purchase by private company out of capital

4. The specified provisions for the purposes of section 712(2)(b)(i) of the 2006 Act (Companies Act accounts: relevant provisions to determine available profits for redemption or purchase out of capital) are provisions of any of the kinds mentioned in paragraphs 1 and 2 of this Schedule.

Justification of distribution by references to accounts

5. The specified provisions for the purposes of section 836(1)(b)(i) of the 2006 Act (Companies Act accounts: relevant provisions for distribution purposes) are provisions of any of the kinds mentioned in paragraphs 1 and 2 of this Schedule.

SCHEDULE 8

Regulation 13

GENERAL INTERPRETATION

Financial instruments

1. References to "derivatives" include commodity-based contracts that give either contracting party the right to settle in cash or in some other financial instrument, except where such contracts—

(a) were entered into for the purpose of, and continue to meet, the company's expected purchase, sale or usage requirements,

(b) were designated for such purpose at their inception, and

(c) are expected to be settled by delivery of the commodity.

2.—(1) The expressions listed in sub-paragraph (2) have the same meaning as they have in Council Directive 78/660/EEC on the annual accounts of certain types of companies(**a**).

(2) Those expressions are "available for sale financial asset", "business combination", "commodity-based contracts", "derivative", "equity instrument", "exchange difference", "fair value hedge accounting system", "financial fixed asset", "financial instrument", "foreign entity", "hedge accounting", "hedge accounting system", "hedged items", "hedging instrument", "held for trading purposes", "held to maturity", "monetary item", "receivables", "reliable market" and "trading portfolio".

Fixed and current assets

3. "Fixed assets" means assets of a company which are intended for use on a continuing basis in the company's activities, and "current assets" means assets not intended for such use.

Historical cost accounting rules

4. References to the historical cost accounting rules are to be read in accordance with paragraph 30 of Schedule 1 to these Regulations.

Listed investments

5.—(1) "Listed investment" means an investment as respects which there has been granted a listing on—

(a) a recognised investment exchange other than an overseas investment exchange, or

(b) a stock exchange of repute outside the United Kingdom

(2) "Recognised investment exchange" and "overseas investment exchange" have the meaning given in Part 18 of the Financial Services and Markets Act 2000(**b**).

Loans

6. A loan is treated as falling due for repayment, and an instalment of a loan is treated as falling due for payment, on the earliest date on which the lender could require repayment or (as the case may be) payment, if he exercised all options and rights available to him.

Materiality

7. Amounts which in the particular context of any provision of Schedule 1 to these Regulations are not material may be disregarded for the purposes of that provision.

(**a**) O.J. L222 of 14.8.1978, page 11, as amended in particular by Directives 2001/65/EEC, 2003/51/EEC and 2006/46/EEC of the European Parliament and of the Council (O.J. L238 of 27.12.2001, page 28, O.J. L178 of 17.7.2003, page 16 and O.J. L224 of 16.8.2006, page 1).

(**b**) 2000 c.8.

Participating interests

8.—(1) A "participating interest" means an interest held by an undertaking in the shares of another undertaking which it holds on a long-term basis for the purpose of securing a contribution to its activities by the exercise of control or influence arising from or related to that interest.

(2) A holding of 20% or more of the shares of the undertaking is to be presumed to be a participating interest unless the contrary is shown.

(3) The reference in sub-paragraph (1) to an interest in shares includes—

(a) an interest which is convertible into an interest in shares, and

(b) an option to acquire shares or any such interest,

and an interest or option falls within paragraph (a) or (b) notwithstanding that the shares to which it relates are, until the conversion or the exercise of the option, unissued.

(4) For the purposes of this paragraph an interest held on behalf of an undertaking is to be treated as held by it.

(5) In the balance sheet and profit and loss formats set out in Part 1 of Schedule 1 and Part 1 of Schedule 4 to these Regulations, "participating interest" does not include an interest in a group undertaking.

(6) For the purpose of this paragraph as it applies in relation to the expression "participating interest"—

(a) in those formats as they apply in relation to group accounts, and

(b) in paragraph 19 of Schedule 6 (group accounts: undertakings to be accounted for as associated undertakings),

the references in sub-paragraphs (1) to (4) to the interest held by, and the purposes and activities of, the undertaking concerned are to be construed as references to the interest held by, and the purposes and activities of, the group (within the meaning of paragraph 1 of that Schedule).

Purchase price

9. "Purchase price", in relation to an asset of a company or any raw materials or consumables used in the production of such an asset, includes any consideration (whether in cash or otherwise) given by the company in respect of that asset or those materials or consumables, as the case may be.

Realised profits and losses

10. "Realised profits" and "realised losses" have the same meaning as in section 853(4) and (5) of the 2006 Act.

Staff costs

11.—(1) "Social security costs" means any contributions by the company to any state social security or pension scheme, fund or arrangement.

(2) "Pension costs" includes—

(a) any costs incurred by the company in respect of any pension scheme established for the purpose of providing pensions for persons currently or formerly employed by the company,

(b) any sums set aside for the future payment of pensions directly by the company to current or former employees, and

(c) any pensions paid directly to such persons without having first been set aside.

(3) Any amount stated in respect of the item "social security costs" or in respect of the item "wages and salaries" in the company's profit and loss account must be determined by reference to payments made or costs incurred in respect of all persons employed by the company during the financial year under contracts of service.

EXPLANATORY NOTE

(This note is not part of the Regulations)

These Regulations specify the form and content of the accounts and directors' report of companies subject to the small companies regime under Part 15 of the CA 2006 (c.46) ("the 2006 Act"). Section 381 of the 2006 Act defines what is meant by "small companies regime". The Regulations replace provisions previously contained in the Schedules to Part 7 of the Companies Act 1985 (c.6) ("the 1985 Act") and in the Schedules to Part 8 of the Companies (Northern Ireland) Order 1986 (S.I. 1986/1032 (N.I. 6)) ("the 1986 Order"). They extend to the whole of the United Kingdom, reflecting the extent of the 2006 Act.

The Regulations come into force on 6th April 2008, and apply in relation to financial years beginning on or after that date (regulation 2). The corresponding provisions of the 1985 Act or the 1986 Order continue to apply to accounts and directors' reports for financial years beginning before that date.

The Regulations continue the implementation of the following Directives-

Council Directive 78/660/EEC on the annual accounts of certain types of companies ("the Fourth Directive") (O.J.L222 of 14.8.1978, page 1), and

Council Directive 83/349/EEC on consolidated accounts ("the Seventh Directive") (O.J. L193 of 18.7.1983, page 1).

Regulation 3(1) of, and Schedule 1 to, the Regulations specify the form and content of the individual accounts of a company which is subject to the small companies regime and which is preparing Companies Act individual accounts. Schedule 1 re-enacts Schedule 8 to the 1985 Act and Schedule 8 to the 1986 Order, with one substantive modification.

Paragraph 36(4) of Schedule 1 implements article 1.5 of Directive 2006/46 of the European Parliament and the Council of 14th June 2006 amending the Fourth and Seventh Directives and Council Directives 86/635/EEC on the annual accounts and consolidated accounts of banks and other financial institutions and 91/674/EEC on the annual accounts and consolidated accounts of insurance undertakings (O.J. L224 of 16th August 2006, pages 1 to 7). The Directive is also to be implemented by the Large and Medium-sized Companies and Groups (Accounts and Reports) Regulations 2008, the CA 2006 (Amendment) (Accounts and Reports) Regulations 2008, and by the Financial Services Authority using powers under the Financial Services and Markets Act 2000 (c.8).

Paragraph 36(4) of Schedule 1 gives companies the option of including financial instruments in the accounts at a fair value provided that they may be so included under international accounting standards adopted under the IAS Regulation (as defined in section 474(1) of the 2006 Act) on or before 5th September 2006, and provided that the disclosures required by such standards are made.

Regulation 4 of, and Schedule 2 to, the Regulations re-enact the requirements of Part 1 of Schedule 5 to the 1985 Act and Part 1 of Schedule 5 to the 1986 Order for small companies. They concern information about related undertakings which must be provided in the notes to a company's individual accounts, whether they are Companies Act accounts or IAS accounts.

Regulation 5 of, and Schedule 3 to, the Regulations re-enact the requirements of Part 1 of Schedule 6 to the 1985 Act and Part 1 of Schedule 6 to the 1986 Order as they apply to small companies. They concern information about directors' remuneration which must be provided in the notes to a company's individual accounts, whether they are Companies Act accounts or IAS accounts.

Regulation 6 of, and Schedule 4 to, the Regulations make provision about Companies Act individual accounts which may be delivered to the registrar of companies for a small company under section 444 of the 2006 Act. Schedule 4 re-enacts Schedule 8A to the 1985 Act and Schedule 8A to the 1986 Order.

Regulation 7 of, and Schedule 5 to, the Regulations specify information to be included in the directors' report which a company's directors are required to prepare under section 415 of the 2006 Act. Schedule 5 re-enacts the provisions in Schedule 7 to the 1985 Act and Schedule 7 to the 1986 Order as they apply to small companies, with two modifications – the thresholds for disclosure of political donations and expenditure and charitable donations have been raised from £200 to £2000 (paragraphs 2 and 4), and provision is now made for disclosure of donations to independent election candidates (paragraph 2).

Regulation 8 of, and Part 1 of Schedule 6 to, the Regulations specify the form and content of Companies Act group accounts which a parent company subject to the small companies regime may choose to prepare, although not required to do so (see section 398 of the 2006 Act). The Schedule re-enacts Schedule 4A to the 1985 Act and Schedule 4A to the 1986 Order as they apply to small companies, save that paragraphs 9, 13 and 17 have been simplified to facilitate convergence with international accounting standards.

Regulations 9 and 10 apply the provisions of Schedule 3 (information in notes to accounts about directors' benefits) and Part 2 of Schedule 6 (information in notes about related undertakings) to Companies Act or IAS group accounts which the directors of a small parent company choose to prepare. Part 2 of Schedule 6 re-enacts Part 2 of Schedule 5 to the 1985 Act and Part 2 of Schedule 5 to the 1986 Order.

Regulation 11 makes provision for exemptions from Companies Act group accounts which may be delivered to the registrar of companies for a small parent company under section 444 of the 2006 Act.

Regulation 12 of, and Schedule 7 to, the Regulations define the term "provisions" for the purposes of the Regulations and for the purposes of sections 677(3)(a) (Companies Act accounts: relevant provisions for purposes of financial assistance), 712(2)(b)(i) (Companies Act accounts: relevant provisions to determine available profits for redemption or purchase out of capital) and 836(1)(b)(i) (Companies Act accounts: relevant provisions for distribution purposes) of the 2006 Act.

Regulation 13 of, and Schedule 8 to, the Regulations contain general interpretation provisions.

A transposition note has been prepared which sets out how Directive 2006/46 is to be transposed into UK law. An Impact Assessment of the effect that the implementation of Directive 2006/46 will have on the costs of business, charities or voluntary bodies has also been prepared. Both are available from the Department for Business, Enterprise and Regulatory Reform, Corporate Law and Governance Directorate, 1 Victoria Street, London SW1. They are also available electronically at www.berr.gov.uk. Copies have also been placed in the libraries of both Houses of Parliament. Otherwise, an Impact Assessment has not been produced for these Regulations as they have only a negligible impact on the costs of business, charities or voluntary bodies.

Appendix C Small company accounts exemptions decision chart

The decision chart below is designed to determine whether a company qualifies in any particular year to be treated as small or medium-sized, and hence whether it is entitled to special provisions in the preparation of its annual accounts, and whether it is entitled to prepare and file abbreviated accounts.

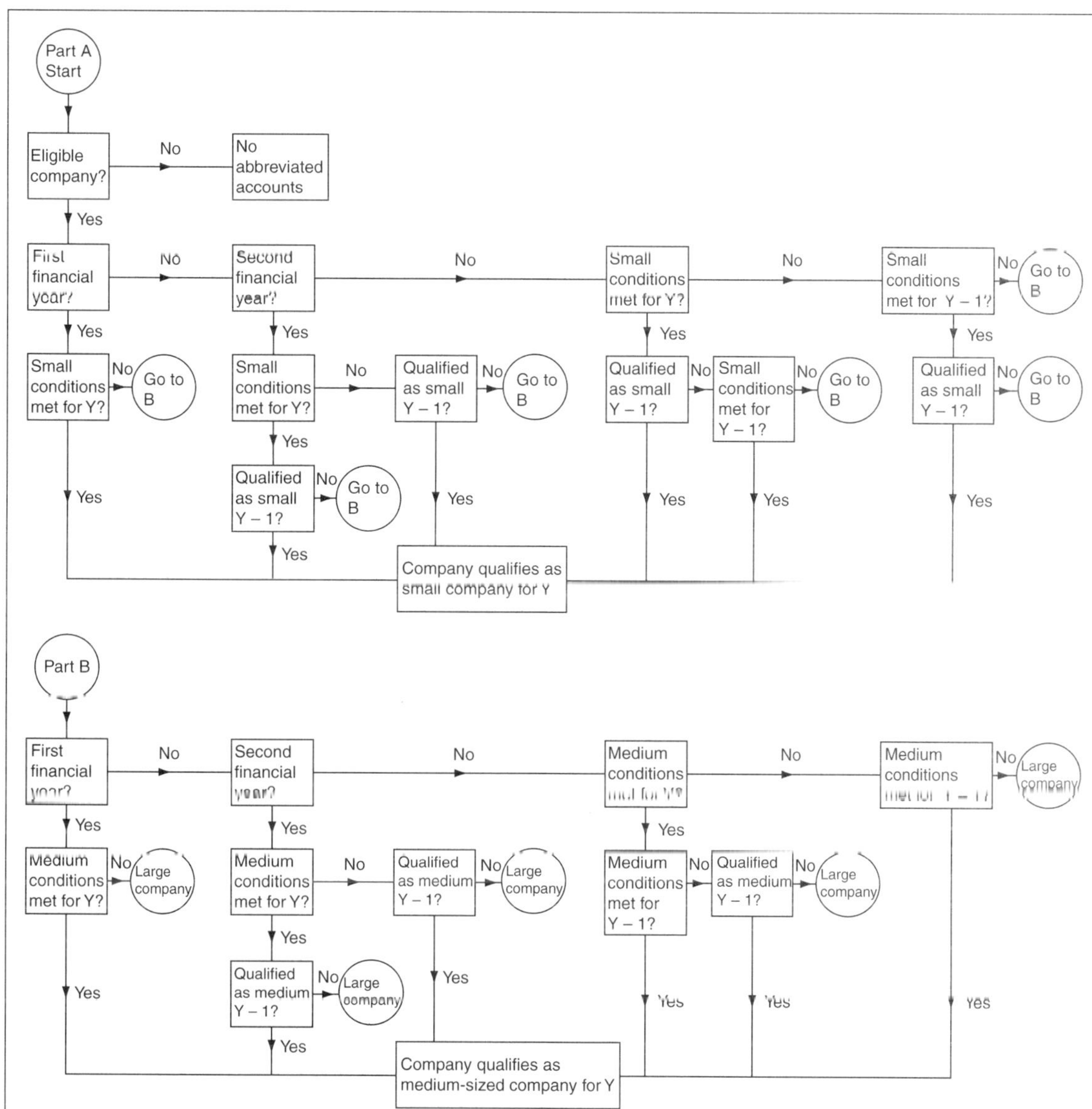

Terms, expressions, etc. used in the chart are explained as follows.

'Eligible company?'

The following companies are not eligible and are not therefore entitled to prepare small company
s. 384 accounts or to file abbreviated accounts, irrespective of size:

- public companies;
- *s. 384(2)* members of 'ineligible' (see below) groups;
- a company carrying on an insurance market activity; and
- a company that is an authorised insurance company, a banking company, an e-money issuer, a
s. 384(1) MiFID investment firm or a UCITS management company (see **5.1**).

A group is 'ineligible' if any of its members is a public company; a body corporate (other than a company (i.e. other than a company as defined by the CA 2006)) whose shares are admitted to trading on a regulated market in an EEA State; a person (other than a small company) who has permission under Part 4 of the FSMA 2000 to carry on a regulated activity; a small company that is an authorised insurance company, a banking company, an e-money issuer, an MiFID investment firm or a UCITS management company; or a person who carries on insurance market activity (CA 2006 384(2)).

A company is a 'small company' for this purpose of ineligibility if it qualified as small in relation to its last financial year ending on or before the end of the financial year to which the accounts relate.

s. 480(2) A dormant company member of an ineligible group may prepare small company accounts.

'No abbreviated accounts'

The company is not entitled to file abbreviated accounts.

'Years'

Y = current financial year

Y – 1 = preceding financial year

'First financial year?'

In a company's first year of incorporation, it will qualify as small or medium-sized, as appropriate, provided it meets the qualifying conditions in its first financial year.

'Qualifying conditions'

In order to qualify as small or medium-sized, as the case may be, the qualifying conditions set out in **5.2** must be satisfied.

Note: Part B of the chart should only be used after following the logic route of Part A.

'Qualified as small (medium)?'

Did the company qualify as small (or medium-sized) in Y – 1?

'Large company'

The company, being neither small nor medium-sized, is not entitled to prepare accounts in accordance with the relevant special provisions. The term 'large' is not used in the legislation.

Appendix D Small and subsidiary company audit exemptions decision chart

The decision chart below is designed to determine whether a company qualifies in any particular year to exemption from audit.

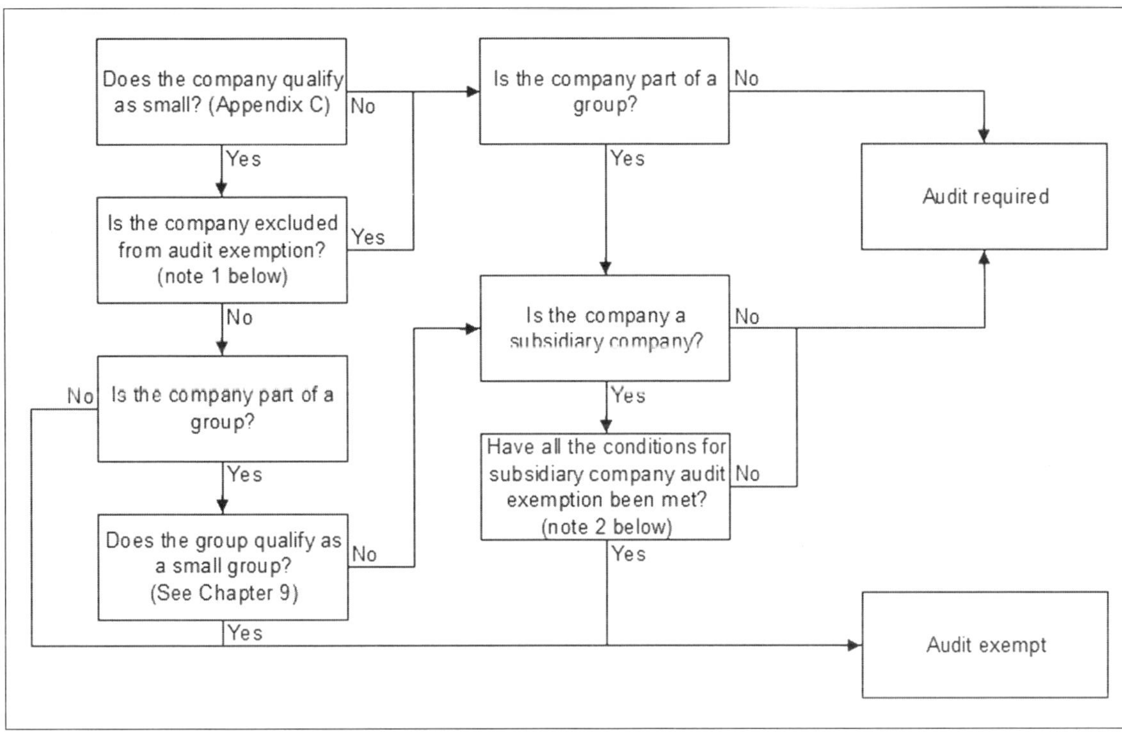

Note 1 – companies excluded from audit exemption

A company is not entitled to the small companies audit exemption conferred by CA 2006 s. 477 if it was at any time within the financial year in question:

- a public company;
- a company that is an authorised insurance company, a banking company, an e-money issuer, a MiFID investment firm or a UCITS management company, or carries on insurance market activity; or
- a special register body (as defined under the Trade Union and Labour Relations (Consolidation) Act 1992) or an employers' association (as defined under the Industrial Relations (Northern Ireland) Order 1992). *s. 478*

Note 2 – Subsidiaries of EEA companies – audit exemption

In accordance with CA 2006 s. 479A, a subsidiary company (irrespective of its size) is exempt from audit if it fulfils all of the following conditions:

(a) its parent undertaking is established under the law of an EEA state;
(b) all of the subsidiary company's shareholders agree the exemption in respect of the financial year in question;

(c) the parent gives a guarantee (under s. 479C) of all the outstanding liabilities to which the subsidiary is subject at the end of the financial year until they are satisfied in full;
(d) the company is included in the consolidated accounts drawn up by the parent undertaking. These accounts must be prepared in accordance with Directive 83/349/EEC (the Seventh Company Law Directive) or international accounting standards;
(e) the consolidated accounts drawn up by the parent must disclose the use of the exemption by the subsidiary;
(f) the directors of the subsidiary must file the following documents at Companies House on or before the date that they file the subsidiary's accounts:
   (i) written notice of the agreement in (b);
   (ii) a written statement by the parent of the guarantee in (c);
   (iii) a copy of the consolidated annual report and accounts referred to in (d) and the auditor's report on those accounts;
(g) the company is not quoted (as defined by s.385);
(h) the company is not an authorised insurance company, a banking company, an e-money issuer, a MiFID investment firm or a UCITS management company, or carries on insurance market activity; and
(i) the company is not a special register body (as defined under the Trade Union and Labour Relations (Consolidation) Act 1992) or an employers' association (as defined under the Industrial Relations (Northern Ireland) Order 1992).

Appendix E Financial Reporting Standard for Smaller Entities (FRSSE) (effective April 2008) accounts checklist

The table below contains a financial statements disclosure checklist derived from the FRSSE and can be used for financial statements prepared for accounting periods ***beginning on or after 6 April 2008.***

The checklist assumes that the company meets the definition of a small company and that application of the FRSSE is available. The checklist provides only a summary of the requirements and it is recommended that the FRSSE itself and the definitions contained therein are also reviewed. (On its publication in 2008, the current FRSSE contained certain transitional arrangements which are also not covered in the checklist.)

FRSSE disclosure checklist		
	FRSSE para	**Y/N or N/A**
GENERAL		
Do the accounts prepared for the company include: (a) a balance sheet as at the last day of the financial year; and (b) a profit and loss account?	**2.1**	
True and fair view		
Do the accounts give a true and fair view of the results and position of the company?	**2.2**	
Have the directors of the company, in determining how amounts are presented within the accounts, had regard to the substance of the reported transaction or arrangement, in accordance with generally accepted accounting principles or practice?	**2.2**	
If there are special circumstances in which compliance with any provisions of the FRSSE or Companies Act causes inconsistencies with the requirement to give a true and fair view, the directors must depart from that provision to the extent necessary to give a true and fair view. Have particulars of the departure, the reasons for it and its effect been included in a note to the accounts as follows: (a) a statement that there has been a departure from the requirements of the FRSSE or Companies Act and that the departure is necessary to give a true and fair view; (b) a statement of the treatment that the FRSSE or Companies Act would normally require and a description of treatment adopted; (c) a statement of the reasons why the treatment prescribed would not give a true and fair view; and (d) a description, with quantification, of how the position shown in the accounts is different as a result of the departure (except where, quantification is already evident in the accounts themselves, or the effect cannot reasonably be quantified, in which case the directors shall explain the circumstances)?	**2.3**	

Where a departure continues in subsequent accounts, have the disclosures been made in all subsequent accounts and have comparative amounts for the previous period been included? Where a departure affects only the comparative amounts, have disclosures been given for those comparative amounts?	**2.4**	
Where there is any doubt about whether applying provisions of FRSSE would be sufficient to give a true and fair view, has an adequate explanation been included in the notes to the accounts of the transaction or arrangement concerned and the treatment adopted?	**2.5**	
Where compliance with the provisions of companies legislation as to the matters to be included in a company's individual accounts or in notes to those accounts would not be sufficient to give a true and fair view, has the necessary additional information been given in the accounts or in a note to them?	**2.18**	
Accounting principles and policies		
Do the accounts state that they have been prepared in accordance with the Financial Reporting Standard for Smaller Entities (effective April 2008)?	**2.6**	
Do the accounts include: (a) a description of each material accounting policy followed; (b) details of any changes to the accounting policies followed in the preceding period including, in addition to the disclosures necessary for prior period adjustment, a brief explanation of why each new accounting policy is thought more appropriate and an indication of the effect of the change on the results for the current period; and (c) a description of any change in estimation technique (if material) and, where practicable, the effect on the results for the current period?	**2.7**	
Do the accounts include the accounting policies adopted by the company in determining the amounts to be included in respect of items shown in the balance sheet or in determining the profit or loss (including such policies with respect to the depreciation and diminution in value of assets)?	**2.8**	
Are the accounting policies and estimation techniques consistent with the requirements of the FRSSE and of companies legislation (or other equivalent legislation)?	**2.9**	
Where a choice is permitted, have the most appropriate policies and techniques been selected, considering the entities particular circumstances for the purpose of giving a true and fair view, taking account of the objectives of relevance, reliability, comparability and understandability?	**2.9**	
Have the accounting policies been applied consistently within the same accounts and from one financial year to the next?	**2.10**	
Have they been reviewed regularly to ensure that they remain the most appropriate to the entity's particular circumstances for the purpose of giving a true and fair view?	**2.10**	
Following a change in accounting policy, have the amounts for the current and corresponding periods been restated on the basis of the new policies?	**2.10**	
In determining the aggregate amount of any item, has the amount of each individual asset or liability been determined separately (i.e. without netting off income and expenditure or assets and liabilities)?	**2.11**	

Going concern		
When preparing accounts, have the directors assessed whether there are significant doubts about the entity's ability to continue as a going concern?	**2.12**	
Have any material uncertainties, of which the directors are aware in making their assessment, been disclosed?	**2.12**	
Where the period considered by the directors in making this assessment has been limited to a period of less than one year from the date of approval of the accounts, has that fact been stated?	**2.12**	
If the directors determine after the balance sheet date either that they intend to liquidate the entity or to cease trading, or that they have no realistic alternative but to do so, have the accounts not been prepared on a going concern basis?	**2.12**	
Prudence		
Have all amounts been determined on a prudent basis?	**2.13**	
Accruals		
Have the accounts, with the exception of cash flow information, been prepared on the accruals basis of accounting?	**2.14**	
Have all income and charges relating to the financial year to which the accounts relate been taken into account, without regard to the date of payment or receipt?	**2.14**	
Prior period adjustments		
Have all prior period adjustments been accounted for by restating the comparative figures for the preceding period in the primary statements and notes and adjusting the opening balance of reserves for the cumulative effect?	**2.15**	
Has the cumulative effect of the adjustments been noted at the foot of the statement of total recognised gains and losses of the current period?	**2.15**	
Has the effect of prior period adjustments on the results for the preceding period been disclosed where practicable?	**2.15**	
Formats – general rules		
Have the company's individual accounts complied, at a minimum, with the provisions set out in the FRSSE as to the form and content of the balance sheet and profit and loss account and additional information to be provided by way of notes to the accounts in order to give a true and fair view?	**2.16** **2.19**	
Have the directors adopted the same format in preparing the accounts as in previous financial years of the company unless in their opinion there are special reasons for a change?	**2.17**	
Have the reasons for any change in format been explained in a note to the accounts in which the new format is first adopted?	**2.17**	
If there is no amount to be shown for an item in respect of the financial year to which the accounts relate and for the immediately preceding financial year, has it been excluded?	**2.20**	
Where the special nature of the company's business requires it, have the directors adapted the arrangement, headings and sub-headings of items in the balance sheet or profit and loss account to which an Arabic number is assigned in the formats?	**2.21**	

Have items to which Arabic numbers are assigned in any of the formats been combined for any financial year if: (a) their individual amounts are not material to assessing the state of affairs or profit and loss of the company for that year; or (b) their combination facilitates that assessment of the balance sheet or profit and loss account?	**2.22**	
Where this applies, have the individual amounts of any items which have been combined been disclosed in a note to the accounts?	**2.22**	
Have corresponding amounts for the previous period been shown for every item disclosed in the balance sheet, profit and loss account and notes to the accounts?	**2.23**	
Where there is no amount to be shown for an item in the balance sheet or profit and loss account for the current accounting period but a corresponding amount can be shown for the previous accounting period, has the corresponding amount been shown?	**2.23**	
Where a corresponding amount is not comparable with that for the current accounting period, has it been adjusted and particulars of the adjustment and reasons for it been disclosed in a note to the accounts?	**2.23**	
Have corresponding amounts been omitted in relation to any amounts stated in the notes to the accounts for the items listed below: (a) details of additions, disposals, revaluations, transfers and cumulative depreciation of fixed assets; (b) transfers to or from reserves and provisions and the source and application of any transfers; (c) details of a company's shareholdings in subsidiary undertakings; and (d) details of a company's significant holding in undertakings other than subsidiary undertakings.	**2.23**	
If not given in the company's primary statements has a note been included of any amount set aside or proposed to be set aside, or withdrawn or proposed to be withdrawn from reserves?	**2.24**	
For each reserve disclosed separately in the accounts, has the following information been provided: (a) the amount of the reserve at the beginning and the end of the financial year; (b) any amounts transferred to or from the reserves during the year; and (c) the source and application of the amounts transferred?	**2.24**	
For the aggregate of all items shown as creditors in the balance sheet, has the aggregate of the amounts which fall due for payment more than five years after the end of the current period been disclosed?	**2.25**	
In respect of the above disclosure, have amounts payable or repayable by instalments and those payable or repayable otherwise than by instalments been separately disclosed?	**2.25**	
For each item shown under creditors, has the aggregate amount of any debts included where any security has been given by the company been disclosed?	**2.26**	
Has either Balance Sheet Format 1 or 2, as set out in SI 2008/409 Sch 1, been adopted (see **Chapter 6**).	**2.27**	
Has either Profit and Loss Format 1 or 2, as set out in SI 2008/409 Sch 1, been adopted (see **Chapter 6**).	**2.28**	
For both the balance sheet and the profit and loss account, has the order of the headings and sub-headings in the chosen format been followed?	**2.27** **2.29**	

Approving and signing of accounts		
Have the company's annual accounts been approved by the board of directors and signed on behalf of the board on the balance sheet by a director of the company?	**2.30** **2.36** **14.4**	
Has the date on which the accounts have been approved by the board of directors been disclosed in the accounts?	**2.30**	
Does the balance sheet contain, in a prominent position above the signature, a statement that the accounts have been prepared in accordance with the special provisions in part 15 of the CA 2006 relating to small companies?	**2.30**	
Does the copy of the company's balance sheet which is delivered to the Registrar and every copy of the balance sheet which is published by or on behalf of the board state the name of the person who signed the balance sheet on behalf of the board?	**2.31** **2.32** **14.4**	
Delivery to the Registrar		
Does the copy of the accounts to be delivered to the Registrar include in a prominent position the registered number of the company and has it been signed by, and state the name of, the directors who signed on behalf of the board and registered auditors as appropriate?	**2.35**	
Exemptions from audit		
Where a company meets the conditions for exemption from audit (see **Chapter 11**), and has taken advantage of that exemption, does the balance sheet contain a statement by the directors that: (a) for the year in question, the company was entitled to exemption from audit (under s. 475 and 477 of CA 2006); (b) mo member or members eligible to do so have deposited a notice requesting an audit within the specified time period; and (c) the directors acknowledge their responsibilities for complying with the requirements of CA 2006 with respect to accounting records and for preparing accounts which give a true and fair view of the state of affairs of the company as at the end of the financial year and of its profit or loss for the financial year in accordance with the requirements of s. 394 and 395 (duty to prepare individual company accounts and applicable accounting framework), and which otherwise comply with the requirements of CA 2006 relating to accounts, so far as applicable to the company?	**2.37**	
Where the directors have taken advantage of the exemption from audit due to the fact that the company is dormant, and the company has during the financial year in question acted as an agent for any person, has the fact that it has so acted been stated?	**2.38**	
Liability Limitation Agreement		
Where exemption from audit is not available, or the directors have not taken advantage of the exemption from audit and the company has entered into a liability limitation agreement with its auditors, have the principal terms of the agreement and either the date of the resolution approving the agreement or the agreement's principal term or the date of the resolution waiving the need for such approval been disclosed in the notes to the accounts?	**3.39**	
PROFIT AND LOSS ACCOUNT		
General		
Have all gains or losses recognised in the accounts for the period been included in the profit and loss account or the statement of total recognised gains and losses?	**3.1**	

Are only profits realised at the balance sheet date included in the profit and loss account?	**3.1**	
Have all liabilities which have arisen in respect of the period or in respect of the previous financial year, including those which have become apparent between the balance sheet date and the date on which it is signed, been included?	**3.1**	
Are all gains and losses which have been excluded from the profit and loss account specifically permitted or required to be taken direct to the reserves by the FRSSE or by companies legislation or equivalent legislation?	**3.2**	
Where an amount relating to any preceding financial year is included in the profit or loss account, has the effect of its inclusion been stated?	**3.3**	
Where the company has supplied geographical markets outside the United Kingdom during the financial year, has the percentage of turnover that is attributable to those markets been separately disclosed?	**3.4**	
Exceptional items		
Have all exceptional items (other than those included in **3.6** (below)) been credited or charged in arriving at the profit or loss on ordinary activities by inclusion under the statutory format headings to which they relate?	**3.5**	
Have these exceptional items each either individually or as an aggregate of items of a similar type, been disclosed separately by way of a note or on the face of the profit and loss account if that degree of prominence is necessary to give a true and fair view?	**3.5**	
Has an adequate description of each exceptional item been given to enable its nature to be understood?	**3.5**	
Has the effect been stated of any transactions that are exceptional by virtue of size or incidence even though they fall within the ordinary activities of the company?	**3.5**	
Have the following items, including provisions in respect of such items, been shown separately on the face of the profit and loss account after operating profit (which is normally profit before income from shares in groups undertakings) and before interest: (a) profits or losses on the sale or termination of an operation; (b) costs of a fundamental reorganisation or restructuring having a material effect on the nature and focus of the reporting entity's operations; and (c) profits or losses on the disposal of fixed assets?	**3.6**	
Profit or loss on disposal		
Has the profit or loss on disposal of an asset been accounted for in the profit and loss account of the period in which the disposal occurred as the difference between the net sale proceeds and the net carrying amount, whether carried at historical cost (less any provisions made) or at a valuation?	**3.7**	
Does the profit or loss on disposal of a previously acquired business include the attributable amount of purchased goodwill that has previously been eliminated against reserves as a matter of accounting policy and has not previously been charged in the profit and loss account?	**3.7**	
Disclosure of auditor remuneration		
Where the accounts are audited, has the remuneration of the company's auditor, including sums paid in respect of expenses, been disclosed in a note to the accounts, including the nature and estimated monetary value of any benefits in kind?	**3.8**	

Where more than one person has been appointed as a company's auditor in respect of the period to which the accounts relate, has the remuneration of each person been disclosed separately?	**3.8**	
PROFIT AND LOSS ACCOUNT		
Basic principles		
Has revenue been recognised under an exchange transaction with a customer, when, and to the extent that, it obtains the right to consideration in exchange for its performance? At the same time, has it recognised a new asset, typically a debtor?	**4.1**	
Where payment from a customer is received in advance of performance, has a liability equal to the amount received, representing its obligation under the contract been recognised? When the seller obtains the right to consideration through performance, has the liability been reduced and the amount of the reduction in the liability simultaneously been reported as revenue?	**4.2**	
A seller may obtain a right to consideration when some, but not all, of its contractual obligations have been fulfilled. Where a seller has partially performed its contractual obligations, has revenue been recognised to the extent that it has obtained the right to consideration through its performance?	**4.3**	
Has revenue been measured at the fair value of the right to consideration? *Subject to paragraphs* ***4.5 – 4.6*** *or other evidence to the contrary, this will normally be the price specified in the contractual arrangement, net of discounts, value added tax and similar sales taxes.*	**4.4**	
Where the effect of the time value of money is material to reported revenue, has the amount of revenue recognised been at the present value of the cash inflows expected to be received from the customer in settlement? Has the unwinding of the discount been credited to finance income representing a gain from a financing transaction?	**4.5**	
Where at the time revenue is recognised on a transaction there is a significant risk that there will be default on the amount of consideration due and the effect is material to reported revenue, has an adjustment to the price specified in the contractual arrangement been made to the amount of revenue to be recognised?	**4.6**	
Have any adjustments to a debtor as a result of changes in the time value of money and credit risk been excluded from within revenue?	**4.7**	
Turnover		
Are the items included within turnover (which may be described as 'sales' in a seller's accounts) the revenue resulting from exchange transactions under which a seller supplies to customers the goods or service that it is in business to provide? *Turnover should exclude other exchange transactions such as the sale of fixed assets.*	**4.8/ 4.9**	
Contracts for services		
If there are distinguishable phases of a single contract for which the value of each phase can be reliably estimated, has the contract been accounted for as two or more separate transactions?	**4.10**	
Have only contracts for services which involve the provision of a single service, or a number of services which constitute a single project, been accounted for as long-term contracts?	**4.11**	
Where contract activity falls into different accounting periods and it is concluded that the effect is material, has the contract for services been accounted for as a long-term contract?	**4.12**	

In determining whether contracts should be accounted for as long-term contracts, has the aggregate effect of all such contracts on the accounts as a whole been considered?	**4.12**	
Where the substance of a contract is that the seller's contractual obligations are performed gradually over time, has revenue been recognised as the contract activity progresses to reflect the seller's partial performance of its contractual obligations?	**4.13**	
Does the amount of revenue reflect the accrual of the right to consideration as contract activity progresses by reference to value of the work performance?	**4.13**	
Where the substance of the contract is that a right to consideration does not arise until the occurrence of a critical event, has revenue only been recognised once that event occurs?	**4.14**	
Does the amount of revenue recognised on any contract for services reflect any uncertainties as to the amount that the customer will accept and pay?	**4.15**	
STATEMENT OF TOTAL RECOGNISED GAINS AND LOSSES		
Where there are recognised gains and losses in addition to the results included in the profit and loss account, has a primary statement been presented showing the total of recognised gains and losses and its components with the same prominence as the profit and loss account?	**5.1**	
Are the components the gains and losses recognised in the period insofar as they are attributable to shareholders, excluding transactions with shareholders?	**5.1**	
FIXED ASSETS AND GOODWILL		
Disclosure		
Has the following information been provided for all fixed assets and goodwill:	**6.1**	
(a) the cost or valuation at the beginning and the end of the year; and	**6.1**	
(b) the effect of any:	**6.1**	
(i) revaluation made during the year;	**6.1**	
(ii) acquisitions during the year;	**6.1**	
(iii) disposals during the year; and	**6.1**	
(iv) transfers during the year?	**6.1**	
Has the following information been provided in respect of provisions for depreciation or diminution in value:	**6.2**	
(a) the cumulative amount of such provision as at the beginning and end of the year;	**6.2**	
(b) the amount of any such provisions made during the year;	**6.2**	
(c) the amount of any adjustments made on disposal during the year; and	**6.2**	
(d) the amount of any other adjustments made during the year?	**6.2**	

Research and development		
Has the cost of fixed assets acquired or constructed in order to provide facilities for research and development activities over a number of accounting periods been capitalised and written off over their useful lives through the profit and loss account?	**6.3**	
Has expenditure on pure and applied research been written off in the period of expenditure through the profit and loss account?	**6.4**	
Has development expenditure been written off in the period of expenditure except in the following circumstances when it may be deferred to future periods:	**6.5**	
(a) there is a clearly defined project; and	**6.5**	
(b) the related expenditure is separately identifiable; and	**6.5**	
(c) the outcome of the project has been assessed with reasonable certainty as to:	**6.5**	
(i) its technical feasibility; and	**6.5**	
(ii) its ultimate commercial viability considered in the light of factors such as likely market conditions (including competing products), public opinion, consumer and environmental legislation; and	**6.5**	
(d) the aggregate of the deferred development costs, any further development costs, and related productions, selling and administration costs is reasonably expected to be exceeded by related future sales or other revenues; and	**6.5**	
(e) adequate resources exist, or are reasonably expected to be available, to enable the project to be completed and to provide any consequential increases in working capital?	**6.5**	
In the foregoing circumstances has development expenditure been deferred only to the extent that its recovery can be reasonably regarded as assured?	**6.6**	
If an accounting policy of deferral of development expenditure is adopted, has it been applied to all development projects that meet the criteria in paragraph 6.5?	**6.7**	
If development costs have been deferred to future periods, have they been amortised?	**6.8**	
Does the amortisation commence with the commercial production or application of the product, service process, or system and is it allocated on a systematic basis to each accounting period by reference to either the sale or use of the product, service, process or system or the period over which they are expected to be sold or used?	**6.8**	
Has deferred development expenditure for each product been reviewed at the end of each accounting period and where the circumstances that justified the deferral of expenditure no longer apply has the expenditure been written off immediately project by project?	**6.9**	
Has the amount of deferred development expenditure carried forward at the beginning and end of the period been disclosed under intangible assets in the balance sheet or in the notes to the balance sheet?	**6.10**	
Has the reason for capitalising these costs and the period over which they are being depreciated been disclosed in a note to the accounts?	**6.10**	
If development costs have not been treated as a realised loss, has this been stated together with an explanation of the circumstances relied upon by the directors to justify their decision?	**6.10**	

Other intangible assets and goodwill		
Have positive purchased goodwill and purchased intangible assets been capitalised?	**6.11**	
Have internally generated goodwill and intangible assets not been capitalised?	**6.11**	
Has any intangible asset purchased with a business been recognised separately from the purchased goodwill if its value can be measured reliably?	**6.12**	
Have capitalised goodwill and intangible assets been depreciated on a straight-line (or more appropriate) basis over their useful economic lives, which shall not exceed 20 years?	**6.13**	
Has the period chosen for depreciating goodwill and the reasons for choosing that period been disclosed in a note to the accounts?	**6.13**	
Is the residual value assigned to goodwill zero?	**6.14**	
If for any intangible asset a higher residual value is assigned, has this value been established reliably?	**6.14**	
Have the useful economic lives been reviewed at the end of each reporting period and revised if necessary, subject to the constraints that the reviewed life shall not exceed 20 years from the date of acquisition?	**6.15**	
Has the carrying amount at the date of revision been depreciated over the reviewed estimate of remaining useful economic life?	**6.15**	
Ensure that goodwill and intangible assets have not been revalued.	**6.16**	
If an acquisition appears to give rise to negative goodwill, have fair values been checked to ensure that those of the acquired assets have not been overstated and those of the acquired liabilities have not been understated?	**6.17**	
Has the remaining negative goodwill up to the fair values of the non-monetary assets acquired been released to the profit and loss account over the lives of those assets?	**6.17**	
Has any additional negative goodwill been recognised in the profit or loss account over the period expected to benefit from it?	**6.17**	
Has the amount of negative goodwill on the balance sheet and the period(s) in which it is being written back been disclosed?	**6.17**	
Tangible fixed assets		
*Checklist questions concerning FRSSE paragraphs from **6.19-6.26** apply to all tangible fixed assets other than investment properties.*		
Are any tangible fixed assets initially measured at cost, then written down to their recoverable amount if necessary?	**6.19**	
Has the initial carrying amount of a tangible fixed asset received as a gift or donation by a charity been its current value, (i.e. the lower of replacement cost and recoverable amount), at the date it is received?	**6.19**	
Where there is no record of the purchase price or production cost of an asset, or any such record cannot be obtained without unreasonable expense or delay, is the value ascribed the earliest available record of its value?	**6.19**	
Have particulars been given of any case where the purchase price or production cost of any asset is for the first time determined in this way?	**6.19**	

Have all costs that are directly attributable to bringing the tangible fixed asset into working condition for its intended use been included in its measurement?	**6.20**	
Have other costs been excluded?	**6.20**	
Where a policy of capitalising finance costs (such as interest) is adopted, have finance costs that are directly attributable to the construction of tangible fixed assets been capitalised as part of the cost of those assets? *Ensure the total amount of finance costs capitalised during a period does not exceed the total amount of finance costs incurred during that period.*	**6.20**	
Where applicable, do the notes to the accounts disclose that finance costs are included in determining the cost of the asset and the amount of the finance costs so included?	**6.20**	
During extended periods in which active development is interrupted, has capitalisation of directly attributable costs, including finance costs, been suspended?	**6.21**	
Did capitalisation cease when substantially all the activities that were necessary to get the tangible fixed asset ready for use were complete, even if the asset was not yet brought into use?	**6.21**	
Has subsequent expenditure been capitalised if: (a) it enhances the economic benefits of a fixed asset in excess of the previously assessed standard of performance (i.e. if it is an 'improvement'); or (b) It replaces or restores a component that has been separately depreciated over its useful economic life?	**6.22**	
Where an entity adopts an accounting policy of revaluation in respect of a tangible fixed asset, is its carrying amount its market value (or the best estimate thereof) as at the balance sheet date?	**6.23**	
Where the directors believe that market value is not an appropriate basis, has current basis (the lower of replacement cost and recoverable amount) been used instead?	**6.23**	
Where a tangible fixed asset is revalued, have all tangible fixed assets of the same class (i.e. having a similar nature, function or use in the business) been revalued, without necessarily applying a policy of revaluation to all classes of tangible fixed assets?	**6.23**	
It may be possible to establish with reasonable reliability the values of certain tangible fixed assets, other than properties, by reference to active second-hand markets or appropriate publicly available indices. For other tangible fixed assets, including property, has a valuation been performed by an experienced valuer (i.e. one who has recognised and relevant recent professional experience, and sufficient knowledge of the state of the market, in the location and category of the tangible fixed asset being valued) at least every five years?	**6.24**	
Has it been updated by an experienced valuer in the intervening years where it is likely that there has been a material change in value?	**6.24**	
Have revaluation losses caused only by changing market prices been recognised in the statement of total recognised gains and losses until the carrying amount of the asset reaches its depreciated historical cost?	**6.25**	
Have other revaluation losses been recognised in the profit and loss account?	**6.25**	

Have revaluation gains been recognised in the statement of total recognised gains and losses, except to the extent (after adjusting for subsequent depreciation) that they reverse revaluation losses on the same asset that were previously recognised in the profit and loss account?	**6.26**	
To that extent, have they been recognised in the profit and loss account?	**6.26**	
Has the subsequent adjustment to depreciation achieved the same overall effect that would have been reached had the original downward revaluation reflected in the profit and loss account not occurred?	**6.26**	
Where tangible fixed assets have been revalued has either – the comparable amounts determined under the historical cost accounting rules (i.e. the aggregate historical cost amount that would have been included had the assets not been revalued, reflecting any write-downs to recoverable amount that would have been necessary); or the differences between those amounts and the corresponding amounts actually shown in the balance sheet been shown separately in the balance sheet or in a note to the accounts?	**6.27**	
Where tangible fixed assets are constantly being replaced and their value is not material to assessing the company's state of affairs and the quantity, value and composition are not subject to material variation are these included at a fixed quantify and value?	**6.28**	
Where tangible fixed assets have been revalued, has the year in which they were valued been disclosed?	**6.29**	
If tangible fixed assets have been revalued in the current financial year, have the names of the persons who valued them or particulars of their qualifications for doing so and the bases of the valuation been disclosed?	**6.29**	
Investments		
Have fixed asset investments initially been measured at cost? Or, alternatively, have they been measured at a market value determined as at the date of their last valuation or on any other value determined on a basis which appears to the directors to be appropriate (in which case, the method for adopting it must be disclosed in a note to the accounts)?	**6.30**	
Have gains and losses been recognised (in the profit and loss account or statement of total recognised gains and losses) on the same basis as in paragraph **6.25** and **6.26** above?	**6.30**	
Where fixed asset investments have been revalued have either – the comparable amounts determined under the historical cost accounting rules (i.e. the aggregate historical cost amount that would have been included had the assets not been revalued, reflecting any write-downs to recoverable amount that would have been necessary) or the differences between those amount and the corresponding amounts actually shown in the balance sheet been shown separately in the balance sheet or in the note to the accounts?	**6.31**	
Has the aggregate amount of listed investments included under each item of investments shown in the balance sheet been disclosed?	**6.32**	
For each item has the following been disclosed: (a) the aggregate market value of the listed investments where it differs from its balance sheet amount; and (b) both the market value and the stock exchange value of any investments, of which the market value is taken as being higher than the stock exchange value?	**6.32**	

Where the company has at the end of the financial year a significant holding in an undertaking (which is not a subsidiary undertaking of the company) which represents 20% or more of the nominal value of any class of shares in the undertaking, or more than 20% of the book value of the investing company's total assets, have the following been stated in relation to the undertaking:		
(a) the name of the undertaking;	**6.33**	
(b) if the undertaking is incorporated outside of the United Kingdom, the country in which it is incorporated;	**6.33**	
(c) if it is unincorporated, the address of its principal place of business;	**6.33**	
(d) the identity and proportion of the nominal value of each class of shares held;	**6.33**	
(e) the aggregate amount of the capital and reserves of the undertaking as at the end of the most recent financial year ending with or before that of the investing company; and	**6.33**	
(f) its profit or loss for that year?	**6.33**	
Revaluation reserve		
Have gains or losses arising on the revaluation of assets that have been recognised in the statement of total recognised gains and losses been credited, or debited, to a separate revaluation reserve?	**6.34**	
Have amounts been transferred from the revaluation reserve to the profit or loss account when they have been realised?	**6.35**	
Has the treatment for taxation purposes of amounts credited or debited to the revaluation reserve been disclosed in a note to the accounts?	**6.36**	
Depreciation		
Checklist paragraphs from ***6.38-6.43*** *apply to all tangible fixed assets other than investment properties.*	**6.37**	
Has the cost (or revalued amount) less estimated residual value of a tangible fixed asset been depreciated on a systematic basis over its useful economic life?	**6.38**	
Does the depreciation method reflect as fairly as possible the pattern in which the asset's economic benefits are consumed by the entity?	**6.38**	
Has the depreciation charge for each period been recognised as an expense in the profit and loss account unless it is permitted to be included in the carrying amount of another asset?	**6.38**	
Where a tangible fixed asset comprises two or more major components with substantially different useful economic lives, has each component been accounted for separately for depreciation purposes and depreciated over its individual useful economic life?	**6.39**	
Have the useful economic lives and residual values of tangible fixed assets been reviewed regularly and, if necessary, revised?	**6.40**	
On revision, has the carrying amount of the tangible fixed asset at the date of revision less the revised residual value been depreciated over the revised remaining useful economic life?	**6.40**	
If there has been a change in the depreciation method, does it meet the requirement that the new method will give a fairer presentation of the results and of the financial position?	**6.41**	

Have the following been disclosed in the accounts for (1) land and buildings and (2) other tangible fixed assets in aggregate:		
(a) the depreciation methods used;	**6.42**	
(b) the useful economic lives or the depreciation rates used; and	**6.42**	
(c) where material, the financial effect of a change during the period in either the estimate of useful economic lives or the estimate of residual values?	**6.42**	
Where there has been a change in the depreciation method used has the effect, if material, and the reason for change been disclosed in the period of change?	**6.43**	
Write-downs to recoverable amount		
*Checklist paragraphs **6.45 – 6.48** apply to capitalised goodwill and all fixed assets other than investment properties and financial instruments (except investments in subsidiaries, associates, and joint ventures).*	**6.44**	
Have fixed assets and goodwill been carried in the balance sheet at no more than recoverable amount?	**6.45**	
If the net book amount of a fixed asset or goodwill is considered not to be recoverable in full at the balance sheet date (perhaps as a result of obsolescence or a fall in demand for a product), has the net book amount been written down to the estimated recoverable amount, which shall then be written off over the remaining useful economic life of the asset?	**6.45**	
If the recoverable amount of a tangible fixed asset or investment subsequently increases as a result of a change in economic conditions or in the expected use of the asset, has the net book amount been written back to the lower of recoverable amount and the amount at which the asset would have been recorded had the original write-down not been made?	**6.46**	
If the recoverable amount of an intangible asset or capitalised goodwill subsequently increases, has the net book amount been written back only if an external event caused the original write-down and subsequent external events clearly and demonstrably reverse the effects of that event in a way that was not foreseen when the original write-down was calculated?	**6.47**	
Have write-downs and any reversals to recoverable amount been charged or credited to the profit and loss account for the period?	**6.48**	
Have write-downs of revalued tangible fixed assets that reverse previous revaluation gains simply as a result of changing market prices been recognised in the statement of total recognised gains and losses to the extent that the carrying amount of the asset is greater than its depreciated historical cost?	**6.48**	
Are any amounts not shown in the profit and loss account disclosed (either separately or in aggregate) in a note to the accounts?	**6.48**	
Where fixed assets are not actually revalued in the balance sheet but their value is considered by the director, has a note to the accounts been included stating the following:		
(a) that the directors have considered the value of some or all of the fixed assets of the company, without actually revaluing those assets;	**6.49**	
(b) that the directors are satisfied that the aggregate value of those assets at the time in question is or was not less than the aggregate amount at which they were then stated in the company's accounts; and	**6.49**	

(c) that the assets affected are accordingly stated in the accounts on the basis that a revaluation of the company's fixed assets took place at that time?	**6.49**	
Investment properties		
Have investment properties not been subject to periodic charges for depreciation except for properties held on lease, which shall be depreciated at least over the period when the unexpired term is 20 years or less?	**6.50**	
Have investment properties been included in the balance sheet at their market value and has the carrying value been displayed prominently either on the face of the balance sheet or in the notes?	**6.51**	
Have the names of the persons making the valuation, or particulars of their qualifications been disclosed together with the bases of valuation used by them?	**6.52**	
If a person making a valuation is an employee or officer of the company or group that owns the property has this fact been disclosed?	**6.52**	
Ensure that any changes to the market value of investment properties have not been taken to the profit and loss account, and instead taken to the statement of total recognised gains and losses (being a movement on an investment revaluation reserve), unless a deficit (or its reversal) on an individual investment property is expected to be permanent, in which case it shall be charged (or credited) in the profit and loss account of the period.	**6.53**	
Government grants		
Subject to paragraph **6.55**, have government grants been recognised in the profit and loss account so as to match them with the expenditure towards which they are intended to contribute?	**6.54**	
To the extent that the grant is made as a contribution towards expenditure on a fixed asset, in principle it may be deducted from the purchase price or production cost of that asset. However, the option to deduct government grants from the purchase price or production costs of fixed assets is not available to companies governed by the accounting and reporting requirements of UK companies legislation. In such cases, has the amount so deferred been treated as deferred income?	**6.54**	
If a government grant is recognised in the profit and loss account have the conditions for its receipt been complied with and is there reasonable assurance that the grant will be received?	**6.55**	
Have potential liabilities to repay grants either in whole or in part in specified circumstances been provided for only to the extent that repayment is probable?	**6.56**	
Has the repayment of a government grant been accounted for by setting off the repayment against any unamortised deferred income relating to the grant?	**6.56**	
Has any excess been charged immediately to the profit and loss account?	**6.56**	
Have the following statements been disclosed in the accounts:		
(a) the effects of government grants on the results for the period and/or the financial position of the entity; and (b) where the results of the period are affected materially by the receipt of forms of government assistance other than grants, the nature of that assistance and, to the extent that the effects on the accounts can be measured, an estimate of those effects?	**6.57**	

LEASES		
Hire purchase and leasing		
Have those hire purchase contracts which are of a financing nature been accounted for on a basis similar to that set out below for finance leases?	**7.1**	
Conversely, have other hire purchase contracts been accounted for on a basis similar to that set out below for operating leases?	**7.1**	
Accounting for lessees		
Have finance leases been recorded in the balance sheet of a lessee as an asset and as an obligation to pay future rentals?	**7.2**	
At inception, was the lease recorded both as an asset and as a liability at the fair value of the asset?	**7.2**	
In those cases where the fair value of the asset does not give a realistic estimate of the cost to the lessee of the asset and of the obligation entered into, has a better estimate been used?	**7.3**	
Does this better estimate approximate to the present value of the minimum lease payments, derived by discounting them at the interest rate implicit in the lease?	**7.3**	
Has the total finance charge under a finance lease been allocated to accounting periods during the lease term so as to produce a constant periodic rate of charge on the remaining balance of the obligation for each accounting period, or a reasonable approximation thereto (e.g. the straight-line method may provide such reasonable approximation)?	**7.4**	
Has the rental under an operating lease been charged on a straight-line basis over the lease term even if the payments are not made on such a basis, unless another systematic and rational basis is more appropriate?	**7.5**	
Have any incentives to sign a lease, in whatever form they may take, been spread by the lessee on a straight-line basis over the lease term or, if shorter than the full lease term, over the period to the review date on which the rent is first expected to be adjusted to the prevailing market rate?	**7.6**	
Have assets leased under a finance lease been depreciated over the shorter of the lease term or its useful life?	**7.7**	
In the case of a hire purchase contract that has the characteristics of a finance lease, has the asset been depreciated over its useful life?	**7.7**	
Accounting by lessors		
Has the amount due from the lessee under a finance lease been recorded in the balance sheet of the lessor as a debtor at the amount of the net investment in the lease after making provision for items such as bad and doubtful rentals receivable?	**7.8**	
Have the total gross earnings under finance leases been recognised on a systematic and rational basis (normally a constant periodic rate of return on the lessor's net investment)?	**7.9**	
Has rental income from an operating lease been recognised on a straight-line basis over the period of the lease, even if payments are not made on such a basis, unless another systematic and rational basis is more representative of the time pattern in which the benefit from the leased asset is receivable?	**7.10**	
Have assets held for use in operating leases by a lessor been recorded as fixed assets and depreciated over their useful life?	**7.11**	

Manufacturer / dealer lessor		
Ensure that a manufacturer or dealer lessor does not recognise a profit under an operating lease. If there is a selling profit under a finance lease has it been restricted to the excess of the fair value of the asset over the manufacturer's or dealer's cost less any grants receivable by the manufacturer or dealer towards the purchase, construction or use of the asset?	**7.12**	
Sale and leaseback transactions – accounting by the seller/lessee		
In a sale and leaseback transaction that results in a finance lease, has any apparent profit or loss (i.e. the difference between the sale price and the previous carrying value) been deferred and amortised in the accounts of the seller/lessee over the shorter of the lease term and the useful life of the asset?	**7.13**	
If the leaseback is an operating lease, have the following conditions been met:		
(a) any profit or loss has been recognised immediately, provided it is clear that the transaction is established at fair value;	**7.14**	
(b) if the sale price is below fair value any profit or loss has been recognised immediately, except that if the apparent loss is compensated for by future rentals at below market price it shall to that extent be deferred and amortised over the remainder of the lease term (or, if shorter, the period during which the reduced rentals are chargeable); or	**7.14**	
(c) if the sale price is above fair value, has the excess over fair value been deferred and amortised over the shorter of the remainder of the lease term and the period to the next rent review (if any)?	**7.14**	
Sale and leaseback transactions – accounting by the buyer/lessor		
Has the buyer/lessor accounted for a sale and leaseback in the same way as other leases, using methods in paragraphs **7.8-7.12**?	**7.15**	
Disclosure by lessees		
Have the following been disclosed:		
(a) either:	**7.16**	
(i) the gross amounts of assets that are held under finance leases together with the related accumulated depreciation for (1) land and buildings and (2) other fixed assets in aggregate; or	**7.16**	
(ii) has the information in (i) been integrated with it, such that the totals of gross amount, accumulated depreciation, net amount and depreciation allocated for the period for (1) land and buildings and (2) other fixed assets in aggregate for assets held under finance leases are included with similar amounts for owned fixed assets? Where this is the treatment, have the net amount of assets held under finance leases and the amount of depreciation allocated for the period in respect of assets under finance leases included in the overall total been disclosed separately?	**7.16**	
(b) the amounts of obligations related to finance leases (net of finance charges allocated to future periods)? Are these disclosed separately from other obligations and liabilities, either on the face of the balance sheet or in the notes to the accounts?	**7.16**	
(c) the amount of any commitments existing at the balance sheet date in respect of finance leases that have been entered into but whose inception occurs after the year end?	**7.16**	

In respect of operating leases, has the lessee disclosed the payments that it is committed to make during the next year, analysed into those in which the commitment expires within that year, those expiring in the second to fifth years inclusive, and those expiring over five years from the balance sheet date?	**7.17**	
Disclosure by lessors		
Have the following been disclosed:		
(a) the gross amounts of assets held for use in operating leases and the related accumulated depreciation charges;	**7.18**	
(b) the cost of assets acquired, whether by purchase or finance lease, for the purpose of letting under finances leases; and	**7.18**	
(c) the net investment in (i) finance leases and (ii) hire purchase contracts at each balance sheet date?	**7.18**	
CURRENT ASSETS		
Stocks and long-term contracts		
Have stocks been stated in the accounts at the total of the lower of cost and net realisable value of the separate items of stock or of groups of similar items?	**8.1**	
Where there is no record of the purchase price or production cost of stock has the value ascribed been the earliest available record of its value?	**8.2**	
Have particulars been given of any case where the purchase price or production cost of any asset is for the first time determined in this way?	**8.2**	
Have finance costs (such as interest) that are directly attributable to the acquisition, construction or production of stock been included as part of the cost?	**8.3**	
In such cases, do the notes to the accounts disclose that finance costs are included in determining the cost of the asset and the amount of finance cost so included?	**8.3**	
Have stocks which are constantly being replaced, and their value is not material to assessing the company's state of affairs and their quantity, value and composition are not subject to material variation, been included at a fixed quantity and value?	**8.4**	
Have distribution costs been excluded from production costs of stocks?	**8.5**	
Have long-terms contracts been assessed on a contract-by-contract basis and reflected in the profit and loss account by recording turnover and related costs as contract activity progresses?	**8.6**	
Has turnover been ascertained in a manner appropriate to the stage of completion of the contract, the business and the industry in which it operates?	**8.6**	
Where it is considered that the outcome of a long-term contract can be assessed with reasonable certainty before its conclusion, has the prudently calculated attributable profit been recognised in the profit and loss account as the difference between the reported turnover and related costs for that contract?	**8.7**	
Have long-term contacts been disclosed in the balance sheet as follows:		

(a) the amount by which recorded turnover is in excess of payments on account has been classified as 'amounts recoverable on contracts' and separately disclosed within debtors; (b) the balance of payments on account (in excess of the amount (i) matched with turnover and (ii) offset against long-term contract balances) has been classified as payments on account and separately disclosed within creditors; (c) the amount of long-term contracts, at costs incurred, net of amounts transferred to cost of sales, after deducting foreseeable losses and payments on account not matched with turnover, have been classified as 'long-term contract balances' and separately disclosed within the balance sheet heading 'stocks'? Has the balance sheet note disclosed separately the balances of: (i) net cost less foreseeable losses; and (ii) applicable payments on account; (d) the amount by which the provision or accrual for foreseeable losses exceeds the costs incurred (after transfers to cost of sales) has been included within either 'provisions for liabilities' or 'creditors' as appropriate?	**8.8**	
Consignment stock Where consignment stock is in substance an asset of the dealer, has the stock been recognised as such on the dealer's balance sheet, together with a corresponding liability to the manufacturer? Has any deposit been deducted from the liability and the excess classified as a trade creditor? Where stock is not in substance an asset of the dealer, has the stock been excluded on the dealer's balance sheet until the transfer of title has crystallised? Has any deposit in this case been included under 'other debtors'?	**8.9**	
Debt factoring Where the entity has transferred to the factor all significant benefits and all significant risks relating to the debts, and has no obligation to repay the factor, have the debts been removed from the entity's balance sheet and no liability been recognised in respect of the proceeds received from the factor? Has a profit or loss been recognised, calculated as the difference between the carrying amount of the debts and the proceeds received?	**8.10**	
Where the entity has retained significant benefits and risks relating to factored debts have the factored debts been shown gross (after providing for bad debts, credit protection charges and any accrued interest) separately on the face of the balance sheet, if the following conditions have been met: (a) there is no doubt that the entity's exposure to loss is limited to a fixed monetary amount; (b) amounts received from the factor are secured only on the debts factored; (c) the debts factored are capable of separate identification; (d) the debt factor has no recourse to other debts or assets; (e) the entity has no right to reacquire the debts in the future; and (f) the factor has no right to return the debts even in the event of the cessation of the factoring agreement?	**8.11**	
Have any amounts received from the factor in respect of those debts, to the extent that they are not returnable, been shown as deductions therefrom on the face of the balance sheet (a 'linked presentation')?	**8.11**	
Do the accounts include a note stating that the entity is not required to support bad debts in respect of factored debts and that the factors have stated in writing that they will not seek recourse other than out of factored debts?	**8.11**	

Has the interest element of the factor's charges been recognised as it accrues and included in the profit and loss account with other interest charges?	**8.11**	
In other cases, have gross assets (equivalent in amount to the gross amount of the debts) been shown on the balance sheet of the entity within assets and a corresponding liability in respect of the proceeds received from the factor been shown with liabilities?	**8.12**	
Have the interest elements of the factor's charges and other factoring costs been recognised as they accrue and included in the profit and loss account with other interest charges?	**8.12**	
Current asset investments		
Have current asset investments initially been stated in the accounts at the lower of cost and net realisable value? (Alternatively, have they been measured at the current cost?)	**8.13**	
Have gains and losses been recognised (in the profit and loss account or statement of total recognised gains and losses) using the basis applied to tangible fixed assets in paragraphs **6.25** and **6.26**?	**8.13**	
Where listed shares are held as a current asset investment, has the following information been disclosed: (a) the aggregate market value of those investments where it differs from their balance sheet amount; and (b) both the market value and the stock exchange value of any investments, of which the market value is taken as being higher than the stock exchange value?	**8.14**	
Start-up costs and pre-contract costs		
Have start-up costs been accounted for on a basis consistent with the accounting treatment of similar costs incurred as part of the entity's on-going activities?	**8.15**	
In cases where there are no such similar costs, have start-up costs that do not meet the criteria for recognition as assets under another specific requirement of the FRSSE been recognised as expenses when they were incurred?	**8.15**	
Have pre-contract costs been expensed as incurred, except those directly attributable costs that have been recognised as an asset when it is virtually certain that a contract will be obtained and the contract is expected to result in future net cash inflows with a present value no less than all amounts recognised as an asset?	**8.16**	
Have costs incurred before the asset recognition criteria have been met been expensed?	**8.16**	
TAXATION		
General		
Has tax (current and deferred) been recognised in the profit and loss account, except to the extent that it is attributable to a gain or loss that is or has been recognised directly in the statement of total recognised gains and losses (in which case the tax shall also be recognised directly in that statement)?	**9.1**	
Have the material components of the (current and deferred) tax charge (or credit) for the period been disclosed separately?	**9.2**	

Have any special circumstances that affect the overall tax charge or credit for the period, or may affect those of future periods, been disclosed by way of a note to the profit and loss account and have their individual effects been quantified?	**9.3**	
Have the effects of a fundamental change in the basis of taxation been included in the tax charge or credit for the period and separately disclosed on the face of the profit and loss account?	**9.3**	
Deferred tax		
Has deferred tax been recognised in respect of all timing differences that have originated but not reversed by the balance sheet date?	**9.4**	
Has deferred tax been excluded on: (a) revaluation gains and losses unless, by the balance sheet date, the entity has entered into a binding agreement to sell the asset and has revalued the asset to the selling price; or (b) taxable gains arising on revaluations or sales if it is more likely than not that the gain will be rolled over into a replacement asset?	**9.4**	
Have unrelieved tax losses and other deferred tax assets been recognised only to the extent that it is more likely than not that they will be recovered against the reversal of deferred tax liabilities or other future taxable profits?	**9.5**	
Has deferred tax been recognised when the tax allowances for the cost of a fixed asset are received before or after the depreciation of the fixed asset is recognised in the profit and loss account?	**9.6**	
If and when all the conditions for retaining the tax allowances have been met, has the deferred tax been reversed?	**9.6**	
Has deferred tax not been recognised on permanent differences?	**9.7**	
Has deferred tax been measured at the average tax rates that would apply when the timing differences are expected to reverse, based on tax rates and laws that have been enacted by the balance sheet date?	**9.8**	
If an entity adopts a policy of discounting, have all deferred tax balances that have been measured by reference to undiscounted cash flows and for which the impact of discounting is material been discounted?	**9.9**	
When discounting is used, has the unwinding of the discount been shown as a component of the tax change and been disclosed separately?	**9.9**	
Has the deferred tax balance and its material components been disclosed?	**9.10**	
Has the movement between the opening and closing net deferred tax balances, and the material components of this movement, been disclosed?	**9.11**	
If assets have been revalued, or if their market values have been disclosed in a note, has the amount of tax that would be payable or recoverable if the assets were sold at those values been disclosed?	**9.12**	
Tax on dividends		
Have outgoing dividends and similar amounts payable been recognised at an amount that includes any withholding tax but excludes other taxes, such as attributable tax credits?	**9.13**	
Have incoming dividends and similar income receivable been recognised at an amount that includes any withholding tax but excludes other taxes, such as attributable tax credits?	**9.14**	

Has any withholding tax suffered been shown as part of the tax change?	**9.14**	
Value added tax (VAT)		
Has turnover shown in the profit or loss account excluded either VAT on taxable outputs or VAT imputed under the flat rate VAT scheme?	**9.15**	
Has irrecoverable VAT allocated to fixed assets and to other items disclosed separately in the accounts been included in their cost where practicable and material?	**9.15**	
PENSIONS		
Is the cost of a defined contribution scheme equal to the contributions payable to the scheme for the accounting period?	**10.1**	
Has the cost been recognised within operating profit in the profit and loss account?	**10.1**	
Have particulars been given of any pension commitments included under any provision shown in the company's balance sheet and any such commitments for which no provision has been made?	**10.2**	
Where any such commitment relates wholly or partly to pension payable to past directors of the company, have separate details been given of that commitment, so far as it relates to such pensions?	**10.2**	
Have the following disclosures been made in respect of a defined contribution scheme: (a) the nature of the scheme (i.e. defined contribution); (b) the cost for the period; and (c) any outstanding or prepaid contributions at the balance sheet date?	**10.3**	
Where a company participates in a defined benefit scheme, reference should be made to Appendix II of the FRSSE 'Accounting for retirement benefits: defined benefit schemes'. The disclosure checklist does not cover this Appendix.	**10.4**	
PROVISIONS, CONTINGENT LIABILITIES AND CONTINGENT ASSETS		
Provisions		
Paragraphs 11.2-11.8 are not applied to pensions, deferred tax or leases which are covered by more specific requirements of the FRSSE.	**11.1**	
Has a provision been recognised when it is probable (i.e. more likely than not) that a present obligation exists, as a result of a past event, and that it will require a transfer of economic benefits in settlement that can be estimated reliably?	**11.2**	
Is the amount recognised the best estimate of the expenditure required to settle the obligation at the balance sheet date?	**11.2**	
Where the effect of the time value of money is material, is the amount of the provision the present value of the expenditure expected to be required to settle the obligation?	**11.2**	
If discounting has been used, has the unwinding of the discount been shown as other finance costs adjacent to interest?	**11.2**	
Where some or all of the expenditure required to settle a provision may be reimbursed by another party (e.g. through an insurance claim), has the reimbursement been recognised, as a separate asset, only when it is virtually certain to be received if the entity settles the obligation?	**11.3**	
Has the expense relating to the provision been presented net of the recovery in the profit and loss account?	**11.3**	

Have gains from the expected disposal of assets been excluded from the measurement of the provision?	**11.3**	
Have provisions been reviewed at each balance sheet date and then adjusted to reflect the current best estimate?	**11.4**	
Has a provision only been used for expenditure for which the provision was originally recognised?	**11.5**	
For each class of provision has the following information been provided (except where the movement consists of the application of a provision for the purpose for which it was established): (a) the amount of the provision at the beginning and the end of the financial year; (b) any amounts transferred to or from the provision during the year; (c) the source and application of the amounts transferred; and (d) details of each material provision included under 'other provisions' in the company's balance sheet in any case where the amount of that provision is material?	**11.6**	
Contingent liabilities and contingent assets		
Are contingent liabilities and contingent assets not recognised?	**11.7**	
Have the following been disclosed for contingent liabilities, except where their existence is remote, and probable for contingent assets: (a) a brief description of the nature of the contingent item; (b) an estimate of its financial effect (where practicable); and (c) its legal nature?	**11.8**	
Have details been provided where any valuable security has been provided by the company in connection with a contingent liability?	**11.9**	
Where practicable, has the aggregate amount, or estimated amount, or contracts for capital expenditure been disclosed?	**11.10**	
Have details of any other financial commitments not provided for which are relevant to assessing the company's state of affairs also been disclosed?	**11.10**	
Have details been given of any charge on the assets of the company to secure the liabilities of any other person, including, where practicable, the amount secured?	**11.11**	
FINANCIAL INSTRUMENTS, SHARE CAPITAL AND SHARE-BASED PAYMENTS		
General		
Has a financial instrument, or its component parts, been classified as a financial liability, a financial asset or an equity instrument in accordance with the substance of the contractual arrangement rather than its legal form?	**12.1**	
Have the finance costs of borrowings been allocated to periods over the term of the borrowings at a constant rate on the carrying amount?	**12.2**	
Have all finance costs been charged in the profit and loss account?	**12.2**	
Have borrowings initially been stated in the balance sheet at the fair value of consideration received?	**12.3**	
Has the carrying amount of borrowings been increased by the finance cost in respect of the reporting period and reduced by payments made in respect of the borrowings in that period?	**12.3**	

Where an arrangement fee is such as to represent a significant additional cost of finance when compared with the interest payable over the life of the instrument, has it been treated as in paragraph **12.2**?	**12.4**	
Where this is not the case, has it been charged in the profit and loss account immediately?	**12.4**	
Has any amount of convertible debt issued been separately disclosed from other liabilities?	**12.5**	
Have any dividends relating to a financial instrument or a component that is a financial liability been recognised as expenses in the profit and loss account?	**12.6**	
Have distributions to holders of equity instruments been debited by the entity directly to equity, net of any related income tax benefit?	**12.6**	
If any dividends have been declared after the balance sheet date, have the dividends not been recognised as a liability at the balance sheet date?	**12.6**	
Are the following stated in the notes to the accounts:		
(a) the aggregate amount of dividends paid in the financial year (other than those for which a liability existed at the immediately preceding balance sheet date); (b) the aggregate amount of dividends that the company is liable to pay at the balance sheet date; and (c) the aggregate amount of dividends that are proposed before the date of approval of the accounts, and not otherwise disclosed in (a) or (b)?	**12.7**	
If any fixed cumulative dividends on the company's shares are in arrears, has the amount of the arrears and the period for which each class of dividends is in arrears been disclosed?	**12.8**	
The company's share capital		
Has the following information been disclosed with respect to the company's share capital: (a) where shares of more than one class have been allotted, the number and aggregate nominal value of share of each class allotted; (b) for any part of the allotted share capital that consists of redeemable shares: (i) the earliest and latest dates on which the company has the power to redeem those shares; (ii) whether those shares must be redeemed in any event or are liable to be redeemed at the option of the company or of the shareholder; and (iii) whether any (and, if so, what) premium is payable on redemption?	**12.9**	
If the company has allotted any shares during the period, has the following information been disclosed: (a) the classes of shares allotted; and (b) for each class, the number allotted, their aggregate nominal value, and the consideration received by the company for the allotment?	**12.10**	
Has the amount of allotted share capital and the amount of called up share capital which has been paid up been separately disclosed?	**12.11**	
Have the number, description and amount of shares in the company held by or on behalf of its subsidiary undertakings been disclosed unless the subsidiary undertaking is concerned as a personal representative or a trustee?	**12.12**	

Share based payments		
Has the entity accounted for share-based payment arrangements (including transactions with employees or others providing similar services) as follows:	**12.13**	
For cash-settled share-based payment transactions (a) An entity shall recognise the goods or services received or acquired when it obtains the goods or as the services are received. If the goods or services received or acquired do not qualify for recognition as assets, they shall be recognised as expenses. The entity shall recognise a corresponding liability. (b) The amount of the goods or services and the corresponding liability recognised shall be the best estimate of the expenditure required to settle the liability at the balance sheet date. The liability shall be remeasured at each balance sheet date and at the date of settlement. (c) Information shall be disclosed in a note to describe the principal terms and conditions of cash-settled share-based payment transactions that exist during the period, including their current and potential financial effect.	**12.13**	
For equity-settled share-based payment arrangements	**12.13**	
(d) Information shall be disclosed in a note to describe the principal terms and conditions of any equity-settled share-based payment arrangement that exist during the period including, the number of shares and the number of employees and others potentially involved, the grant date, any performance conditions and over what periods these apply and, where applicable, any option exercise prices.	**12.13**	
Where the terms of the arrangement provide the counterparty with the choice of whether the entity settles the transaction in cash or by issuing equity instruments, has the transaction been accounted for as a cash-settled transaction in accordance with paragraph **12.13 (a) – (c)**? Has the liability been measured at the best estimate of the amount required to settle it at the balance sheet date if the counterparty were to opt for cash settlement? If the obligation is eventually settled by the issue of equity instruments, has the liability previously recognised been treated as the proceeds of issue of those instruments?	**12.14**	
Where the entity and not the counterparty has the choice of settlement method, has the arrangement been treated as either an equity-settled transaction in accordance with paragraph **12.13(d)** or as a cash-settled transaction in accordance with paragraph **12.13 (a) – (c)**, as appropriate to the entity's circumstances?	**12.15**	
FOREIGN CURRENCY TRANSLATION		
Transactions in foreign currencies		
Where sums originally denominated in foreign currencies have been brought into account under any items shown in the balance sheet or profit and loss account, has the basis on which those sums have been translated into local currency been disclosed?	**13.1**	
Subject to paragraphs **13.4** and **13.6**, has each asset, liability, revenue or cost arising from a transaction denominated in a foreign currency been translated into the local currency at the exchange rate in operation on the date on which the transaction occurred?	**13.2**	
If the rates do not fluctuate significantly, has an average rate for a period been used as an approximation?	**13.2**	
Where the transaction is to be settled at a contracted rate, has that rate been used?	**13.2**	

Where a trading transaction is covered by a related or matching forward contract, has the rate of exchange specified in that contract been used?	**13.2**	
Subject to paragraph **13.6**, which relates to the treatment of foreign equity investments financed by foreign currency borrowings, have no subsequent translations been made once non-monetary assets have been translated and recorded?	**13.3**	
At each balance sheet date, have monetary assets and liabilities denominated in a foreign currency been translated by using the closing rate or, where appropriate, the rates of exchange fixed under the terms of the relevant transactions?	**13.4**	
Where there are related or matching forward contracts in respect of trading transactions, have the rates of exchange specified in those contracts been used?	**13.4**	
Have all exchange gains or losses on settled transactions and unsettled monetary items been reported as part of the profit or loss for the period from ordinary activities?	**13.5**	
Where a company has used foreign currency borrowings to finance, or to provide a hedge against, its foreign equity investments and the conditions set out below apply, have the equity investments been denominated in the appropriate foreign currencies and the carrying amounts translated at the end of each accounting period at closing rates for inclusion in the investing company's accounts?	**13.6**	
Where investments are treated in this way, have any exchange differences arising been taken to reserves and the exchange gains or losses on the foreign currency borrowings then been offset, as a reserve moment, against these exchange differences?	**13.6**	
For the above treatment to be permitted, do the following conditions apply: (a) in any accounting period, exchange gains or losses arising on the borrowings may be offset only to the extent of exchange differences arising on the equity investments; (b) the foreign currency borrowings, whose exchange gains or losses are used in the offset process, shall not exceed, in the aggregate, the total amount of cash that the investments are expected to be able to generate, whether from profits or otherwise; and (c) the accounting treatment adopted shall be applied consistently from period to period?	**13.6**	
Incorporating accounts of foreign entities		
When preparing accounts for a company and its foreign entities (which includes the incorporation of the results of associated companies or foreign branches into those of an investing company) has the closing rate/ net investment method of translating the local currency accounts been used?	**13.7**	
Have any exchange differences arising from the retranslation of the opening net investment in a foreign entity at the closing rate been recorded as a movement on reserves?	**13.8**	
Has the profit and loss account of a foreign entity accounted for under the closing rate/net investment method been translated at the closing rate or at an average rate for the period?	**13.9**	

Where an average rate is used, has the difference between the profit and loss account translated at an average rate and at the closing rate been recorded as a movement on reserves?	**13.9**	
Has the average rate used been calculated by the method considered most appropriate for the circumstances of the foreign entity?	**13.9**	
In those circumstances where the trade of the foreign entity is more dependent on the economic environment of the investing company's currency than that of its own reporting currency, have the transactions of the foreign operation been reported as though all of its transactions had been entered into by the investing company itself in its own currency (as in paragraph **13.2 – 13.5**)?	**13.10**	
Has the method used for translating the accounts of each foreign entity been applied consistently from period to period unless its financial and other operational relationships with the investing company change?	**13.11**	
Where foreign currency borrowings have been used to finance, or provide a hedge against, group equity investments in foreign entities, have exchange gains and losses on the borrowings, which would otherwise have been taken to the profit and loss account, been offset as reserve movements against exchange differences arising on the retranslation of the net investments provided that: (a) the relationships between the investing company and the foreign entities concerned justify the use of the closing rate method for consolidation purposes; (b) in any accounting period, the exchange gains and losses arising on foreign currency borrowings have been offset only to the extent of the exchange differences arising on the net investments in foreign entities; (c) the foreign currency borrowings, whose exchange gains or losses are used in the offset process, have not exceeded, in the aggregate, the total amount of cash that the net investments are expected to be able to generate, whether from profits or otherwise; and (d) the accounting treatment is applied consistently from period to period?	**13.12**	
Where the provisions of paragraph **13.6** have been applied in the investing company's accounts to a foreign equity investment that is neither a subsidiary nor an associated company, has the same offset procedure been applied in the consolidated accounts?	**13.12**	
POST BALANCE SHEET EVENTS		
Have the amounts recognised in the entity's accounts been adjusted to reflect adjusting events after the balance sheet date?	**14.1**	
Have non-adjusting events after the balance sheet date not resulted in adjustment in the accounts?	**14.2**	
Has each material category of non-adjusting event after the balance sheet date included disclosure of the following: (a) the nature of the event; and (b) an estimate of its financial effect or a statement that such an estimate cannot be made?	**14.3**	

RELATED PARTY DISCLOSURES		
Where the reporting entity: (a) purchases, sells or transfers goods and other assets or liabilities; or (b) renders or receives services; or (c) provides or receives finance or financial support (irrespective or whether a price is charged) to, from or on behalf of a related party, have details of such material transactions been disclosed, including: (i) the names of the transacting related parties; (ii) a description of the relationship between the parties; (iii) a description of the transactions; (iv) the amounts involved; (v) any other elements of the transactions necessary for an understanding of the accounts; (vi) the amounts due to or from related parties at the balance sheet date and provisions for doubtful debts due from such parties at that date; and (vii) amounts written off in the period in respect of debts due to or from related parties?	**15.1**	
Have any personal guarantees given by directors in respect of borrowings by the reporting entity been disclosed in the notes to the accounts?	**15.2**	
Have amounts included in the profit and loss account under 'investment income' and 'other interest receivable and similar income' that were received, or are receivable from group undertakings, been shown separately?	**15.3**	
Have amounts included in the profit and loss account under 'interest payable and similar charges' paid, or payable, to group undertakings, been shown separately?	**15.4**	
Have commitments which are undertaken on behalf of or for the benefit of (a) any parent undertaking or fellow subsidiary undertaking, or (b) any subsidiary undertaking of a company, been disclosed separately from those commitments disclosed under paragraphs **10.2** and **11.8 – 11.11** and have commitments undertaken under (a) been disclosed separately from those undertaken under (b)?	**15.5**	
Have other transactions with related parties been disclosed on an aggregate basis unless disclosure of an individual transaction, or connected transactions, is necessary for an understanding of the impact of the transactions on the accounts of the reporting entity or is required by law?	**15.6**	
Has no disclosure as a related party transaction been made of: (a) pension contributions paid to a pension fund; (b) emoluments in respect of services as an employee of the reporting entity; or (c) transactions with the parties listed below simply as a result of their role as: (i) providers of finance in the course of their business in that regard; (ii) utility companies; (iii) government departments and their sponsored bodies; or (iv) a customer, supplier, franchiser, distributor or general agent?	**15.7**	
When the reporting entity is controlled by another party, has there been disclosure of the related party relationship and the name of that party and, if different, the name of the controlling party?	**15.8**	
If the controlling party or ultimate controlling party is not known, has that fact been disclosed?	**15.8**	
Has this information been disclosed irrespective of whether any transactions have taken place between the controlling parties and the reporting entity?	**15.8**	

Where the company is a subsidiary undertaking, has the following information been given with respect to the company (if any) regarded by the directors as being the company's ultimate parent company:		
(a) the name of that company; and (b) its country of incorporation if outside the United Kingdom and if known to the directors?	**15.9**	
Parent undertaking drawing up accounts for larger group		
Where the company is a subsidiary undertaking, (a) for the largest group of which it is a member for which group accounts are drawn up, and (b) for the smallest such group of undertakings, has the following information been given with respect to the parent undertaking: (i) the name of the parent undertaking; (ii) the country of incorporation, if outside the United Kingdom; (iii) if unincorporated, the address of its principal place of business; and (iv) if copies of either of the group accounts refereed to in (a) or (b) above are available to the public, the address from which they may be obtained?	**15.10**	
Directors' benefits: advances, credit and guarantees		
Has information about the following directors' benefits been provided in the notes to the accounts (the directors of a company being the persons who were a director at any time in the financial year to which the accounts relate): (a) advances and credits granted by the company to its directors; and (b) guarantees of any kind entered into by the company on behalf of its directors?	**15.11**	
Has the following information been disclosed for an advance or credit: (a) its amount; (b) an indication of the interest rate; (c) lis main conditions; and (d) any amounts repaid?	**15.12**	
Has the following information been disclosed for a guarantee? (a) Its main terms; (b) the amount of the maximum liability that may be incurred by the company (or its subsidiary), and (c) any amount paid and any liability incurred by the company (or its subsidiary) for the purpose of fulfilling the guarantee (including any loss incurred by reason of enforcement of the guarantee)?	**15.13**	
Have the totals of amounts stated in paragraphs **15.12 (a)** and **(d)**, and **15.13 (b)** and **(c)**, been disclosed in the notes to the accounts?	**15.14**	
Have the requirements of this section 15 of the FRSSE been applied in relation to every advance, credit or guarantee subsisting at any time in the financial year to which the accounts relate: (a) whenever it was entered into; (b) whether or not the person was a director of the company in question at the time it was entered into; and (c) in the case of an advance, credit or guarantee involving a subsidiary undertaking of that company, whether or not that undertaking was such a subsidiary undertaking at the time it was entered into?	**15.15**	

Subsidiary undertakings		
Where at the end of the financial year the company has subsidiary undertakings, has the following information been disclosed: (a) the name of each subsidiary undertaking; and (b) with respect to each subsidiary undertaking if it is incorporated outside the United Kingdom, the country in which it is incorporated; or if it is unincorporated, the address of its principal place of business?	**15.16**	
Holdings in subsidiary undertakings		
In relation to shares of each class held by the company in a subsidiary undertaking, have the following been stated: (a) the indentity of the class; and (b) the proportion of the nominal value of the shares of that class represented by those shares?	**15.17**	
Have the shares held by the company itself been distinguished from those attributed to the company which are held by or on behalf of a subsidiary undertaking?	**15.17**	
Financial information about subsidiary undertakings		
Have the following been disclosed in respect of each subsidiary undertaking: (a) the aggregate amount of its capital and reserves as at the end of its relevant financial year; and (b) its profit and loss for that year? The information in **15.18** is not required if: (a) the company is exempt by virtue of ss. 400 and 401 of the CA 2006 from the requirement to prepare group accounts; or (b) the company's investment in the subsidiary undertaking is included in the company's accounts by way of the equity method of valuation; or (c) the subsidiary undertaking is not required by any provision of the CA 2006 to deliver a copy of its balance sheet for its relevant financial year and does not otherwise publish that balance sheet in the United Kingdom or elsewhere, and the company's holding is less than 50 per cent of the nominal value of the shares in the undertaking; or (d) it is not material.	**15.18** **15.19**	
Membership of certain undertakings		
Where at the end of the financial year the company is a member of a qualifying and material undertaking, has the following information been given: (a) the name and legal form of the undertaking; and (b) the address of the undertaking's registered office (whether in or outside the United Kingdom) or, if it does not have such an office, its head office (whether in or outside the United Kingdom)?	**15.21 /** **15.23**	

Where the undertaking is a qualifying partnership has the following been stated either: (a) that a copy of the latest accounts of the undertaking has been or is to be appended to the copy of the company's accounts sent to the registrar under s. 444 of the CA 2006; or (b) the name of at least one body corporate (which may be the company) in whose group accounts the undertaking has been or is to be dealt with on a consolidated basis? *This is not required if the notes to the company's accounts disclose that the company is exempt because the partnership is dealt with on a consolidated basis in group accounts prepared by (I) a member of the partnership established under law, or (II) a parent undertaking of such a member.*	**15.22** **15.24**	
CONSOLIDATED ACCOUNTS		
Where the directors of a company subject to the small companies regime have prepared group accounts for the year as well as preparing individual accounts for the year, have the accounting practices and disclosure requirements set out in FRSs 2,6,7 and, as they apply in respect of consolidated accounts, FRSs 5, 9,10,11 and 28 been regarded as standard? *If the reporting entity is part of a group that prepares publicly available consolidated accounts, it is entitled to the exemptions given in FRS 8 paragraph 3 (a)-(c).*	**16.2**	
Form and content of small group accounts		
Where a small company has prepared individual accounts in accordance with the legal requirements reflected in the FRSSE and is preparing group accounts in respect of the same year, have paragraphs 16.4 to 16.8 been applied?	**16.3**	
In preparing group accounts, has the entity had regard to the legal requirements reflected in the FRSSE and the provisions of schedule 6 of the Small Companies and Groups (Accounts and Directors' Report) Regulations 2008 (SI 2008/409)? *Any references in that schedule to compliance with the provisions of 'Schedule 6' shall be construed as references to the legal requirements reflected in the FRSSE.*	**16.4**	
In preparing group accounts, have details been shown in the notes to the group accounts of: (a) advances and credits granted to the directors of the parent company, by that company, or by any of its subsidiary undertakings; and (b) guarantees of any kind entered into on behalf of the directors of the parent company, by that company or by any of its subsidiary undertakings?	**16.5**	
Has the balance sheet format set out in paragraph 2.27 been modified as follows? For item B.III 'Investments' substitute: 'B III Investments 1. Shares in group undertakings 2. Interests in associated undertakings 3. Other participating interests 4. Loans to group undertakings and undertakings in which a participating interest is held 5. Other investments other than loans 6. Others.'	**16.6**	

Has the profit and loss account format set out in paragraph **2.29** been modified as follows? For the item headed 'Income from participating interests' substitute: 'Income from interests in associated undertakings' and 'Income from other participating interests'.	**16.7**	
Where group accounts are prepared does the balance sheet contain in a prominent position above the signature required by paragraph 2.30, a statement that they are prepared in accordance with the special provisions in part 15 of the CA 2006 relating to small companies?	**16.8**	
DIRECTORS' REMUNERATION		
Has the overall total of the following items been disclosed in respect of directors' remuneration: (a) the overall amount of remuneration paid to or receivable by directors in respect of qualifying services; (b) the overall amount of money paid to or receivable by directors and the net value of assets (other than money, share options or shares) received or receivable by directors, under long term incentive schemes in respect of qualifying services; and (c) the overall value of any company contributions paid, or treated as paid, to a pension scheme in respect of directors' qualifying services and by reference to which the rate or amount of any money purchase benefits that may become payable will be calculated?	**17.1**	
In the case of money purchase schemes and defined benefit schemes, has the number of directors (if any) to whom retirement benefits are accruing in respect of qualifying services been disclosed?	**17.1**	
Has disclosure been made of aggregate amounts of any compensation to directors or past directors in respect of loss of office, including benefits other than in cash, and the estimated money value of such benefits and their nature?	**17.2**	
Has disclosure been made of the aggregate amount of any consideration paid to, or receivable by, third parties for making available the services of any person: (a) as a director of the company; or (b) while director of the company, as director of any subsidiary undertaking, or otherwise in connection with the management of the affairs of the company or any of its subsidiary undertakings?	**17.3**	
In reference to 'consideration', has disclosure been made of benefits other than cash and the estimated money value of such benefits and their nature?	**17.3**	
THE DIRECTORS' REPORT		
Have the directors of the company prepared a directors' report for each individual financial year of the company?	**18.1**	
Have the following disclosures been made in the directors' report: (a) the principal activities of the company;	**18.1**	
(b) details of the company's directors;	**18.1**	
(c) political donations and expenditure;	**18.1**	
(d) charitable donations;	**18.1**	
(e) acquisition of own shares; and	**18.1**	
(f) employment, etc of disabled persons?	**18.1**	

Where the company is a parent and chooses to prepare group accounts, is the directors' report a group report relating to the undertakings included in the consolidation?	**18.3**	
The principal activities of the company		
Have the principal activities (being the various classes of business in which the company operates) of the company and its subsidiaries during the year been stated?	**18.4**	
Details of the company's directors		
Have the names been stated of the persons who, at any time during the financial year, were directors of the company?	**18.5**	
Disclosure of qualifying third party indemnity provisions		
If, when a director's report is approved, any qualifying third party indemnity provision (whether made by the company or otherwise) is in force or was in force during the financial year for the benefit of one or more directors of the company (or of an associated company), has the report stated that such provision is or was in force?	**18.6**	
Political donations and expenditure and charitable donations		
If the company or the company and its subsidiaries, has in the financial year made any political donation to any political party or other political organisation, or made any political donation to any independent election candidate, or incurred any political expenditure and the amount of the donation or expenditure or (as the case may be) the aggregate amount of all donations and expenditure exceeded £2,000, has the directors' report disclosed the following particulars: (a) for political donations – the name of each political party, other political organisation or independent election candidate to whom such a donation has been made and the total amount given to that party, organisation or candidate by way of such donations in the financial year; and (b) for political expenditure – the total amount incurred by way of such expenditure in the financial year?	**18.7**	
If the company, or the company and its subsidiaries made any contribution to a non-EU political party, has a statement been included in the directors' report regarding the amount of the contribution or, if it has made two or more such contributions in the year, the total amount of the contributions?	**18.8**	
If the company, or the company and its subsidiaries, has in the financial year given money for charitable purposes that exceeds £2,000 has the amount given for each of the purposes for which money has been given been disclosed?	**18.9**	
Acquisition of own shares		
Where the company acquires its own shares, either by purchase or acquisition by forfeiture, has the directors' report stated: (a) the number and nominal value of shares purchased, the aggregate consideration paid for the shares and the reasons for the purchase; (b) the number and nominal value of shares acquired; (c) the maximum number and nominal value of shares acquired or charged during the year; and (d) the number and nominal value of such shares acquired which were disposed of in the year?	**18.10**	

Has the amount of money received been disclosed where the shares were disposed of for money?	**18.10**	
In each case above, has the percentage of the called-up share capital which they represent been stated?	**18.10**	
In each case above, where shares have been charged, has the amount of the charge been stated?	**18.10**	
Employment, etc of disabled persons		
Where the average number of employees exceeds 250, has a statement been included describing the policy which the company has adopted for: (a) giving full and fair consideration to applications for employment by disabled persons, having regard to their particular aptitude and abilities; (b) continuing employment and appropriate training for employees of the company who became disabled during the period when they were employed by the company; and (c) otherwise for the training, career development and promotion of disabled persons employed by the company?	**18.11**	
Statement as to disclosure of information to auditors		
Where a small company chooses not to take advantage of the exemption in the CA 2006 relating to the audit of accounts, has a statement been included in the directors' report that, so far as each of the directors at the time the report is approved are aware: (a) there is no relevant audit information of which the company's auditors are unaware; and (b) the directors have taken all steps that they ought to have taken to make themselves aware of any relevant audit information and to establish that the auditors are aware of that information?	**18.12**	
Approval and signing of the directors' report		
Has the directors' report been approved by the board of directors and signed on behalf of the board by a director or the secretary of the company?	**18.13**	
Has every copy of the directors' report which is published by or on behalf of the board stated the name of the person who signed it on behalf of the board?	**18.13**	
Has the copy of the directors' report which is delivered to the registrar stated the name of the person who signed it on behalf of the board?	**18.14**	
If the directors' report is prepared in accordance with the small companies regime, has a statement been included to that effect in a prominent position above the signature?	**18.15**	

Appendix F Small company abbreviated accounts checklist

As small companies more frequently produce abbreviated accounts than medium-sized companies, the following checklist provides a guide to the appropriate disclosure requirements in producing 'abbreviated accounts' for delivery by small companies to the Registrar of Companies. This applies where the company prepares UK GAAP accounts. Abbreviated accounts are not available s. 444(3)
for filing where IAS accounts are prepared.

References in this checklist to 'full accounts' include 'small company individual accounts' in accordance with SI 2008/409 Sch 1 and references to Sch below refer to this statutory instrument.

Checklist for the availability and content of abbreviated accounts for small companies

A company which qualifies as small is entitled to deliver abbreviated accounts to the Registrar of Companies (CA 2006 s. 444).

1. Complete the following information:

	2013	2012	2011	
Turnover	£	£	£	
Balance sheet total	£	£	£	
Employees				
Dormant?	Yes/No	Yes/No	Yes/No	s. 1169

Refer to **Chapter 5** and **Appendix C** to determine the size of the company
Refer to **Chapter 7** for the definition of a dormant company.

Are abbreviated accounts appropriate?	√ or N/A
2. Based on the above information (a) The company qualifies as: (i) small (if so, answer **3** to **11**); (ii) dormant (if so, answer **5, 6** and **8** to **12**), } abbreviated accounts may be prepared	
(b) The company is: (i) ineligible; or (ii) other (i.e. neither 'small' nor 'medium-sized'). } if so, abbreviated accounts *not* appropriate	
Directors' statements and signature 3. Directors are required to state in a prominent position above the approval signature on the balance sheet that the accounts are prepared in accordance with the provisions of CA 2006 relating to small companies. (s. 450(3))	
4. Where advantage is taken of audit exemption, the directors are required to confirm or acknowledge: (s. 475–476)	
(a) company's entitlement to audit exemption;	
(b) members have not required the company to obtain an audit (CA 2006 s. 476); (c) duty to keep accounting records (CA 2006 s. 386); (d) duty to prepare true and fair view accounts (CA 2006 ss. 393–394).	

s. 475(2) *s. 480*	5. If the company is dormant and is exempt from the provisions relating to the audit of accounts, a statement is required as in **4** above.	
s. 450	6. Abbreviated balance sheet must be signed by a director (in accordance with CA 2006 s. 450) on behalf of the board.	
	Special auditor's report	
s. 449(1)	***(Not applicable where 'dormant company' under CA 2006 s. 480 or advantage taken of small company audit exemption)***	
s. 449(2)	7. Where abbreviated accounts are filed, the special auditor's report is required to state that in the auditor's opinion: (a) the small company is entitled to deliver abbreviated accounts prepared in accordance with the relevant provision (s. 444(1)–(3));	
	(b) the accounts are properly prepared in accordance with that relevant provision.	
s. 449(3)	If the auditor's report on the full annual accounts was qualified, the special report must reproduce the text in full (with further material necessary to understand a qualification).	
s. 449(3)	The special auditor's report must also reproduce any statement contained in the full auditor's report under s. 498(2) or (3) (proper accounting records or failure to obtain necessary information, etc.). If the auditor's report on the full accounts is unqualified but contains an emphasis of matter paragraph, the APB considers that it is necessary for the auditor to include such a paragraph (together with any further material necessary to understand it) in the special auditor's report.	
	8. No directors' report.	
s. 444(3)	9. No profit and loss account.	
Sch 4.1 (1) *Sch 4 formats*	10. Balance sheet – abbreviated version (a) Only format headings with letter or Roman number need be shown (in the order and presentation of SI 2008/409 Sch 4). (b) For debtors *and* creditors, show aggregate amounts falling due: (i) within one year; (ii) after more than one year (unless shown in notes).	
s. 444(6)	(c) The name and signature of a director (see **6** above).	
Sch 4.2	11. Notes – show only:	
Sch 4.3	(a) accounting policies adopted – including: • depreciation and diminution in value of assets; and • statement of preparation in accordance with the FRSSE (if applicable);	
Sch 4.4	(b) Share capital:	
Sch 4.4(1)	(i) number and aggregate nominal value of allotted shares of each class;	
Sch 4.5	(ii) share allotments during the year – state classes allotted and reason for allotment and for each class of shares, the number allotted, their aggregate nominal value and the consideration received by the company;	
Sch 4.4(2)	(iii) redeemable shares – redemption dates and option details *(Preference shares as financial liabilities).*	
Sch 4.6(1)–(3)	(c) Fixed assets: • movements – only format headings with letter or Roman number (i.e. movements in tangible fixed assets, intangible fixed assets, and fixed asset investments for the categories in total) need be shown, including cost or valuation and accumulated depreciation at beginning and end of year; additions, disposals, revaluations, and depreciation provisions;	
Sch 4.7	• fair value disclosure of financial fixed assets, if applicable.	

(d) Creditors and indebtedness: (i) liabilities repayable in more than five years amount due for repayment, other than by instalments, after more than five years from the balance sheet date; amount repayable by instalments, after more than five years;		*Sch 4.8*
(ii) aggregate amount of *secured* liabilities.		*Sch 4.8(2)*
(e) Foreign currencies – basis for translating sums denominated in foreign currencies.		*Sch 4.9*
(f) Comparative figures (in accordance with accounting standards). Where corresponding amounts are not comparable, adjust and give particulars of and reasons for adjustment.		
(g) Particulars of subsidiary undertakings. For disclosure details see **SI 2008/409 Sch 2** at **Appendix B**		*Sch 2.1–3*
(h) Particulars of holdings in undertakings (other than subsidiary undertakings) where holdings exceed 20 per cent ('significant holdings'). (For disclosure details see **SI 2008/409 Sch 2** at **Appendix B**.)		*Sch 2.5–8*
(i) Parent undertakings (name and country of incorporation or principal business address if unincorporated).		*Sch 2.9*
(j) Ultimate parent company.		*Sch 2.10*
(k) Directors' benefits: advances, credits and guarantees. **Chapter 10**		*s. 413*
Dormant company – acting as agent 12. Where an audit-exempt dormant company (under s. 480) has acted as agent for any person during the financial year, that fact must be disclosed in the notes to the accounts.		*Sch 4.10*

Appendix G Selected reading and reference material

This appendix provides a selection of the websites and literature to which this book might form a companion.

Useful websites

Financial Reporting Council	www.frc.org.uk
International Accounting Standard Board	www.ifrs.org
International Auditing and Assurance Standards Board	www.ifac.org/IAASB
Department for Business, Innovation and Skills (BIS)	www.bis.gov.uk
Companies House	www.companieshouse.gov.uk
Legislation and statutory instruments	www.legislation.gov.uk
Institute of Chartered Accountants in England and Wales	www.icaew.com
Institute of Chartered Accountants of Scotland	www.icas.org.uk
Accountancy Magazine	www.accountancymagazine.com

Legislation and regulation

Companies Act 2006	HMSO (Her Majesty's Stationery Office)
Companies Act 2006 – Explanatory notes	HMSO
Companies Act 2006 – Tables of origins and destinations	HMSO

Accounting and Auditing Standards

Accounting Standards 2013/14	Wolters Kluwer (UK) Ltd
Auditing Standards 2013/14	Wolters Kluwer (UK) Ltd
International Accounting Standards	
Bound volume of International Financial Reporting Standards (Complete text)	IFRS Foundation
IFRS for Small and Medium-sized Entities (July 2009)	IFRS Foundation

Checklists

Company Accounts Disclosure Checklist	SWAT UK Ltd	Wolters Kluwer (UK) Ltd
Unlisted Companies Accounts UK GAAP Checklist (Accountants' Digest 565, December 2011)	S Hastie	Wolters Kluwer (UK) Ltd

FRC/Auditing Practices Board

The Auditor's Statement on the Summary Financial Statement in the United Kingdom	APB Bulletin 2008/3 (April 2008)
The Special Auditor's Report on Abbreviated Accounts in the United Kingdom	APB Bulletin 2008/4 (April 2008)
Auditor's Reports on Revised Accounts and Reports in the United Kingdom	APB Bulletin 2008/5 (April 2008)
The 'Senior Statutory Auditor' under the United Kingdom Companies Act 2006	APB Bulletin 2008/6 (April 2008)
Miscellaneous Reports by Auditors Required by the United Kingdom Companies Act 2006	APB Bulletin 2008/9 (October 2008)
Guidance on smaller entity audit documentation	APB Practice Note 26 (Revised) (December 2009)
Compendium of Illustrative Auditor's Reports on United Kingdom Public Sector Financial Statements for periods ended on or after 15 December 2010 (Revised)	APB Bulletin 2010/2 (Revised March 2012)

Index